AF769524

Introduction to Investor-State Arbitration

Introduction to Investor-State Arbitration

Yves Derains
Josefa Sicard-Mirabal

Wolters Kluwer

Published by:
Kluwer Law International B.V.
PO Box 316
2400 AH Alphen aan den Rijn
The Netherlands
E-mail: international-sales@wolterskluwer.com
Website: lrus.wolterskluwer.com

Sold and distributed in North, Central and South America by:
Wolters Kluwer Legal & Regulatory U.S.
7201 McKinney Circle
Frederick, MD 21704
United States of America
Email: customer.service@wolterskluwer.com

Sold and distributed in all other countries by:
Air Business Subscriptions
Rockwood House
Haywards Heath
West Sussex
RH16 3DH
United Kingdom
Email: international-customerservice@wolterskluwer.com

Printed on acid-free paper.

ISBN 978-90-411-8400-9

e-Book: ISBN 978-90-411-8401-6
web-PDF: ISBN 978-90-411-8402-3

© 2018 Kluwer Law International BV, The Netherlands

All rights reserved. No part of this publication may be reproduced, stored in a retrieval system, or transmitted in any form or by any means, electronic, mechanical, photocopying, recording, or otherwise, without written permission from the publisher.

Permission to use this content must be obtained from the copyright owner. More information can be found at: lrus.wolterskluwer.com/policies/permissions-reprints-and-licensing

Printed in the United Kingdom.

Table of Contents

Foreword

Foreign private investment constitutes an extremely significant contribution to the development of the economy of the host State. However, foreign investors are reluctant to invest abroad as they fear their interests will be expropriated or discriminated against or that they and their capital will be trapped in the host State. For centuries, the only protection they could find was that of their own State through diplomatic protection which often took the ugly face of boat gun diplomacy and sometimes was at the origin of wars. Investor-State arbitration put an end to that unsatisfactory situation. It replaced the recourse to the force with a recourse to the law and in this regard constitutes a real progress of civilization. The creation of the International Centre for the Settlement of Investment Disputes (ICSID), under the auspices of the International Bank for Reconstruction and Development (World Bank) by the Washington Convention in 1965, was the first step. It was followed by about 3,000 bilateral treaties and several multilateral treaties which provide the investors and the host State with the protection of international law through investor-State arbitration, under the aegis of various institutions, among which the International Court of Arbitration of the International Chamber of Commerce (ICC) is proud to play a significant role. The existence of investor-State arbitration has contributed to the ever-increasing rise in globalization during the last fifty years. Thousands of investors from one corner of the world are investing in markets on the other corner of the globe providing services, technology or capital. This would not be possible if both the investor and the host State did not know that disputes in this respect will be resolved peacefully under the rule of law.

Investor-State arbitration is now under the public watch and facing many challenges. While many books have been written on the subject, the authors have accomplished a remarkably clear and concise explanation of at times very complex issues. This work will acquaint students and lay people alike with basic legal concepts and policies while providing background by highlighting interesting and important cases.

The combination of the authors' practical and academic backgrounds enhances the delivery and approach to the substantive and sometimes difficult concepts of investor-State arbitration allowing the reader to become familiar with them without great difficulty.

I am delighted with this book and anticipate it will be useful for anyone interested in international investor-State arbitration.

Alexis Mourre

List of Abbreviations

AAA	American Arbitration Association
BIT	Bilateral Investment Treaty
CAFTA-DR	Dominican Republic-Central America Free Trade Agreement
CETA	EU-Canada Comprehensive Economic and Trade Agreement
CIETAC	Chinese International Economic and Trade Arbitration Commission
CJEU	Court of Justice of the European Union
CPTPP	Comprehensive and Progressive Agreement for Trans-Pacific Partnership
DCF	Discounted Cash Flow
DIS	German Arbitration Institute
EBIT	Earnings Before Interest and Taxes
EBITDA	Earnings Before Interest, Taxes, Depreciation and Amortisation
ECHR	European Court of Human Rights
ECT	Energy Charter Treaty
EU	European Union
Euratom	European Atomic Energy Community
FAA	Federal Arbitration Act
FCPA	Foreign Corrupt Practices Act
FET	Fair and Equitable Treatment
FMV	Fair Market Value
FPS	Full Protection and Security
FSIA	Foreign Sovereign Immunities Act
FTC	NAFTA Free Trade Commission
HKIAC	Hong Kong International Arbitration Centre
IBA	International Bar Association

IBA Guidelines	IBA Guidelines on Conflicts of Interest in International Arbitration
IBA Rules	IBA Rules on the Taking of Evidence in International Arbitration
ICAA	International Commercial Arbitration Act
ICC	International Chamber of Commerce
ICC Guidance Note	ICC Guidance Note for the Disclosure of Conflicts by Arbitrators
ICDR	International Centre for Dispute Resolution
ICJ	International Court of Justice
ICSID	International Centre for the Settlement of Investment Disputes
ICSID Convention	Washington Convention on the Settlement of Investment Disputes Between States and Nationals of Other States
ILC	International Law Commission
ILC Articles on State Responsibility or ILC Articles	ILC Articles on Responsibility of States for Internationally Wrongful Acts
ISDS	Investor-State Dispute Settlement
IVS	International Valuation Standards
LCIA	London Court of International Arbitration
MFN	Most-Favored-Nation Treatment
MIT	Multilateral Investment Treaty
NAFTA	North American Free Trade Agreement
NBK	National Bank of Kazakhstan
New York Convention	New York Convention on the Recognition and Enforcement of Foreign Arbitral Awards
NHA	National Highway Authority
NPM	Non-precluded Measures
NT	National Treatment
PCA	Permanent Court of Arbitration
PCIJ	Permanent Court of International Justice
SCC	Arbitration Institute of the Stockholm Chamber of Commerce
SIAC	Singapore International Arbitration Centre
TFEU	Treaty on the Functioning of the EU
TPP	Trans-Pacific Partnership Agreement
TTIP	Transatlantic Trade and Investment Partnership
UK	United Kingdom

UN	United Nations
UNCITRAL	United Nations Commission on International Trade Law
UNCITRAL Model Law	UNCITRAL Model Law on International Commercial Arbitration
UNCITRAL Rules on Transparency	UNCITRAL Rules on Transparency in Treaty-based Investor-State Arbitration
UNCTAD	United Nations Conference on Trade and Development
US	United States
VCLT	Vienna Convention on the Law of Treaties
VIAC	Vienna International Arbitral Centre
WTO	World Trade Organization

Acknowledgements

This book would not have been achieved without the active support of Ana Gerdau de Borja Mercereau, associate at Derains & Gharavi. She helpfully contributed to several chapters and conducted a tireless war against material inconsistencies. We are very grateful to her.

Yves Derains & Josefa Sicard-Mirabal

I would like also to express my appreciation to a number of former students who assisted me with research of certain topics. I thank Jadranka Jakovcic, Clémence Prévot and María Feliz Ball. I also thank Mara Vento for her contribution to the Evidence chapter. A special word of gratitude to Veronika Timoveefa for her considerable contribution in research and drafting of some chapters.

Finally, I would like to acknowledge my husband, Antonio, and my other family members for their support, encouragement and love.

Josefa Sicard-Mirabal

CHAPTER 1

Introduction to Investor-State Arbitration

Investor-State arbitration is a unique development in international law, wherein an investor (individual or company) is provided with a direct right of action against a State, most commonly stemming from a bilateral or multilateral investment treaty (MIT). These treaties typically provide protection against expropriation, breach of fair and equitable treatment (FET), full protection and security (FPS), national treatment (NT), most-favored-nation treatment (MFN), and prevent arbitrary/unreasonable or discriminatory measures. A State is liable to pay compensation for breaching the obligations set forth in the treaty.

Commentators note that the investor and a State do not need to have a clear contractual relationship or 'privity' and therefore term the investor-State arbitration regime as 'arbitration without privity'. Indeed, the breach of a treaty in many instances involves a State action (e.g., a tax measure that the investor alleges is expropriatory) but does not arise out of the breach of a contractual provision.

Commentators have explained that the investor-State arbitration regime actors might approach issues from different perspectives (such as the public international law paradigm or the commercial arbitration paradigm, common law and civil law backgrounds). Each of these paradigms has differing fundamental assumptions underlying them and can result in different decisions based on the choice of paradigm.

It should be borne in mind that the investor-State regime is not subject to the common law doctrine of *stare decisis* and as such, decisions of one tribunal do not bind other tribunals.

Investor-State arbitration has also been under criticism for several years. Some of the criticisms relate to vague standards or to conflict of interests when an arbitrator also sits as a counsel. Others point to deeper systemic or conceptual problems within the system, such as the lack of legitimacy in arbitration, improper empowerment to corporate entities, incompatibility with European Union (EU) law, no clear mechanism for reviewing an award, and lack of transparency, to name only a few. Supporters of the regime, on the other hand, point out that the regime promotes the rule of law instead of diplomatic or even military persuasion in international relations and provides valuable protections to investors who might otherwise be susceptible to national courts that might be subject to domestic pressures.

§1.01 INTRODUCTION

Arbitration is a procedure for the settlement of disputes where the parties grant to private persons the power to issue a binding decision (the arbitral award) that is enforceable at law. Arbitration is the routine way to resolve disputes in international commercial relations where recourse to State courts is the exception. This is the result of the combined action of the States and economic circles during the second part of the twentieth century.

The movement started when, on the basis of a draft prepared by the International Chamber of Commerce (ICC), the United Nations (UN) adopted in 1958 the New York Convention on the Recognition and Enforcement of Foreign Awards (New York Convention).[1] The trend continued and was reinforced with the entering into force on 14 October 1966 of the 1965 Washington Convention on the Settlement of Investment Disputes between States and Nationals of Other States (ICSID Convention). This Convention, under the aegis of the World Bank, creates a specific organization, the International Center for the Settlement of Investment Disputes (ICSID) and provides conciliation and arbitration rules for investment disputes.

Two other important milestones were the 1976 United Nations Commission on International Trade Law (UNCITRAL) Rules on Arbitration and the 1985 UNCITRAL Model Law on International Commercial Arbitration (UNCITRAL Model Law).

This chapter is intended to provide a broad overview of investor-State arbitration that will be developed and discussed further in subsequent chapters. This chapter will examine in a general manner the differences between institutional arbitration and ad hoc arbitration. This is followed by a comparison between international commercial arbitration and investor-State arbitration (also referred to as international investment arbitration), it will briefly list the sources of investment law and will end with criticisms hurled at investment arbitration.

§1.02 INSTITUTIONAL ARBITRATION VERSUS AD HOC ARBITRATION

Arbitration is a consensual process that emanates from the parties agreement. Arbitrations are typically conducted by either one or three arbitrator(s). The arbitral tribunal, as it is usually called, is the equivalent of a judge or panel of judges in a State court. The difference is that the process is tailored in accordance with the parties' needs and

1. Convention on the Recognition and Enforcement of Foreign Arbitral Awards (UNCITRAL), ILM 1046 (1968).

wishes. For example, the parties generally select the arbitrators, and, as a result, the parties maintain an important degree of control over the skills of who is to determine the outcome of their dispute. Normally, arbitrators are very experienced lawyers and experts in the field in which they are called to decide.

In international commercial arbitration and investor-State arbitration, parties have the option to choose between institutional or administered arbitration and ad hoc or non-administered arbitration. To make an educated choice on institutional or ad hoc arbitration one must appreciate the differences between them as well as the advantages and disadvantages of each.

[A] Institutional Arbitration

Institutional arbitration is one in which a specialized institution assumes the role of administering the arbitration process. There are many arbitral institutions around the globe from which to choose. Some institutions are distinguished by the subject matter of their disputes: commercial, investor-State, energy, for example. Others are distinguished by their scope, e.g., domestic, regional and international. Each institution has its own set of rules, which provide a framework for the arbitration, and its own form of administration to assist in the process. Some of the popular arbitral institutions are the following.

The International Centre for Settlement of Investment Disputes (ICSID)

Based in Washington, D.C., and operating under the auspices of the World Bank, ICSID was established pursuant to the 1965 Washington Convention on the Settlement of Investment Disputes between States and Nationals of Other States (ICSID Convention).[2] ICSID is a specialized organization that deals exclusively with investor-State disputes, and it has its own particular rules. For further information, *see* www.icsid.org.

The International Court of Arbitration of the International Chamber of Commerce (ICC)

The ICC, which is based in Paris, was established in 1923. It is probably the best-known international commercial arbitration institution.[3] For further information, *see* www.iccwbo.org.

2. Washington Convention on the Settlement of Investment Disputes between States and Nationals of Other States (opened for signature 18 March 1965, entered into force 14 Oct. 1966).
3. The ICC also administers investor-State arbitrations. In 2017, the number of filings in which States or State entities were included was approximately 15% according to the ICC 2017 Statistical Report. Four cases were filed in 2017 on the basis of a bilateral investment treaty. The ICC has administered thirty-nine cases so far, which listed ICC arbitration as one of the dispute resolution options available to the parties in the field of investor-State disputes.

The London Court of International Arbitration (LCIA)

The LCIA, which is based in London, was established in 1892. It is Europe's second leading international arbitration institution and is very well known internationally. The LCIA has affiliated arbitral institutions in Dubai (DIFC-LCIA), India (LCIA India) and Mauritius (LCIA-MIAC). For further information, *see* www.lcia.org.

The American Arbitration Association (AAA) and Its International Arm, the International Centre for Dispute Resolution (ICDR)

Established in 1926, it is the best-known institution in the United States (US). The AAA administers a large number of domestic disputes, while the ICDR administers international arbitrations pursuant to its International Rules of Arbitrations. For further information, *see* www.adr.org.

The Permanent Court of Arbitration (PCA)

The PCA was established in 1899 to facilitate arbitration and other forms of dispute resolution between States. Currently the PCA provides dispute resolution services for disputes involving States, State entities, intergovernmental organizations and private parties. Its cases are generally administered under the UNCITRAL Arbitration Rules. For further information, *see* www.pca-cpa.org.

There are also regional and national institutions involved in international arbitration, such as the German Arbitration Institute (DIS), the Arbitration Institute of the Stockholm Chamber of Commerce (SCC), the Swiss Chambers' Arbitration Institution, the Vienna International Arbitral Centre (VIAC), the Milan Chamber of Arbitration, the Chinese International Economic and Trade Arbitration Commission (CIETAC), the Singapore International Arbitration Centre (SIAC) and the Hong Kong International Arbitration Centre (HKIAC).

The advantages of institutional arbitration include:

(1) Pre-established set of rules and procedures.
(2) Oversight and administrative assistance from the institution.[4]
(3) A list of qualified arbitrators to choose from in some institutions.
(4) Assistance in encouraging reluctant parties to proceed with arbitration.
(5) An established process format with a proven record. Such format seeks to ensure that the arbitration proceedings begin in a timely manner.

4. The role of the institution may vary depending on the institutional rules, but it may include the following: (a) oversight of the parties and the tribunals' proper application of its own rules (*see* Art. 1, Appendix I of the Statutes of the ICC Court; Art. D of the Constitution of the LCIA Court; and Art. 1 of the SCC Rules), (b) assisting in the formation or constitution of the arbitral tribunal and matters pertaining thereto (*see* Arts 12–15 of the ICC Rules, Art. 5 of the LCIA Rules, and Art. 5-11 of the ICDR Rules), (c) Determination of the seat of the arbitration if not otherwise agreed to by the parties (*see* Art. 18 of ICC Rules and Art. 16(1) of LCIA Rules), (d) consolidation of parallel proceedings (*see* Art. 10 of ICC Rules), (e) scrutiny and approval of the award under the ICC system (*see* Art. 34 of the ICC Rules), (f) determination of fees and expenses (*see* Appendix III of ICC Rules).

The primary disadvantages of institutional arbitration include:

(1) Administrative fees for services provided.
(2) Bureaucracy from within the institution, which can lead to delays and additional costs.
(3) The parties and the arbitrators may be required to meet unrealistic time frames set forth in the relevant rules.

[B] Ad Hoc Arbitration

Ad hoc arbitration is one that is not administered by an institution. Under ad hoc arbitration, the parties decide the (procedural) 'rules' of their arbitration. The parties will therefore have to determine all aspects of the arbitration themselves – for example, the number of arbitrators, appointing the arbitrators, the applicable law and the procedure for conducting the arbitration.

However, in ad hoc arbitrations parties commonly choose to incorporate pre-existing rules on non-administered arbitrations. This offers the parties the certainty of rules to govern their arbitration without the oversight of an institution.

The most used pre-existing rules in ad hoc arbitrations are the UNCITRAL Rules.[5] If the parties do not choose any pre-existing rules of non-administered arbitration, then only the rules of the place of the arbitration (lex arbitri) will govern the ad hoc arbitration.

The arbitration agreement, whether reached before or after a dispute has arisen, may simply state that 'disputes between parties will be arbitrated'. It is preferable to indicate the place or seat of the arbitration as this will have a significant impact on several vital issues such as the procedural laws governing the arbitration and the

5. UNCITRAL was established by the United Nations (UN) to help harmonize and unify laws around the world related to international business and trade. It does this in part by promoting uniform practices and procedures and by creating model laws and rules, such as the UNCITRAL Arbitration Rules. UNCITRAL does not itself administer or become involved in individual arbitrations. The UNCITRAL Arbitration Rules are a set of procedural rules covering all aspects of the arbitration process, which parties may agree to in part or in whole to help resolve their international disputes. They were adopted in 1976, then revised in 2010 and 2013. The UNCITRAL Arbitration Rules have been used to govern a broad range of procedures, including: disputes between private commercial parties; disputes between States and foreign investors (investment arbitration); disputes between two countries (State-to-State disputes). Their 2013 revision included a new provision for investor-State arbitration initiated pursuant to a treaty providing for the protection of investments or investors, referring to the UNCITRAL Rules on Transparency in Treaty-Based Investor-State Arbitration ('Rules on Transparency'). The UNCITRAL Rules are also often used as guidelines. The UNCITRAL Model Law on International Commercial Arbitration of 1985, with amendments as adopted in 2006 '… is designed to assist States in reforming and modernizing their laws on arbitral procedure so as to take into account the particular features and needs of international commercial arbitration. It covers all stages of the arbitral process from the arbitration agreement, the composition and jurisdiction of the arbitral tribunal and the extent of court intervention through to the recognition and enforcement of the arbitral award. It reflects worldwide consensus on key aspects of international arbitration practice having been accepted by States of all regions and the different legal or economic systems of the world'. For further information, *see* http://www.uncitral.org/uncitral/en/uncitral_texts/arbitration/1985Model_arbitration.html (accessed 25 May 2018).

enforceability of the award. If the parties cannot agree on the details of the arbitration, as noted above, it will be the rules of the place of the arbitration or lex arbitri that will govern.

Some advantages of ad hoc arbitration include the following:

(1) More cost effective and faster: If the parties approach the arbitration with cooperation, ad hoc proceedings have the potential to be more flexible, faster and cheaper than institutional proceedings. The absence of administrative fees alone may provide an excellent incentive to use the ad hoc procedure.
(2) Flexibility: In the ad hoc process, flexibility is paramount. This enables the parties to decide the dispute resolution procedure themselves. Note, however, that this will require a greater degree of effort, cooperation and expertise from the parties.

Some of the disadvantages of ad hoc proceedings include the following:

(1) The arbitration process can become very complicated. Parties wishing to include an ad hoc arbitration clause seeking to agree to the terms of arbitration after a dispute has arisen have the option of negotiating a complete set of rules that meet their needs. However, this approach can require considerable time, attention and expense with no guarantee that the terms agreed to will address all future issues or eventualities. Furthermore, if parties have not agreed on arbitration terms before any dispute arises, it is less likely that they will cooperate in doing so once a dispute has arisen. In ad hoc arbitrations, parties commonly designate an 'appointing authority' to appoint arbitrators. This serves to ensure that if the parties cannot agree on appointments and challenges of the arbitrators, an institution can step in to assist in the process. Institutions such as the ICC, the PCA, LCIA and ICDR serve as appointing authorities under UNCITRAL Rules for a fee.
(2) May not be cheaper: Parties sometimes believe that ad hoc may be cheaper than institutional arbitration because they forgo the administration fee. In reality and practice, this may not be the case. The benefits of having an arbitral institution administer the arbitration may outweigh the risks of increased time and costs associated with having to seek court intervention to resolve procedural issues that may arise in an ad hoc arbitration. This may especially be the case in complex disputes. Moreover, the arbitrators fix their own fees, without the control of an institution.

§1.03 INTERNATIONAL COMMERCIAL ARBITRATION VERSUS INVESTOR-STATE ARBITRATION

The protection of foreign investment has been at the origin of tension for centuries. The exercise of diplomatic protection or espousal in favor of national investors abroad by powerful States was supported with the threat or the use of force, the so-called gunboat diplomacy.[6] Fortunately, after years of development in the commercial field, arbitration was used to provide peaceful solutions to the disputes resulting from international investments, as a substitute for diplomatic protection.

The conclusion of State contracts, i.e., contracts entered into between private parties with States or State agencies in connection with a foreign investment, is at the origin of this new role of arbitration. These contracts almost systematically contain an arbitration clause that allows the investor not to be subject to the courts and sometimes to the legal order of the State where the investment is made. Indeed, the prohibition for a State or State agencies to have recourse to arbitration, still in force in some jurisdictions, has been generally eliminated for international relations.[7] Moreover, it is now broadly admitted that a State may not rely on its own national legislation to deny that it had the legal capacity to enter into an otherwise valid arbitration agreement.[8]

The use of the techniques inherent to commercial arbitration to resolve disputes arising from investment contracts was also largely facilitated when the ICSID Convention of 1965 entered into force.

Such investor-State arbitrations are based on arbitration agreements entered into between the host State and the investor. It could be an arbitration clause in a joint-venture agreement or in a concession contract or host States foreign investment law. In addition, it could be also a submission to arbitration agreed between the State and the investor after the dispute arises.

These investor-State arbitrations, based on an arbitration agreement included in a contract or in relation to a contract, are very similar to international commercial arbitrations. As a matter of fact, the arbitration institutions that were mainly involved in the field of commercial arbitration have adapted their rules to facilitate their participation in the field of investor-State arbitration.[9]

---

6. *See* Andrew Newcombe & Lluis Paradell, *Law And Practice of Investments Treaties: Standards of Treatment*, 8 (Wolters Kluwer 2009).
7. *See*, e.g., in France, the *Cour de cassation* (Supreme Court) has ruled since 1966 in the famous *Galakis* case that the prohibition for the State to enter into arbitration agreements does not apply to international relations (*Trésor Public v. Galakis*, Cour de cassation, 1re civil, Case No. 61-12.255, Judgement of 2 May 1966, 96 Journal du Droit international 684 (1969)). The English Arbitration Act 1966 abolished the restriction under the Crown applications. Yet, in a number of jurisdictions/countries where the concept of administrative contract exists, disputes relating to this type of contract cannot be arbitrated. It is often the case of concession contracts between the State and a foreign investor.
8. *See*, e.g., Art. 177(2) of the Swiss Federal Statute on Private International Law providing that '[a] state, or an enterprise held by, or an organization controlled by a state, which is party to an arbitration agreement, cannot invoke its own law in order to contest its capacity to arbitrate or the arbitrability of a dispute covered by the arbitration agreement.' Likewise, Art. 2 of the 2011 Spanish Arbitration Law sets forth that, in the case of international arbitration, States and the entities under their aegis may not invoke the prerogatives of their own legal systems in connection with matters subject to arbitration.
9. When the ICC International Court of Arbitration revised its Rules in 2012, it did not any longer indicate under Art. 1(1) that its function was to provide for the settlement of 'business disputes' of an international character, but only states that it administers the resolution of 'disputes' seeking to include investment disputes. But, more significantly, the new Rules excluded the role of ICC National Committees in the nomination process of arbitrators when 'one or more of the parties is a state or claims to be a state entity'. This exception was included to eliminate the fear of States that representatives of business circles might play a role in the appointment of arbitrators

To attract investments many countries have adopted a national law guaranteeing rights protecting foreign investments. They are often called investment codes. They generally include provisions defining the notions of 'investment' and of 'investor', and substantive rules such as FET, protection from arbitrary and discriminatory measures, compensation in case of nationalization and expropriation, NT and MFN, the right to free transfer of funds, etc. Most of them also include provisions concerning the settlement of disputes between the host State and the investor by international arbitration.

However, although there are still a number of international investment proceedings based on arbitration agreements included in a contract between the State and the investor, they are today a minority. The legal basis for investor-State arbitrations is found either in national law on investment protection or, and it is the overwhelming majority, in bilateral investment treaties (BITs) or in multilateral investment treaties (MITs).

BITs are treaties entered into by two Contracting States with a view to protecting the investments of their nationals made in the territory of the other Contracting State. Similar to investment codes, BITs typically provide a definition of 'investment' and 'investor', and of the nationality of the Contracting States and contain an undertaking by each State toward the other that the investments of its national on the former's territory will enjoy certain rights: FET, NT, MFN treatment, compensation in the event of expropriation or damage to the investment and guarantees of free transfers of funds. In particular, they include a clause under which the host State grants the investor the right to settle through arbitration disputes with the State relating to its investment in case it does not elect to sue the State in its national courts. The investor generally has the choice between several arbitration institutions or ad hoc arbitration. To date, more than 3,000 BITs have entered into force.

A number of MITs are a source of investor-State arbitration. The three following MITs deserve to be specially mentioned:

(1) the North American Free Trade Agreement (NAFTA) between Mexico, Canada and the US, which entered into force in 1994;
(2) the Energy Charter Treaty (ECT) which entered into legal force in April 1998 and was acceded by fifty-one States, as well as the European Community and the European Atomic Energy Community (Euratom) so far;
(3) the Dominican Republic-Central America Free Trade Agreement (CAFTA-DR), between the Dominican Republic, El Salvador, Costa Rica, Guatemala, Honduras, Nicaragua, and the US, which entered into force in 2006.

---

with, again, the view of attracting investment disputes. Likewise, Art. 1(1) of the UNCITRAL Model Law, as amended in 2006, stresses that it applies to international arbitration but highlights in its footnote n. 2 that the term 'commercial' must be interpreted broadly, including 'investment'.

The current discussions relating to the Trans-Pacific Partnership Agreement (TPP)[10] and the Transatlantic Trade and Investment Partnership (TTIP)[11] would also lead to the creation of large, multilateral trade and investment agreements.

A few characteristics that distinguish investor-State arbitrations from commercial arbitrations must be pointed out:

- The first characteristic is that when arbitration is not based on an arbitration clause included in an investment contract, the host State makes a general offer to arbitrate foreign investors at large in its national investment laws, or to certain categories of foreign investors in BITs or MITs to which the host State is a party. No consent to arbitrate exists between the parties until the investor has accepted this offer. In general, an investor accepts the host State's offer by instituting arbitration proceedings. This has been famously described by Professor Jan Paulsson as 'arbitration without privity'.[12]
- The second characteristic concerns the applicable law. The general practice in international commercial arbitration is that the arbitrators apply the rules of law chosen by the parties to govern the substance of the dispute. In the absence of such a choice, the arbitrators apply the law or the rules of law that they determine to be appropriate. The situation is different in investor-State arbitration in particular when the jurisdiction of the arbitrators does not result from an arbitration agreement.

When the State and the investor have entered into an investment contract, the dispute is essentially about the rights and obligations of the parties under the contract, as in international commercial arbitration. The arbitrator must decide on the basis of the specific law chosen by the parties to govern their contract which is often that of the State, sometimes combined with the general principles of international law. As a matter of fact, it is the spirit of Article 42(1) of the ICSID Convention that states that '[t]he Tribunal shall decide a dispute in accordance with such rules of law as may be agreed by the parties. In the absence of such agreement, the Tribunal shall apply the law of the Contracting State party to the dispute (including its rules on the conflict of laws) and such rules of international law as may be applicable.' Moreover, when the law of the State is applicable to long-term investment contracts or concession contracts, the parties may agree on freezing clauses or 'stabilization' clauses to protect their investment from adverse changes to the legal and fiscal environment.

When the arbitrators' jurisdiction is grounded on an investment law or a treaty on investment protection, the arbitrators are no longer dealing with strictly contractual

10. The TPP is being negotiated between the following States: Australia, Brunei Darussalam, Canada, Chile, Japan, Malaysia, Mexico, New Zealand, Peru, Singapore, and Vietnam. Details of the TPP are available on the website of the Office of the United States Trade Representative, *see* https://ustr.gov/trade-agreements/free-trade-agreements/trans-pacific-partnership (accessed 25 May 2018). The United States formally withdrew from the TPP in January 2017.
11. Details of the TTIP are available on the website of the Office of the United States Trade Representative, *see* https://ustr.gov/ttip (accessed 25 May 2018). The United States have not formally withdrawn from TTIP, but negotiations have been put on pause.
12. Jan Paulsson, *Arbitration Without Privity*, 10(2) ICSID Rev. 254–257 (1995).

obligations. They must decide whether the State has actually implemented the guarantees that the investor alleges it enjoys under that law or under that treaty. This does not follow the traditional rule in international commercial arbitration.

In fact, the exact relationship between international commercial arbitration and investment (or investor-State arbitration) has also led to an academic interest. Commentators point out how each of the regimes might have fundamental assumptions that can lead to different results based on the choice of the paradigm selected:[13]

- Transparency is the third characteristic of investor-State arbitration. Even if one is to argue that confidentiality is not the primary rule in international commercial arbitration, an arbitration case remains within the purview of the parties and the public at large has no interest in it. The presence of the State in investor-State arbitration changes the perspective, in particular when the investor is complaining about national tax or environmental policies. In a resolution of 16 December 2013, the General Assembly of the UN stressed 'the need for provisions on transparency in the settlement of such treaty-based investor-State disputes to take account of the public interest involved in such arbitrations'. Obviously, this is so because the consequences of a host State breaching its obligations under a treaty result in a direct impact to its citizens.

This concern explains why not only the awards and decisions are available on the ICSID website or other websites but also why most of the submissions of the parties, particularly when mandated by certain MITs such as NAFTA, are also available. More generally, in 2013 UNCITRAL adopted the Rules on Transparency in Treaty-based Investor-State Arbitration (UNCITRAL Rules on Transparency). These rules apply to any investor-State arbitration under the UNCITRAL Rules on the basis of treaties concluded on or after 1 April 2014.

According to these rules and subject to exceptional decisions of the arbitrators enforcing confidentiality,[14] the documents submitted in the proceeding are available to the public. Moreover, non-disputing parties to the treaty may be allowed to make submissions and the hearings are public:[15]

- A special characteristic of ICSID must be mentioned. According to Article 53(1) of the ICSID Convention, an award rendered pursuant to the Convention is

13. Anthea Roberts, *Clash of Paradigms: Actors and Analogies Shaping the Investment Treaty System*, 107 Am. J. Intl. L. 45–49, 58–63 (2013).
14. *See* Art. 7 of the UNCITRAL Rules on Transparency: '1. Confidential or protected information, as defined in paragraph 2 and as identified pursuant to the arrangements referred to in paragraphs 3 and 4, shall not be made available to the public pursuant to articles 2 to 6. 2. Confidential or protected information consists of: (a) Confidential business information; (b) Information that is protected against being made available to the public under the treaty; (c) Information that is protected against being made available to the public, in the case of the information of the respondent State, under the law of the respondent State, and in the case of other information, under any law or rules determined by the arbitral tribunal to be applicable to the disclosure of such information; or (d) Information the disclosure of which would impede law enforcement.'
15. *See* Arts 2–6 of the UNCITRAL Rules on Transparency.

binding upon the parties and is not subject to any control by national courts.[16] The only available remedy is the annulment procedure before an annulment committee contemplated by the ICSID Convention itself.[17] Article 54(1) of the Convention requires the Contracting States to enforce the award on presentation of a certified copy of the award by the Secretary General of ICSID.[18] Thus, the ICSID Convention envisions a self-contained regime. In commercial arbitration and in non-ICSID Investor-State arbitrations, a party must seek enforcement of the arbitral award in domestic courts, in general, pursuant to the New York Convention.[19]

§1.04 BRIEF OVERVIEW OF SOURCES OF INVESTMENT LAW

As already mentioned throughout the chapter, investment law is composed of three legal sources: international law (A), investment contracts between investors and States (B) and domestic law (C).

[A] International Law

The main legal instruments relating to investment are investment treaties. These primarily aim at protecting the foreign investor in the host State. The treaty is the most important source of international law.

The main reference in this area of the law is the Vienna Convention on the Law of Treaties (VCLT), adopted on 23 May 1969 that entered into force on 27 January 1980. It is a combination of codification and progressive development of international law. Article 2(a) of the VCLT defines 'treaty' as 'an international agreement concluded between states in written form and governed by international law, whether embodied in a single instrument or two or more related instruments and whatever its particular designation'.

16. ICSID Convention, Art. 53(1): 'The award shall be binding on the parties and shall not be subject to any appeal or to any other remedy except those provided for in this Convention. Each party shall abide by and comply with the terms of the award except to the extent that enforcement shall have been stayed pursuant to the relevant provisions of this Convention.'
17. ICSID Convention, Art. 52(1): 'Either party may request annulment of the award by an application in writing addressed to the Secretary-General on one or more of the following grounds: (a) that the Tribunal was not properly constituted; (b) that the Tribunal has manifestly exceeded its powers; (c) that there was corruption on the part of a member of the Tribunal; (d) that there has been a serious departure from a fundamental rule of procedure; or (e) that the award has failed to state the reasons on which it is based.'
18. ICSID Convention, Art. 54(1): 'Each Contracting State shall recognize an award rendered pursuant to this Convention as binding and enforce the pecuniary obligations imposed by that award within its territories as if it were a final judgment of a court in that State. A Contracting State with a federal constitution may enforce such an award in or through its federal courts and may provide that such courts shall treat the award as if it were a final judgment of the courts of a constituent state.'
19. In countries such as France, where the domestic law is more favorable to the enforcement of arbitral awards than the New York Convention, enforcement is sought pursuant to local law.

The definition of treaty under Article 2(a) of the VCLT deals only with treaties concluded between States that are in writing. Moreover, the VCLT deals only with international agreements that are governed by international law. States may enter into contracts where the national law of one of the parties governs, for example, commercial contracts. These are international agreements that do not fall within the VCLT.

Professor Francisco Orrego Vicuña once commented on the difference between a treaty and a contract by saying that:

> Not long ago teachers of international law used to explain that treaties are like contracts, only between states. Today it is necessary to explain that contracts are like treaties, only between individuals and the state. Paradoxical as it may seem, these different explanations respond to the changing reality underlying the process of globalization of the law. What used to be a useful comparison between international law and a separate domestic legal framework treaties and contracts has now become a part of a single legal structure which encompasses both contracts and treaties as well as a host of other instruments.[20]

Treaties have no governing law clause – the treaty is the governing law. Disputes arising out of the treaty are normally heard before international arbitral tribunals.

[B] Investment Contracts

Investment contracts are agreements between a foreign investor and a host State or instrumentality of a State setting forth the terms and conditions of an investment project in the territory of the host State. These international contracts may take the form of a concession agreement or a development agreement. Disputes may be heard in courts or arbitration, and the governing law clause is normally the law of the host State.

At this juncture, it is important to distinguish when a State is acting in its sovereign capacity *(jure imperii)* versus its commercial or business capacity *(jure gestionis)*. Justice Souter of the US Supreme Court, in *Saudi Arabia v. Nelson* said that:

> Under the restrictive, as opposed to the absolute, theory of foreign sovereign immunity, a state is immune from the jurisdiction of foreign courts as to its sovereign or public acts (*jure imperii*), but not as to those that are private or commercial in character (*jure gestionis*) ... a state engages in commercial activity under the restrictive theory where it exercises only those powers that can also be exercised by private citizens, as distinct from those powers peculiar to sovereigns. Put differently, a foreign state engages in commercial activity for purposes of the restrictive theory only where it acts in the manner of a private player within the market.[21]

---

20. *See* Francisco Orrego Vicuña, *Of Contracts and Treaties in the Global Market*, 8 Max-Planck Y.B. U.N. L. 341 (2004).
21. *Saudi Arabia v. Nelson*, 507 U.S. 349, 359–360 (1993).

[C] Foreign Investment Laws

Foreign investment laws seek to promote and control foreign investment and set standards that are applied to protect the investor. Normally, such legislation provides the basic provisions of the desired investment, incentives and guarantees, investment controls, and sets out the administration of the foreign investment process. Domestic law applies to and regulates both domestic and foreign investment. It consists of all laws and regulations of the host State, including, for example, investment laws and codes, tax codes, mining and other natural resource laws, as well as environmental laws and labor regulation.

§1.05 INVESTMENT ARBITRATION CRITICISM AND BACKLASH

Professor Karl-Heinz Böckstiegel has discussed the future of both commercial and investor-State arbitration.[22] In his lecture, Professor Böckstiegel expressed his view that in regard to commercial arbitration many domestic arbitration laws still need improvement, and that national court systems need to be adjusted for purposes of implementing the New York Convention along with addressing modern arbitration issues. He predicted that investment arbitration will continue to grow in spite of the criticisms that will inevitably continue.

Despite its growth, investor-State arbitration has been the object of much criticism. Some of the criticism warrants consideration while others are based on misconceptions and inaccurate information. This in turn has resulted in more careful scrutiny of the investor-State arbitration regime at large.

A 2012 Report issued by the Corporate European Observatory and the Transnational Institute delves into certain criticisms and starts off its executive summary by saying: 'The last two decades have witnessed the silent rise of a powerful international investment regime that has ensnared hundreds of countries and put corporate profit before human rights and the environment.'[23]

The report goes on to enumerate its key findings, including, that the number of investment arbitrations and sums of monies involved has surged in the past two decades; that such provides huge profits to lawyers at the expense of the taxpayer; that the investment lawyers and arbitrators are a small, elitist group; and that the investment arbitration world is becoming integrated with the speculative financial world, among others.

22. Karl-Heinz Böckstiegel, *Commercial and Investment Arbitration: How Different Are They Today? – The Lalive Lecture 2012*, 28(4) Arb. Intl. 577, 589–590 (2012).
23. *Profiting from Injustice, How Law Firms, Arbitrators and Financiers are Fueling an Investment Arbitration Boom*, Corporate Europe Observatory and the Transnational Institute (Nov. 2012), pp. 1, 7–9.

Moreover, a number of countries have denounced ICSID – Bolivia, Ecuador and Venezuela,[24] and others such as India, Indonesia and South Africa have initiated the process of terminating investment treaties.[25]

Nationalist and Protectionist Agenda Reinvigorated in 2016 to Present

More recently, there have been political evolutions that have brought about changes in trade and investment policy in a number of countries. The new policies point to a protectionist and nationalist agenda. Sovereign States fear alternative dispute resolution for the threats it imposes on the authority of domestic legislation, giving power to corporations via non-transparent processes.[26] For all intents and purposes, a nationalist and protectionist approach hinders globalization and as such reduces international trade and investment. Some examples of US policy changes under the Trump administration include the US withdrawal from the TPP, which is a free trade agreement between Canada and ten countries in the Asia-Pacific region, and from the TTIP, a proposed trade agreement between the US and the EU. The Trump administration is renegotiating the NAFTA with Mexico and Canada and recently imposed tariffs on steel and aluminum, which affects the World Trade Organization (WTO). The United Kingdom (UK), a central hub for many international investment treaties, will also be seeing an upheaval of its BITs after BREXIT, particularly intra-EU BITs that will likely result in termination and re-negotiation.

On 6 March 2018, the Court of Justice of the European Union (CJEU) issued its ruling on the compatibility of intra-EU BITs with EU law in *Slovak Republic v. Achmea BV*.[27] The CJEU determined that arbitration provisions found in BITs concluded between the EU Member States are incompatible with EU law. In the CJEU's opinion, BITs establish a mechanism for settling disputes between an investor and a Member State by an arbitral tribunal which falls outside the judicial system of the EU and as such cannot ensure the full effectiveness of EU law were a dispute to require the interpretation or application of EU law.

---

24. Bolivia denounced in 2007, *see* http://arbitrationblog.kluwerarbitration.com/2017/08/12/life-icsid-10th-anniversary-bolivias-withdrawal-icsid/ (accessed 25 May 2018); Ecuador denounced in 2009, *see* https://uk.practicallaw.thomsonreuters.com/2-422-1266?transitionType=Default&contextData=(sc.Default)&firstPage=true&bhcp=1 (accessed 25 May 2018); Venezuela denounced in 2012, *see* https://www.iisd.org/itn/2012/04/13/venezuelas-withdrawal-from-icsid-what-it-does-and-does-not-achieve/ (accessed 25 May 2018). It is however interesting to note that in the beginning of 2018 Ecuador started negotiating new investment treaties.
25. India's terminations began in 2016, *see* https://www.bakermckenzie.com/en/insight/publications/2017/05/withdrawal-from-investment-treaties (accessed 25 May 2018); Indonesia's terminations began in 2014, *see* https://www.bakermckenzie.com/en/insight/publications/2017/05/withdrawal-from-investment-treaties (accessed 25 May 2018); South Africa's terminations began in 2012, *see* http://www.nortonrosefulbright.com/knowledge/publications/118456/bilateral-investment-treaties-in-south-africa (accessed 25 May 2018).
26. James McBride, *How Are Trade Disputes Resolved?* (13 Mar. 2018), https://www.cfr.org/backgrounder/how-are-trade-disputes-resolved (accessed 25 May 2018).
27. *Slowakische Republik (Slovak Republic) v. Achmea BV*, CJEU Case No. C-284/16, Judgment of 6 March 2018, http://curia.europa.eu/juris/document/document.jsf?text=&docid=199968&pageIndex=0&doclang=EN&mode=req&dir=&occ=first&part=1&cid=404057 (accessed 25 May 2018).

The CJEU decision will no doubt have implications going forward. At present there are more than 190 BITs between EU Member States. Based on the ruling, investors will not be able to commence arbitration proceedings under BITs between EU Member States. There are, however, questions left unanswered. For example, it is not clear how the CJEU ruling will affect pending disputes against EU Member States under intra-EU BITs or its impact on arbitration under the ECT, which entered into force in April 1998 and to which the EU is a party.

As a matter of fact, the recent investment protection treaties concluded by the EU have replaced international arbitration by a permanent court with an appeals court. It is the case of the Free Trade Agreement of 2016 between the EU and Vietnam and of the EU-Canada Comprehensive Economic and Trade Agreement (CETA) of the same year. The same solution was adopted in April 2018 in the EU-Mexico new agreement and in a similar agreement between the EU and Singapore.

New Zealand has signed agreements to exclude compulsory investor-State dispute settlement (ISDS) with five countries in the Comprehensive and Progressive Agreement for Trans-Pacific Partnership (CPTPP). The Minister for Trade and Export Growth, David Parker, said the agreements are 'side letters' with the same treaty-level status as the Agreement.

New Zealand has signed additional side letters with Brunei Darussalam, Malaysia, Peru and Vietnam. New Zealand has also signed a side letter to exclude investor-State dispute resolution with Australia, the source of 80% of investment from the CPTPP nations into New Zealand.

Canada and Chile have joined New Zealand in a declaration about ISDS. In their view, this joint declaration 'is an acknowledgement of public concerns about [investor-State dispute settlement (ISDS)] ... [a]long with Canada and Chile'. They indicated to have pledged to work together to promote transparency.[28] This declaration was signed in early March 2018. The CPTPP, which was also signed in March 2018, is in the process of ratification and projected to come into force later in 2018 or early 2019.[29] The side letters and declaration add to work that had already narrowed the scope for investors to make investor-State claims under the CPTPP. Minister Parker, said that '[w]e have tackled it [ISDS] from several different directions. We have also made it clear that we will oppose including ISDS in any future free trade agreements involving New Zealand.'

The terms of the side letters vary. Some exclude the use of ISDS between New Zealand and other countries entirely, while other side letters allow arbitration to proceed only if the relevant government agrees.[30]

28. International Centre for Trade and Sustainable Development, *Countries Sign Pacific Rim Trade Deal, Call for 'Expeditious' Ratification Process*, https://www.ictsd.org/bridges-news/bridges/news/countries-sign-pacific-rim-trade-deal-call-for-%E2%80%9Cexpeditious%E2%80%9D-ratification (accessed 25 May 2018).
29. *Ibid.*
30. The side letters and joint declaration on ISDS are available on the Website of the New Zealand's Ministry of Foreign Affairs and Trade (MFAT), https://www.mfat.govt.nz/en/trade/free-trade-agreements/free-trade-agreements-concluded-but-not-in-force/cptpp/resources/#joint (accessed 25 May 2018).

Another more extreme approach that is picking up steam from certain scholars and critics calls for the total dismantling of the investor-State system and the creation of a new system altogether.[31] This approach alleges arbitrators' inherent lack of impartiality and inability to be objective when chosen by a party, the overt bias against States and the difficulty States have in finding acceptable arbitrators, the flawed nature of challenging an arbitrator's appointment, the inevitable rise of issue conflict with arbitrator's who are continuously recycled within the system, and the most pressing issue: the inability of any clear mechanism for reviewing or appealing an award.[32] This approach calls for the suspension of any new investment treaties, terminating existing treaties or eliminating certain problematic provisions within the treaties, looking ultimately to tear down the system and rebuild it.[33]

§1.06 CONCLUSION

Investor-State arbitration is a unique development in international law as it provides investors a direct way to sue a sovereign. This right is born from international bilateral and multilateral treaties signed by States. Prior to this development, investors' only recourse for the expropriation of their assets was to seek diplomatic protection or 'espousal' from their own governments. Diplomatic protection was never given as States would weigh many factors before acceding to espouse the investor's claims. Moreover, investors need to exhaust all legal recourse and remedies in the host State before seeking diplomatic protection. The absence of States' agreement under treaties to resolving disputes by investor-State arbitration would revert us back to the diplomatic protection era and perhaps even the gunboat diplomacy.

It should be borne in mind that the essence of international investment agreements has been, and will continue to be, chiseled by the corresponding economic, political and legal eras in which they are negotiated. When globalization increases, it is right to assume that trade will grow and investment agreements will increase along with the need for continued protection of foreign investments. If, however, a more protectionist and nationalist era is upon us, we may see the opposite taking place. It behoves all parties concerned to work towards the consolidation of a transparent international investment order that protects and balances the interests of investors, States and its citizens.

Questions

(1) What are the main distinctions between international investment arbitration and international commercial arbitration?
(2) Why do States enter into treaties to protect and promote foreign investment?

31. George Kahale III, *Rethinking ISDS*, TDM, ISSN 1875-4120 February 2018, www.transnational-dispute-management.com.
32. *Ibid.*
33. *Ibid.*

(3) Why is international arbitration seen as an attractive method of dispute resolution for investment disputes?
(4) What are some advantages and disadvantages to holding investment arbitrations under institutional arbitration rules as opposed to an ad hoc proceeding?
(5) What is the applicable law in investor-State arbitration?
(6) How are investor-States arbitration awards enforced?

CHAPTER 2

Investment and Investor

Investor-State arbitration offers protection to investors that make an investment in a State that has accepted to arbitrate disputes resulting from its acts or omissions affecting certain investments. A State may consent to arbitrate in a contract, in a national law on foreign investment or in investment treaties. An investor may consent to arbitrate by concluding a contract or by commencing arbitration based on a national law or an investment treaty.

In general, jurisdiction is normally acquired over the person (*ratione personae*) and over the matter (*ratione materiae*). This is also the case in investor-State arbitration. *Ratione personae* jurisdiction is acquired based on the nationality of the investor and jurisdiction *ratione materiae* is acquired based on the existence of an investment.

The expression 'investment' may have different meanings according to its context. Definitions of 'investment' in business, economy, finance or law will therefore vary. In investment arbitration, the notion of 'investment' is crucial because it triggers the application of an investment treaty or of a law on the protection of foreign investments, a pillar of the tribunal's jurisdiction.

The notion of 'investor' is another pillar of arbitral jurisdiction. An investor may be a natural or a legal person. An investor's right to arbitrate against the State is usually straightforward when this right has its basis on an investment contract with an arbitration agreement. Yet a State's offer to arbitrate contained in its national law on foreign investment or in its investment treaties is limited to certain predefined categories of 'investors'.

In addition to satisfying treaty requirements in relation to the notions of 'investment' and 'investor', a claimant in investment arbitration has to satisfy the standard rule on jurisdiction *ratione temporis*. This rule requires nationality on the date of injury (*dies a quo*) and on the date of submission of the claim for resolution (i.e., filing the request for arbitration) (*dies ad quem*). The ICSID

Convention requires specific critical dates depending on whether a natural or a legal person brings the investment claim.

Finally, an arbitral tribunal may deny jurisdiction *ratione temporis* when the investor's nationality results from acquiring nationality through fraudulent means or from material error by national authorities granting nationality. Moreover, in some cases tribunals may dismiss claims as inadmissible because of abuse of process.

§2.01 INTRODUCTION

The purpose of investor-State arbitration is to offer protection to investors that make an investment in a State that has accepted to have disputes resulting from its acts affecting certain investments to be submitted to arbitration. The acceptance of the State may be found in a contract, in a national law on foreign investments or in BIT or ann MIT.

The investor accepts to arbitrate against a State by concluding a contract with the State providing for investor-State arbitration or by commencing arbitration based on a national law on foreign investment or on an investment treaty. Because the investor is not a 'party' to the investment treaty, some scholars have referred to investment treaty arbitration as 'arbitration without privity'.[1]

In order for arbitrators to have jurisdiction, it is necessary that the dispute relates to an investment covered by the contract, the law or the treaty. The concept of 'investment' lacks a precise definition in international treaties and in the arbitration jurisprudence (§2.02). The protection of the 'investor' mainly depends on its nationality; nationality is a concept subject to various definitions (§2.03).

§2.02 THE CONCEPT OF INVESTMENT

The word 'investment' has several different meanings according to the context: business, tax, economy, finances, law, etc. Consequently, the recourse to common sense to recognize an investment is not of much help, contrary to the hope of some authors.[2] In the field of arbitration, the notion of investment is particularly important when it triggers the applicability of a treaty or of a law on the protection of foreign investments that, subsequently, will be the basis of the arbitrators' jurisdiction.

The notion of investment has been called the 'the cursed notion of the ICSID system'.[3] The regrettable confusion about the notion of investment increases when the discussion is no longer limited to ICSID arbitration and is extended to other procedures such as UNCITRAL arbitration. Many authors are concerned that the very concept of

1. *See*, for example, Jan Paulsson, *Arbitration Without Privity*, 10(2) ICSID Rev. (1995).
2. *See* Eduardo Silva Romero, *Por un regreso al sentido ordinario de la palabra 'inversión'*, 10 Revista Peruana de Arbitraje 25 (2010).
3. Walid Ben Hamida, *La notion d'investissement: la notion maudite du système CIRDI ?*, 4 Les cahiers de l'arbitrage 33 (2007).

investment arbitration be based on such an unstable notion. However, this supposed instability has not jeopardized the development of investment arbitration.

Although there is no uniformity on the definition of investment in the major applicable legal texts, two main approaches result from the efforts of arbitral tribunals and scholars to propose a definition: the subjective approach and the objective approach.

[A] The Absence of a Uniform Definition of the Concept of 'Investment' in Legal Instruments

There is no definition of the concept of investment in the ICSID Convention. There is no uniformity in this regard in MITs and BITs that in most cases provide examples of investment rather than a proper definition. When there is an attempt to provide one, it is very broad and, consequently, not very useful in practice.

[1] The Absence of a Definition under Article 25 of the ICSID Convention

Article 25(1) of the ICSID Convention reads that:

> The jurisdiction of the Centre shall extend to any legal dispute arising directly of an investment, between a Contracting State (or any constituent subdivision or agency of a Contracting State designated to the Centre by that State) and a national of another Contracting State, which the parties to the dispute consent in writing to submit to the Centre. When the parties have given their consent, no party may withdraw its consent unilaterally.

Although is it clear that the existence of an investment is a mandatory requisite to ICSID jurisdiction, no definition of investment can be found in the ICSID Convention. This is not the result of an oversight. The *travaux préparatoires* reveal that the omission was intentional. Article 30(i) of the first draft defined the notion of investment as follows: '"investment" means any contribution of money or other assets of economic value for an indefinite period or, if the period be defined, for not less than five years'.[4] However, no agreement was reached on that wording or on any other. The view of the majority was that investment was an evolving concept that could not be reduced to a frozen definition. Moreover, a definition was not felt necessary on the ground that the consent of the parties to ICSID intervention could be a sufficient confirmation that their dispute was originating from an investment. The negotiators' assumption was that the parties would agree to arbitration under the ICSID rules in a contract when the investment was made or after the occurrence of the dispute. They had not foreseen that in a near future many States would give a blind agreement to ICSID jurisdiction in-laws on the protection of investments, bilateral or multilateral treaties. Neither had they foreseen

4. *Convention on the Settlement of Investment Disputes between States and Nationals of Others States, Documents Concerning the Origin and the Formulation of the Convention* vol. I (ICSID 1970), p. 116.

the difficulties that the absence of a definition of investment would create in this context.

[2] *The Definitions in Other Multilateral Treaties*

[a] *NAFTA*

The NAFTA definition under its Article 1139 is enterprise-based. It refers to an 'enterprise' owned or controlled by an investor as a type of investment as well as to assets linked to the activities of an enterprise: equity and debt securities of an enterprise, a loan to an enterprise, any interest in an enterprise entitling the owner to a share of the income and/or profits of the enterprise, any interest in an enterprise entitling the owner to a share of the assets of the enterprise upon its dissolution, business real estate, and interests arising from the commitment of capital or other resources. Certain monetary claims are expressly excluded from the definition.

[b] *The Energy Charter Treaty*

Article 1(6) of the ECT defines 'investment' as follows:

> 'Investment' means every kind of asset, owned or controlled directly or indirectly by an Investor and includes:
>
> (a) tangible and intangible, and movable and immovable, property, and any property rights such as leases, mortgages, liens, and pledges;
> (b) a company or business enterprise, or shares, stock, or other forms of equity participation in a company or business enterprise, and bonds and other debt of a company or business enterprise;
> (c) claims to money and claims to performance pursuant to contract having an economic value and associated with an Investment;
> (d) Intellectual Property;
> (e) Returns;
> (f) any right conferred by law or contract or by virtue of any licences and permits granted pursuant to law to undertake any Economic Activity in the Energy Sector.
>
> A change in the form in which assets are invested does not affect their character as investments and the term 'Investment' includes all investments, whether existing at or made after the later of the date of entry into force of this Treaty for the Contracting Party of the Investor making the investment and that for the Contracting Party in the Area of which the investment is made (hereinafter referred to as the 'Effective Date') provided that the Treaty shall only apply to matters affecting such investments after the Effective Date.
>
> 'Investment' refers to any investment associated with an Economic Activity in the Energy Sector and to investments or classes of investments designated by a Contracting Party in its Area as 'Charter efficiency projects' and so notified to the Secretariat.

Two points must be noted: (1) the given list of assets is not exhaustive but contains just examples and (2) the protection of the ECT is reserved to investments in the energy sector under precise conditions.

[3] The Various Definitions in Bilateral Treaties

Traditionally, BITs have defined 'investment' as an asset or an interest, providing as the ECT a non-exhaustive list such as movable and immovable property, shares, stocks and debentures of companies or interests in the property of such companies, loans and portfolio transactions, mortgages, liens and pledges, contractual rights, claims to money, intellectual property rights and goodwill, concessions conferred by law or by contract.

The China-Pakistan Free Trade Agreement[5] of 2006 is a good example. Its Article 46 provides the following definition:

> For the purpose of this Chapter,
>
> 1. The term 'investment' means every kind of asset invested by investors of one Party in accordance with the laws and regulations of the other Party in the territory of the latter, and particularly, though not exclusively, includes:
>
> (a) movable and immovable property and other property rights such as mortgages, pledges and similar rights;
> (b) shares, debentures, stock and any other kind of participation in companies;
> (c) claims to money or to any other performance having an economic value associated with an investment;
> (d) intellectual property rights, in particular copyrights, patents, trade-marks, trade-names, technical process, know-how and goodwill;
> (e) business concessions conferred by law or under contract permitted by law, including concessions to search for, cultivate, extract or exploit natural resources.

Further to the non-exhaustiveness of the list, which is stressed in the text, the circularity of the definition is noteworthy: 'The term "investment" means every kind of asset invested by investors.' It is not specific to this treaty. Article 1(1) of the 1997 Italy-Pakistan BIT[6] reads that investment 'mean[s] any kind of property invested ... by a natural or legal person ...' and the 1994 Bolivia-Chile BIT does not hesitate to state in Article I(2) that 'investment refers to every kind of assets and rights in relation to an investment'.[7]

The difficulties of interpretation resulting from such broad and sweeping definitions of the concept of investment are described below. They have prompted a new generation of treaties including definitions that are more restrictive. The 2012 US Model

5. Free Trade Agreement between the Government of the Islamic Republic of Pakistan and the Government of the People's Republic of China (24 Nov. 2006).
6. Agreement between the Government of the Islamic Republic of Pakistan and the Government of the Italian Republic on the Promotion and Protection of Investments (19 Jul. 1997).
7. Agreement between the Republic of Bolivia and the Republic of Chile on the Reciprocal Promotion and Protection of Investments (22 Sep. 1994) (original in Spanish, free translation).

BIT provides a good example: it states that investment means every asset that has the characteristics of an investment; this is obviously a tautology, but such definition has the advantage to point out that the list it provides are just examples of the forms that an investment may take:

> 'investment' means every asset that an investor owns or controls, directly or indirectly, that has the characteristics of an investment, including such characteristics as the commitment of capital or other resources, the expectation of gain or profit, or the assumption of risk. Forms that an investment may take include:
>
> (a) an enterprise;
> (b) shares, stock, and other forms of equity participation in an enterprise;
> (c) bonds, debentures, other debt instruments, and loans;[8]
> (d) futures, options, and other derivatives;
> (e) turnkey, construction, management, production, concession, revenue- sharing, and other similar contracts;
> (f) intellectual property rights;
> (g) licenses, authorizations, permits, and similar rights conferred pursuant to domestic law;[9,10] and
> (h) other tangible or intangible, movable or immovable property, and related property rights, such as leases, mortgages, liens, and pledge.

The 2016 Free Trade Agreement between the EU and Vietnam refers to 'every kind of asset ... that has the characteristics of an investment, including such characteristics as the commitment of capital or other resources, the expectation of gain or profit, the assumption of risk and for a certain duration'.[11] The CETA between the EU and Canada adopt the same definition in its Article 8(1). However, these new treaties do not provide for resolution of investment disputes by traditional arbitration but by a permanent Tribunal with an appellate procedure.[12]

8. Some forms of debt, such as bonds, debentures, and long-term notes, are more likely to have the characteristics of an investment, while other forms of debt, such as claims to payment that are immediately due and result from the sale of goods or services, are less likely to have such characteristics.
9. Whether a particular type of license, authorization, permit, or similar instrument (including a concession, to the extent that it has the nature of such an instrument) has the characteristics of an investment depends on such factors as the nature and extent of the rights that the holder has under the law of the Party. Among the licenses, authorizations, permits, and similar instruments that do not have the characteristics of an investment are those that do not create any rights protected under domestic law. For greater certainty, the foregoing is without prejudice to whether any asset associated with the license, authorization, permit, or similar instrument has the characteristics of an investment.
10. The term 'investment' does not include an order or judgment entered in a judicial or administrative action.
11. EU-Vietnam Free Trade Agreement (2016), Trade in Services, Investment and E-Commerce, Chapter I on 'General Provisions', Art. 4(p).
12. *See*, for example, Comprehensive Economic and Trade Agreement (CETA) between Canada, of the one Part, and the European Union and its Member States, of the Other Part (2016), Art. 8.27 and Art. 8.28.

[B] The Investment in Arbitration Jurisprudence

Article 25 of the ICSID Convention limits the jurisdiction of ICSID arbitrators to disputes arising from an investment. This has led ICSID arbitrators to develop what is known as the 'double barrel' or 'double keyhole' approach: to retain jurisdiction, ICSID arbitrators should check first whether the dispute relates to an investment pursuant to the requirements of applicable treaty and, then, that it is 'arising of an investment' according to Article 25 of the ICSID Convention. However, this approach has not generated a uniform definition of the concept of investment and the proposed definitions have found little support outside of ICSID arbitration.

[1] The ICSID Jurisprudence

ICSID arbitrators appear to be divided into two main groups: those who believe in the existence of an objective concept of investment and apply with more or less flexibility the so-called *Salini test* (a); and those who prefer a subjective case-by-case approach and rely mainly on the parties' agreement in the applicable BIT (b).

[a] The Objective Approach

The basic characteristics of an investment were enumerated in 2001 by the *Salini v. Morocco*[13] tribunal: (a) a contribution, (b) an assumption of risk, (c) a duration and (d) a contribution to the economic development of the host State of the investment. The idea was that these characteristics were requisites that should be objectively met as a condition for the jurisdiction of ICSID arbitrators. This became known as the *Salini test*.[14]

However, subsequent ICSID tribunals did not uniformly apply the *Salini test*. Some considered that it had to be strictly applied.[15] Others reduced the number of

13. *Salini Costruttori S.p.A. and Italstrade S.p.A. v. Kingdom of Morocco*, ICSID Case No. ARB/00/4, Decision on Jurisdiction (16 Jul. 2001), 42 ILM 609, 622 (2003), para. 52: 'The doctrine generally considers that investment infers: contributions, a certain duration of performance of the contract and a participation in the risks of the transaction ... In reading the Convention's preamble, one may add the contribution to the economic development of the host State of the investment as an additional condition. In reality, these various elements may be interdependent. Thus, the risks of the transaction may depend on the contributions and the duration of performance of the contract. As a result, these various criteria should be assessed globally even if, for the sake of reasoning, the Tribunal considers them individually here.'
14. In fact, the *Salini* case was not the first to introduce a definition of investment in addition to that of the treaty. In *Fedax N.V. v. The Republic of Venezuela*, ICSID Case No. ARB/96/3, Decision of the Tribunal on Objections to Jurisdiction (11 Jul. 1997), 37 ILM 1378, 1387 (1998), the tribunal indicated that an investment is characterized by 'a certain duration, a certain regularity of profit and return, assumption of risk, a substantial commitment and a significance for the host State's development'.
15. *See*, among other decisions, *Bayindir Insaat Turizm Ticaret Ve Sanayi A.S. v. Islamic Republic of Pakistan*, ICSID Case No. ARB/03/29, Decision on Jurisdiction (14 Nov. 2005), paras 130 et seq.; *Jan de Nul N.V. and Dredging International N.V. v. Arab Republic of Egypt*, ICSID Case No. ARB/04/13, Decision on Jurisdiction (16 Jun. 2006), para. 91.

criteria to three, as the *LESI* tribunal in 2006,[16] which considered that the contribution to the economic development of the host State of the investment was difficult to prove and was implicitly covered by the three first criteria of *Salini*. However, these criteria were increased to six when in 2009, the *Phoenix* Tribunal[17] added as conditions, observance of the law of the host State and good faith in making the investment. This position, however, was not followed a year later by the *Saba Fakes*[18] tribunal, which retained only the first three criteria of the *Salini* test; it did not retain the contribution to the host State development because an investment, which is expected to be fruitful, might turn out to be an economic disaster while nevertheless remaining an investment. It also rejected the condition of good faith because it was not contemplated by the text of the ICSID Convention and that of legality of the investment because such condition should be included in a BIT. This approach was confirmed by the *Quiborax* tribunal in 2010:

> The Tribunal appreciates that the element of contribution to the development of the host State is generally regarded as part of the well-known four-prong Salini test. Yet, such contribution may well be the consequence of a successful investment; it does not appear as a requirement. If the investment fails, it may end up having made no contribution to the host State development. This does not mean that it is not an investment.[19]

Consequently, it seems that for the majority of those arbitrators which believe that a general concept of investment should be referred to in order to establish their jurisdiction pursuant to Article 25 of the ICSID Convention, only the three first criteria of the *Salini test* should be met:

(1) a contribution;
(2) an element of risk;
(3) a certain duration.

[b] The Subjective Approach

Other tribunals have rapidly concluded that the *Salini test* had no solid basis under the ICSID Convention. In 2008, the *Biwater* tribunal pointed out that:

---

16. *LESI, SpA and Astaldi, SpA v. People's Democratic Republic of Algeria*, ICSID Case No. ARB/05/3, Decision on Jurisdiction (12 Jul. 2006), para. 72(iv).
17. *Phoenix Action, Ltd. v. The Czech Republic*, ICSID Case No. ARB/06/5, Award (15 Apr. 2009), para. 100.
18. *Saba Fakes v. Republic of Turkey*, ICSID Case No. ARB/07/20, Award (14 Jul. 2010), paras 110–111.
19. *Quiborax S.A., Non Metallic Minerals S.A. and Allan Fosk Kaplún v. Plurinational State of Bolivia*, ICSID Case No. ARB/06/2, Decision on Jurisdiction (27 Sep. 2012), para. 220.

> In the Tribunal's view, there is no basis for a rote, or overly strict, application of the five[[20]] Salini criteria in every case. These criteria are not fixed or mandatory as a matter of law. They do not appear in the ICSID Convention ...
>
> Further, the *Salini Test* itself is problematic if, as some tribunals have found, the 'typical characteristics' of an investment as identified in that decision are elevated into a fixed and inflexible test, and if transactions are to be presumed excluded from the ICSID Convention unless each of the five criteria are satisfied. This risks the arbitrary exclusion of certain types of transaction from the scope of the Convention. It also leads to a definition that may contradict individual agreements (as here), as well as a developing consensus in parts of the world as to the meaning of 'investment' (as expressed, e.g., in bilateral investment treaties). If very substantial numbers of BITs across the world express the definition of 'investment' more broadly than the *Salini Test*, and if this constitutes any type of international consensus, it is difficult to see why the ICSID Convention ought to be read more narrowly.[21]

This position was confirmed by an ICSID annulment committee in 2009 in *Malaysian Historical Salvors v. Malaysia*.[22] The *Alpha Projecktholding* tribunal adopted a similar reasoning in 2010:

> The ICSID Convention does not define the term 'investment'. Given the absence of a definition, both parties refer to illustrative criteria developed in various arbitration awards, most notably the award in *Salini v. Morocco*. However, the elements of the so-called Salini test, which some tribunals have applied mandatorily and cumulatively (i.e., if one feature is missing, a claimed investment will be ruled out of ICSID jurisdiction), are not found in Article 25(1) of the ICSID Convention. In applying the criteria in this manner, these tribunals have sought to apply a universal definition of 'investment' under the ICSID Convention, despite the fact that the drafters and signatories of the Convention decided that it should not have one. This Tribunal will not follow that approach and will not impose additional requirements beyond those expressed on the face of Article 25(1) of the ICSID Convention and the UABIT.
>
> The Tribunal is particularly reluctant to apply a test that seeks to assess an investment's contribution to a country's economic development. Should a tribunal find it necessary to check whether a transaction falls outside any reasonable understanding of 'investment', the criteria of resources, duration, and risk would seem fully to serve that objective. The Tribunal recognizes that elements discussed in the *Salini* test might be of some use if a tribunal were concerned that a BIT or contract definition of 'investment' was overreaching and captured transactions that manifestly were not investments under any acceptable definition. Indeed, a number of tribunals and *ad hoc* committees have treated the *Salini* elements as non binding, non-exclusive means of identifying (rather than defining) investments that are consistent with the ICSID Convention. However, in most

20. The *Biwater* tribunal saw five and not four criteria as in *Salini*, as follows: (a) duration, (b) regularity of profit, (c) assumption of risk, (d) substantial commitment, and (e) contribution to the development of the host State.
21. *Biwater Gauff (Tanzania) Ltd. v. United Republic of Tanzania*, ICSID Case No. ARB/05/22, Award (24 Jul. 2008), paras 312, 314.
22. *Malaysian Historical Salvors, SDN, BHD v. The Government of Malaysia*, ICSID Case No. ARB/05/10, Decision of the Application for Annulment (16 Apr. 2009), para. 79.

> cases –including, in the Tribunal's view, this one – it will be appropriate to defer to the States' definition of investment in a BIT or a contract.[23]

The *Abaclat* tribunal showed the same preference for the definition of the BIT in 2011:

> Considering that these criteria [The Salini criteria] were never included in the ICSID Convention, while being controversial and having been applied by tribunals in varying manners and degrees, the Tribunal does not see any merit in following and copying the *Salini* criteria. The *Salini* criteria may be useful to further describe what characteristics contributions may or should have. They should, however, not serve to create a limit, which neither the Convention itself nor the Contracting Parties to a specific BIT intended to create.[24]

The conclusion is that a significant number of ICSID tribunals appear to be reluctant to refer to an objective concept of 'investment' and prefer to rely on the definition to be found in the applicable BIT.

[2] The Jurisprudence of Non-ICSID Tribunals

Non-ICSID tribunals do not have to bother with the absence of a definition of the concept of investment in Article 25(1) of the ICSID Convention, which is not applicable. They consider only the definition of the applicable BIT and retain jurisdiction if they find the alleged investment on the list. This approach was perfectly explained by the *Mytilineos* tribunal constituted pursuant to the UNCITRAL Rules:

> It is the established practice of ICSID tribunals to assess whether a specific transaction qualifies as an 'investment' under the ICSID Convention, independently of the definition of investment in a BIT or other applicable investment instrument, in order to fulfill the *ratione materiae* prerequisite of Article 25 of the Convention. This requirement is set out in Article 25(1) of the Convention, which confines the jurisdiction of ICSID arbitration tribunals to 'legal dispute[s] arising directly out of an investment' without defining 'investment'.
>
> ... However, this later *ratione materiae* test for the existence of an investment in the sense of Article of the 25 ICSID Convention is one specific to the ICSID Convention and does not apply in the context of *ad hoc* arbitration provided for in BITs as an alternative to ICSID.
>
> In the present *ad hoc* arbitration under the UNCITRAL Rules one would therefore have to conclude that the only requirements that have to be fulfilled in order to confer *ratione materiae* jurisdiction on this Tribunal are those under the BIT.[25]

---

23. *Alpha Projecktholding mgbh v. Ukrain Alpha Projektholding GmbH v. Ukraine*, ICSID Case No. ARB/07/16, Award (8 Nov. 2010), paras 311–312.
24. *Abaclat and Others v. Argentine Republic*, ICSID Case No. ARB/07/5 (formerly *Giovanna a Beccara and Others v. The Argentine Republic*), Decision on Jurisdiction and Admissibility (4 Aug. 2011), para. 364. *See also Philip Morris Brands Sarl, Philip Morris Products S.A. and Abal Hermanos S.A. v. Oriental Republic of Uruguay*, ICSID Case No. ARB/10/7 (formerly *FTR Holding SA, Philip Morris Products S.A. and Abal Hermanos S.A. v. Oriental Republic of Uruguay*), Decision on Jurisdiction (2 Jul. 2013), para. 187.
25. *Mytilineos Holdings SA v. The State Union of Serbia & Montenegro and Republic of Serbia*, Partial Award on Jurisdiction (UNCITRAL) (8 Sep. 2006), paras 112, 117–118.

However, there are two notable exceptions. Two tribunals considered, as the 2012 US Model BIT does, that the fact that the lists of investments included in most BITs are not exhaustive is an evidence that they are just mere examples of what an investment could be provided it meet the characteristics of an objective concept of investment under international law. The *Romak* tribunal stressed:

> First, the approach advanced by Romak deprives the term 'investments' of any inherent meaning, which is contrary to the logic of Article 1(2) of the BIT. Indeed, as already mentioned, the categories of investments enumerated in Article 1(2) of the BIT are not exhaustive, and do not constitute an all encompassing definition of 'investment'. Both Parties agree that this is the case. Therefore, there may well exist categories different from those mentioned in the list which, nevertheless, could properly be considered investments protected under the BIT. Accordingly, there must be a benchmark against which to assess those non-listed assets or categories of assets in order to determine whether they constitute an 'investment' within the meaning of Article 1(2). The term 'investment' has a meaning in itself that cannot be ignored when considering the list contained in Article 1(2) of the BIT.[26]

The *Aps Finance and Trade* tribunal found that when the Contacting States make a list of what constitutes an investment in a BIT they 'explicitly or implicitly refer to an "objective" definition given by international law'.[27] It added that in a case where the Contracting States contemplated that disputes might be resolved alternatively under the ICSID Convention or the UNCITRAL Rules, the consequences is that they 'inevitably intended to refer to what constitutes "investment" under the ICSID Convention as concretely applied in the relevant case law'.[28]

Those are strong arguments that show that the definition of the concept of investment remains hotly disputed among arbitrators. This generates a lack of foreseeability that is difficult to explain to the parties because the same economic operation may be considered as protected or not protected by the same BIT, depending on whether the arbitrators define their jurisdiction *ratione materiae* by a mere reference to the list of investments provided in the treaty or rely on an objective concept of investment in the light of the *Salini test*.

Whatever the applicable arbitration rules, it seems that there is at least an agreement to exclude from the concept of investment commercial transactions. The *Joy Mining Machinery* tribunal in 2004 was explicit in this regard:

> The Tribunal is also mindful that if a distinction is not drawn between ordinary sales contracts, even if complex, and an investment, the result would be that any sales or procurement contract involving a State agency would qualify as an investment. International contracts are today a central feature of international trade and have stimulated far reaching developments in the governing law, among

26. *Romak S.A. (Switzerland) v. The Republic of Uzbekistan*, UNCITRAL, PCA Case No. AA280, Award (26 Nov. 2009), para. 180.
27. *Alps Finance and Trade AG v. The Slovak Republic*, UNCITRAL, Award (5 Mar. 2011), para. 239.
28. *Ibid.*

> them the United Nations Convention on Contracts for the International Sale of Goods, and significant conceptual contributions. Yet, those contracts are not investment contracts, except in exceptional circumstances, and are to be kept separate and distinct for the sake of a stable legal order. Otherwise, what difference would there be with the many State contracts that are submitted every day to international arbitration in connection with contractual performance, at such bodies as the International Chamber of Commerce and the London Court of International Arbitration?[29]

However, there is also a degree of inconsistency in this respect. In 2012, the *Deutsche Bank v. Sri Lanka*[30] ICSID tribunal found that a hedging agreement was an investment under the Germany-Sri Lanka BIT.[31]

§2.03 THE PROTECTED INVESTOR

The investor may be a natural or a legal person. The right of investors to arbitrate against the State is not seriously disputable when it concluded with the State an investment contract that includes an arbitration clause. The issue is more complicated when the investor intends to rely on the offer to arbitrate that the State has made to foreign investors in its national investment law or to certain categories of foreign investors in BITs or MITs to which this State is a party. In the first case, the investor must meet the definition of a foreigner under national investment law. In the second case, the investor must meet the conditions laid down by the definition of 'investor' in the particular BIT of MIT:

> The fundamental issue is that of the nationality of the investor, although some BITs and MITs contain definition of the investor which also includes permanent residents of the contracting parties.[32] With regard to investment laws, the investor must not be a national of the host State since the very purpose of the law is to foster foreign investment by granting a special protection to foreign investors. Concerning BITs or MITs, the investor must also be a national of a country which is a party to a treaty binding on the host State. Although the nationality of natural persons has given rise to controversies, it is essentially the nationality of corporations which is at the origin of the more serious difficulties. The date at which the nationality must be taken into consideration is also an important factor.

29. *Joy Mining Machinery Limited v. Arab Republic of Egypt*, ICSID Case No. ARB/03/11, Award on Jurisdiction (6 Aug. 2004), para. 58.
30. *Deutsche Bank AG v. Democratic Socialist Republic of Sri Lanka*, ICSID Case No. ARB/09/2, Award (31 Oct. 2012), para. 312(iii).
31. This award was subject to annulment proceedings, which were discontinued on 9 Sep. 2016.
32. For instance, the Argentina-Canada BIT defines the investor as follows: 'The term "investor" includes any natural person who makes the investment possessing the citizenship or permanently residing in a Contracting Party in accordance with its laws.' Article 201 of NAFTA contains a similar definition of 'national', whereby permanent residents are considered as nationals. Likewise, Art. 1(7) of the ECT refers not only to nationals but also to individuals who are 'permanently residing' in a contracting party.

[A] Natural Persons

Arbitral tribunals tend to determine whether a person is a national of a particular country by application of the law of the country whose nationality is claimed.[33] In case such nationality is disputed the tribunal will not hesitate to determine it. As stressed in the *Soufraki* award:

> It is accepted in international law that nationality is within the domestic jurisdiction of the State, which settles, by its own legislation, the rules relating to the acquisition (and loss) of its nationality ... But it is no less accepted that when, in international arbitral or judicial proceedings, the nationality of a person is challenged, the international tribunal is competent to pass [judgement] upon that challenge. It will accord great weight to the nationality law of the State in question and to the interpretation and application of that law by its authorities. But it will in the end decide for itself, whether, on the facts and law before it, the person whose nationality is at issue was or was not a national of the State in question and when, and what follows from that finding. Where, as in the instant case, the jurisdiction of an international tribunal turns on an issue of nationality, the international tribunal is empowered, indeed bound, to decide that issue.[34]

However, the situation of dual nationals, i.e., persons who have the nationality of the host State, in addition to the nationality of the State on whose basis he or she claims protection, creates a specific problem in ICSID arbitration. Dual nationals are expressly excluded under Article 25(2)(a) of the ICSID Convention which reads that:

> 2) 'National of another Contracting State' means:
>
> (a) any natural person who had the nationality of a Contracting State other than the State party to the dispute on the date on which the parties consented to submit such dispute to conciliation or arbitration as well as on the date on which the request was registered pursuant to paragraph (3) of Article 28 or paragraph (3) of Article 36, but does not include any person who on either date also had the nationality of the Contracting State party to the dispute;

The application of the rule raises difficulty when a dual national investor claims that his or her effective nationality is not that of the host State. According to the prevailing definition of nationality in international law, such as expressed in the *Nottebohm*[35] case when the International Court of Justice (ICJ) found that nationality is a 'legal bond having at its basis a social fact of attachment, a genuine connection of

33. Pursuant to Art. 1 of the 2012 US Model BIT, '"national" means for the United States, a natural person who is a national of the United States as defined in Title III of the Immigration and Nationality Act'. Article 201 of NAFTA reads that 'national means a natural person who is a citizen or permanent resident of a Party and any other natural person referred to in Annex 201.1'. In turn, Annex 201.1 provides that 'national also includes: (a) with respect to Mexico, a national or a citizen according to Arts 30 and 34, respectively, of the Mexican Constitution; and (b) with respect to the United States, "national of the United States" as defined in the existing provisions of the Immigration and Nationality Act'.
34. *Hussein Nuaman Soufraki v. The United Arab Emirates*, ICSID Case No. ARB/02/7, Award (7 Jul. 2004), para. 55.
35. *Nottebohm Case (Liechtenstein v. Guatemala), Second Phase*, ICJ Judgment (6 Apr. 1955), 1955 ICJ Reports 4, 23.

existence, interests and sentiments, together with reciprocal rights and duties'. On the basis of Article 25(2)(a) of the ICSID Convention, arbitral tribunals refuse to rely on the effective nationality and do not consider that a dual national is entitled to protection.[36]

In ICSID arbitration, the solution should be the same *mutatis mutandi*, when a BIT or MIT contains a definition of 'investor' that includes not only nationals but also natural persons who are permanent residents under the applicable domestic law, if that resident is not a national of a country party to the ICSID Convention, since Article 25(2)(a) of the Convention requires the investor to be a national of a Contracting State.

With regard to non-ICSID investor-State arbitration, the situation of dual nationals depends only on the text of the relevant applicable treaty or investment law. For example, Article 1 of the US Model BIT addresses the dual nationality issue in its definition of 'investor of a Party': 'a natural person who is a dual national shall be deemed to be exclusively a national of the State of his or her dominant and effective nationality'. Failing such definition, the tribunal in the *García Armas v. Venezuela* case held that in the absence of express limitation excluding dual nationals or requiring dominant and effective nationality it was not possible to devoid of effect the nationality granted freely by a State and accepted as valid by the other.[37] This solution was upheld by the Paris Court of Appeal on 25 April 2017[38] in setting aside proceedings.

[B] Legal or Juridical Persons

A legal person's nationality is that of the State of its seat or its place of incorporation or formation. Consequently, a legal person must have its seat or must have been incorporated in another State to rely on the investment law of a State protecting foreign investors. However, it will be insufficient when the investment law also requires that the investor be under foreign control.[39]

Although most BITs protect legal persons that are legally constituted or incorporated in a contracting party, granting protection to investors by the mere fact of incorporation, some of them provide protection to legal entities incorporated in a

36. *See Champion Trading Company, Ameritrade International, Inc. v. Arab Republic of Egypt*, ICSID Case No. ARB/02/9 (formerly *Champion Trading Company, Ameritrade International, Inc., James T. Wahba, John B. Wahba, Timothy T. Wahba v. Arab Republic of Egypt*), Decision on Jurisdiction (21 Oct. 2003), pp. 16–17.
37. *Serafín García Armas and Karina García Gruber v. The Bolivarian Republic of Venezuela*, UNCITRAL, PCA Case No. 2013-3, Decision on Jurisdiction (15 Dec. 2014), para. 200.
38. Paris Court of Appeal, pôle 1, 1re ch., *République bolivarienne du Venezuela v. Monsieur Serafín García Armas and Mme Karina García Gruber*, Judgment (25 Apr. 2017). *See* comments by Walid Ben Hamida, *L'investisseur protégé: Paris le paradis arbitral des binationaux et des investisseurs souverains*, 4 Les Cahiers de l'Arbitrage 674 (2017).
39. *See*, for example, the Venezuelan law on promotion and protection of investments (Decree No. 356 of 3 Oct. 1999) which, after indicating that an 'international investment' must be owned or effectively controlled by foreign natural or legal persons, defines 'international investor' in its Art. 3(4), as follows: 'The owner of an international investment or whom effectively controls it.' (Free translation of Spanish original: 'El propietario de una inversión internacional, o quien efectivamente la controle.')The application of this law is discussed in the *Venoklim* award; *see Venoklim Holding B.V. v. Bolivarian Republic of Venezuela*, ICSID Case No. ARB/12/22, Award (3 Apr. 2015), paras 141 et seq.

non-contracting party controlled by natural or legal persons holding the nationality of the other contracting party.[40] Failing such a specific requisite, the huge majority of arbitral tribunals is of the view that control is irrelevant and that a treaty's silence with respect to control means that incorporation in another contracting party is sufficient.

This position was clearly expressed in the *Tokios Tokelès v. Ukraine* case. The Lithuanian Tokios had created a Ukrainian subsidiary that brought a claim against Ukraine under Lithuania-Ukraine BIT. Tokios Tokelès itself was 99%-owned by Ukrainian nationals. According to Lithuanian law, applicable under the BIT, the place of incorporation was enough to determine the nationality of a legal person, and there was no control requirement in the BIT. The majority of the arbitrators[41] decided that Tokios could rely on the BIT because:

> Article 1(2)(b) of the Ukraine-Lithuania BIT defines the term 'investor', with respect to Lithuania, as 'any entity established in the territory of the Republic of Lithuania in conformity with its laws and regulations... The Treaty contains no additional requirements for an entity to qualify as an 'investor' of Lithuania.[42]

In ICSID arbitration, the control of a legal person by nationals of a Contracting State is taken into consideration only when the investor is a legal person of the same nationality as the host State, provided it has been contemplated by the Contracting Parties. Article 25(2)(b) of the Washington Convention reads:

---

40. *See*, for example, Agreement on Encouragement and Reciprocal Protection of Investments between the Kingdom of the Netherlands and the Argentine Republic (20 Oct. 1992), Art. 1(b): 'the term "investor" shall comprise with regard to either Contracting Party: ... ii. without prejudice to the provisions of paragraph (iii) hereafter, legal persons constituted under the law of that Contracting Party and actually doing business under the laws in force in any part of the territory of that Contracting Party in which a place of effective management is situated; and iii. legal persons, wherever located, controlled, directly or indirectly, by nationals of that Contracting Party'. The Protocol to this Agreement seeks to define 'control' within the meaning of Art. 1(b)(iii), as follows: 'B. With reference to Article 1, paragraph b) (iii) the Contracting Party in the territory of which the investments are undertaken may require proof of the control invoked by the investors of the other Contracting Party. The following facts, *inter alia*, shall be accepted as evidence of the control: i. being an affiliate of a legal person of the other Contracting Party; ii. having a direct or indirect participation in the capital of a company higher than 49% or the direct or indirect possession of the necessary votes to obtain a predominant position in assemblies or company organs.' Adopting a slightly different test on legal persons, combining the 'control' requirement with the 'incorporation' and 'seat' requirements, *see* Agreement Between the Government of the Federal Republic of Ethiopia and the Government of the Republic of France for the Reciprocal Promotion and Protection of Investments (25 Jun. 2003), Art. 1(3): 'The term "company" means any legal person constituted on the territory of one Contracting Party in accordance with the legislation of that Party and having its head office on the territory of that Party, or controlled directly or indirectly by the nationals of one Contracting Party, or by legal persons having their head office in the territory of one Contracting Party and constituted in accordance with the legislation of that Party.'
41. Interestingly, the president of the tribunal, Professor Prosper Weil, expressed a minority view, considering that a legal person controlled by nationals of the host State could not enjoy the protection of the BIT.
42. *Tokios Tokelés v. Ukraine*, ICSID Case No. ARB/02/18, Decision on Jurisdiction (29 Apr. 2004), para. 28. *See also Saluka Investments B.V. v. The Czech Republic*, UNCITRAL, Partial Award (17 Mar. 2006), in which a similar decision was based on Art. 1(b) of the Czech-Republic-Netherlands BIT, which reads that: 'the term "investors" shall comprise: (i) natural persons having the nationality of one of the Contracting Parties in accordance with its law; (ii) legal persons constituted under the law of one of the Contracting Parties'. (paras 222 et seq.).

> any juridical person which had the nationality of a Contracting State other than the State party to the dispute on the date on which the parties consented to submit such dispute to conciliation or arbitration and any juridical person which had the nationality of the Contracting State party to the dispute on that date and which, because of foreign control, the parties have agreed should be treated as a national of another Contracting State for the purposes of this Convention.

In the 2016 World Investment Report, the United Nations Conference on Trade and Development (UNCTAD) noted on the basis of the available information that since 2010, about one-third of ISDS claims had been filed by claimant entities that were ultimately owned by a parent in a third country not party to the treaty on which the claim was based.[43]

Finally, some investment treaties contain denial-of-benefits clauses excluding nationals of third States that, through shell or mailbox companies, claim treaty protection. For instance, the Canada-Mongolia BIT[44] provides in Article 18(2) that a contracting party may deny BIT benefits to investments of an investor that is an enterprise of the other contracting party 'if investors of a non-Party own or control the enterprise and the enterprise has no substantial business activities in the territory of the Party under whose law it is constituted or organized'.

[C] Date of Nationality

[1] Jurisdiction Ratione Temporis

On comity grounds, States have historically required 'continuous nationality' under international law and, particularly, in diplomatic protection. Espousing a claim and thus interfering with how another State handled internal affairs required 'continuous nationality' until the date of dispute resolution (*dies ad quem*). But when States empowered individuals to pursue their claims directly against other States, the requirement that nationality exist on the date of dispute resolution was relaxed.[45]

In investor-State arbitration, the standard rule on jurisdiction *ratione temporis* requires nationality on the date of injury (*dies a quo*) and on the date of submission of the claim for resolution (i.e., filing the request for arbitration) (*dies ad quem*). For example, in *García Armas v. Venezuela* the majority of the tribunal held that jurisdiction required that the investor possess the nationality of the relevant State: (a) on the date of injury (unless the treaty provides otherwise) and (b) on the date of the request for arbitration pursuant to terms of the BIT.[46] The *Pey Casado v. Chile* tribunal upheld the same nationality critical dates.[47]

43. UNCTAD, *2016 World Investment Report, Investor Nationality: Policy Challenges* (United Nations 2016), p. 171.
44. Agreement between Canada and Mongolia for the Promotion and Protection of Investments (8 Sep. 2016).
45. *See Loewen Group, Inc. and Raymond L. Loewen v. United States of America*, ICSID Case No. ARB(AF)/98/3, Award (26 Jun. 2003), para. 230.
46. *Serafín García Armas and Karina García Gruber v. The Bolivarian Republic of Venezuela*, UNCITRAL, PCA Case No. 2013-3, Decision on Jurisdiction (15 Dec. 2014), paras 215–217. It is

In ICSID arbitration, Article 25(2)(a) of the ICSID Convention requires that a natural person possess the nationality of a Contracting State that is not a party to the dispute on two dates: on the date when he or she consents to arbitrate, and on the date when the Secretary General registers the request for arbitration. In investment treaty arbitrations, the date of consent is the date of the request for arbitration, which often does not coincide with the date when the Secretary General registers the request under Article 28(3)[48] of the ICSID Convention. For instance, the *Kim et al. v. Uzbekistan* tribunal applied the investment treaty and the ICSID Convention requirements on nationality of natural persons, finding that the critical dates applying to the claimants were: (a) 'the date of the alleged breach', (b) 'the date the claim was submitted to ICSID' and (c) 'the date the claim was registered by ICSID'.[49]

The three critical dates in relation to nationality in *Kim et al. v. Uzbekistan* above should be understood in the context of natural persons. Article 25(2)(b) of the ICSID Convention does not require nationality on the registration date for legal persons. Rather, a legal person shall possess the nationality of a Contracting State other than the State party to the arbitration 'on the date on which the parties consented to submit such dispute' to arbitration. ICSID tribunals also consider other nationality date requirements such as those provided under the relevant investment treaty or investment legislation. Except for the ICSID Convention critical dates, non-ICSID tribunals will also consider these other nationality date requirements.

The ICJ held in the *Arrest Warrant* case that 'jurisdiction must be determined at the time that the act instituting proceedings were filed'.[50] This means that jurisdiction persists regardless of later events. Arbitral tribunals have therefore rejected, for instance, allegations that investors were no longer interested parties.[51]

In *El Paso v. Argentina*, the arbitral tribunal rejected Argentina's allegation that subsequent events such as El Paso's sale of its shares in the Argentine invested companies led to the tribunal's lack of jurisdiction over El Paso. According to the tribunal, the text of the ICSID Convention and the US-Argentina BIT[52] do not require

noteworthy that the Paris Court of Appeal set aside the Decision on the ground that this tribunal's majority had also found that the date when the investment was made was irrelevant for jurisdiction purposes, reading in the applicable treaty the requirement that the date of the investment be taken into consideration: Paris Court of Appeal, pôle 1, 1re ch., *République bolivarienne du Venezuela v. Monsieur Serafín García Armas and Mme Karina García Gruber*, Judgement (25 Apr. 2017).

47. *Victor Pey Casado and President Allende Foundation v. Republic of Chile*, ICSID Case No. ARB/98/2, Award (8 May 2008), para. 414.
48. ICSID Convention, Art. 28(3): 'The Secretary-General shall register the request unless he finds, on the basis of the *information* contained in the request, that the dispute is manifestly outside the jurisdiction of the Centre. He shall forthwith notify the parties of registration or refusal to register.'
49. *Vladislav Kim and others v. Republic of Uzbekistan*, ICSID Case No. ARB/13/6, Decision on Jurisdiction (8 Mar. 2017), paras 190–191.
50. *Case Concerning the Arrest Warrant (Democratic Republic of the Congo v. Belgium)*, Judgment (14 Feb. 2002), 2002 ICJ Reports 3, 13, p. 26.
51. Christoph H. Schreuer et al., *The ICSID Convention: A Commentary*, 92 (2nd ed., Cambridge University Press 2014).
52. Treaty between the Argentine Republic and the United States of America Concerning the Reciprocal Encouragement and Protection of Investment (14 Nov. 1991).

'continuous ownership of the investment'.[53] Otherwise, expropriation by the host State could easily defeat these treaties' purpose. The tribunal rejected that the investment's sale in October 2003 after the critical dates of consent to arbitrate (submission of request for arbitration) and arbitration registration in June 2003 could affect jurisdiction, unless the right to claim compensation had been included in the sale.[54]

Tribunals have exceptionally required 'continuous nationality' from the date of injury until the date of dispute resolution (*dies ad quem*).[55] In the ICSID Additional Facility *Loewen* arbitration, the US raised, among other things, jurisdictional objections against Loewen Group after the 2001 merits hearing. Loewen Group had filed a voluntary application under the US Bankruptcy Code leading to a reorganization plan. Pursuant to the reorganization of its business operations Loewen Group ceased to exist as a Canadian company, reorganized as a US corporation. Before ceasing to exist Loewen Group 'assigned all of its right, title and interest to the NAFTA claim to a newly created corporation (discreetly called Nafcanco – a play on the words NAFTA and Canada)'.[56]

Nafcanco's only asset was the NAFTA claim, and its only business was the pursuit of this claim. The arbitral tribunal noted that NAFTA expressly required nationality on the submission date (*dies a quo*) in Articles 1116 and 1117 but was silent on 'whether nationality must continue to the time of resolution of the claim'.[57] Applying international law, the tribunal explained that the requirement of continuous nationality until resolution of the dispute (*dies ad quem*) was expressly relaxed in certain treaties but not in NAFTA:

> When investment claims were negotiated and resolved only at a governmental level, any change in nationality of the claimant defeated the only reason for the negotiations to continue. The claiming government no longer had a citizen to protect. This history has changed as the nature of the claim process has changed. As claimants have been allowed to prosecute claims in their own right more often, provision has been made for amelioration of the strict requirement of continuous nationality. But those provisions have been specifically spelled out in the various treaties that TLGI cites as proof that international law has changed. Thus, in the claims settlement agreement between Iran and the United States arising out of the hostage crisis, the requirement of continuous nationality was specifically altered in the agreement. Many of the bilateral investment treaties, the so-called 'BITs', contain specific modifications of the requirement. But such specific provisions in

53. *El Paso Energy International Company v. The Argentine Republic*, ICSID Case No. ARB/03/15, Decision on Jurisdiction (27 Apr. 2006), para. 135.
54. *Ibid.*, paras 135–136.
55. *Loewen Group, Inc. and Raymond L. Loewen v. United States of America*, ICSID Case No. ARB(AF)/98/3, Award (26 Jun. 2003).
56. *Ibid.*, para. 220.
57. *Loewen Group, Inc. and Raymond L. Loewen v. United States of America*, ICSID Case No. ARB(AF)/98/3, Award (26 Jun. 2003), para. 226. *See also*, NAFTA, Arts 1116 and 1117: 'Article 1116: Claim by an Investor of a Party on Its Own Behalf 1. An investor of a Party may submit to arbitration under this Section a claim that another Party has breached an obligation under: … Article 1117: Claim by an Investor of a Party on Behalf of an Enterprise 1. An investor of a Party, on behalf of an enterprise of another Party that is a juridical person that the investor owns or controls directly or indirectly, may submit to arbitration under this Section a claim that the other Party has breached an obligation under: …'

> other treaties and agreements only hinder TLGI's contentions, since NAFTA has no such specific provision.[58]

Therefore, the *Loewen* tribunal found that '[s]uch a naked entity as Nafcanco, even with its catchy name, cannot qualify as a continuing national' in the arbitration.[59] Yet subsequent investment awards have not endorsed the *Loewen* strict standard on 'continuous nationality' until the date of dispute resolution.

[2] Changes in Investor Nationality

An arbitral tribunal may deny jurisdiction *ratione temporis* when an investor's nationality change results from fraudulent acquisition of nationality or from material error by national authorities granting nationality. However, if the change in nationality is not fraudulent and does not result from a material error, it may nevertheless constitute, in certain cases, abuse of process. For example, tribunals have discussed abuse of process when ruling on corporate restructuring of an investment seeking to obtain treaty protection otherwise unavailable. When found, the abuse of process objection in investment arbitration leads to non-admissibility of claims.

On the distinction between jurisdictional and admissibility objections, Professor Jan Paulsson explains that a jurisdictional objection is when a claim cannot be brought to the forum seized, whereas an admissibility objection is when a claim cannot 'be heard at all (or at least not yet)'.[60] The *Philip Morris v. Australia* tribunal distinguished between the *ratione temporis* jurisdictional objection and abuse of process as an admissibility objection in relation to corporate restructuring.

According to the *Philip Morris* tribunal, the critical date as the date of the alleged breach is essential for jurisdiction *ratione temporis* based on a treaty breach.[61] Therefore, when a treaty breach and thus an investment dispute exist, corporate restructuring after the date of breach leads to lack of jurisdiction *ratione temporis*.[62] In turn, an abuse of process objection can succeed when 'an investor who is not protected by an investment treaty restructures its investment in such a fashion as to fall within the scope of protection of a treaty in view of a specific foreseeable dispute'.[63] The threshold for an abuse of process finding is high, subject to an objective test not requiring bad faith evidence.[64] The tribunal went on to define the 'foreseeability' test in abuse of process as 'reasonable prospect' that a measure giving rise to treaty claims will materialize, as follows:

---

58. *Loewen Group, Inc. ibid.*, para. 229.
59. *Ibid.*, para. 237.
60. Jan Paulsson, *Jurisdiction and Admissibility*, in *Liber Amicorum in honour of Robert Briner*, 601, 617 (ICC Publishing 2005).
61. *Philip Morris Asia Limited v. Commonwealth of Australia*, PCA Case No. 2012-12, Award on Jurisdiction and Admissibility (17 Dec. 2015), para. 529.
62. *Ibid.*, para. 539.
63. *Ibid.*
64. *Ibid.*

> [F]oreseeability rests between the two extremes posited by the tribunal in *Pac Rim v. El Salvador* – 'a very high probability and not merely a possible controversy'. On this basis, the initiation of a treaty-based investor-State arbitration constitutes an abuse of rights (or an abuse of process, the rights abused being procedural in nature) when an investor has changed its corporate structure to gain the protection of an investment treaty at a point in time when a specific dispute was foreseeable. The Tribunal is of the opinion that a dispute is foreseeable when there is a reasonable prospect, as stated by the *Tidewater* tribunal, that a measure which may give rise to a treaty claim will materialise.[65]

The tribunal went on to find that Philip Morris had failed to prove that the alleged tax and business reasons 'were determinative for the restructuring'. [66] Thus, the tribunal concluded that its claims were inadmissible because 'the main and determinative, if not sole, reason for the restructuring was the intention to bring a claim under the Treaty, using an entity from Hong Kong'.[67]

New developments in treaty making also seek to deal with abuse in corporate restructuring. Article 16(3) of the 2018 Draft Model BIT of the Netherlands entitles the host State to deny the benefits of treaty protection in some restructuring cases, as follows:

> The responding Contracting Party may deny the benefits of this Section to an investor within the meaning of Article 1(b) of this Agreement, which has changed its corporate structure with a main purpose to gain the protection of this Agreement at a point in time where a dispute had arisen or was foreseeable. This particularly includes situations where an investor has changed its corporate structure with a main purpose to submit a claim to its original home state.[68]

Moreover, the *Micula et al. v. Romania* award provides a good example of fraud allegations in relation to a natural person's acquisition of nationality. On the jurisdictional objection about treaty-required nationality of one of the claimants, Mr Viorel Micula, the tribunal dismissed Romania's allegations that he had not fulfilled the five-year residence requirement in Sweden. It pointed out that the Swedish decision granting nationality was unrelated to the arbitration and that it would be deferential to the Swedish authorities. In its view, 'the Tribunal would only be inclined to disregard the decision of the Swedish authorities if there was convincing and decisive evidence that Viorel Micula's acquisition of Swedish nationality was fraudulent or at least resulted from a material error'.[69]

In *Arif v. Moldova*, Moldova argued that the decree granting French nationality to Mr Arif was invalid. The tribunal relied on 'strong and convincing evidence that Mr Arif acquired French nationality in accordance with French law'.[70] It went on to find that Moldova had failed to show that Mr Arif's nationality 'was obtained fraudulently or

65. *Ibid.*, paras 529, 539, 554.
66. *Ibid.*, para. 584.
67. *Ibid.*, paras 584, 588.
68. Netherlands Draft Model BIT of 2018.
69. *Ioan Micula and others v. Romania, ICSID Case No. ARB/05/20*, Decision on Jurisdiction and Admissibility (24 Sep. 2008), para. 95.
70. *Mr. Franck Charles Arif v. Republic of Moldova*, ICSID Case No. ARB/11/23, Award (8 Apr. 2013), para. 356.

resulted from a material error of the French authorities'.[71] Thus, the tribunal refused to exercise control over the French authorities' decision granting Mr Arif French nationality.

§2.04 CONCLUSION

While a State may consent to arbitrate in a contract, in a national law on foreign investment or in investment treaties, an investor may consent to arbitrate by concluding a contract or by commencing arbitration based on a national law or an investment treaty.

In investment arbitration, the notion of 'investment' is one of the pillars of arbitral jurisdiction, because it triggers the application of an investment treaty or of a law on the protection of foreign investments. The notion of 'investor' as a natural or legal person is another pillar of arbitral jurisdiction.

Having satisfied investment treaty requirements on the categories of protected 'investments' and 'investors', a claimant in investment arbitration may confront jurisdiction *ratione temporis* issues. With some variations depending on the applicable law, the standard rule on jurisdiction *ratione temporis* requires nationality on the date of injury (*dies a quo*) and on the date of submission of the claim for resolution (i.e., filing the request for arbitration) (*dies ad quem*).

Fraudulent acquisition of nationality or material error by national authorities granting nationality may lead to lack of jurisdiction *ratione temporis*. In addition, in some cases tribunals may dismiss claims as inadmissible because of abuse of process in corporate restructuring.

Questions

(1) What is arbitration without privity?
(2) What is the difference between the objective and the subjective tests on the definition of 'investment'?
(3) Please discuss the application of the *Salini test* versus the application of the 'investment' definition under an investment treaty.
(4) What law applies to the investor's nationality?
(5) Could entities without legal personality qualify as an 'investor' under the ICSID Convention
(6) What is the relevance of 'effective nationality' for jurisdiction *ratione personae*?
(7) Please discuss *Loewen*'s 'continuous nationality' requirement.
(8) Please discuss different types of denial clauses in investment treaties.
(9) What is the difference between lack of jurisdiction *ratione temporis* and non-admissibility for abuse of process?

71. *Ibid.*, para. 357.

(10) What factors have arbitral tribunals considered when ruling on allegations of abuse of process in relation to changes of nationality?

CHAPTER 3

Jurisdiction of the Arbitral Tribunal

To issue a binding award that will be enforced pursuant to the New York Convention, within the ICSID system or any national law, the arbitral tribunal must have proper jurisdiction to decide the dispute at hand. Under the well-accepted principle of international law 'competence-competence', it is the tribunal that decides on its own jurisdiction. Contrary to judges, arbitrators do not have general adjudicative powers. Arbitrators' powers are derived from the parties' agreement as recognized by the law.

Jurisdictional issues in investment arbitration differ from those that are traditionally encountered in international commercial arbitration. In commercial arbitration, there are two or more private actors who are in dispute and who provide for arbitration in their contract, or concluding a *compromis* or submission once the dispute has already arisen. The governing law of such relationship is usually domestic law.

In investor-State arbitration, on the other hand, the jurisdictional requirements are in most cases imposed by bilateral and multilateral investment treaties. The applicable governing law is international law.

The difference stems from the fact that in investor-State disputes one of the principal actors is a sovereign State and as such, generally has immunity protecting it from being sued by private individuals.

The crux of jurisdiction in both commercial and investor-State arbitration is that an agreement by all the relevant parties must be present. In investor-State arbitration, said agreement comes under the guise of consent to arbitration by the investor after the dispute has arisen.

§3.01 INTRODUCTION

Consent is the foundation of arbitration. This is true for commercial and investor-State arbitration. In investment arbitration, host States express their consent via treaties, national laws or direct agreement with the investor. Investors must also consent to the arbitration. In contractual agreements, consent is implied by the parties' agreement. Under treaties, the investor express and perfects consent either by bringing a claim (e.g., filing a request for arbitration) or providing notice via a communication letter prior to filing a claim.

The date of filing the claim has an impact on certain factors, including the investor's nationality, the irrevocability of either party's consent, and the exclusion of other available legal remedies.

Before commencing the arbitration, there may be various preconditions that may limit consent. Such conditions may include a waiting or cooling-off period, engaging in amicable or settlement negotiations over a certain period. Many treaties also contain fork-in-the-road or *electa una via* provisions. These clauses address the issue that arises when a party chooses arbitration over local litigation, or local litigation depending on the treaty's language.

This chapter will explore the notion of consent to jurisdiction in investor-State dispute resolution (§3.02), which may be conditioned on the fulfilment of pre-existing requirements (§3.03). Once there is effective consent, there may arise the issue of the scope of consent (§3.04). Unless there is a clause providing for exclusive arbitral jurisdiction, there may be multiple proceedings engaged with regard to the same set of facts. Finally, this chapter will discuss the implications of such parallel proceedings (§3.05).

§3.02 CONSENT

The foundation of arbitration is consent. Both parties must agree to submit their dispute to arbitration. Such agreement or consent is key in determining the jurisdiction of an arbitral tribunal in commercial and investment arbitration. As such, the proceedings may at times begin with hearings and a separate award on jurisdiction before the arbitrators proceed to consider the merits of the dispute.

The particularity of investor-State arbitration concerns the involvement of a sovereign State as one of the parties. Consent to jurisdiction may be expressed in different ways. It has become universally accepted by arbitral tribunals that a State may issue a public offer to arbitrate disputes and that the investor accepts the offer by submitting a request for arbitration.

Article 25(1) of the ICSID Convention includes consent as one of the conditions for the jurisdiction of the Centre. No particular formalities are required for consent to be effective, except that it must be in writing and it must be explicit.[1] When parties give

1. Christoph H. Schreuer, *The ICSID Convention. A Commentary*, §§ 379, 191 (2nd ed., Cambridge University Press 2009); *Cable Television of Nevis, Ltd. and Cable Television of Nevis Holdings, Ltd.*

their consent, no party may withdraw it unilaterally.[2] Its irrevocability is grounded in a well-established principle of international customary law: *pacta sunt servanda*.[3]

A practical aspect of consenting to arbitration that will be discussed in greater detail concerns the various methods by which consent can be expressed (A). This section will then examine the way in which the investor may consent to arbitral jurisdiction and in particular the moment when both parties' consent is considered effective (B).

[A] Modalities for Expressing Consent

Consent to investor-State arbitration (whether institutional or ad hoc) can be offered in the arbitration clause of the investor-State agreement (1), in the host State's domestic legislation (2), and in BITs or MITs (3).

[1] Agreement Between the Host State and the Investor

Arbitration clauses are commonly included into contracts concluded by investors and sovereign States, thus providing consent to the arbitral forum for any future disagreements. Additionally, parties may agree to submit a dispute that has already arisen to arbitration by means of a '*compromis*'.[4] Various arbitral institutions provide model arbitration clauses to avoid unnecessary issues regarding the validity and effectiveness of arbitration agreements. ICSID has notably developed an elaborate set of model clauses that cover a whole range of situations.[5]

The benefit of the direct agreement is the possibility to custom-tailor dispute resolutions provisions. Parties are free to negotiate narrow arbitration clauses, including certain types of disputes, or broad ones, typically referring to any and all disputes that may arise in respect of or in connection with the contract. Parties may also draft a clause including a reference to a particular BIT or MIT.[6] This way, if a dispute arises, the parties will initiate arbitral proceedings pursuant to dispute resolution provision of the relevant treaty.

---

v. Federation of St. Kitts and Nevis, ICSID Case No. ARB/95/2, Award (13 Jan. 1997), para. 4.17 (The Tribunal held that the references in the court documentation to the ICSID clause in the agreement were merely statements of fact and did not amount to consent by any person to ICSID jurisdiction).

2. Christoph H. Schreuer, *The ICSID Convention. A Commentary*, 254–255 (2nd ed., Cambridge University Press 2009).
3. *See Forminster Enterprises Limited (Cyprus) v. Czech Republic*, UNCITRAL, Award (15 Dec. 2014).
4. Peter Muchlinski, Federico Ortino & Christoph Schreuer, *The Oxford Handbook of International Investment Law*, 832 (Oxford University Press 2008).
5. ICSID, *Model Clauses*, http://icsidfiles.worldbank.org/icsid/icsid/staticfiles/model-clauses-en/main-eng.htm (accessed 27 Mar. 2018).
6. Peter Muchlinski, Federico Ortino & Christoph Schreuer, *The Oxford Handbook of International Investment Law*, 832 (Oxford University Press 2008); *Ceskoslovenska Obchodni Banka, A.S. v. The Slovak Republic*, ICSID Case No. ARB/97/4, Decision on Jurisdiction (24 May 1999), 5 ICSID Reports 335, paras 49–59.

It should be noted that the parties' consent need not be recorded in a single instrument.[7] In *Amco v. Indonesia*, the tribunal held that:

> while a consent in writing to ICSID arbitration is indispensable, since it is required by Article 25(1) of the Convention, such consent in writing is not to be expressed in a solemn, ritual and unique formulation. The investment agreement being in writing, it suffices to establish that its interpretation in good faith shows that the parties agreed to ICSID arbitration, in order for the ICSID Tribunal to have jurisdiction over them.[8]

For example, the investor may make an investment application containing an arbitration provision. If a competent organ of the State approves this application, there is mutual consent to arbitration.[9]

Generally, arbitral tribunals adopt a liberal stance towards the validity and extent of arbitration agreements. In particular, they accept to hear cases arising out of multiple contractual documents, where only one or several but not all of them contain arbitration provisions.[10]

[2] Consent to Arbitration Contained in Host State Legislation

A host State may give consent to arbitration by legislative means, often via its domestic investment code. Similar to direct agreements between the investor and the State, States may give their consent with respect to an existing or future dispute. While this method of consent to arbitral jurisdiction does not raise many issues now, this was not the case until the prominent *SPP v. Egypt* decision recognized for the first time the binding nature of the public offer to arbitrate contained in a host State law.[11] Indeed, at the time of the signature of the ICSID Convention, it was already recognized that 'a host State might in its investment promotion legislation offer to submit disputes arising out of certain classes of investments to the jurisdiction of the Centre, and the investor might give his consent thereto in writing'.[12] However, Egypt argued in the *SPP* arbitration (and other States have advanced similar arguments)[13] that its investment legislation was only meant to inform the investor about the dispute resolution options available and a separate agreement to arbitrate had to be entered into between the

7. Peter Muchlinski, Federico Ortino & Christoph Schreuer, *The Oxford Handbook of International Investment Law*, 832–833 (Oxford University Press 2008).
8. *Amco Asia Corporation and others v. Republic of Indonesia*, ICSID Case No. ARB/81/1, Decision on Jurisdiction (25 Sep. 1983), 1 ICSID Reports 400.
9. Peter Muchlinski, Federico Ortino & Christoph Schreuer, *The Oxford Handbook of International Investment Law*, 832 (Oxford University Press 2008).
10. *See*, for example, Pierre Lalive, *The First 'World Bank' Arbitration (Holiday Inns v. Morocco)—Some Legal Problems*, 51 Brit. Y.B. Intl. L. 156–159 (1980); *SOABI v. Senegal*, Decision on Jurisdiction (1 Aug. 1984).
11. *Southern Pacific Properties (Middle East) Limited v. Arab Republic of Egypt*, ICSID Case No. ARB/84/3, Decision on Jurisdiction (14 Apr. 1988), para. 70.
12. *Report of the Executive Directors of the World Bank that accompanied the 1965 Convention on the Settlement of Investment Disputes between States and Nationals of Other States*, 1 ICSID Reports 28, para. 24.
13. *See* for example, *Inceysa Vallisoletana S.L. v. Republic of El Salvador*, ICSID Case No. ARB/03/26, Award (2 Aug. 2006), 15–16.

parties.[14] The arbitral tribunal concluded that the language of Egyptian law was sufficiently imperative to constitute an offer to arbitrate that was binding on the State and could be accepted by the investor. Here, two separate events are required for the consent to jurisdiction to be effective: offer by the host State (a) and acceptance by the investor (b).

[a] Offer by Host State

A provision containing a host State's consent to arbitration may be explicit, or it may require additional actions by the host State to establish consent.[15] When the provision containing host State's consent is not clear, this may lead to additional disputes as to its meaning.[16]

It is crucial to specify that not every investment law or code contains an offer to arbitrate disputes, even if there is a reference to dispute resolution in the text. The offer must be unequivocal and it should not require any further actions on behalf of the parties. In *Biwater v. Tanzania*, the arbitral tribunal considered that dispute resolution options presented in the State investment law followed by a condition 'as may be mutually agreed by the parties' did not constitute a 'unilateral, standing offer' because it required further mutual assent by both the State and the investor.[17]

Even if the language of the offer is sufficiently firm, it may limit the investor's options of bringing the claim. The text of the law may limit the categories of investors or type of investment, with regard to which it consents to arbitral jurisdiction, which would preclude certain investors from being able to validly accept the State's offer. In addition, the host State's offer, 'may be subject to certain conditions, time limits or formalities', like investment authorization or acceptance of the offer within certain period of time.[18]

[b] Acceptance by Investor

Legislative provisions containing host State's consent to arbitration operates as an offer to arbitrate: 'in order to perfect an arbitration agreement, that offer must be accepted by the investor'.[19] One way to accept the offer is by submitting a request for arbitration, i.e., instituting arbitral proceedings.[20] However, bearing in mind that an outstanding

14. *Southern Pacific Properties (Middle East) Limited v. Arab Republic of Egypt*, ICSID Case No. ARB/84/3, Decision on Jurisdiction (14 Apr. 1988).
15. Christoph H. Schreuer, *The ICSID Convention. A Commentary*, 200 (2nd ed., Cambridge University Press 2009).
16. *See*, e.g., *Southern Pacific Properties (Middle East) Limited v. Arab Republic of Egypt*, ICSID Case No. ARB/84/3, Decision on Jurisdiction (14 Apr. 1988), para. 70.
17. *Biwater Gauff (Tanzania) Ltd. v. United Republic of Tanzania*, ICSID Case No. ARB/05/22, Award (24 Jul. 2008), paras 329–330.
18. Christoph Schreuer, *Consent to Arbitration (updated 02/2007)*, 6, https://www.transnational-dispute-management.com/article.asp?key=555 (accessed 27 Mar. 2018).
19. *Ibid.*, p. 5.
20. In *Tradex v. Albania*, the tribunal held that 'it can now be considered as established and not requiring further reasoning that such consent can also be effected unilaterally by a Contracting

offer may be altered or revoked at any time before it is accepted, it is advisable for the investor to give its consent in writing at the earliest possible.[21] In this respect, other ways in which an investor can give its consent are for example through an investment agreement with the host State, through a simple communication to the host State,[22] or a statement contained in an application for an investment license.[23]

[3] Consent Through Bilateral or Multilateral Investment Treaties

[a] General Considerations

States may express a public offer to arbitrate in dispute resolution provisions of a BIT or MIT. This modality of the State's consent to arbitration was first recognized by the *AAPL v. Sri Lanka* tribunal.[24] The binding nature of this type of offer was considered more controversial than the previously described options because in this case the agreement, a treaty, is made between two or more States. While in the case of legislation it is interpreted as a unilateral act of the State, which can engage its responsibility, in a treaty, States emit reciprocal engagements that should arguably be enforced only as against the Contracting States themselves.[25] The investor in this scenario is a third-party beneficiary of the treaty protections, including the right to arbitrate its investment disputes with the host State.

In contrast to the offer to arbitrate contained in national legislation, the dispute resolution provisions of an international treaty take into account the fact that the treaty was concluded between specific States. Accordingly, only the investors who satisfy the nationality requirement of the other contracting party or parties may benefit from the arbitration provision contained in the treaty.[26]

State in its national laws the consent becoming effective at the latest if and when the foreign investor files its claim with ICSID making use of the respective national law'. *See Tradex Hellas S.A. v. Republic of Albania*, ICSID Case No. ARB/94/2, Decision on Jurisdiction (24 Dec. 1996), pp. 186–187.

21. Christoph Schreuer, *Consent to Arbitration (updated 02/2007)*, 5, https://www.transnational-dispute-management.com/article.asp?key = 555 (accessed 27 Mar. 2018).
22. This was the case in *SPP v. Egypt*, where the investor sent a letter to the Minister of Tourism of Egypt a year before commencing the arbitration. *See Southern Pacific Properties (Middle East) Limited v. Arab Republic of Egypt*, ICSID Case No. ARB/84/3, Decision on Jurisdiction (14 Apr. 1988).
23. UNCTAD, *Consent to Arbitration*, 14, http://unctad.org/fr/Docs/edmmisc232add2_en.pdf (accessed 25 May 2018).
24. *Asian Agricultural Products Ltd. v. Republic of Sri Lanka*, ICSID Case No. ARB/87/3, Award (27 Jun. 1990).
25. *See* Jan Paulsson, *Arbitration Without Privity*, 10(2) ICSID Rev. (1995).
26. Andrea Marco Steingruber, *Consent in International Arbitration*, §§ 11.45, 201 (Oxford University Press 2012).

[b] Consent Contained in Bilateral Treaties

In practice, the vast majority of investor-State arbitrations are now commenced based on the advance offer to arbitrate contained in BITs. The reason for this development is the proliferation of bilateral protection treaties and the pervasiveness of references to ICSID or other arbitration rules in final provisions of the BITs.[27]

An arbitration agreement is perfected when an eligible foreign investor accepts the offer extended by the State. An offer to arbitrate may be accepted in several ways, as it was discussed earlier in this chapter. It is a generally accepted practice that an offer of consent is accepted when an investor institutes arbitration proceedings. This was confirmed by the tribunal in *Generation Ukraine v. Ukraine*.[28]

Many dispute resolution clauses in modern BITs express consent to ICSID arbitration 'on the part of the two Contracting States … for the benefit of nationals of the other State party to the treaty'.[29] Article 8 of the 1980 BIT between the United Kingdom and Sri Lanka is an example of a simple ICSID clause:

> Each Contracting Party hereby consents to submit to the International Centre for the Settlement of Investment Disputes (herein referred to as 'the Centre') for settlement by conciliation or arbitration under the Convention … any legal disputes arising between that Contracting Party and a national or company of the other Contracting Party concerning an investment of the latter in the territory of the former.[30]

A treaty dispute resolution provision referring to arbitration does not necessarily contain the host State's consent. Sometimes additional action by the host State may be required, like giving its consent once the dispute has emerged.[31] Moreover, dispute resolution provisions may provide for several alternatives prior to instituting arbitral proceedings. These alternatives may, for example, include mandatory prior negotiation, other ways of amicable dispute resolution like mediation, or national courts of the host State. Some of the alternatives, such as amicable dispute resolution and resolution of dispute before national courts, will be elaborated later in this chapter, when discussing cooling-off period and exhaustion of local remedies.

As mentioned earlier, the scope of the dispute resolution provisions may be tailored to include all kinds of potential disputes. Alternatively, the arbitration clause in a BIT may be tailored more narrowly to encompass only certain types of disputes. Problems arise when the provision is vague, which may cause a dispute before even

---

27. *Ibid.*, paras 11.46–11.47.
28. The *Generation Ukraine v. Ukraine* tribunal held that 'it is firmly established that an investor can accept a State's offer of ICSID arbitration contained in a bilateral investment treaty by instituting ICSID proceedings. There is nothing in the BIT to suggest that the investor must communicate its consent in a different form directly to the State … It follows that the Claimant validly consented to ICSID arbitration by filing its Notice of Arbitration at the ICSID Centre'. *See Generation Ukraine, Inc. v. Ukraine*, ICSID Case No. ARB/00/9, Award (16 Sep. 2003), paras 12.2–12.3.
29. UNCTAD, above n. 23, at 17.
30. *United Kingdom-Sri Lanka BIT*, 19 ILM 886, 888 (1980).
31. UNCTAD, *Consent to Arbitration*, 7, http://unctad.org/fr/Docs/edmmisc232add2_en.pdf (accessed 25 May 2018).

initiating an arbitral proceeding. In *Compañía de Aguas del Aconquija, S. A. and Vivendi Universal v. Argentina,*[32] for example, the contentious provision was Article 8 of the BIT between France and Argentina, containing consent for 'any dispute relating to investment'.[33] The ad hoc committee held that:

> Article 8 deals generally with disputes relating to investments made under this Agreement between one Contracting Party and an investor of the other Contracting Party. It is those disputes which may be submitted, at the investor's option, either to national or international adjudication. Article 8 does not use a narrower formulation, requiring that the investor's claim allege a breach of the BIT itself. Read literally, the requirements for arbitral jurisdiction in Article 8 do not necessitate that the Claimant allege a breach of the BIT itself: it is sufficient that the dispute relate to an investment made under the BIT.[34]

In contrast, the tribunal in *SGS v. Pakistan*[35] reached the opposite conclusion. Referring to Article 9 of the BIT between Switzerland and Pakistan, which contains consent with respect to 'disputes with respect to investments', the tribunal concluded that it did not have jurisdiction with respect to contract claims which did not also constitute 'breaches of the substantive standards of the BIT.[36]

Another potential issue may arise if a host State decides to withdraw from or denounce the treaty. As alluded to before, it is advisable that the investor accepts the offer early on to avoid side effects of the host State's denunciation of the treaty. Once the offer is accepted and the arbitration agreement is perfected, 'it remains in existence even if the States parties to the BIT agree to amend or terminate the treaty'.[37] Effects of denunciation shall be given special attention and will be discussed in detail below.

[c] Consent Contained in Multilateral Treaties

The mechanism of consent through a multilateral treaty operates in the same way as a BIT, which is discussed above. MITs are less common than bilateral treaties, but the two most important ones, namely NAFTA and the ECT, have given rise to a number of investment arbitrations.

32. *Compañiá de Aguas del Aconquija S.A. and Vivendi Universal S.A. v. Argentine Republic*, ICSID Case No. ARB/97/3 (formerly *Compañía de Aguas del Aconquija, S.A. and Compagnie Générale des Eaux v. Argentine Republic*), Award (21 Nov. 2000).
33. Christoph Schreuer, *Consent to Arbitration (updated 02/2007)*, 9, https://www.transnational-dispute-management.com/article.asp?key = 555 (accessed 27 Mar. 2018).
34. *Compañiá de Aguas del Aconquija S.A. and Vivendi Universal S.A. v. Argentine Republic*, ICSID Case No. ARB/97/3 (formerly *Compañía de Aguas del Aconquija, S.A. and Compagnie Générale des Eaux v. Argentine Republic*), Decision on Annulment (3 Jul. 2002), para. 55.
35. *SGS Société Générale de Surveillance S.A. v. Islamic Republic of Pakistan*, ICSID Case No. ARB/01/13, Decision on Jurisdiction (6 Aug. 2003).
36. Christoph Schreuer, *Consent to Arbitration (updated 02/2007)*, 10, https://www.transnational-dispute-management.com/article.asp?key = 555 (accessed 27 Mar. 2018).
37. Rudolf Dolzer & Christoph Schreuer, *Principles of International Investment Law*, 259 (2nd ed., Oxford University Press 2012).

NAFTA, entered into by Canada, Mexico and the US, expressly provides that the State parties consent to submit disputes to arbitration.[38] At the same time, it specifies that the investor must also consent to the arbitral forum.[39] The investor may bring the proceedings on behalf of itself or an enterprise incorporated in one of the State parties. To bring a claim, the investor has to follow the procedure set out in the treaty and, in particular, to waive its 'right to initiate or continue before any administrative tribunal or court under the law of any Party, or other dispute settlement procedures'.[40] The waiver requirement is meant to minimize the possibility of parallel proceedings and will be discussed in more detail further below.

The ECT also contains unconditional consent to arbitration for disputes that fall within the ambit of the treaty.[41] The dispute resolution provision of the ECT is very broad and encompasses consent for four different arbitral fora.[42]

[4] Exclusive Choice-of-Forum Clause

An issue arises when, in addition to the dispute resolution provision in a protection treaty, the investor also concludes a contract with the State which contains an exclusive dispute resolution clause. Instinctively, it would appear that the contractual clause should override the BIT provision which is of a more general nature. Such conclusion has not been the case with some arbitral tribunals that have noted that a State should not have the possibility to contract out of its international law obligations subscribed to in the protection treaty.[43] Notwithstanding, one should bear in mind that BITs contain an offer from the State to the investor, and it is the investor that decides to accept it or not.

The principal basis for overcoming the exclusive choice-of-forum clause in the contract concluded between the parties (which is generally in favor of the host State's national courts) is the fundamental distinction between treaty and contract claims (which will be discussed further below). As concluded by the *Vivendi* tribunal, while purely contract claims may be limited by the exclusive choice-of-forum clause, the claims arising out of BIT protections do not fall under this clause and may be litigated pursuant to the treaty dispute resolution provisions. The distinction between a contract

38. NAFTA, Art. 1122. This article specifies in its second paragraph that the consent given therein satisfies the requirements of ICSID for jurisdiction, 1958 New York Convention and Inter-American Convention, thereby indicating a strong commitment to binding arbitration. *See also* Andrea Marco Steingruber, *Consent in International Arbitration*, §§ 11.67–11.68 (Oxford University Press 2012).
39. NAFTA, Art. 1121.
40. *Ibid.*
41. ECT, Art. 26; please note that this article provides for three months of amicable negotiation prior to submitting the dispute to arbitration.
42. ECT, Art. 26(4): the investor may choose among ICSID, ICSID Additional Facility, sole arbitrator or ad hoc arbitration under UNCITRAL Rules, or proceedings under the auspices of the Stockholm Chamber of Commerce.
43. *Compañiá de Aguas del Aconquija S.A. and Vivendi Universal S.A. v. Argentine Republic*, ICSID Case No. ARB/97/3 (formerly *Compañía de Aguas del Aconquija, S.A. and Compagnie Générale des Eaux v. Argentine Republic*), Award (21 Nov. 2000). *See also Gami Investments, Inc. v. The Government of the United Mexican States*, UNCITRAL, Award (15 Nov. 2004).

claim and a treaty claims is not always obvious, in particular where the treaty contains an umbrella clause (*see* below). Some tribunals have concluded that the umbrella clause elevates contract claims to the status of treaty claims. As such, one may wonder whether in this case, the exclusive choice-of-forum clause should prevent such claims from being heard by a tribunal constituted on the basis of the BIT dispute resolution provisions.

[5] Consent of Constituent Subdivisions or Agencies of the State

Under the ICSID Convention, there is a specific procedure required for the consent of a constituent subdivision or an agency of the host State.[44] In addition to the consent given by such an entity itself, it also has to be specifically designated to the Centre, and the consent of the subdivision or agency should be approved by the State.[45] These two acts should be clearly distinguished, because they serve different functions and are both required for the jurisdiction of the Centre over the subdivision or agency.[46] On the other hand, there is no formal requirement for State approval of consent: it may take various forms and does not have to be communicated directly to the Centre. However, given that jurisdiction depends on this requirement, it is advisable for investors wanting to bring claims against a State subdivision or agency to obtain said approval.[47]

The question of consent by constituent subdivision or agency should be distinguished from the issue of attribution of responsibility for actions of such a subdivision or agency to the State.[48] States have raised this issue at the jurisdiction stage to assert that the investor does not have a claim against the State itself, but against its subdivision or agency, which is a separate legal entity, and thus the tribunal's jurisdiction should not extend over it.[49] Tribunals, such as the one in the *Jan de Nul* case, have rightly concluded that this issue should be dealt with at the merits stage.[50]

[B] The Moment When Consent Becomes Perfected and Irrevocable

The arbitral tribunal only has jurisdiction if at the time when the proceedings are instituted, both parties have given effective consent, which was not withdrawn or otherwise affected. Under ICSID, the precise moment of consent also triggers a number of consequences. In particular, investor's nationality has to satisfy the BIT and ICSID

44. ICSID Convention, Art. 25(3): 'Consent by a constituent subdivision or agency of a Contracting State shall require the approval of that State unless that State notifies the Centre that no such approval is required.'
45. Christoph H. Schreuer, *The ICSID Convention. A Commentary*, §§ 903–904, 338 (2nd ed., Cambridge University Press 2009).
46. *Ibid.*, §§ 905, p. 338.
47. *Ibid.*, §§ 909–910, p. 339.
48. *See* discussion on attribution in Ch. 9 on Damages, §9.02.
49. *See Jan de Nul N.V. and Dredging International N.V. v. Arab Republic of Egypt*, ICSID Case No. ARB/04/13, Decision on Jurisdiction (16 Jun. 2006).
50. *Ibid.*, para. 89.

conditions at the time of consent.[51] Moreover, under Article 25(1) of the ICSID Convention, when consent is perfected it becomes irrevocable.

Irrevocability of the State's consent is clearly in the interest of foreign investors. Consequently, while the general method of accepting the State's public offer to arbitrate is by instituting the proceedings. Irrevocability of consent under the ICSID Convention is an expression of the fundamental principle of international law, *pacta sunt servanda*.[52] It seems logical that this maxim, which applies to consent to arbitration contained in a contract or *compromis*, should also govern consent based on legislation or treaty.

It should be noted that where there are other jurisdictional requirements that are not satisfied at the moment of the investor's acceptance, consent to jurisdiction becomes perfected at the moment when the last condition is satisfied.[53] After this point, the State may not directly withdraw its offer, whether by changing its legislation or by denouncing the BIT. The State is equally precluded from indirectly revoking its consent. In particular, it may not rely on Article 25(4) notification to exclude a specific class of disputes from its consent.[54] Denouncing the ICSID Convention[55] would not allow the State to indirectly revoke its consent to jurisdiction either, because Article 72 of the Convention precludes such notice from affecting the rights of investors arising out of the State's consent to jurisdiction.[56]

§3.03 PRECONDITIONS TO ARBITRATION

When the State issues a public offer to arbitrate via its legislation or an investment treaty, the investor's acceptance cannot add or subtract any conditions from the initial offer. As such, the investor is required to fulfil all the conditions that a State may include in its offer to arbitrate for the arbitral tribunal to have jurisdiction over the dispute. The two most common preliminary conditions include a cooling-off period (A) and the exhaustion of local remedies requirement (B).

51. Loukas A. Mistelis, *Concise International Arbitration*, 70 (Kluwer Law International 2010): 'The Centre only has jurisdiction if both the host State and the investor's State of nationality are Contracting States. The critical date for assessing the fulfillment of this jurisdictional requirement is the date of the institution of ICSID proceedings. This requirement is fulfilled if consent to jurisdiction is given prior to the ratification of the Convention but the Convention enters into force before the institution of proceedings (*Holiday Inns v. Morocco; see also Amco v. Indonesia (I) (DA); LETCO v. Liberia; Cable TV v. St. Kitts and Nevis).*'
52. Andrea Marco Steingruber, *Consent in International Arbitration*, § 11.109 (Oxford University Press 2012).
53. *Ibid.*, § 11.99.
54. *Alcoa Minerals v. Jamaica*, Decision on Jurisdiction (6 Jul. 1975), 4 YBCA 206 (1979); *Kaiser Bauxite Company v. Jamaica*, ICSID Case No. ARB/74/3, Decision on Jurisdiction (6 Jul. 1975).
55. The Convention expressly provides for the possibility of denunciation on six months' notice in Art. 71.
56. ICSID Convention, Art. 72: 'Notice by a Contracting State pursuant to Articles 70 or 71 shall not affect the rights or obligations under this Convention of that State or of any of its constituent subdivisions or agencies or of any national of that State arising out of consent to the jurisdiction of the Centre given by one of them before such notice was received by the depositary.'

In general, preconditions to arbitration postpone the initiation of arbitral proceedings. Investors, who may have lost an important part of their investment, sometimes find it unnecessarily lengthy or costly to comply with the State's conditions, such as respecting an eighteen-month negotiation period or attempting to litigate in the national courts for a year before bringing the arbitration. Hence, some investors have relied on the most-favored-nation provision to try to benefit from more favorable dispute resolution provisions of another treaty concluded by the same host State (C). In addition, there exists a debate among arbitral tribunals as to whether the aforementioned preconditions actually affect their jurisdiction or whether they are merely admissibility requirements (D).

[A] Cooling-Off Period

A 'cooling-off' period, or amicable negotiation period, is a reprieve granted to the parties before they are allowed to institute arbitral proceedings. During this period, the parties engage in a good faith attempt of negotiating a settlement or attempting another peaceful dispute resolution mechanism, such as mediation or conciliation. They are not, however, required to reach any particular result.[57]

While the amicable negotiation clause can be seen as giving the parties a last chance to find a peaceful resolution to their dispute and preserve the relationship, many investors have come to see it more as a dilatory tactic employed by the State to postpone arbitration. The most common cooling-off period is six months,[58] but it may go up to twelve months or even more.[59] It is sensible to surmise that an investor, whose investment has been expropriated and lost all or most of its value, would be disinclined to wait any period of time before proceeding in claiming compensation.

A particular issue that has given rise to disputes is the point in time when the cooling-off period starts to run and its duration. Generally, the investor has to notify the State that a dispute has arisen. Arbitral tribunals have taken different views on the requisite form for said notification. The more formalistic view is to require a formal notification announcing that the investor is beginning the amicable negotiation period pursuant to the relevant treaty, which is the majority position taken by tribunals. On the other hand, in *Burlington v. Ecuador* the tribunal held that the mere evidence of controversy, i.e., an informal notice, would suffice to satisfy the notification requirement.[60]

57. *Murphy v. Ecuador*, ICSID Case No. ARB/08/4, Decision on Jurisdiction (15 Dec. 2010), para. 135. *See also* Crina Baltag, *Not Hot Enough: Cooling-Off and the Recent Developments under the Energy Charter Treaty*, 6 Indian J. Arb. L. 190 (2017).
58. Crina Baltag, *Not Hot Enough: Cooling-Off and the Recent Developments under the Energy Charter Treaty*, 6 Indian J. Arb. L. 190 (2017). For example, Switzerland-Kenya BIT (2009): three-month cooling off period; Switzerland-Croatia BIT (1997): six-month cooling-off period.
59. For example, Indonesia-Spain BIT (1995).
60. *Burlington Resources Inc. v. Republic of Ecuador*, ICSID Case No. ARB/08/5 (formerly *Burlington Resources Inc. and others v. Republic of Ecuador and Empresa Estatal Petróleos del Ecuador* (PetroEcuador)), Decision on Jurisdiction (2 Jun. 2010), para. 337.

[B] Exhaustion of Local Remedies

[1] The Principle

Under customary international law, exhaustion of local remedies is associated with the notion of diplomatic protection. The International Law Commission (ILC) Draft Articles on Diplomatic Protection in Article 14 state: 'A State may not present an international claim in respect of an injury to a national or other person referred to in draft article 8 before the injured person has, subject to draft article 15, exhausted all local remedies.' Based on this principle, the general rule, with limited exceptions, is that a State can only exercise diplomatic protection for its nationals once all local remedies have been exhausted.[61]

In investor-State arbitration, only a limited number of treaties require the exhaustion of local remedies. This requirement was a common feature of international investment agreements during the 1970s and the 1980s.[62]

When the exhaustion of local remedies is required, the conditions to determine whether an investor may eventually bring its case to international arbitration fall into three categories:[63]

(1) Some treaties allow an investor access to international arbitration if domestic courts have failed to deliver a decision within a given period of time.[64]
(2) Other treaties limit the right of an investor to eventually bring its case to arbitration to circumstances where the decision rendered by domestic courts fails to fully settle the dispute.[65]
(3) A third category of treaties allows recourse to international arbitration in case the decision rendered by domestic courts is contrary to the norms of

61. *See*, for example, *Interhandel case, Switzerland v. United States of America*, Judgment (21 Mar. 1959), ICJ Reports 6, 25 (1959); *Elettronica Sicula S.p.A. (ELSI) case, United States v. Italy*, Judgement (20 Jul. 1989), ICJ Reports 15, 31 (1989).
62. Joachim Pohl, Kekeletso Mashigo & Alexis Nohen, *Dispute Settlement Provisions in International Investment Agreements: A Large Sample Survey*, OECD Working Papers on International Investment, 2012/02 (OECD Publishing 2012), para. 27.
63. *Ibid.*, at para. 28.
64. For example, Art. 10(3) of the Argentina-Netherlands BIT (1992) states: 'If within a period of eighteen months from submissions of the dispute to the competent organs mentioned in paragraph (2) above, these organs have not given a final decision or if the decision of the aforementioned organs has been given but the parties are still in dispute, then the investor concerned may resort to international arbitration or conciliation.'
65. For example, Art. 9(3) of the Austria-Philippines BIT from 2002, which states: 'If such a dispute between an investor of one Contracting Party and the other Contracting Party continues to exist after a period of six months, the investor shall be entitled to submit the case either to: (a) international arbitration of the International Centre for Settlement of Investment Disputes established pursuant to the Convention on the Settlement of Investment Disputes Between States and Nationals of other States opened for signature at Washington D.C. on 18 March 1965 (ICSID Convention), or (b) an arbitrator or international ad hoc arbitral tribunal established under the Arbitration Rules of the United Nations Commission on International Trade Law (UNCITRAL).'

> international law or it is manifestly unjust or constitutes a denial of justice.[66]

Under ICSID arbitration, Article 26 of the ICSID Convention expressly recognizes the possibility for States to 'require the exhaustion of local administrative or judicial remedies as a condition of [their] consent to arbitration under this Convention'. At the same time, Article 26 of the ICSID Convention 'constitutes an express waiver of the rule of exhaustion of local remedies in ICSID arbitrations',[67] The relevant portion of the provision reads as follows: 'Consent of the parties to arbitration under this Convention shall, unless otherwise stated, be deemed consent to such arbitration to the exclusion of any other remedy.'

According to the tribunal in *Lanco International v. Argentina*, the exclusivity rule in the first sentence of Article 26 'means that there is no need to exhaust domestic procedures before initiating ICSID arbitration, unless otherwise stipulated'.[68] In *Generation Ukraine v. Ukraine*, the tribunal followed this same reasoning. In particular, it held that, should a State wish to require exhaustion of local remedies as a condition of consent to ICSID arbitration, such requirement 'must be contained in the instrument in which such consent is expressed, i.e., the BIT itself'. [69]

The tribunal in *Maffezini v. Spain* stated that 'the language of Article 26 makes clear that unless a Contracting State has conditioned its consent to ICSID arbitration on the prior exhaustion of domestic remedies, no such requirement will be applicable. Article 26 thus reverses the traditional international law rule, which implies the exhaustion requirement unless it is expressly or implicitly waived'.[70]

The *Hochtief v. Argentina* tribunal held that there is no obligation to continue litigation upon the expiration of the eighteen months, regardless of the court's reaching a final - or any - decision on the matter. Perhaps even more importantly, the investor does not have to accept the court decision - if it is rendered within the eighteen months - as the final resolution of the dispute, and may nevertheless bring the case in arbitration thereafter.[71] Thus, it is understood that when the dispute resolution clause requires the investor to resort to local courts and attempt litigation for a certain period of time (generally, eighteen months), the investor only has to begin said litigation.

66. According to Art. 9(3) of the Italy-Uruguay BIT from 1990, the investor may proceed to international arbitration if the court decision is in contrast to norms of international law, with the contents of the present agreement, or if it is manifestly unjust or constitutes a denial of justice.
67. *Mr. Franck Charles Arif v. Republic of Moldova*, ICSID Case No. ARB/11/23, Award (8 Apr. 2013), para. 333.
68. *Lanco International Inc. v. Argentine Republic*, ICSID Case No. ARB/97/6, Preliminary Decision on Jurisdiction (8 Dec. 1998), para. 37.
69. *Generation Ukraine, Inc. v. Ukraine*, ICSID Case No. ARB/00/9, Award (16 Sep. 2003), para. 13.5.
70. *Emilio Agustin Maffezini v. The Kingdom of Spain*, ICSID Case No. ARB/97/7, Decision on Jurisdiction (25 Jan. 2000), para. 22.
71. *Hochtief AG v. The Argentine Republic*, ICSID Case No. ARB/07/31, Decision on Jurisdiction (24 Oct. 2011), paras 40–44.

[2] Bypassing the Exhaustion of Local Remedies Requirement Based on Futility Exception

Exhaustion of local remedies can be an imposing requirement for investors. If investors were to comply with the exhaustion of local remedies provision (which often coexists with the amicable negotiation requirement), it could take them two years or even longer to access the arbitral forum. This is all the more problematic where it is well established that the national jurisdiction which has to be seized as a precondition to arbitration could never render a final decision on the matter within eighteen months.

Arbitral tribunals have relied on the customary international law, in particular, the futility exception, to overcome the exhaustion of local remedies requirement in finding jurisdiction. As mentioned above, this exception dates back to international law before investor-State arbitration. At that time, investors had no direct recourse against the host State and had to rely on their own country to espouse their claim by offering diplomatic protection. Exhaustion of local remedies was a compulsory requirement for commencing the proceedings under diplomatic protection, and futility was an exception to this requirement.[72]

Given that customary international law requirement of exhaustion of local remedies required the parties to litigate until a final and binding decision in the local courts, it could effectively become a bar to diplomatic protection where the State's judicial apparatus was unduly slow and costly. As such, the ILC, in its attempt to codify the state of customary international law on diplomatic protection, recognized the following exceptions to the exhaustion of local remedies condition:

- Local remedies do not provide a reasonable possibility of redress.
- Undue delay in proceedings attributable to the State whose responsibility is sought.
- No relevant connection between the State whose responsibility is sought and the injured person.
- The 'injured person is manifestly precluded from pursuing local remedies'.[73]
- The State has waived the exhaustion of local remedies requirement.[74]

BITs have profoundly changed the paradigm of dispute settlement in the context of foreign investment. Thus, the requirement to submit the dispute to national courts prior to instituting arbitral proceedings contained in investment treaties is not the same as the traditional exhaustion of local remedies in the context of diplomatic protection. However, arbitral tribunals have followed the same logic as the ILC in limiting the effect of BIT clauses requiring preliminary litigation in national courts where this condition effectively serves no purpose and would only delay the investor's arbitration remedy.

72. *Elettronica Sicula S.p.A. (ELSI) case, United States v. Italy*, Judgement (20 Jul. 1989), ICJ Reports 15 (1989).
73. International Law Commission Draft Articles on Diplomatic Protection, Art. 15.
74. *Ibid.*

As stated by the tribunal in *Abaclat v. Argentina*, 'there must be a real chance in practice that the Host State, through its courts, would address the issue in a way that could lead to an effective resolution of the dispute'.[75] In that case, the arbitrators considered that they were not specifically applying the futility exception, as it is understood under customary international law, but rather weighing the State's interests in being able to address the investor's grievances in its national courts as opposed to the latter's interests in being able to bring its claims in arbitration.[76]

Indeed, there are a number of arbitral awards disregarding the exhaustion of local remedies clause in relation to Argentina. Argentina, when dealing with a major financial crisis issued laws that not only affected many foreign investors but also provided for stays of judicial proceedings and impossibility for the State to enter into any settlements, whether judicial or others. Tribunals opined that the measures taken by Argentina rendered recourse to Argentine courts effectively futile.[77]

The *ICS v. Argentina* also discussed the futility exception to exhaustion of local remedies,[78] emphasizing, however, the criterion of 'obvious futility, where the relief sought is patently unavailable'.[79] Finding that the parties' experts provided two conflicting opinions as to the availability of effective relief through Argentinian courts, the tribunal concluded that it could not hold that local remedies would have been completely ineffective, and found no compelling reason to exempt ICS from complying with the requirement.[80]

Based on the cases on the subject, one can gauge that arbitral tribunals tend to have a liberal approach in interpreting the preconditions to arbitration.

[C] The Application of MFN Provisions to Jurisdiction

The MFN clause is present in many investment treaties and is usually found among the substantive protections afforded to the investor. This is essentially a non-discrimination provision seeking to establish equality between all foreign investors with regard to their investment in the same host State.[81] For example, the Germany-Argentina BIT provides that:

> Neither Contracting Party shall subject nationals or companies of the other Contracting Party, as regards their activity in connection with investments in its

75. *Abaclat and Others (Case formerly known as Giovanna a Beccara and Others) v. Argentine Republic*, ICSID Case No. ARB/07/5, Decision on Jurisdiction and Admissibility (4 Aug. 2011), para. 582.
76. *Ibid.*, at § 584.
77. *See Ambiente Ufficio S.P.A. and others v. The Argentine Republic*, ICSID Case No. ARB/08/9, Decision on Jurisdiction and Admissibility (8 Feb. 2013), para. 607.
78. *See ICS Inspection and Control Services Limited v. The Argentine Republic*, P.C.A. Case No. 2010-9, Award on Jurisdiction (10 Feb. 2012).
79. *Ibid.*, para. 269.
80. *Ibid.*
81. *Case concerning rights of nationals of the United States of America in Morocco, France v. United States of America*, Judgment (27 Aug. 1952), ICJ Reports 176, 187 (1952).

territory, to treatment less favourable than it accords to its own nationals or companies or to nationals or companies of any third State.[82]

MFN clauses may take different forms. It is possible to distinguish four principal types of such provisions:

(1) Broad MFN clause that covers 'all matters'.[83]
(2) Clause with general wording.[84]
(3) MFN attached to the FET clause.[85]
(4) Narrow MFN clause.[86]

Whereas the first type of MFN clauses does not raise the question whether it applies to dispute resolution provisions (indeed, it may be expressly stated in the treaty that such is the case), the issue is much less clear as regards the other types. The mechanism of an MFN provision relies on the *ejusdem generis* principle. According to this rule, an investor can only enjoy the more favorable treatment that is afforded to other foreign investors if it falls under the subject matter of the MFN clause.[87] Hence, if the subject matter of the MFN clause is limited to the level of import tax, then its beneficiary may only enjoy more favorable tax regime and not any other type of more favorable treatment. Following the same logic, if the MFN is related to the FET provision, then its beneficiary should only be able to benefit from a more favorable substantive treatment.

Arbitral tribunals have not been uniform on this subject. Indeed, it is possible to distinguish two main contradictory lines of decisions: on the one hand, *Maffezini v. Spain* and, on the other hand, *Plama v. Bulgaria*.[88] The *Maffezzini* tribunal was first to hold that the MFN clause in the Argentina-Spain BIT 'embraces the dispute settlement provisions of this treaty' thus effectively allowing the claimant to bypass the exhaustion of local remedies provision by relying on the Chile-Spain BIT, which provided for arbitration only preceded by a six-month cooling-off period.[89]

82. Germany-Argentina BIT, Art. 3.
83. Julie A. Maupin, *MFN-Based Jurisdiction in Investor-State Arbitration: Is There Any Hope For a Consistent Approach?*, 14 J. Intl. Econ. L. 157, 163–165 (2011). For example, Belgium-Luxembourg BIT.
84. *See*, for example, Germany-Argentina BIT, Art. 3(1)-(2) (1991).
85. For example, the MFN clause in question in the *Maffezini* case. *Emilio Agustin Maffezini v. The Kingdom of Spain*, ICSID Case No. ARB/97/7, Decision on Jurisdiction (25 Jan. 2000).
86. For example, Interpretive Declaration to the Panama-Argentina BIT (1996).
87. Article 9(1) of its 1978 Draft Articles on Most-Favored-Nation Treatment: 'Under a most-favored-nation clause the beneficiary State acquires, for itself or for the benefit of persons or things in a determined relationship with it, only those rights which fall within the limits of the subject-matter of the clause.' *Draft Articles on MFN clauses with commentaries*, text adopted by the International Law Commission at its thirtieth session, II(Part Two) Yearbook of the International Law Commission 27 (1978).
88. *Emilio Agustin Maffezini v. The Kingdom of Spain*, ICSID Case No. ARB/97/7, Decision on Jurisdiction (25 Jan. 2000). *Plama Consortium Limited v. Republic of Bulgaria*, ICSID Case No. ARB/03/24, Decision on Jurisdiction (8 Feb. 2005).
89. *Emilio Agustin Maffezini v. The Kingdom of Spain*, ICSID Case No. ARB/97/7, Decision on Jurisdiction (25 Jan. 2000), paras 63–64.

The *Maffezzini* award sparked outrage in the arbitration community and especially among the States parties to investment treaties with MFN clauses.[90] In point of fact, it may appear farfetched that consent to arbitration could be implied by way of an MFN clause that only concerns 'treatment' of the investor or investment. The *Maffezzini* view is not shared by all the tribunals that have had an opportunity to treat this issue since.

The *Plama v. Bulgaria* tribunal spearheads the opposing view on the interpretation of the MFN clause in regard to jurisdiction. The facts of the case are different from *Maffezzini*, which may explain the difference in outcomes. In the latter, there was fundamental consent to the forum and the type of disputes to be submitted to the forum, and the claimant simply wanted to avoid the eighteen-month litigation in national courts. In *Plama*, on the other hand, the applicable treaty contained a very restrictive arbitration clause, which provided for an ad hoc procedure and only with regard to expropriation claims.[91] The BIT between Bulgaria and Cyprus had the following dispute resolution clause:

> The legality of the expropriation shall be checked at the request of the concerned investor through the regular administrative and legal procedure of the contracting party that had taken the expropriation steps. ... If within 3 months after the beginning of the consultations no agreement is reached, the amount of the compensation at the request of the concerned investor shall be checked either in a legal regular procedure of the Contracting Party which had taken the measure on expropriation or by an international 'Ad hoc' Arbitration Court.

The claimant attempted to import into this treaty a dispute resolution clause providing for ICSID arbitration from another BIT signed between Bulgaria and Finland.

Notwithstanding the difference in facts, the reasoning adopted by the *Plama* tribunal is transposable to *Maffezzini*. The tribunal noted that the arbitration provision in a treaty, much as a contractual arbitration clause, is separable from the rest, and the States could not have intended that dispute resolution provisions in the BIT may be substituted by others imported by operation of the MFN clause unless it is expressly provided for in the treaty itself.[92] Other arguments that have found support with later tribunals include a discussion of the 'most favorable' language: in particular, it is possible to doubt whether a dispute resolution clause without an exhaustion of local remedies requirement is indeed more favorable than a clause without such a condition.[93]

The debate among the tribunals is not settled, and it appears that they are more or less reluctant to rely on the MFN clause to overcome preconditions to arbitration depending on the reasonableness of the latter.

90. *Plama Consortium Limited v. Republic of Bulgaria*, ICSID Case No. ARB/03/24, Decision on Jurisdiction (8 Feb. 2005), pp. 64–65.
91. *Ibid.*
92. *Ibid.*, para. 212.
93. *Ibid.*, para. 208. *See also Daimler Financial Services AG v. Argentine Republic*, ICSID Case No. ARB/05/1, Award (22 Aug. 2012), pp. 103–105.

[D] Procedural, Jurisdictional or Admissibility Nature of the Preconditions to Arbitration

While this section is entitled 'Preconditions to Arbitration', it is unclear whether the cooling-off and exhaustion of local remedies clauses constitute restrictions to the consent to jurisdiction, or whether they are merely procedural or admissibility requirements. If these preconditions were to be considered jurisdictional in nature, and the claimant did not comply with them, then the arbitration agreement would not be formed, and the tribunal would not have the jurisdiction to hear the claim. The non-fulfilment of admissibility requirements, on the other hand, does not affect the existence of the agreement to arbitrate and, thus, the tribunal's jurisdiction.[94]

Cases where the tribunals found this to be a jurisdictional requirement include *Goetz v. Burundi*[95] and *Enron* and *Ponderosa Assets v. Argentine Republic.*[96] This, however, appears to be a minority view. The majority of arbitral tribunals consider that it is possible to waive the compulsory amicable negotiation period.[97] Likewise, Dolzer and Schreuer adopt the following position:

> The view that periods foreseen for negotiations are not of a jurisdictional nature is preferable. By the time the tribunal makes a decision on this issue, any waiting period is likely to have elapsed. Under these circumstances insistence on the compliance with the waiting period before the institution of proceedings would make little sense and would merely compel the claimant to start new proceedings.[98]

Similar to cooling-off clauses, the compulsory resort to local courts condition has also given rise to the debate as to whether it affects the fundamental jurisdiction of the tribunal or merely the admissibility of certain claims.[99]

The *Abaclat* tribunal concluded that exhaustion of local remedies is a procedural requirement, which only relates to the way in which Argentina's consent is to be implemented. According to this interpretation, this precondition to arbitration does not

94. Alejandro López Ortiz, Patricia Ugalde-Revilla, et al., *The Role of National Courts in ICSID Arbitration*, in *ICSID Convention after 50 Years: Unsettled Issues*, 338 (Crina Baltag Editor, Kluwer Law International 2017).
95. *Antoine Goetz et consorts v. République du Burundi*, ICSID Case No. ARB/95/3, Award (10 Feb. 1999).
96. *Enron Corporation and Ponderosa Assets, L.P. v. Argentine Republic*, ICSID Case No. ARB/01/3 (also known as: *Enron Creditors Recovery Corp. and Ponderosa Assets, L.P. v. The Argentine Republic*), Decision on Jurisdiction (14 Jan. 2004).
97. Andrea Marco Steingruber, *Consent in International Arbitration*, 196 (Oxford University Press 2012), making reference in n. 63 to *Ethyl v. Canada* (Award on Jurisdiction), *Wena v. Egypt* (Decision on Jurisdiction), *Lauder v. Czech Republic* (Award), *SGS v. Pakistan* (Decision on Jurisdiction), *Biwater v. Tanzania* (Award).
98. Rudolf Dolzer & Christoph Schreuer, *Principles of International Investment Law*, 36 (2nd ed., Oxford University Press 2012).
99. Martin Dietrich Brauch, *IISD Best Practices Series: Exhaustion of Local Remedies in International Investment Law*, 17 (International Institute for Sustainable Development 2017), https://www.iisd.org/sites/default/files/publications/best-practices-exhaustion-local-remedies-law-investment-en.pdf (accessed 28 May 2018).

affect the fundamental issue of whether the State has given its consent to arbitral jurisdiction.[100]

In *Maffezini v. Spain*, on the contrary, the tribunal interpreted the time-limited exhaustion of local remedies requirement as jurisdictional,[101] considering it a mandatory condition of consent. Where the investor does not comply with this requirement, a tribunal should dismiss the case on jurisdictional grounds, absent an alternative basis to establish its jurisdiction.[102] Following the same reasoning, *Daimler* tribunal affirmed that 'all BIT-based dispute resolution provisions [...] are by their very nature jurisdictional'.[103]

The *Abaclat v. Argentina* tribunal highlighted the distinction between jurisdiction and admissibility:

> although a lack of jurisdiction or admissibility may both lead to the same result of a tribunal having to refuse to hear the case, such refusal is of a fundamentally different nature and therefore carries different consequences:
>
> (i) While a lack of jurisdiction *stricto sensu* means that the claim cannot at all be brought in front of the body called upon, a lack of admissibility means that the claim was neither fit nor mature for judicial treatment;
> (ii) Whereby a decision refusing a case based on a lack of arbitral jurisdiction is usually subject to review by another body, a decision refusing a case based on a lack of admissibility can usually not be subject to review by another body;
> (iii) Whereby a final refusal based on a lack of jurisdiction will prevent the parties from successfully re-submitting the same claim to the same body, a refusal based on admissibility will, in principle, not prevent the claimant from resubmitting its claim, provided it cures the previous flaw causing the inadmissibility.[104]

§3.04 THE SCOPE OF CONSENT TO JURISDICTION

Once the initial obstacles to acceding to arbitral jurisdiction, if any, have been overcome, there remains the issue of the scope of consent. The arbitrators may not exceed the mission given to them by the parties. As such, they may only decide the claims, which are covered by the consent. Depending on the instrument containing the parties' consent, the tribunal may have jurisdiction only with regard to contract claims, which are governed by national law (generally, that of the host State). This is similar to commercial arbitration, where private parties bring claims for non-performance against one another. On the other hand, where the offer to arbitrate is contained in an

100. *Ibid.*, para. 496.
101. *Emilio Agustin Maffezini v. The Kingdom of Spain*, ICSID Case No. ARB/97/7, Decision on Jurisdiction (25 Jan. 2000).
102. *Ibid.*, p. 18.
103. *Daimler Financial Services AG v. Argentine Republic*, ICSID Case No. ARB/05/1, Award (22 Aug. 2012), para. 193.
104. *Abaclat and Others v. Argentine Republic*, ICSID Case No. ARB/07/5 (formerly *Giovanna a Beccara and Others v. The Argentine Republic*), Decision on Jurisdiction (4 Aug. 201), para. 247.

international treaty, the arbitral tribunal constituted on its basis has the jurisdiction to hear treaty claims. Here, the investor may claim compensation for breaches of the substantive protections afforded to it by the treaty; these claims are governed by international law.

To understand fully the potential scope of tribunals' jurisdiction, it is important to differentiate between breaches of treaty and contract (A). It will then be discussed that, in certain circumstances, contract claims may be lifted to the level of treaty claims in the presence of the so-called umbrella clause (B).

[A] Breaches of Treaty and Breaches of Contract

Although it may appear to be clear, the distinction between treaty and contract claims is not so evident in practice. The jurisdiction of an arbitral tribunal over a contract claim can often be subject of debate and be an initial matter for the tribunal to resolve, after parties have submitted their claims. While a contract claim is related to a breach of the contract concluded by the parties and governed by national law, a breach of treaty refers to treaty violations and is governed by international law.

Apart from the fact that an investor and a host State are bound by the applicable treaty, foreign investment may also involve a contract reflecting the rights and obligations between the parties. Concession agreements are a significant example of such contracts. While the rights of the investor under each of these instruments are different, they may sometimes overlap. Often, the foreign investor does not have an agreement directly with the State but may have a contract concluded with a State-owned company or a government agency. When a State-owned company or the agency breaches a contract concluded with a foreign investor, the latter may have both contract and treaty claims against the host State.[105] This has an impact on determination of jurisdiction, because the tribunal may only hear the claims based on the instrument to which the arbitration provision conferring jurisdiction upon it pertains.[106]

The distinction between treaty claims and contract claims was established by the ICSID annulment committee in *Vivendi Universal S.A. v. Argentine Republic.*[107] The ad hoc committee stated that:

> In accordance with this general principle (which is undoubtedly declaratory of general international law), whether there has been a breach of the BIT and whether there has been a breach of contract are different questions. Each of these claims will be determined by reference to its own proper or applicable law – in the case of the BIT, by international law; in the case of the Concession Contract, by the proper law of the contract.[108]

105. Katia Yannaca-Small, *Improving the System of Investor-State Dispute Settlement*, OECD Working Papers on International Investment, 2006/01, 25 (OECD Publishing 2006).
106. *Ibid.*
107. *Compañiá de Aguas del Aconquija S.A. and Vivendi Universal S.A. v. Argentine Republic*, ICSID Case No. ARB/97/3 (formerly *Compañía de Aguas del Aconquija, S.A. and Compagnie Générale des Eaux v. Argentine Republic*), Decision on Annulment (3 Jul. 2002).
108. *Ibid.*, para. 96.

Further elaborating on the complexity of contract and treaty claims, the *Vivendi* tribunal held that BITs 'set an independent standard' from that contained in contracts and a State could breach a treaty without breaching a contract and vice versa:[109]

> Where the fundamental basis of the claim is a treaty laying down an independent standard by which the conduct of the parties is to be judged, the existence of an exclusive jurisdiction clause in a contract between the claimant and the respondent state or one of its subdivisions cannot operate as a bar to the application of the treaty standard.[110]

The distinction between contract and treaty claims becomes of particular importance when the two instruments have incompatible dispute resolution provisions. In *Lanco v. Argentina* and *Salini v. Morocco*, the investor was allowed to refer a contract dispute to an arbitral tribunal on the basis of a treaty despite the existence of a separate dispute settlement clause in the contract. In *Lanco v. Argentina*, the tribunal held that the exclusive jurisdiction clause in favor of national courts did not prevent the submission of disputes to ICSID on two main grounds.[111] First, the wording of Article 26 of the ICSID Convention is such that 'the consent of the parties to arbitration is considered consent to such arbitration to the exclusion of any other remedy'.[112] Second, 'since administrative jurisdiction cannot be selected by mutual agreement, the weight to be accorded to the contractual choice which the parties had made ought to be diminished'.[113] In *Salini v. Morocco*, the tribunal concluded that the dispute resolution clause in the relevant BIT 'overrode the contractual jurisdiction clause' and obliged the host State to comply with its own offer of jurisdiction with regard to BIT claims and breach of contract claims.[114]

The distinction between these different types of claims finds its source in the test of triple identity.[115] To the extent that a dispute might involve the same parties, object

109. Katia Yannaca-Small, *Improving the System of Investor-State Dispute Settlement*, OECD Working Papers on International Investment, 2006/01, 27 (OECD Publishing 2006).
110. *Compañiá de Aguas del Aconquija S.A. and Vivendi Universal S.A. v. Argentine Republic*, ICSID Case No. ARB/97/3 (formerly *Compañía de Aguas del Aconquija, S.A. and Compagnie Générale des Eaux v. Argentine Republic*), Decision on Annulment (3 Jul. 2002), para. 101.
111. Katia Yannaca-Small, *Improving the System of Investor-State Dispute Settlement*, OECD Working Papers on International Investment, 2006/01, 26 (2006).
112. *Lanco International Inc. v. Argentine Republic*, ICSID Case No. ARB/97/6, Preliminary Decision on Jurisdiction (8 Dec. 1998), para. 36.
113. Katia Yannaca-Small, *Improving the System of Investor-State Dispute Settlement*, OECD Working Papers on International Investment, 2006/01, 26 (OECD Publishing 2006).
114. *Salini Costruttori S.p.A. and Italstrade S.p.A. v. Kingdom of Morocco*, ICSID Case No. ARB/00/4, Decision on Jurisdiction (31 Jul. 2001), para. 61. But *see Joy Mining Machinery Limited v. Arab Republic of Egypt*, ICSID Case No. ARB/03/11, Award on Jurisdiction (6 Aug. 2004), paras 72–79: the tribunal held that 'a basic general distinction can be made between commercial aspects of a dispute and other aspects involving the existence of some form of State interference with the operation of the contract involved'. Commercial aspects of a dispute, according to the tribunal, should be settled 'as agreed to in the Contract, including the resort to arbitration if and when available'.
115. *Enron Corporation and Ponderosa Assets, L.P. v. Argentine Republic*, ICSID Case No. ARB/01/3 (also known as: *Enron Creditors Recovery Corp. and Ponderosa Assets, L.P. v. The Argentine Republic*), Decision on Jurisdiction (Ancillary Claim) (2 Aug. 2004), para. 49.

and cause of action[116] it might be considered a dispute where it is virtually impossible to separate the contract issues from the treaty issues and to draw any jurisdictional conclusions from a distinction between them. A purely contractual claim, however, will normally find difficulty in passing the jurisdictional test of treaty-based tribunals, which will of course require allegation of a specific violation of treaty rights as the foundation of their jurisdiction. As the annulment committee held in *Vivendi*, '[a] treaty cause of action is not the same as a contractual cause of action; it requires a clear showing of conduct which is in the circumstances contrary to the relevant treaty standard.'[117]

Issues that arise in relation to umbrella and fork-in-the-road provisions, which will be discussed below, illustrate that the distinction between contract and treaty claims may be unsustainable and cause contradictory results in practice.

[B] Umbrella Clause

The 'umbrella clause' is a provision found in many bilateral and multilateral investment treaties and is commonly used to provide additional protection to investors. Such protection is aimed at covering investment agreements that host States have concluded with foreign investors prior to the entry into force of the relevant treaty. Under such clauses the host State undertakes to comply with all its obligations arising out of investment contracts.[118] As such, a violation of the contract with the foreign investor also amounts to a breach of the said clause in the BIT. An example of such a treaty provision is Article 10(1) of the ECT, which provides as follows:

> Each Contracting Party shall observe any obligations it has entered into with an Investor or an Investment of an Investor of any other Contracting Party.

Interpretation and, consequently, scope and effect of umbrella clauses differ among various commentators. Christoph Schreuer states that:

> umbrella clauses have been added to some BITs to provide additional protection to investors beyond the traditional international standards. They are often referred to as 'umbrella clauses' because they put contractual commitments under the BIT's protective umbrella. They add the compliance with investment contracts, or other undertakings of the host State, to the BIT's substantive standards. In this way, a violation of such a contract becomes a violation of the BIT.[119]

The formulation of umbrella clauses in investment agreements varies significantly. Because of this diversity, the proper interpretation of the clause depends on the specific wording of the particular treaty, its ordinary meaning, context, the object and

116. *Lauder v. Czech Republic*, UNCITRAL Final Award (3 Sep. 2001), paras 161, 163.
117. *Compañiá de Aguas del Aconquija S.A. and Vivendi Universal S.A. v. Argentine Republic*, ICSID Case No. ARB/97/3 (formerly *Compañía de Aguas del Aconquija, S.A. and Compagnie Générale des Eaux v. Argentine Republic*), Decision on Annulment (3 Jul. 2002), para. 75.
118. Anthony C. Sinclair, *The Origins of the Umbrella Clause in the International Law of Investment Protection*, 20(4) Arb. Intl. 411–434 (2004).
119. *See* Katia Yannaca-Small, *Improving the System of Investor-State Dispute Settlement*, OECD Working Papers on International Investment, 2006/01 (OECD Publishing 2006).

purpose of the treaty as well on negotiating history or other indications of the parties' intent.[120]

There is a string of decisions that illustrates the uncertainty associated with the multiple issues related to umbrella clauses. The main question that the tribunals faced in *SGS v. Pakistan*, *SGS v. Philippines* and *SGS v. Paraguay* is whether the umbrella clause elevates contract claims to the level of treaty violations, which evidently affected the jurisdiction of the arbitrators to hear all the claims in the same forum.[121]

The *SGS v. Pakistan* tribunal was the first to deal with the interpretation of an umbrella clause. The unprecedented position the tribunal found itself may in part explain why it interpreted the clause narrowly, holding that the claimant needed to introduce 'clear and convincing evidence'[122] that the parties to the investment treaty intended that the umbrella clause elevates a contract breach to the level of a treaty breach. Indeed, the BIT clause provided for 'observance of commitments', which does not necessarily refer to contracts concluded by the State.[123] Since the claimant failed to provide clear and convincing evidence, the tribunal rejected its proposed interpretation of umbrella clause and denied the claim, thus refusing to adjudicate the contract breach concerned.[124]

The tribunal in *SGS v. Philippines* criticized the reasoning of *SGS v. Pakistan* tribunal and held that the umbrella clause did indeed elevate contractual breaches to the level of treaty violation. According to the arbitration tribunal, a distinction must be made between the observance and performance of State obligations, such as contracts concluded with investors and the 'extent or content' of these obligations.[125] The issue of the 'extent' of these obligations remains contractual in nature, and thus should be governed by the applicable national law.[126]

While interpreting the umbrella clause in an extensive fashion, the tribunal, nevertheless, declined its jurisdiction in this case, because of the exclusive choice-of-forum clause in the contract between the investor and the State. This decision highlights the paradoxical effect of the umbrella clause operating to elevate contract breaches to the level of treaty violations: the exclusive choice-of-forum clause in the contract is also covered by its operation and, as such, disregarding this clause would arguably be a violation of the State's international law obligations. The tribunal concluded that a generally worded BIT dispute resolution clause could not override the

120. *Ibid.*
121. *SGS Société Générale de Surveillance S.A. v. Islamic Republic of Pakistan*, ICSID Case No. ARB/01/13, Decision on Jurisdiction (6 Aug. 2003); *SGS Société Générale de Surveillance S.A. v. Republic of the Philippines*, ICSID Case No. ARB/02/6, Decision on Jurisdiction (29 Jan. 2004); *SGS Société Générale de Surveillance S.A. v. The Republic of Paraguay*, ICSID Case No. ARB/07/29, Decision on Jurisdiction (12 Feb. 2010).
122. *SGS Société Générale de Surveillance S.A. v. Islamic Republic of Pakistan*, ICSID Case No. ARB/01/13, Decision on Jurisdiction (6 Aug. 2003), para. 167.
123. *Ibid.*, para. 166.
124. *Ibid.*
125. *SGS Société Générale de Surveillance S.A. v. Republic of the Philippines*, ICSID Case No. ARB/02/6, Decision on Jurisdiction (29 Jan. 2004), para. 128 (emphasis in the original).
126. Vlad Zolia, *Effect and Purpose of 'Umbrella Clauses' in Bilateral Investment Treaties: Unresolved Issues*, TDM 5, 26 (2005), https://www.transnational-dispute-management.com/article.asp?key=603 (accessed 27 Mar. 2018).

more specific and carefully negotiated choice-of-forum clause in the contract between the host State and the investor.[127] The tribunal based its decision, first of all, on the principle of *generalia specialibus non derogant*: the BIT dispute resolution clause being a more general provision, it cannot override a more specific clause contained in the contract. Second, the arbitral panel suggested that the treaty is meant to provide a general framework for the protection of the investors and 'not to override or replace the actually negotiated investment arrangements made between the investor and the host State'.[128]

Although decisions by investment tribunals are not binding on subsequent tribunals, *SGS v. Philippines* and later cases involving the interpretation and application of umbrella clause followed a similar pattern, recognizing the choice-of-forum agreement by either staying the arbitration proceedings until the contractual dispute is decided by the chosen court or declining their own jurisdiction.[129]

However, in yet another case brought by SGS, this time against Paraguay, the tribunal went even further in its reasoning than its predecessors.[130] In addition to accepting its jurisdiction to hear the breach of contract claims elevated to the level of treaty violation by virtue of an umbrella clause, the tribunal concluded that there was no issue of inadmissibility regardless of the exclusive choice-of-forum clause. The arguments advanced by the *SGS v. Paraguay* tribunal can be characterized as grounded in public international law – as opposed to 'contractual freedom' reasoning followed by in the *SGS v. Philippines* case – as it was held that the State should not be able to contract out of its international law obligations by including 'an implied waiver of BIT rights into every investment agreement that specifies a dispute resolution mechanism other than ICSID'.[131]

Tribunals' interpretations varied with respect to the effect of the placement of the umbrella clause within the BIT. The Tribunal in the aforementioned case *SGS v. Pakistan* held that the placement of the clause near the end of the Swiss-Pakistan BIT was indicative of an intention of the Contracting Parties 'that [Article 11] was not meant to project a substantive obligation'.[132] The Tribunal held that had the Contracting Parties intended to create a substantive obligation through the umbrella clause it would logically have been placed 'among the substantive "first order" obligations'.[133] On the other hand, the *SGS v. Philippines* tribunal did not consider the placement of the

127. *SGS Société Générale de Surveillance S.A. v. Republic of the Philippines*, ICSID Case No. ARB/02/6, Decision on Jurisdiction (29 Jan. 2004), paras 134, 153.
128. *Ibid.*, para. 141.
129. Andrea Schulz, *The Future Convention on Exclusive Choice of Court Agreements and Arbitration: Parallel Proceedings and Possible Treaty Conflicts, In Particular with ICSID and the New York Convention on the Recognition and Enforcement of Foreign Arbitral Awards*, Prel. Doc. No. 32, 18 (2005). *See also Bureau Veritas, Inspection, Valuation, Assessment and Control, BIVAC B.V. v. The Republic of Paraguay*, ICSID Case No. ARB/07/9, Decision on Jurisdiction (29 May 2009).
130. *SGS Société Générale de Surveillance S.A. v. The Republic of Paraguay*, ICSID Case No. ARB/07/29, Decision on Jurisdiction (12 Feb. 2010).
131. *Ibid.*, para. 177.
132. *SGS Société Générale de Surveillance S.A. v. Islamic Republic of Pakistan*, ICSID Case No. ARB/01/13, Decision on Jurisdiction (6 Aug. 2003), paras 169–170.
133. *Ibid.*, para. 170.

clause to be a decisive factor. In its reasoning, the tribunal maintained that 'it is difficult to accept that the same language in other Philippines BITs is legally operative, but that it is legally inoperative in the Swiss-Philippines BIT merely because of its location'.[134]

A crucial issue in respect of umbrella clauses is the scope and nature of the obligations undertaken.[135] Differences are drawn between umbrella clauses that refer to 'commitments',[136] 'any obligation'[137] and 'any other obligation'.[138] Further, some umbrella clauses refer to obligations 'entered into' by a State, while others refer to obligations 'assumed' by the State.[139] The degree to which the object of the obligations is specified is yet another distinction among various BITs. An example of a broadly phrased umbrella clause can be found in Article 2(2)(c) of the 1991 US-Argentina BIT, which states: 'Each Party shall observe any obligation it may have entered into with regard to investments.'[140] These variations raise the question whether the obligation referred to is a contractual obligation between the State and the investor or whether it could extend to unilateral obligations undertaken by the State through, *inter alia*, promises, legislative acts or administrative measures.[141]

§3.05 PARALLEL PROCEEDINGS

Due to the existence of more than 3,000 BITs and the continued globalization, investors often have a choice of multiple fora to bring their claims. It is not unusual in international arbitration that the same cause of action is adjudicated in more than one forum simultaneously. The same dispute, or two closely related disputes, may result in parallel proceedings before different arbitral tribunals (or between a national court and an arbitral tribunal), thus imposing a risk of conflicting decisions. Besides the fact that it causes an unnecessary waste of money, the issue of parallel proceedings imposes legal uncertainty in terms of available legal remedies. In determining whether two or more cases are the same and thus parallel, factors to be looked at are whether there is sufficient identity of parties, of subject matter of the dispute and of the cause of action. This constitutes the so-called 'triple identity' test.[142]

Several procedural mechanisms have been adopted to avoid or mitigate the undesirable effects of parallel proceedings. Those are the principles of lis pendens, res

134. *SGS Société Générale de Surveillance S.A. v. Republic of the Philippines*, ICSID Case No. ARB/02/6, Decision on Jurisdiction (29 Jan. 2004), para. 124.
135. Katia Yannaca-Small, *Improving the System of Investor-State Dispute Settlement*, OECD Working Papers on International Investment, 2006/01 (OECD Publishing 2006).
136. Belgium and Luxembourg-Saudi Arabia BIT (2002), Art. 7(2).
137. Greek Model BIT 2001, Art. 11(2).
138. Greece-Argentina BIT 1999 (not in force), Art. 2(3).
139. Katia Yannaca-Small, *Improving the System of Investor-State Dispute Settlement*, OECD Working Papers on International Investment, 2006/01, 10 (OECD Publishing 2006).
140. US-Argentina BIT (1991), Art. 2(2)(c).
141. *Ibid.*
142. Pedro J. Martinez-Fraga & Harout Jack Samra, *The Role of Precedent in Defining Res Judicata in Investor-State Arbitration*, 32 Nw. J. Intl. L. & Bus. 419 (2012).

judicata, *electa una via* and consolidation of proceedings (upon parties' mutual consent or if there is an express treaty provision allowing consolidation of claims).[143]

When the two claims are being pursued at the same time, the issue is categorized as one of lis pendens.[144] The tribunal may choose to stay its proceedings 'if it is satisfied that it would be in the interests of justice to do so'.[145] When the two claims are pursued subsequently, there already being a judgment from the first court; the matter is treated as a question of res judicata.[146] It is important to note that the principle of res judicata 'only applies to decisions within the same legal order, namely those of other international tribunals applying public international law [having] no application to the decisions of national courts'.[147]

The importance of this distinction between proceedings under national and international law is succinctly provided in *Elettronica Sicula S.p.A. (ELSI) (United States of America v. Italy)*, where the Tribunal stated that:

> Compliance with municipal law and compliance with the provisions of a treaty are different questions. What is a breach of treaty may be lawful in the municipal law and what is unlawful in the municipal law may be wholly innocent of violation of a treaty provision.[148]

The following four features of investment arbitration are contributing to and raising possibilities of parallel proceedings:[149]

(1) Bilateralism. Separate identity of a tribunal constituted according to the treaty provisions or applicable rules imposes the risk that the same dispute may be adjudicated by a judicial body of a respective host State.
(2) Non-exclusivity. Treaties rarely exclude 'all recourse to state courts'.[150] Therefore, when allowed, an investor may pursue proceedings both before an arbitral tribunal and before a competent national body.
(3) Exclusion of local remedies. Similarly, as with non-exclusivity rule, if a treaty does not explicitly require exhaustion of local remedies, parties are not obliged to do so. That again leaves enough room for the parties to start parallel proceedings.
(4) Multiple investor claims. In a case where multiple investors involved in a single dispute want to pursue separate actions, there may be as much

143. Campbell McLachlan QC, Laurence Shore & Matthew Weiniger, *International Investment Arbitration: Substantive Principles*, 80, 125 (2nd ed., Oxford International Arbitration Series 2007).
144. *Ibid.*, p. 81.
145. *Ibid.*, p. 130.
146. *Ibid.*, p. 81.
147. *Ibid.*, p. 84.
148. *Elettronica Sicula S.p.A. (ELSI) case, United States v. Italy*, Judgement (20 July 1989), ICJ Reports 15 (1989).
149. *Ibid.*, ICJ Reports 87 (1989).
150. *Ibid.*, p. 88.

proceedings as there are investors. For example, in *Lauder v. Czech Republic*,[151] an investor brought an arbitration proceeding against the State. At the same time, the company that managed the investor's investment brought a separate arbitration proceeding against the State.[152] Although the allegations against the State and the evidence in both cases were substantially the same, the State chose not to consolidate the cases.[153] Ultimately, that resulted in two opposing decisions. The question that arose in the second out of two decisions was whether the second decision amounted to violation of the principle of res judicata. The tribunal rejected this submission with the following reasoning:

> The parties in London arbitration differ from the parties in this arbitration. Mr. Lauder is the controlling shareholder of CME Media Ltd, whereas in this arbitration a Dutch holding company being part of the CME Media Ltd Group is the Claimant. The two arbitrations are based on different bilateral investment treaties, which grant comparable investment protection, which, however, is not identical. Both arbitrations deal with the Media Council's interference with the same investment in the Czech Republic. However, the Tribunal cannot judge whether the facts submitted to the two tribunals for decision are identical ...'[154]

The following sections will discuss the different procedural tools that may be used to avoid parallel proceedings including a fork-in-the-road clause (A) and a waiver of domestic remedies (B). Thereafter, the effects of res judicata in the context of investment arbitration shall be addressed (C).

[A] Fork-in-the-Road

ISDS provisions are a major component of investment treaties[155] – they provide fora for investors in case of a treaty breach. ISDS provisions list the institutions to which investors may submit their claim. Nowadays, the majority of ISDS treaty provisions provide recourse to both domestic courts and international arbitration,[156] giving parties a choice regarding the forum for the submission of their dispute. The divergence emerges as to whether that choice is final and exclusive.

151. *Lauder v. Czech Republic*, UNCITRAL Final Award (3 Sep. 2001).
152. *CME Czech Republic B.V. v. The Czech Republic*, UNCITRAL, Award (14 Mar. 2003).
153. *Lauder v. Czech Republic*, UNCITRAL Final Award (3 Sep. 2001), para. 118.
154. *CME Czech Republic B.V. v. The Czech Republic*, UNCITRAL, Award (14 Mar. 2003), para. 432.
155. Joachim Pohl, Kekeletso Mashigo & Alexis Nohen, *Dispute Settlement Provisions in International Investment Agreements: A Large Sample Survey*, OECD Working Papers on International Investment, 2012/02, 7 (OECD Publishing 2012).
156. *Ibid.*, From 1970 onwards, full ISDS sections (or annexes) began to appear in the treaties. These treaties featured two innovations: (a) they provided recourse to international arbitration as a dispute settlement mechanism, and (b) while ISDS was initially limited to claims arising under the expropriation clause, those treaties provided ISDS for claims arising under other substantive treaty provisions. The first treaty to contain such specific ISDS section and to propose international arbitration as a dispute settlement mechanism is the Belgium/Luxembourg-Indonesia BIT from 1970.

More than a third of the treaties that provide a choice between domestic judicial review and international arbitration specify that a choice, once made by the investor, is final and exclusive.[157] That provision is the so-called fork-in-the-road clause, also known as the principle of *electa una via*. Fork-in-the-road clauses provide that, once the case is brought to domestic courts, an investor cannot initiate international arbitration proceedings, and vice versa. In other words, where the tribunal would otherwise have jurisdiction pursuant to a treaty, a party may lose the ability 'to avail itself of such jurisdiction' by choosing to submit the claim before the State court (or other competent authority).[158] Parties are precluded from, simultaneously or subsequently, resorting to any other potentially available dispute resolution mechanism. Such provision can be found in Article 26 of ICSID Convention:

> Consent of the parties to arbitration under this Convention shall, unless otherwise stated, be deemed consent to such arbitration to the exclusion of any other remedy. A Contracting State may require the exhaustion of local administrative or judicial remedies as a condition of its consent to arbitration under this Convention.

There are certain indications that the tribunals rely on in determining whether a final and binding choice of forum has been made by the investor. First of all, proceedings in the national courts must have been instituted before the request of arbitration is filed.[159] However, more importantly, domestic proceedings must concern the same cause of action and the same subject matter, as well as being brought among the same parties, as those involved in the arbitration. If the investor wants to bring a claim based on a BIT violation in arbitration, then it would only be precluded under the *electa una via* provision if the domestic proceedings also concern an alleged breach of a right conferred on the investor by the BIT. The State must also be the defendant in the domestic proceedings, which may not always be possible depending on the applicable administrative law.[160]

There are treaties that, on the contrary, leave the choice between international arbitration and domestic court proceedings reversible until a specified event occurs.[161] Some treaties allow the simultaneous pursuit of the claim in both domestic courts and international arbitration until a specified event occurs.[162]

157. *Ibid.*, para. 22.
158. Campbell McLachlan QC, Laurence Shore & Matthew Weiniger, *International Investment Arbitration: Substantive Principles*, 90 (2nd ed., Oxford International Arbitration Series 2007).
159. Christoph Schreuer, *Travelling the BIT Route – Of Waiting Periods, Umbrella Clauses and Forks in the Road*, 5 J. World Inv. & Trade 248 (2004).
160. *Ibid.*
161. Article 10(2) of the Austria-Mexico BIT from 1998 provides as follows, allowing switching from domestic court proceedings to international arbitration until the first instance decision of a domestic court is rendered: 'If an investor of a Contracting Party or his investment that is an enterprise initiates proceedings before a national tribunal with respect to a measure that is alleged to be a breach of this Agreement, the dispute may only be submitted to arbitration under this Part if the competent national tribunal has not rendered judgment in the first instance on the merits of the case.'
162. Article 11(2) of the Germany-Madagascar BIT from 2006 states that the choice between the domestic courts and international arbitration has to be made if the dispute cannot be settled within six months.

Another difficulty posed by fork-in-the-road clauses would be that investment treaties often divide jurisdiction for potential disputes on grounds of different basis of the claim. More precisely, the determination as to whether a dispute shall be submitted to local courts or international arbitration tribunal will depend on whether a dispute at issue presents a contract or a treaty claim. This, however, represents a big risk of parallel proceedings. Namely, by pleading different types of causes of action (contract and treaty claim, while in fact the subject matter in both claims is the same or substantially intertwined), parties can have the same matter being tried both before the local courts and in arbitration. Switch from the conventional ICSID approach that divided treaty claims from contract claims occurred with the *Pantechniki S.A. Contractors & Engineers v. Republic of Albania* case.[163] In *Pantechniki*, the sole arbitrator held that the relevant test, as taken from the *Vivendi* Annulment decision,[164] was whether the 'fundamental basis of a claim sought to be brought before the international forum is autonomous of claims to be heard elsewhere'.[165] In this case, the BIT claims did not have an autonomous existence outside the prior contractual claims brought before Albanian courts and therefore the election of one forum or the other was final.[166] Consequently, the conclusion was that the claimant's earlier court proceedings precluded it from recourse to arbitration before ICSID under the 1991 Albania-Greece BIT.[167]

Other arbitral tribunals have also highlighted the extreme effects of strict application of the triple identity test, which would deprive the fork-in-the-road clause of much of its practical effect.[168] As noted by the arbitral tribunal in *Chevron v. Ecuador*, '[n]ational legal systems do not commonly provide for the State to be sued in respect of a breach of treaty as such, even though actions for breach of a national law giving effect to a treaty might be possible.'[169] The tribunal notes that the triple identity test was developed for the questions of res judicata and might not be appropriate to decide the issues of fork-in-the-road. In this case, the tribunal considered that it did not have to make a conclusion on the standard to be applied because the specific wording of the applicable *electa una via* clause meant it was not triggered. To be triggered, the clause provided that the dispute must have been submitted to domestic courts by the 'national or company concerned' whereas litigation before the national courts had not been instituted by the claimants in the arbitration. As such, the tribunal rejected the State's fork-in-the-road objection to jurisdiction.[170]

---

163. *Pantechniki S.A. Contractors & Engineers (Greece) v. The Republic of Albania*, ICSID Case No. ARB/07/21, Award (30 Jul. 2009).
164. *Compañiá de Aguas del Aconquija S.A. and Vivendi Universal S.A. v. Argentine Republic*, ICSID Case No. ARB/97/3 (formerly *Compañía de Aguas del Aconquija, S.A. and Compagnie Générale des Eaux v. Argentine Republic*), Decision on Annulment (3 Jul. 2002), para. 55.
165. *Pantechniki S.A. Contractors & Engineers (Greece) v. The Republic of Albania*, ICSID Case No. ARB/07/21, Award (30 Jul. 2009), para. 61.
166. *Ibid.*, para. 63.
167. *Ibid.*, paras 67– 68.
168. *See Chevron Corporation and Texaco Petroleum Corporation v. The Republic of Ecuador*, UNCITRAL, PCA Case No. 2009-23, Third Interim Award on Jurisdiction and Admissibility (27 Feb. 2012).
169. *Ibid.* Part IV, pp. 23–24.
170. *Ibid.*, p. 26.

The purpose of the fork-in-the-road in international investment arbitration is to avoid situations of uncertainty and unpredictability that dispute resolution at multiple fora may bring. In addition to a possible violation of principle of *ne bis in idem*, (not twice the same thing) it may give rise to duplicative or contradictory decisions on the same matter and between the same parties, and double enforcement and execution proceedings.

[B] Waiver

Another provision that may sometimes be confused with an *electa una via* clause is a waiver, which is, however, not as common as the fork-in-the-road. It pursues the same objective as the fork-in-the-road clause in so that it aims at eliminating parallel proceedings. Here, in order to accede to arbitration, the investor must waive its right to litigate the claims in domestic courts. An example of this clause may be found in NAFTA Article 1121:

> An investor ... waive[s its] right to initiate or continue before any administrative tribunal or court under the law of any Party, or other dispute settlement procedures.

In *Marvin Roy Feldman v. Mexico*, the arbitral tribunal analyzed the operation of the waiver clause and distinguished it from the exhaustion of local remedies requirement.[171] According to the tribunal, NAFTA Article 1121 is not a confirmation or restatement of the customary international rule on exhaustion of local remedies, but rather indicates preference for international arbitration as opposed to domestic litigation, provided there is a waiver of the latter.[172] This is true with regard to damages claims only, leaving open to the investor 'proceedings for injunctive, declaratory or other extraordinary relief' before the domestic courts.[173]

Generally, it should be noted that the waiver requirement is particular to NAFTA and does not appear very often in other protection treaties.

[C] Res Judicata and Lis Pendens

The principles of res judicata and lis pendens are both procedural devices that were originally developed in relation to traditional court litigation. Res judicata, or claim preclusion, refers to the idea that the same case may not be adjudicated twice, and is a fundamental principle of international law.[174] Once there has been a final decision, whether made by domestic courts or by an arbitral tribunal, the parties should not have

171. *Marvin Roy Feldman Karpa v. United Mexican States*, ICSID Case No. ARB(AF)/99/1 (also known as *Marvin Feldman v. Mexico*), Award (16 Dec. 2002).
172. *Ibid.*, para. 73.
173. NAFTA, Art. 1121(2)(b).
174. *Application of the Convention on the Prevention and Punishment of the Crime of Genocide* (*Bosnia and Herzegovina v. Serbia and Montenegro*), Judgment (26 Feb. 2007), ICJ Reports 43, 90 (2007).

an opportunity to re-litigate the same claims. Lis pendens refers to pending proceedings and allows a court or tribunal to decline to hear a claim or suspend their proceedings if the same claim was first brought in a different forum having jurisdiction. This tool is aimed at avoiding conflicting decisions on the same subject matter.

In the context of investor-State arbitration, res judicata is not interpreted in the same way as under national laws. Judgments rendered by domestic courts are not binding on the arbitral tribunal that is subsequently constituted. In fact, if the arbitrators had to comply with the national judgments, regardless of the due process issues affecting these decisions, the FET standard, which includes protection from abuse of process, would be left meaningless.

The annulment committee in *Lucchetti v. Peru* drew the distinction between the effects of res judicata at national and international levels. According to this ad hoc committee, '[w]hile an international judgment which is res judicata will in principle constitute a legal obstacle to a new examination of the same matter, res judicata at national level produces its legal effects at national level and will in international judicial proceedings not be more than a factual element.'[175] As highlighted by this committee, if the national judgments had the effect of res judicata in the international arena, this would allow the States to redefine the scope of res judicata under its law to avoid its international law obligations.

According to Article 53(1) of the ICSID Convention, the 'award shall be binding on the parties and shall not be subject to any appeal or to any other remedy except those provided for in this Convention'. As such, an ICSID award is final with respect to the specific claims brought between the same parties and would preclude a future arbitral tribunal from reconsidering the same facts. The 'sameness' is determined by reference to the triple identity test, which is discussed above in relation to the fork-in-the-road clause. For example, the tribunal in *CME v. Czech Republic* refused to accept the effect of res judicata of a previous award related to the same facts where the parties to the two arbitration proceedings were not exactly the same and they were based on two different BITs.[176] Curiously, the tribunal also held that, at any rate, the respondent State had waived any and all res judicata and lis pendens objections when it expressly refused to consolidate the proceedings.[177]

§3.06 CONCLUSION

The question of jurisdiction is of the utmost importance in investor-State arbitration since it goes to the heart of the arbitrators' power to adjudicate claims brought by investors. Due to the specificity of ISDS, where private individual parties have direct access to a forum where they may litigate against sovereign States, the issues that arise

175. *Empresas Lucchetti, S.A. and Lucchetti Peru, S.A. v. The Republic of Peru*, ICSID Case No. ARB/03/4 (also known as: *Industria Nacional de Alimentos, A.S. and Indalsa Perú S.A. v. The Republic of Peru*), Decision on Annulment (5 Sep. 2007), para. 87.
176. *CME Czech Republic B.V. v. The Czech Republic*, UNCITRAL, Award (14 Mar. 2003), paras 432–433.
177. *Ibid.*, para. 431.

in relation to jurisdiction are also different with regard to more traditional commercial arbitration.

The main similarity between these types of arbitration is the preeminence of consent. However, there are a number of originalities in relation to consent in investor-State arbitration, since the State may make an offer of arbitration in its laws or in a protection treaty, which can be accepted at a later date by the foreign investor. This has become known as arbitration without privity,[178] since there is no longer a need for contractual relationship between the parties to have an agreement to arbitrate.

This lack of privity leads to certain procedural consequences that are particular to investor-State jurisdiction. Notably, the State may impose restrictions on its consent in its legislation or in the BIT, which would be binding on the investor seeking to bring a claim. There is a debate among the arbitral tribunals whether so-called 'preconditions to arbitration' constitute a limit on the arbitrators' jurisdiction or whether they are merely related to admissibility. Moreover, given the hardship some of these conditions may cause to the foreign investor, many tribunals have accepted to overlook them based on the doctrine of futility, or by relying on an MFN clause to import a less restrictive dispute resolution provision into the applicable treaty.

Yet, another particularity of investor-State arbitration lies in the fact that there are multiple potential sources for investors' claims. An investor may have directly concluded a contract with the State, in which case there will be contract breaches for which it may seek compensation. On the other hand, by the same actions and independently of the contract, the State may have also violated the protection treaty and the international obligations it has undertaken. In this latter case, the investor may bring treaty claims, which sometimes coexist with the contract claims, but may also be the only claims available to the investor where no contract was concluded between the parties. Arbitral tribunals may have jurisdiction to hear both types of claims if the dispute resolution provisions in the treaty are compatible with those of the contract. However, there may be conflicts where the investment contract contains an exclusive choice-of-forum clause designating the domestic courts of the State party.

Due to the multiplicity of types and sources of claims available in relation to the same investment, there is an increased risk of parallel proceedings in ISDS. Strict application of the triple identity test, which conditions the applicability of the traditional doctrines of res judicata and lis pendens aimed at preventing multiple litigations of the same issues, leads to the multiplication of simultaneous proceedings. States have attempted to limit this by inserting fork-in-the-road and waiver clauses in protection treaties. However, the practical effect of such provisions is yet again restricted by the triple identity test. To give a meaning to these clauses, some arbitral tribunals have interpreted the triple identity test in a less stringent manner, to take into account the factual circumstances that form the basis of the claim, and not the precise identity between the causes of action and the parties. The goal should be to reduce or eliminate parallel proceedings to avoid wasteful spending of time and resources, in addition to removing the uncertainty of conflicting outcomes.

178. *See* Jan Paulsson, *Arbitration without Privity*, 10(2) ICSID Rev. 232 (1995).

Questions

(1) Why is consent to arbitration so important?
(2) Is there a difference between a State's consent to arbitrate under an investment treaty and arbitration under a contract?
(3) What is the purpose of a fork-in-the-road clause?
(4) Why do States include waiting periods in investment treaties? Should compliance with such requirements be considered jurisdictional, or do they relate to admissibility?
(5) What is the most fundamental distinction between a contract claim and a treaty claim?
(6) How would a State breach a treaty (its BIT) as opposed to only breaching a contract?
(7) There appear to be two types of umbrella clauses: one is a general statement that a particular treaty covers all disputes relating to investment; and the second is a more specific clause that says a State 'shall abide by its obligations'. Should these provisions be read to produce equivalent effect?
(8) Investor-State tribunals' decisions at times appear as conflicting when addressing the same legal issues. Does it hurt the system?

CHAPTER 4

Commencing the Arbitration

Possible forums available to investor-State dispute resolution are national courts, ad hoc arbitration, and institutional arbitration. National courts are not popular for their inherent perceived bias in favor of the State. Nevertheless, this bias does not diminish the fact that many arbitration clauses and treaties include exhaustion of local remedies as a prerequisite for the State's consent to arbitrate.

Ad hoc arbitration, not administered by an institution, leaves up to the parties' discretion all aspects of the arbitration, including the number of arbitrators, their appointment, rules of procedure, and venue. To overcome this procedural void, the parties often select the UNCITRAL Arbitration Rules to govern their ad hoc arbitration.

Institutional arbitration, administered by a specialized arbitral institution, provides a structured framework for the arbitration. Similar to ad hoc arbitrations, arbitral institutions place importance on the seat of the arbitration, which, according to certain arbitration rules, play a role in the choice of the procedural law of the proceedings, which has significant legal consequences. Nevertheless, the seat has no legal consequence in ICSID arbitration because arbitration is conducted in accordance with international law (the ICSID Convention and the regulations and rules issued pursuant to it) and not national law.

Also, applicable law is of paramount importance in investment arbitration because it defines the parties' rights and obligations towards one another, being procedural or substantive. Institutional, procedural rules seek to prevent the proceedings from being hindered or interrupted due to a procedural obstacle, when the parties do not cooperate. The law of the arbitral seat or lex arbitri may have procedural or substantive aspects depending on local laws. But the impact of lex arbitri is limited in the context of investor-State disputes brought under the ICSID Convention, which detaches itself from the seat of arbitration. Substantive law or *lex causae* is the set of rules to be applied by the arbitral tribunal to settle the dispute on its merits.

Finally, the process of constituting the arbitral tribunal includes considerations about nomination and appointment methods, independence and impartiality of arbitrators, disclosure obligations and challenge procedures.

§4.01 INTRODUCTION

The particularity of investment disputes is that they involve an individual or company, who wants to bring a claim against a foreign State, or its subdivision. Until the development of investor-State arbitration in the twentieth century, the most common method of asserting one's rights against a State was to ask your home State to espouse your claim and bring an action for diplomatic protection. With the globalization and growth of international business, States began to realize not just the need to attract foreign investment, but also to protect their own investors abroad. Accordingly, States adopted national laws regulating foreign investment (e.g., investment code) and entered into treaties with other States providing for the protection of the investments of foreign investors.

The default forum for investors to bring a claim against a host State is the host State's national court. However, investors are often reluctant to go to the national courts of another State due to their perceived lack of neutrality. A common aspect of investment treaties and investment codes is to supply legal tools, which provide a different, neutral forum for investors to assert their rights against the host State. The dawn of arbitration and, especially, the creation of ICSID in 1965, have greatly advanced the options of the investor by introducing a transnational State-independent forum for dispute resolution.

Arbitration is an agreed-upon, private form of justice where the parties select, subject to the rules governing the proceedings, the individuals who will have the power to render a final and binding decision on the outcome of their case. Yet, the legitimacy of arbitration would be greatly undermined if there were no procedural safeguards against the bias of the decision-makers, which is why there is a requirement that the arbitrators be independent and impartial.

This chapter introduces the considerations facing investors in selecting the appropriate forum in which to bring their disputes (§4.02). The next section covers the question of applicable law (§4.03). This is followed by a description of the process of constituting the arbitral tribunal (§4.04).

§4.02 FORUM SELECTION

The forums available to the investor for the resolution of foreign investment disputes can be grouped into three categories: national courts (A), ad hoc arbitration (B) and institutional arbitration (C). National courts are not a very popular forum for investors due to the inherent perceived bias in favor of the State. That bias, notwithstanding, does not diminish the fact that many arbitration clauses and treaties include exhaustion of local remedies as a prerequisite for the State's consent to arbitrate. Arbitration is certainly more attractive to foreign investors as it offers a neutral forum separate from the adversary State.

As it will be seen, the choice of forum is of vital importance in investment disputes, as it carries significant consequences. Perhaps, one of the most important differences between forums lies in the finality and enforceability of decisions. Judgments rendered by national courts are readily and easily enforced in the State where they are rendered. Arbitration awards 'travel' to many countries, and can be enforced much easier than a national court decision, because of the New York Convention of 1958.[1] Therefore, it is crucial to ensure that the most appropriate forum is selected when drafting the dispute resolution clause and bringing a claim.

[A] National Courts

In most cases, a contract has been concluded between the investor and the host State, which makes national courts the natural forum to judge claims arising out of this relationship.[2] In fact, in the absence of an agreement to arbitrate, or such an option provided for in a treaty, this would be the only forum for investors to bring a claim directly against the State. It is crucial to remember that it is solely the domestic courts of the host State that will be competent in most cases, since courts of other States would have no jurisdiction over the host State due to sovereign immunity.[3]

This forum is not particularly popular with foreign investors for obvious reasons. Given the fact that national courts form part of the State itself, there is a perception of bias against the foreign investor inherent in national judgments. The *Loewen* case[4] is a particularly striking example of such instance. In that case, a Canadian company was involved in a dispute against its American competitor in the State of Mississippi. The jury allocated enormous damages to the American company, which was presented as a family-run business with its roots from Mississippi in contrast to the wealthy foreigner and which eventually bankrupted the Canadian investor.[5] This problem is even more accentuated in case of States with notoriously corrupt legal systems.

Even if the State is prominent for its virtue with regard to due process, the investor may still not want to bring a claim in the host State's national court. A simple reason for that is the procedural disadvantage: national courts will conduct their proceedings according to national rules of procedure and in the language of the host State, in accordance to their legal systems and traditions. And, it is most likely that the

1. Convention on the Recognition and Enforcement of Foreign Arbitral Awards (UNCITRAL), ILM 1046 (1968).
2. Peter Muchlinski, Federico Ortino & Christoph Schreuer, *The Oxford Handbook of International Investment Law*, 694 (Oxford University Press 2008).
3. Christian Tomuschat, *The International Law of State Immunity and Its Development by National Institutions*, 44 Vand. J. Transnatl. L.1105 (2011): 'No member of the international community is authorized to sit in judgment over another sovereign member; par in parem non habet imperium.' *See* generally, Pierre-Hugues Verdier & Erik Voeten, *How Does Customary International Law Change? The Case of State Immunity*, 2 Intl. Stud. Q. 209 (2015).
4. *Loewen Group, Inc. and Raymond L. Loewen v. United States of America*, ICSID Case No. ARB(AF)/98/3, Award (26 Jun. 2003).
5. *Ibid.*

investor will not be familiar with the foregoing, which will be inherently disadvantageous.

The main advantage of having a national court judgment is that it will be easy to execute in the host State. In this case, there is no need to go through the additional process of demanding the recognition and enforcement of the decision. The investor may also have to use the State courts as a forum, when it is a condition to access arbitration or diplomatic protection. Moreover, in some cases, the treaty conditions the host State's consent to arbitration on the exhaustion of local remedies.[6] Albeit often considered as means of delaying the arbitration, this provision seeks to force the investor to at least try to get relief in the national judicial forum before commencing the complex, and at times, expensive process of arbitration.

It is important to keep track of both exhaustion of local remedies and fork-in-the-road clauses in treaties and contracts. In the presence of the former, the investor will be barred from going to arbitration unless he or she has tried bringing the claim in the national courts. On the contrary, if national courts are selected as the forum when there is a fork-in-the-road clause (or *electa una via* clause), then the investor will be precluded from bringing the same claim in arbitration.[7]

[B] Ad Hoc Arbitration

An ad hoc arbitration refers to a proceeding that is not administered by an institution. It is, thus, left completely up to the discretion of the parties to determine all aspects of the arbitration, such as the number of arbitrators, their appointment, rules of procedure and venue.

The seat, or the country where the proceedings will physically take place, is very important in case of ad hoc arbitration. Most countries will attach consequences to the seat and will not recognize an award annulled in the State of the seat of the arbitration, as Article V(1)(e) of the New York Convention lists the award being 'set aside or suspended by a competent authority of the country in which, or under the law of which, that award was made' as one of the legitimate grounds for non-recognition of a foreign arbitral award.[8] A notable exception to this rule is France, which uses the Article VII's more-favorable-rule provision under the New York Convention to disregard annulment in the State of the seat and enforce even those awards that have been set aside.[9]

6. Peter Muchlinski, Federico Ortino & Christoph Schreuer, *The Oxford Handbook of International Investment Law*, 694 (Oxford University Press 2008): 'Only a few States have conditioned their consent to ICSID jurisdiction on the prior exhaustion of local remedies. A relatively small number of bilateral treaties and a few investment agreements with investors contain such a condition.'
7. *See* generally, Andrea K. Bjorklund, *Yearbook on International Investment Law and Policy, 2013-2014*, 406 (Oxford University Press 2015).
8. New York Convention, Art. V(1)(e).
9. Albert Jan van den Berg, *The New York Convention of 1958: An Overview*, http://www.arbitration-icca.org/media/0/12125884227980/new_york_convention_of_1958_overview.pdf (accessed 29 May 2018), p. 20.

Provided that the parties approach arbitration with cooperation, ad hoc proceedings have the potential to be more flexible and cost effective than institutional proceedings, and therefore, may be better suited for smaller claims. Especially, since the parties will not pay any administration fee to an institution. There is, however, a higher burden on the parties to decide administrative issues themselves, so that the arbitration runs smoothly. If there is a disagreement between the parties, then the arbitration will not be able to go forward since there will be no default rules to fall back on.

In order to overcome a procedural void, the parties often select the UNCITRAL set of procedural arbitration rules to govern their ad hoc arbitration. In fact, the UNCTAD statistics demonstrate that virtually all ad hoc investment arbitrations commenced in the last few years are subject to UNCITRAL Arbitration Rules.[10]

[C] Institutional Arbitration

As the name suggests, institutional arbitration is a proceeding administered by a specialized institution. Each institution has its own set of rules, which provide a framework for the arbitration, and its own form of administration to assist in the process.

In practice, a high number of arbitrations are institutional due to the numerous advantages, both with regard to efficiency and legitimacy. The availability of pre-established rules and procedures provides the parties with a coherent framework for their dispute, which is otherwise largely absent. Domestic laws provide detailed rules of procedure for their domestic judicial systems, but few, if any, for arbitration proceedings. Institutions will fill these gaps with the arbitration equivalent of 'civil procedure'. For example, if one of the parties is hostile and refuses to name an arbitrator, there will be a rule on how to proceed, whereas in an ad hoc arbitration, the proceedings would most likely be delayed at that point.[11]

Similar to ad hoc arbitrations, arbitral institutions also place importance on the seat of the arbitration. Under ICC Rules, for example, the choice of the *situs* constitutes a choice of the procedural or curial law of the proceedings, which has significant legal consequences. However, the same is not the case for ICSID – there is no '*situs*' of the proceedings, as the arbitration is conducted in accordance with international law (i.e., the ICSID Convention and the regulations and rules issued pursuant to it), not any national law. The parties may agree to hold hearings at a location other than ICSID's headquarters in Washington, D.C.,[12] but doing so would be for convenience only. Not

10. UNCTAD (United Nations Conference On Trade And Development) Statistics demonstrate that only 1 non-UNCITRAL ad hoc arbitration was commenced in 2015. Multiple Permanent Court of Arbitration proceedings have also been governed by UNCITRAL Arbitration Rules (eleven such instances in 2015). *Available at* http://investmentpolicyhub.unctad.org/ISDS/Filter ByYear.
11. Nigel Blackaby, Constantine Pastasides, Alan Redfern & Martin Hunter, *Redfern and Hunter on International Arbitration* (Oxford University Press 2009).
12. Convention on the Settlement of Investment Disputes between States and Nationals of Other States (opened for signature 18 March 1965, entered into force 14 Oct. 1966) ('ICSID Convention'), Art. 63.

attaching any consequences to the seat of the arbitration is yet another appeal of ICSID, since the investors do not have to worry that the State will intervene post factum and annul the award in its national court.

The institution will also offer administrative support, both to the parties and the arbitral tribunal. It will allow the arbitration to run smoothly and the administration will make sure that the rules have been followed. In general, one of the main attractions of institutional arbitrations is an established format with a proven track record, which makes awards rendered under its administration more legitimate.[13]

The ICC, the LCIA and the SCC are among the most prominent institutions. However, the primary institution for investor-State dispute resolution is ICSID.

The UNCTAD statistics demonstrate that the vast majority of cases are institutionally based. Fifty-five out of sixty-five arbitrations commenced in 2017 were institutional. Among these, forty-one are under ICSID, which is 63%. Out of the seventy-five arbitrations commenced in 2016, forty-five or 60% selected ICSID as their forum. It should be noted that the ICSID Additional Facility Rules (discussed in more detail below) were also used by the parties with five arbitrations in 2017 and five in 2016.[14]

Although some BITs and other investment instruments provide for other arbitral institutions, such as the ICC,[15] since the majority of investor-State dispute resolution is under ICSID, the discussion will focus mainly on this particular institution.

[1] International Centre for Settlement of Investment Disputes (ICSID)

[a] The Centre

ICSID (or the Centre) is one of the five international organizations that constitute the World Bank Group. Like the other organizations in the Group, it was established by a multilateral treaty, the ICSID Convention, which as of January 2018 has been ratified by 153 States.[16]

The ICSID Convention establishes a forum for settlement of investment-related disputes between a Contracting State and a national of another Contracting State. In addition to nationality requirements being satisfied for the Centre to have jurisdiction, both the State and the investor must have given their written consent to have their dispute resolved by ICSID.[17] Moreover, the dispute must be a legal dispute directly

---

13. Nigel Blackaby, Constantine Partasides, Alan Redfern, Martin Hunter, *Redfern and Hunter on International Arbitration* (Oxford University Press 2009).
14. UNCTAD Statistics, *available at* http://investmentpolicyhub.unctad.org/ISDS/FilterByYear.
15. *See*, for example, Germany-Jordan BIT (concluded on 13 Nov. 2007, ratified on 28 Aug. 2010), Art. 11; Belarus-Croatia BIT (concluded on 26 Jun. 2001, ratified on 14 Jul. 2005), Art. 10.
16. *See* https://icsid.worldbank.org/en/Documents/icsiddocs/List%20of%20Contracting%20States%20and%20Other%20Signatories%20of%20the%20Convention%20-%20Latest.pdf (accessed 29 May 2018).
17. ICSID Convention, Art. 25.

related to an investment.[18] Given these strict jurisdictional requirements, some disputes cannot be brought before the Centre. It should be noted, under certain circumstances, non-ICSID member parties who, nevertheless, want to have the Secretariat of the Centre administer their proceedings, may do so under the ICSID Additional Facility Rules.

Arbitration under ICSID has several unique attributes consciously designed to reflect a balancing of interests between the host States and foreign investors, and to provide a de-politicized and effective mechanism of dispute resolution. Moreover, its affiliation to the World Bank gives an additional incentive for the States to comply with the arbitration award.[19] Although, it should be noted that, it is precisely, the additional 'incentive' that has brought about criticisms of a conflict of interest or bias in the ICSID system.

Among ICSID arbitration features, the most significant is that it is a 'self-contained' system. ICSID arbitration is conducted solely in accordance with the international law provisions of the ICSID Convention and of the regulations and rules adopted pursuant to it. Arbitral awards rendered pursuant to the ICSID Convention are binding on the parties and not subject to any appeal or to any other remedy except for those provided for in the Convention itself. National courts have no power to review the awards in any way. Rather, they must, on simple presentation of a copy of the award certified by ICSID's Secretary General enforce the pecuniary obligations imposed by the award as if it were a final judgment of the national courts.[20]

ICSID's self-contained nature is such that parties may not seek interim, provisional or conservatory measures from a national court unless they have expressly agreed to that effect in the instrument recording their consent to ICSID arbitration.

[b] ICSID Additional Facility Rules

As previously mentioned, the Additional Facility Rules were adopted in 1978 and have since been modified twice, in 2003 and 2006. They have opened access to ICSID arbitration for cases, which fail to satisfy one of the three jurisdictional requirements:

- Nationality (*ratione personae*): an arbitration (or conciliation) can be brought before the Centre even if one of the parties is not a Contracting State or not a national of an ICSID Member State.[21]
- Direct link to an investment (*ratione materiae*): an arbitration (or conciliation) may be administered by the Centre even if the dispute 'do[es] not arise *directly*

18. *Ibid.*
19. For criticisms of the close connection between World Bank and ICSID, *see* Julien Fouret, *The World Bank and ICSID: Family or Incestuous Ties?* 4 Intl. Org. L. Rev. 121 (2007).
20. Convention on the Settlement of Investment Disputes between States and Nationals of Other States (opened for signature 18 March 1965, entered into force 14 Oct. 1966) ('ICSID Convention'), Art. 54.
21. ICSID Additional Facility Rules (April 2006), Sched. C, Ch. II, Art. 2.

out of an investment',[22] provided that the cause is not 'an ordinary commercial transaction'.[23]
- Existence of a legal dispute: Schedule A creates 'fact-finding' proceedings, which may be initiated in the absence of a concrete legal dispute.[24]

It is important to note that the Additional Facility Rules do not extend the jurisdiction of ICSID.[25] They allow the additional types of claims listed above to be administered by the Secretariat of the Centre. It is important to note that the ICSID Convention does not apply to any of the 'recommendations, awards, or reports' rendered under the Additional Facility Rules.[26]

§4.03 APPLICABLE LAW

Applicable law is of paramount importance in dispute resolution since it defines the rights and obligations of the parties towards one another.[27] It gives a paradigm for the parties' relationship and the basis for their claims. In national courts, the question does not always arise since in most domestic and international disputes the law of the forum will apply.[28] National law may at times be referred to interchangeably as, domestic, internal or municipal law. Another national law may supersede the law of the forum if it is more appropriate to govern the dispute, which will be determined according to the choice-of-law rules.[29] Most choice-of-law rules establish the principle of party autonomy: in a significant number of cases, the parties can agree on the law, which will govern their dispute.[30]

International arbitration is different from State courts. First of all, as it is inherently international, thus, there is no single forum whose laws apply. Moreover, there are other sources of applicable law, such as treaties and arbitration rules that affect international arbitration. Thus, determining the applicable law is crucial, as it

22. *Ibid.*, p. 5.
23. *Ibid.*
24. *Ibid.*, Schedule A.
25. Peter Muchlinski, Federico Ortino & Christoph Schreuer, *The Oxford Handbook of International Investment Law*, 704 (Oxford University Press 2008).
26. ICSID Additional Facility Rules (April 2006), Art. 3.
27. Chiara Giorgetti, *Litigating International Investment Disputes: A Practitioner's Guide*, 261 (BRILL 2014).
28. *Ibid.*
29. *See, for example*, Regulation (EC) No. 593/2008 of the European Parliament and of the Council of 17 Jun. 2008 on the law applicable to contractual obligations (Rome I) and Regulation (EC) No. 864/2007 of the European Parliament and of the Council of 11 Jul. 2007 on the law applicable to non-contractual obligations (Rome II). The choice of law rules will elect the law of a State, as opposed to transnational rules or principles. Even in cases where the parties have the autonomy to choose the applicable law, these regulations provide that they must choose a national law.
30. Yas Banifatemi, *The Law Applicable in Investment Treaty Arbitration*, in *Arbitration Under International Investment Agreements: A Guide to the Key Issues*, 193 (Katia Yannaca-Small Editor, Oxford University Press 2010).

will affect the conduct of the proceedings and the outcome of the case on the merits.[31] Similar to national courts, the arbitral tribunals show a lot of deference to the will of the parties.[32] Most importantly, in investor-State arbitration, any national law selected will most likely be applied in conjunction with international law due to the principle that a State cannot escape liability for breaching an international obligation by invoking its national law.[33] Since most investment disputes are based on bilateral and multilateral protection treaties, it is such treaties that will determine the State's international obligations and breach thereof.

When discussing applicable law, a distinction should be made between the procedural (A) and substantive laws (B). The former regulates the conduct of the proceedings: for example, whether there will be oral hearings or only written submissions, applicable rules of evidence, etc. The latter refers to the legal rules, which the arbitrators will use to decide the case on the merits.

[A] Procedural Law

As mentioned above, procedural law means the body of rules, which will govern the conduct of the arbitration itself. It needs to be determined from the outset, since it will regulate each step of the proceeding, such as appointment of the tribunal, hearing schedules. The underlying principle of the law applicable to procedure is party autonomy (1). However, the law of the seat of arbitration, or lex arbitri (2), should also be examined, since it will affect certain procedural questions, as well as the recognition and enforcement of the award.

[1] Party Autonomy

Freedom of choice with regard to the rules of procedure is one of the key attractions of arbitration. In most cases, it will not be problematic, as it will be made automatically by virtue of selecting the institution that will administer the proceedings. For example, by selecting ICSID as the forum, the parties subject themselves to the ICSID Convention Arbitration Rules.[34]

Failing the parties' agreement, the main part of the procedure is determined by the arbitrators. Institutional arbitration rules cover a part of the procedure, and no further participation of the parties is generally required, unless there is a gap. Institutional rules generally have provisions for this type of situations. For example,

31. Chiara Giorgetti, *Litigating International Investment Disputes: A Practitioner's Guide*, 262 (BRILL 2014).
32. Nigel Blackaby, Constantine Pastasides, Alan Redfern & Martin Hunter, *Redfern and Hunter on International Arbitration* (Oxford University Press 2009).
33. Vienna Convention on the Law of Treaties (23 May 1969), 1155 UNTS 331, Art. 27; International Law Commission, Articles on the Responsibility of States for International Wrongful Acts, Art. 3, Official Records of the General Assembly, Fifth-Sixth Session, Supplement No. 10 (A/56/10).
34. ICSID Convention, Art. 44: 'Any arbitration proceeding shall be conducted in accordance with the provisions of this Section and, except as the parties otherwise agree, in accordance with the Arbitration Rules in effect on the date on which the parties consented to arbitration.'

Article 44 of the ICSID Convention allows the parties to agree on the rules to fill the *lacuna(e)*, or allows the arbitrators decide in the absence of agreement.[35] A similar provision is contained in Article 19 of the ICC Rules.[36] Domestic laws may contain a full code of procedure, whereas arbitration rules fit in a small booklet. The latter does not purport to cover any potential procedural questions that may arise. The institutional rules are provisions aimed to prevent the proceedings from being hindered or interrupted due to a procedural obstacle, when the parties are not willing to cooperate. Thus, such institutional rules give the tribunal the authority to settle the issue of procedure.[37]

As noted above, in ad hoc proceedings, the parties will often select the UNCITRAL Arbitration Rules. However, they also have the possibility to define each element of the procedure themselves, which may be useful in a smaller dispute.

In case of gaps, the law of the seat of arbitration may sometimes intervene to provide rules of procedure.[38]

[2] Lex Arbitri

The seat of the arbitration is one of the considerations to take into account when selecting the forum, given that the national law of the seat can affect the proceedings and the award. The rules governing arbitration in the seat of the proceedings is also referred to as 'lex arbitri', which some commentators distinguish from the procedural law because it arguably goes beyond mere procedure.[39]

Indeed, some State laws have 'arbitration codes' or 'laws', providing for applicable procedure rules in the absence of party consensus in an arbitration taking place in that State. For example, Book IV of the French Code of Civil Procedure is dedicated to arbitration: domestic under Title I and international under Title II. Article 1509 states explicitly that the parties may choose the applicable rules of procedure.[40] The rest of the articles provide rules that may apply in the absence of choice: for example, Article 1513 mentions that, absent determination by the parties, the tribunal will decide by a majority of votes.[41] Ostensibly, a rather obvious proposition, but it may be helpful if this aspect is not clear.

35. *Ibid.*
36. ICC Arbitration Rules, Art. 19: 'The proceedings before the arbitral tribunal shall be governed by the Rules and, where the Rules are silent, by any rules which the parties or, failing them, the arbitral tribunal may settle on, whether or not reference is thereby made to the rules of procedure of a national law to be applied to the arbitration.'
37. *See* LCIA Arbitration Rules (2014), Art. 14; SCC Arbitration Rules (2010), Art. 19: 'Subject to these Rules and any agreement between the parties, the Arbitral Tribunal may conduct the arbitration in such manner as it considers appropriate'; SIAC Arbitration Rules (2016), Rule 19: 'The Tribunal shall conduct the arbitration in such manner as it considers appropriate, after consulting with the parties, to ensure the fair, expeditious, economical and final resolution of the dispute.'
38. Nigel Blackaby, Constantine Partasides, Alan Redfern & Martin Hunter, *Redfern and Hunter on International Arbitration*, 184 (Oxford University Press 2009).
39. *Ibid.*
40. French Code of Civil Procedure (*Code de procédure civile*), Art. 1509.
41. *Ibid.*, Art. 1513.

Lex arbitri, however, goes beyond procedural matters.[42] It may stipulate that certain types of disputes are not subject to arbitration under the municipal law.[43] For example, divorce claims cannot be settled by arbitration under French law.[44] This issue goes to the heart of arbitration by assessing whether a specific type of dispute may be resolved in this forum, as opposed to simply giving procedural directives. The most obvious reason why it is difficult to classify lex arbitri as procedural is that different countries have different definitions of what is substantive and what is procedural law.[45]

The impact of lex arbitri is limited in the context of investor-State disputes brought under ICSID, which detaches itself from the concept of the seat of arbitration. This, however, is not the case for arbitrations brought under UNCITRAL, SSC or ICC, for example.

[B] Substantive Law

Substantive law (or *lex causae*) is the set of rules to be applied by the arbitral tribunal to settle the dispute on its merits. The parties have an interest in determining the applicable governing law, which is normally set out in their contract, since it will affect the outcome of their case.[46] The arbitrators, as well focus on the substantive law since it affects the recognition and enforcement of the award.

The role of the arbitrator in determining the applicable law cannot be overstated. Ultimately, the tribunal is the adjudicator, and part of its role is to select and apply a law or laws to settle the dispute. When national courts face the problem of choice of law, they have a specific body of law, part of private international law, including choice-of-law rules, which is applied. In the case of arbitration, there is no national forum. No particular choice of law rules is imperative for the arbitrators, thus granting the arbitrators with broad discretion in their exercise of judgment. On the other hand, the award may be annulled or refused recognition if the arbitrators do not respect the limits of their mission by not applying the law chosen by the parties.[47]

The determination of substantive law is particularly complex in the context of investor-State disputes, because of the particular nature of their relationship and the proliferation of treaties in this area. With regard to the former, the point of contention concerns the investor being a private party, whose rights are generally based on national or municipal law, and whether he or she could have rights in the international

42. Nigel Blackaby, Constantine Pastasides, Alan Redfern & Martin Hunter, *Redfern and Hunter on International Arbitration*, 184 (Oxford University Press 2009).
43. *Ibid.*
44. French Civil Code (*Code civil*) (as revised in 2016), Art. 2060.
45. Nigel Blackaby, Constantine Partasides, Alan Redfern & Martin Hunter, *Redfern and Hunter on International Arbitration*, 184 (Oxford University Press 2009), note 73.
46. Chiara Giorgetti, *Litigating International Investment Disputes: A Practitioner's Guide*, 262 (BRILL 2014).
47. New York Convention, Art. V(1)(c).

order.[48] It has been generally accepted that the investor may engage the State's international responsibility based on the applicable treaty protection, which makes the investor a holder of rights on the international law level.[49] When relying on a BIT, the investor is subject to the treaty's dispute resolution mechanism as well as the selection of law clause. Such clauses often mention the applicability of both domestic and international laws to the resolution of the dispute without specifying the precise scope of application of each one.[50]

The elements to be discussed in relation to the determination of applicable law include the role of the parties (1), as well as the function of the arbitral tribunal (2) and the 'interplay between national and international law' (3).[51]

[1] Determination by the Parties

'The principle of party autonomy is the primary rule governing the arbitration, including in regard to the law applicable to the substance of the dispute.'[52] Just as domestic choice-of-law rules, the rules of most arbitral institutions state that '[t]he Tribunal shall decide a dispute in accordance with such rules of law as may be agreed by the parties.'[53] There is a variety of ways, in which the parties' choice may be manifested.

If the parties are bringing a claim on the basis of a contract, which contains the dispute resolution clause, the situation is rather straightforward. They may include a choice of law clause in the contract, which will be followed by the tribunal. Treaty-based arbitration is more contentious, because the States make the choice of the applicable law on behalf of the investor prior to the dispute even arising. In *AAPL v. Sri Lanka*, the tribunal expressed its reservations on this matter:

48. Hege Elisabeth Kjos, *Applicable Law in Investor-State Arbitration: The Interplay Between National and International Law*, 5 (Oxford University Press 2013).
49. *Ibid.*
50. *See*, for example, Australia-Pakistan BIT (7 Feb. 1998): 'The Arbitral Tribunal shall reach its award by majority vote taking into account the provisions of this Agreement, any agreement between the parties to the dispute and the relevant domestic law of the Party that admitted the investment.' *See also* Argentina-France BIT (3 Jul. 1991): 'The ruling of the arbitral body shall be based on the provisions of this Agreement, the legislation of the Contracting Party which is a party to the dispute, including rules governing conflict of laws, the terms of any private agreements concluded on the subject of the investment, and the relevant principles of international law.'
51. *See*, Hege Elisabeth Kjos, *Applicable Law in Investor-State Arbitration: The Interplay Between National and International Law* (Oxford University Press 2013).
52. Yas Banifatemi, *The Law Applicable in Investment Treaty Arbitration*, in *Arbitration Under International Investment Agreements: A Guide to the Key Issues*, 192 (Katia Yannaca-Small Editor, Oxford University Press 2010).
53. ICSID Convention, Art. 42(1). *See also* ICC Arbitration Rules, Art. 21: 'The parties shall be free to agree upon the rules of law to be applied by the arbitral tribunal to the merits of the dispute'; UNCITRAL Arbitration Rules (as revised in 2010), Art. 35(1): '[t]he arbitral tribunal shall apply the law designated by the parties as applicable to the substance of the dispute'; etc. *See*, more generally, Yas Banifatemi, *The Law Applicable in Investment Treaty Arbitration*, in *Arbitration Under International Investment Agreements: A Guide to the Key Issues*, 193 (Katia Yannaca-Small, Oxford University Press 2010).

the Parties in dispute have had no opportunity to exercise their right to choose in advance the applicable law determining the rules governing the various aspects of their eventual disputes.

In more concrete terms, the prior choice-of-law referred to in the first part of Article 42 of the ICSID Convention could hardly be envisaged in the context of an arbitration case directly instituted in implementation of an international obligation undertaken between two States in favour of their respective nationals investing within the territory of the other Contracting State.[54]

In that case, the tribunal based itself on the conduct of the parties to determine what law the parties had mutually agreed to.[55] *AAPL* was the first case where the tribunal accepted that an investor may bring an ICSID claim based on a dispute resolution provision contained in a BIT. Since then, it has been generally accepted that when an investor brings a claim under a BIT he accepts the offer to arbitrate contained in the protection treaty. As such, he also accepts that choice of law made by the States that signed and ratified the treaty.[56]

Whether contained in a treaty or in a contract, the choice of law clause still has to be interpreted and applied by the tribunal.

[2] The Arbitrator's Role

There are two ways, in which the arbitrators intervene in the determination of the applicable law. First, they interpret the will of the parties under the autonomy principle. Second, in the absence of choice, the arbitrators have to determine the applicable law based on the applicable arbitration rules.

Arbitrator and the Choice-*of-Law Clause*

Even when there is a choice-of-law clause in the contract or the treaty, the arbitrator still has to interpret the clause. For example, the clause may opt for both domestic law of the host State and international law, in which case the tribunal will have to determine which legal questions should be determined according to municipal law and which according to international law.

A specific problem arises when there is a clause in the contract subjecting the dispute to domestic law, but the investor alleges violation of international law by the

54. *Asian Agricultural Products Ltd. v. Sri Lanka*, Award (27 Jun. 1990), ICSID Reports 256 (1997), paras 19–20.
55. Yas Banifatemi, *The Law Applicable in Investment Treaty Arbitration*, in *Arbitration Under International Investment Agreements: A Guide to the Key Issues*, 194 (Katia Yannaca-Small Editor, Oxford University Press 2010).
56. *Antoine Goetz et al. v. Republic of Burundi*, Award (10 Feb. 1999), para. 94: 'Undoubtedly, the applicable law has not been determined here, strictly speaking, by the parties to this arbitration (Burundi and the investors), but rather by the parties to the Bilateral Treaty (Burundi and Belgium). As was the case with the consent of the parties [to the arbitration], the Tribunal deems nevertheless that Burundi accepted the applicable law as determined in the above provision of the Bilateral Treaty by becoming a party to this Treaty, and that claimants did the same by filing their request for arbitration based on the Treaty.' (English translation from XXVI Yearbook of Commercial Arbitration 24, 36 (2001).

State. Tribunals have refused to apply solely municipal law based on customary international law:

> [I]t is a well settled principle of international law that a state cannot rely on a provision of its domestic law to defeat its consent to arbitration ... It is further a well accepted practice that the national law governing by virtue of a choice of law agreement (pursuant to Article 42(1) first sentence of the ICSID Convention) is subject to correction by international law in the same manner as the application of the host state law failing an agreement.[57]

Absence of Choice

The second part of ICSID Article 42(1) provides that in the absence of a party agreement, 'the Tribunal shall apply the law of the Contracting State party to the dispute (including its rules on the conflict of laws) and such rules of international law as may be applicable'.[58] The ICC Rules, on the other hand, provide that 'the arbitral tribunal shall apply the rules of law which it determines to be appropriate'.[59] Under UNCITRAL Model Law, the tribunal shall use the appropriate conflict of law rules to determine the applicable law.[60] Whatever the specific formula, the common thread is that the arbitrators have the possibility to determine the applicable law using a certain degree of discretion.

Most bilateral treaties do not contain a choice of law clause,[61] so the tribunals often have to interpret the second part of ICSID Article 42(1) and similar provisions in other arbitral rules. Contrary to the first phrase of the same article, which commands the interpretation of the parties' will, the second phrase requires the interpretation of the Convention. Under ICSID, it is considered that both domestic law of the host State

57. *Autopista Concesionada de Venezuela, C.A. v. Bolivarian Republic of Venezuela*, ICSID Case No. ARB/00/5, Award (23 Sep. 2003), para. 207.
58. ICSID Convention, Art. 42(1).
59. ICC Arbitration Rules, Art. 21(1).
60. UNCITRAL Arbitration Rules (as revised in 2010), Art. 35(1): 'The arbitral tribunal shall apply the rules of law designated by the parties as applicable to the substance of the dispute. Failing such designation by the parties, the arbitral tribunal shall apply the law which it determines to be appropriate.'
61. Emmanuel Gaillard & Yas Banifatemi, *The Meaning of 'and' in Article 42(1), Second Sentence, of the Washington Convention: The Role of International Law in the ICSID Choice of Law Process*, 18 ICSID Rev. 375, 379 (2003). Yas Banifatemi, *The Law Applicable in Investment Treaty Arbitration*, in *Arbitration Under International Investment Agreements: A Guide to the Key Issues*, 200 (Katia Yannaca-Small Editor, Oxford University Press 2010): 'The vast majority of BITs entered into by countries such as the United States, the United Kingdom, France, or Germany do not contain a clause on the applicable law regarding investment disputes between one of the contracting States and the investors of the other contracting State: as at December 15, 2008 and to the best of the author's knowledge based on the BITs available, none of the 40 BITs entered into by the United States and which are in force contain a clause on the applicable law; a clause on the applicable law can be found in only 12 out of 91 BITs concluded by France and in force, in only 6 out of 91 BITs concluded by the United Kingdom and in force, and in only 8 out of the 114 available BITs concluded by Germany and in force.'

and international law have to be applied,[62] but the question then becomes how to determine their respective application.

[3] Complementary Function of Municipal and International Laws

As mentioned before, even if there is a choice of law in favor of domestic law, international customary law dictates that a State cannot hide behind its national law to avoid its international responsibility.[63] In the absence of choice, the second phrase of ICSID Article 42(1) commands both municipal law and international law to be applied.[64] In general, it would be virtually impossible to conduct investment-related arbitration only relying on one set of laws. The reason for that lies in the particularity of investment law, which has seen a proliferation of legal instruments implemented on national and transnational levels. Since investors most often bring claims based on treaties, international law has to be used to interpret the treaty provisions. However, the scope of international law is limited, and it simply does not regulate a number of private law questions. For example, there is no international property law; therefore, real estate and trademarks are by default subject to domestic law of the host State.[65]

The issue then becomes determining the precise bounds between the two legal orders governing the same dispute. Under most arbitration rules, the tribunal has the liberty to apply the law it considers appropriate.[66] However, ICSID Article 42(1) has been a source of much debate. Historically, the prevailing consensus between academics and tribunals seemed to be that the law of the host State shall have the primary role, and that it is to be supplemented by international law in case of *lacunae,* or corrected if there is an inconsistency.[67] The decision in *Wena Hotels* is widely cited as departing from the aforementioned doctrine in favor of giving both legal orders a role to play:[68]

62. Emmanuel Gaillard & Yas Banifatemi, *The Meaning of 'and' in Article 42(1), Second Sentence, of the Washington Convention: The Role of International Law in the ICSID Choice of Law Process*, 18 ICSID Rev. 375, 380 (2003).
63. *See* above§4.03.
64. *See* above §4.03[B][2].
65. Hege Elisabeth Kjos, *Applicable Law in Investor-State Arbitration: The Interplay Between National and International Law* 5 (Oxford University Press 2013).
66. *See* above §4.03[B][2].
67. *See*, generally, Emmanuel Gaillard & Yas Banifatemi, *The Meaning of 'and' in Article 42(1), Second Sentence, of the Washington Convention: The Role of International Law in the ICSID Choice of Law Process*, 18 ICSID Rev. 375 (2003). *Klöckner Industrie-Anlagen GmbH v. Republic of Cameroon*, Decision on Annulment (3 May 1985), 2 ICSID Reports 95, 122 (1994), para. 69: 'Article 42 of the Washington Convention certainly provides that "in the absence of agreement between the parties, the Tribunal shall apply the law of the Contracting State party to the dispute ... and such principles of international law as may be applicable." This gives these principles (perhaps omitting cases in which it should be ascertained whether the domestic law conforms to international law) a dual role, that is complementary (in the case of a "lacuna" in the law of the State), or corrective, should the State's law not conform on all points to the principles of international law.'
68. Yas Banifatemi, *The Law Applicable in Investment Treaty Arbitration*, in *Arbitration Under International Investment Agreements: A Guide to the Key Issues*, 202 (Katia Yannaca-Small Editor, Oxford University Press 2010).

> What is clear is that the sense and meaning of the negotiations leading to the second sentence of Article 42(1) allowed for both legal orders to have a role. The law of the host State can indeed be applied in conjunction with international law if this is justified. So too international law can be applied by itself if the appropriate rule is found in this other ambit.[69]

The *Wena Hotels* approach is more in line with the flexibility afforded by other arbitration rules.[70] The importance of international law has since been confirmed by other tribunals.[71] Indeed, to the extent that the claim is brought on the basis of an international treaty, international law will inevitably be applied to the merits.[72]

§4.04 CONSTITUTION OF THE ARBITRAL TRIBUNAL

International arbitration is characterized by the parties' ability to select private individuals (or choose a method of their appointment) to hear their case and make a final and binding decision on their dispute. Arbitrators are not judges and their jurisdictional power is only valid for the precise dispute (or type of disputes), for which they are appointed by the parties. The constitution of the arbitral tribunal is thus of high importance, since without a tribunal there can be no arbitration and thus, no decision.

The parties have several options. In an ad hoc arbitration, they can select any number of arbitrators and decide on the method of their appointment. For example, parties can appoint a single arbitrator on whom they both agree. In most institutional arbitrations, the practice is that each party selects an arbitrator, and the two party-appointed arbitrators then agree and nominate the chair or president of the tribunal.[73] This method, however, may be less practical when there are multiple parties to the dispute due to the considerations of fairness. For example, if there were a dispute in which one party is facing three other parties, it would seem unjust to make the

69. *Wena Hotels v. Egypt*, ICSID Case No. ARB/98/4, Decision on Annulment (5 Feb. 2002), para. 40.
70. Emmanuel Gaillard & Yas Banifatemi, *The Meaning of 'and' in Article 42(1), Second Sentence, of the Washington Convention: The Role of International Law in the ICSID Choice of Law Process*, 18 ICSID Rev. 375, 411 (2003).
71. *See*, for example, *Azurix Corp. v. The Argentine Republic*, Decision on Annulment (1 Sep. 2009), para. 146: 'By definition, a treaty is governed by international law, and not by municipal law. It is a fundamental principle that "[a] party may not invoke the provisions of its internal law as justification for its failure to perform a treaty". In any claim for breach of an investment treaty, the question whether or not there has been a breach of the treaty must therefore be determined, not through the application of the municipal law of any State, but through the application of the terms of the treaty to the facts of the case, in accordance with general principles of international law, including principles of the international law of treaties.'
72. Yas Banifatemi, *The Law Applicable in Investment Treaty Arbitration*, in *Arbitration Under International Investment Agreements: A Guide to the Key Issues*, 210 (Katia Yannaca-Small Editor, Oxford University Press 2010).
73. Default arbitration rules do not expressly provide for this method of appointment, but it seems to be the one most often chosen by the parties. However, the ICC Arbitration Rules, under Art. 12, provides that the President of the tribunal is appointed by the Court.

respondents appoint one arbitrator among them given that the first party can make the choice all by itself.[74]

At given times, when parties so choose, an institution may select all arbitrators for a given dispute. Some think that this method offers the advantage of more neutrality, which may be lacking when the parties appoint their own arbitrators, as some parties tend to select individuals who are likely to be favorable to their case. Alternatively, institutions may also have 'lists' of arbitrators – in this case the parties may only appoint their arbitrator from the list maintained by the institution. Although the parties have a say in the selection, they are limited to the persons 'approved' by the institution for their expertise and impartiality.

The most commonly used method for the appointment of arbitrators remains unilateral selection with party-appointed arbitrators choosing the president or chairperson. Surveys demonstrate that one of the most valuable characteristics of international arbitration is the party's ability to select the arbitrators.[75] Unilateral or party appointments gives the parties a sense of more proximity with the process, the impression of a more tailored and controlled process. This is an important distinction between arbitration and court litigation, and an important reason why the parties choose the arbitration as an alternative method of dispute resolution. The perception of proximity and control are factors that earn the parties' trust in the system as a whole. Indeed, studies also show that in more than 50% of the cases, the parties agree to depart from the institutional appointment despite the impeccable reputation of the institutions.[76]

One perception about party appointment that is troublesome is the idea that the party-appointed arbitrator is an arbitrator who 'owes loyalty' to the party that appointed him or her. The rather worrying statistics suggest that in more than 95% of the cases, it is the losing party's arbitrator who pens the dissenting opinion.[77] However, one of the reasons behind this phenomenon may be the fact that the party will most likely nominate someone whose personal views expressed in the past are in line with its case.

---

74. Some countries include the principle of party equality into the definition of public policy and refuse to recognize and enforce arbitral awards made pursuant to arbitration rules, which do not respect this principle. *See Cour de cassation*, Judgment (7 Jan. 1992), *Siemens AG et BKMI Industrienanlagen GmbH v. Dutco Construction Co.* 10 ASA Bulletin 295 (1992) (comments by Charles Jarrosson) (The highest court in France held that having one party nominate its own arbitrator and the over two parties having to nominate an arbitrator joint violates the principle of party equality and, thus, public policy, notwithstanding the fact that the two parties had agreed on the institutional rules that provided for such nomination). This decision induced a change in ICC Rules, which, after the 1998 and 2012 amendments, now allow the Court to appoint all members of the tribunal if joint parties cannot agree on their nominee in Art. 12(8) of the ICC Arbitration Rules.
75. 2015 International Arbitration Survey, *Improvements and Innovations in International Arbitration*, White and Case & School of International Arbitration.
76. Jan Paulsson, *Moral Hazard in International Dispute Resolution*, Inaugural Lecture as Holder of the Michael R. Klein Distinguished Scholar Chair University of Miami School of Law (29 Apr. 2010), p. 8.
77. *Ibid.*

One must remember that arbitrators, party-appointed or otherwise, are neutrals. Likewise, it is crucial to bear in mind that arbitrators have other considerations that they take into account when deciding the dispute before them. First of all, the legitimacy of the institution as a whole depends on their individual performance as an arbitrator. Moreover, the arbitrators will be keen on protecting their reputation to be appointed in the future. They will, therefore, be inclined to adjudicate with the utmost integrity and impartiality. Moreover, arbitrator independence and impartiality is required of the arbitrators, otherwise they may be disqualified.

[A] Independence and Impartiality of Arbitrators

[1] Nature of Independence and Impartiality

Independence and impartiality are fundamental principles of arbitration derived from the arbitrators' duty to the parties, which is the adjudication of the dispute submitted to their jurisdiction in the arbitration agreement.[78] Put simply, since the arbitrators are fulfilling the role of a judge, they have to respect the requirements of due process.

Independence means that there are no unacceptable relationships or connections between an arbitrator and a party or its counsel.[79] It is meant to be an objective condition,[80] which can be verified without inquiring into the state of mind of the arbitrator.

Impartiality means that an arbitrator is subjectively unbiased and not predisposed towards one party. Impartiality is a subjective and more abstract concept than independence, in that it refers to the arbitrator's personal opinions. It is, thus, more difficult to control this requirement and high importance is placed on independence. It has been underlined that '[a]n independent mind is indispensable in the exercise of judicial power.'[81]

Independence and impartiality are two sides of the same coin. They complement one another and are meant to ensure that the arbitrator serves the law rather than one of the parties.

The need for crystal clear due process arises from the contractual relationship between the arbitrator and the parties. Even if an arbitrator is nominated at the initiative of one of the parties, the source of his or her power is bilateral: it is based on the agreement to arbitrate by both parties. The arbitrator, however, is not employed by the parties – there is no relationship of subordination. The classification of an agency contract is not satisfactory either, since an arbitrator is not a representative of either of

78. Dominique Hascher, *Independence and Impartiality of Arbitrators: 3 Issues*, 27(4) Am. U. Intl. L. Rev. 789 (2012).
79. Gary Born, *International Commercial Arbitration* Vol. I, 1474 (Wolters Kluwer 2009).
80. Nigel Blackaby, Constantine Pastasides, Alan Redfern & Martin Hunter, *Redfern and Hunter on International Arbitration*, 267 (Oxford University Press 2009).
81. Emmanuel Gaillard & John Savage (eds), *Fouchard, Gaillard, Goldman On International Commercial Arbitration*, 562 (Kluwer Law International 1999).

the parties;[82] the power he or she is granted is inherently judicial.[83] Fouchard suggests that the contract between the parties and arbitrators has a sui generis form; it cannot be categorized as a known type of civil contract.[84] This contract contains the mixed characteristics of arbitration: contractual in source and judicial in object. The Paris Court of Appeal has also adopted this classification.[85]

The arbitrator's judicial powers derive from a single, common manifestation of the parties to the arbitration proceedings. And, although the arbitrator is bound to comply with the arbitration agreement that the parties adopted, parties are not allowed to go so far as to give instructions on the content of his or her decision.[86] The arbitrator's functions and duties require him or her to rise above the partisan interests of the parties, and not to act in the interests of either party. As the ICC puts it, the arbitrator must determine how to resolve their competing interests.[87]

The growing complexity of international business, the increasing number of multi-party and multi-contract cases, as well as the multiplication of related proceedings, have led to numerous issues concerning independence and impartiality. In addition, changes in legal practice and organizations, including the international expansion and merger of law firms, and the varied nature of the positions occupied by lawyers within law firms, have given rise to novel issues of independence.

The world of arbitration is a small one and there are an increasing number of cases where the same person acts as an arbitrator in one proceeding, while representing a party as their counsel in another. Albeit no express rule prohibits these practices, some may question the impartiality of such an arbitrator, especially if similar questions of law are at stake.[88] This problem is all the more acute in the context of investment disputes, as there is a limited number of issues that come up virtually in every case (e.g., definition of investment, FET, etc.).

[2] Textual Sources

Impartiality and independence are not simply ethical duties of an arbitrator; most primary and secondary sources of international law impose them in some form or other. For example, the New York Convention and, similarly, the Inter-American

82. Dominique Hascher, *Independence and Impartiality of Arbitrators: 3 Issues*, 27(4) Am. U. Intl. L. Rev. 789, 791 (2012).
83. *Ibid.*
84. *Ibid.*
85. *Ibid.*
86. *Ibid.*, p. 790.
87. ICC Note to Parties and Arbitral Tribunals on Conduct of the Arbitration under the ICC Rules of Arbitration (22 Sep. 2016), p. 4.
88. *Saint-Gobain Performance Plastics Europe v. Venezuela* ICSID Case No. ARB/12/13 (Decision on Claimant's Proposal to Disqualify Mr Gabriel Bottini from the Tribunal, 27 Feb. 2013), citing *Republic of Ghana v. Telekom Malaysia Berhard*, Decision of the District Court of the Hague (Civil Law Section), 18 Oct. 2004: 'In this decision, the court ruled that Prof. Emmanuel Gaillard could not simultaneously represent an Italian consortium in its ICSID arbitration against Morocco and serve as arbitrator in a separate investor-State arbitration between Telekom Malaysia and Ghana which turned on similar issues.'

Convention on International Commercial Arbitration,[89] both of which are concerned with the recognition and enforcement of foreign arbitral awards, do not explicitly mention impartiality and independence. However, both of these conventions list among the grounds to refuse recognition and enforcement, the violation of public policy, which has been understood by the States as including the requirements of independence and impartiality.[90]

Institutional rules, which govern most arbitrations, also require that each arbitrator 'be and remain impartial and independent of the parties involved in the arbitration'.[91] SCC and LCIA rules contain virtually the same provisions as those of the ICC, afore quoted. It is also the same for AAA[92] and WIPO.[93] Under the ICSID rules arbitrators are expected to exercise 'independent judgment',[94] which has been subsequently interpreted by the tribunals to encompass both independence and impartiality.[95] Likewise, under the UNCITRAL Model Law, which is often used in ad hoc arbitrations, lack of 'independence and impartiality' is a ground to challenge arbitrators.[96] Moreover, it is sometimes considered a 'mandatory provision'[97] not to be derogated from by the parties.[98] Whatever the textual source of the requirement of impartiality and independence, it seems that their interpretation has been rather uniform.[99]

[B] Duty to Disclose

[1] Burden on the Arbitrator

Due process is only as effective as the procedural safeguards put in place to enforce it. The necessary corollary of independence and impartiality is the duty imposed on the arbitrator to disclose any facts that may affect his or her independent judgment. The

89. Inter-American Convention on International Commercial Arbitration (30 Jan. 975).
90. Reims Court of Appeal (*Cour d'appel de Reims*), *SA J. & P. Avax v. société Tecnimont SPA*, Judgment (2 Nov. 2011), 1 Revue de l'arbitrage 112 (2012) (Comments by Marc Henry).
91. ICC Arbitration Rules, Art. 11(1).
92. AAA Arbitration Rules, Art. VII.
93. WIPO Arbitration Rules, Art. XXII.
94. ICSID Rules of Procedure for Arbitration Proceedings, Art. 14.
95. Nigel Blackaby, Constantine Partasides, Alan Redfern & Martin Hunter, *Redfern and Hunter on International Arbitration*, 275–276 (Oxford University Press 2009).
96. UNCITRAL Arbitration Rules, Art. 11.
97. Nigel Blackaby, Constantine Partasides, Alan Redfern & Martin Hunter, *Redfern and Hunter on International Arbitration*, 267 (Oxford University Press 2009).
98. *Ibid.*: 'Although no doubt the parties are free to agree that a specific disclosed relationship between an arbitrator and a party is not to be considered as sufficiently substantial as to disqualify the person concerned.'
99. Nathalie Bernasconi-Osterwalder, Lise Johnson & Fiona Marshall, *Arbitrator Independence and Impartiality: Examining the dual role of arbitrator and counsel*, IV Annual Forum for Developing Country Investment Negotiators, Background Papers, 5 (27–29 Oct. 2010).

duty to disclose has been characterized as the cornerstone of an arbitrator's duty of independence.[100]

As the International Bar Association (IBA) Guidelines on Conflicts of Interest in International Arbitration (IBA Guidelines) indicate, '[i]f facts or circumstances exist that may, in the eyes of the parties, give rise to doubts as to the arbitrator's impartiality or independence, the arbitrator shall disclose such facts or circumstances to the parties, the arbitration institution or other appointing authority.'[101] Disclosure does not mean that there is necessarily a conflict of interest or bias on behalf of the arbitrator. On the contrary, an arbitrator who makes a disclosure, as opposed to resigning, considers himself or herself unaffected by the circumstances disclosed and thus capable of making a fair and impartial judgment. Most institutions recommend extensive disclosure in case of doubt.

The main goal of the duty to disclose is to give the parties sufficient notice, so that they can make an informed decision when confirming an arbitrator. This is done at an early stage of the proceeding in order to avoid challenges to the validity and enforceability of the award after it is rendered. The duty to disclose persists until the very end of the arbitration with respect to any new facts that may undermine the independence and impartiality of the arbitrator. Certain authors consider that disclosing new facts towards the end of the arbitration should not be judged as stringently, so as to let the proceeding be concluded.[102]

'The obligation to disclose and to investigate potential conflicts rests primarily on the arbitrator.'[103] An arbitrator cannot be declared independent based on his or her lack of actual knowledge due to failure to perform a conflict search. On the other end of the spectrum, there is no duty to make a formal disclosure with regard to the facts that are publicly known, even though it may be encouraged in order to avoid potential challenges.[104]

The IBA Guidelines also mention the obligation for the parties to communicate known direct or indirect connections to the arbitrators. This should in no way dilute the arbitrator's duty to disclose, but rather allow the parties to do their own fact-finding if they feel certain hesitation on behalf of the arbitrator.[105] Both the arbitrator and the party who are aware of a fact, which is not communicated to the other party, can be held jointly responsible for non-disclosure.[106]

100. Ahmed S. El-Kosheri & Karim Y. Youssef, *L'indépendance des arbitres internationaux: le point de vue d'un arbitre*, Bulletin de la Cour internationale d'arbitrage de la CCI, L'indépendence de l'arbitre, Supplément spécial 2007, 45, 53 (2008).
101. IBA Guidelines on Conflicts of Interest in International Arbitration, adopted by resolution of the IBA Council (23 Oct. 2014), Part I: General Standards Regarding Impartiality, Independence and Disclosure, General Standard 3(a).
102. Nigel Blackaby, Constantine Partasides, Alan Redfern & Martin Hunter, *Redfern and Hunter on International Arbitration*, 269 (Oxford University Press 2009).
103. Dominique Hascher, *Independence and Impartiality of Arbitrators: 3 Issues*, 27(4) Am. U. Intl. L. Rev. 789, 794 (2012).
104. *Ibid.*
105. *Ibid.*
106. *Ibid.*

[2] Scope of Disclosure

The existence of the duty to disclose is widely recognized, but its application to specific circumstances is more complex. The questions arising in relation to independence may vary depending on the status of an arbitrator. For example, issues facing academics and non-practicing lawyers are generally different from those facing lawyers practicing within law firms. The type of law firm with which an arbitrator is associated, which may vary from a boutique firm to a large multinational firm or a firm in a network or alliance, will often be significant. Furthermore, the role of an arbitrator within a firm may also have an impact on his or her conflict situation.

Although the types of situations in which independence issues arise are extremely varied, they can be broadly categorized under the following headings:[107]

(i) The arbitrator's relationship with one or several parties.
(ii) The arbitrator's relationship with an entity related to a party.
(iii) The arbitrator's relationship with counsel or an entity linked to counsel.
(iv) The arbitrator's relationship with a State.
(v) The arbitrator's role in a related matter (issue conflicts).

[a] Arbitrator's Relationship with a Party or Parties

The arbitrator may have a direct connection to one of the parties, for example, if he or she has acted as the party's counsel. In such a case, the arbitrator will often feel either prevented from accepting the case or obliged to make a disclosure. The situation is less evident for arbitrators who work in law firms present all around the world. Even if the arbitrator himself or herself does not have a relationship with one of the parties, one of the lawyers in another office of the same firm might, which could lead to disqualification.[108] Depending on the extent of the relationship between the different offices of the same firm, an arbitrator may not even be aware that an international colleague is linked to the party.

Such practices as repeated nomination by the same party or preselection interviews with an arbitrator have also been points of contention.[109] The existence of a conflict in these cases depends on the particular facts at hand. For example, an arbitrator who was contacted by one of the parties solely for purposes of gauging his availability was not disqualified by the Court when challenged by the other party.[110]

107. Anne Marie Whitesell, *Independence in ICC Arbitration: ICC Court Practice Concerning the Appointment, Confirmation, Challenge and Replacement of Arbitrators*, ICC Intl. Ct. Arb. Bull., Special Supplement 2007, Independence of Arbitrators, 7, 8–10 (2008).
108. *See*, for example, *Blue Bank International & Trust (Barbados) Ltd. v. Bolivarian Republic of Venezuela*, ICSID Case No. ARB 12/20, Decision on the Parties' Proposals to Disqualify a Majority of the Tribunal (12 Nov. 2013).
109. Anne Marie Whitesell, *Independence in ICC Arbitration: ICC Court Practice Concerning the Appointment, Confirmation, Challenge and Replacement of Arbitrators*, ICC Intl. Ct. Arb. Bull., Special Supplement 2007, Independence of Arbitrators, 7, 9 (2008).
110. *Ibid.*, p. 15.

[b] *Arbitrator's Relationship with an Entity Linked to a Party*

Given the complexity of modern corporate structures, the relationship with an entity linked to a party, has become increasingly relevant in the context of conflicts of interest. Independence seems to be more frequently challenged in such cases, as opposed to cases in which the link between an arbitrator and a party is more direct.[111] The possible explanation is that arbitrators accept nominations more readily when their connection to one of the parties is tenuous. Moreover, they may be more inclined not to make a disclosure, whether it is because they do not consider the relationship of incidence or because they are not aware of the possible link themselves.

[c] *Arbitrator's Relationship with Counsel or an Entity Linked to Counsel*

Most arbitrators are also practicing lawyers and may be doing so within the structure of a multinational firm. Conflicts and disclosures arise when an arbitrator is related to the counsel or the counsel's firm, or she has previously served on the same tribunal as one of the parties' counsel. This is one reason why some lawyers choose to open solo practices when they decide to become full-time arbitrators.

This issue is of interest in the context of barrister chambers in England. Even though barristers may be members of the same chambers, they are considered to be independent actors and do not share profits among themselves.[112] Yet, for parties and counsel from other countries who are not familiar with this practice, it may be difficult to accept the independence of an arbitrator who practices in the same chambers as the counsel of another party.[113]

Even more interesting is the question of whether a simple acquaintance between an arbitrator and counsel gives rise to a duty to disclose. Given how small the arbitration world is, it would potentially be difficult to find an arbitrator who has not met any of the parties' counsel during a conference or in the course of business.

111. *Ibid.*, p. 9.
112. *See* Marnix A. Leijten & Matthias L. Kuscher, *What Makes Challenges Challenging?*, in *International Arbitration Under Review: Essays in Honour of John Beechey*, 271 (Andrea Carlevaris, Laurent Lévy, Alexis Mourre & Eric A. Schwartz Editor, ICC 2015) (Citing Rix J. in *Laker Airways Inc. v. FLS Aerospace Ltd et al.* [2000] 1 WLR 113: 'It is the essence of practice at the bar ... that ... barristers are all self-employed. This is not a mere matter of form. On the contrary, practicing barristers are prohibited by the rules of their profession from entering partnerships or accepting employment precisely in order to maintain the position where they can appear against or in front of one another.').
113. The ICC Court has been attentive to the position of the parties who are not familiar with the concept of barrister chambers when deciding whether to disqualify an arbitrator. *See* Marnix A. Leijten & Matthias L. Kuscher, *What Makes Challenges Challenging?*, in *International Arbitration Under Review: Essays in Honour of John Beechey*, 272 (Andrea Carlevaris, Laurent Lévy, Alexis Mourre & Eric A. Schwartz, ICC 2015).

[d] Arbitrator's Relationship with a State

This issue is highlighted in the context of investment-related disputes since the respondent is inevitably a State or a State entity. As such, at least one of the arbitrators will always be nominated by the State, and it has a propensity to nominate former government officials or arbitrators who are notorious for defending the State's position in previous cases.[114] Moreover, there is a practice of nominating current or former judges who may arguably be more or less controlled by their States.

In countries with strong centralized governments (which is often the case of developing economies), the choice of potential nominees may be limited, which is why it is important to consider to what extent the relationship between the State and an arbitrator may be disqualifying.

[e] Arbitrator's Role in a Related Matter

This is a question of due process and public policy since it seeks to avoid having arbitrators prejudge the issue or have access to certain information, which will not be available to other members of the tribunal.[115] The arbitrators may hesitate to make a disclosure, since the parties will not be exactly identical to the other case in which they participate or had participated.

This question often comes up in investor-State arbitration specifically, because there are a limited number of legal issues that come up in each case. As such, published doctrinal opinions or participation in the majority ruling on a certain question of law may be challenged as lacking impartiality since the arbitrator has already prejudged the case. It is seen as a conflict issue.

[3] Institutional Guidelines

[a] IBA Guidelines on Conflicts of Interest in International Arbitration

The IBA Guidelines may be very helpful in giving practical guidance to what an arbitrator should disclose.[116] The parties and their counsel frequently consider these

114. *See Saint-Gobain Performance Plastics Europe v. Venezuela*, ICSID Case No. ARB/12/13, Decision on Claimant's Proposal to Disqualify Mr Gabriel Bottini from the Tribunal (27 Feb. 2013) (The two remaining members of the tribunal rejected the proposal to disqualify an arbitrator nominated by Venezuela, who had previously been employed by the government of Argentina to 'Plan and propose a strategy for defending the interests of Argentina in cases where it is either plaintiff or defendant before the courts or arbitration, international or foreign.').
115. *See*, for example, *Caratube International Oil Company LLP and Devincci Salah Hourani v. Republic of Kazakhstan*, ICSID Case No. ARB/13/13, Decision on the Proposal for Disqualification of Bruno Boesch (20 Mar. 2014) (An arbitrator who was the member of the tribunal in a case concerning the same issues and almost all of the same parties as the case in issue was disqualified.).
116. Dominique Hascher, *Independence and Impartiality of Arbitrators: 3 Issues*, 27(4) Am. U. Intl. L. Rev. 789, 796 (2012).

Guidelines in assessing the impartiality and independence of arbitrators, and arbitral institutions and courts also often consult the IBA Guidelines in considering challenges to arbitrators. These Guidelines do not have any legally binding authority and do not override any applicable national law or arbitral rules chosen by the parties.

The IBA Guidelines give a classification of situations, which can fall in the red, orange or green lists. The different colors signify the degree of necessity to disclose certain types of conduct. Red means that disclosure is imperative. Orange list could be described as the grey area in between: it contains the situations that do not give rise to disclosure by default but should be assessed on a case-by-case basis. Green means that, generally, no disclosure is required.

The Red List

The Red List consists of two parts: A 'Non-Waivable Red List' and a 'Waivable Red List'. These lists are by no means exclusive and are meant to indicate situations, in which a third-party objective observer would find that the arbitrator's independence and impartiality are compromised.

The underlying principle of the Non-Waivable Red List is that 'no person can be his or her own judge'.[117] Therefore, acceptance of such a situation cannot cure the conflict. This list includes the case where a manager or director of a company is appointed as an arbitrator in a proceeding to which the company is a party.

The Waivable Red List covers situations that are serious but not as severe. Because of their seriousness, unlike circumstances described in the Orange List, these situations should be considered waivable, but only if and when the parties, being aware of the conflict of interest situation, expressly state their willingness to have such a person act as arbitrator. Notwithstanding a serious conflict of interest, such as those that are described by way of example in the Waivable Red List, the parties may wish to engage such a person as an arbitrator. Here, party autonomy and the desire to have only impartial and independent arbitrators must be balanced.

As mentioned above, according to the IBA Guidelines, disclosure does not imply the existence of a conflict of interest; nor should it by itself result either in a disqualification of the arbitrator or in a presumption regarding disqualification. The purpose of the disclosure is merely to inform the parties of a situation that they may wish to explore further in order to determine whether objectively there are justifiable doubts as to the arbitrator's impartiality or independence. If the conclusion is that there are no justifiable doubts, the arbitrator can act.

Apart from the situations covered by the Non-Waivable Red List, he or she can also act if there is no timely objection by the parties or, in situations covered by the Waivable Red List, if there is a specific acceptance by the parties.

117. IBA Guidelines on Conflicts of Interest in International Arbitration, adopted by resolution of the IBA Council (23 Oct. 2014), Part I: General Standards Regarding Impartiality, Independence and Disclosure, General Standard 2(d), p. 6.

The Orange List

The Orange List is a non-exhaustive list of specific situations that, depending on the facts of a given case, may, in the eyes of the parties, give rise to doubts as to the arbitrator's impartiality or independence. Orange List situations are generally not subject to disclosure. However, an arbitrator needs to assess on a case-by-case basis whether a given situation, even though not mentioned in the Orange List, is nevertheless such as to give rise to justifiable doubts as to his or her impartiality or independence.

A Common Orange List situation is the arbitrator providing previous services for one of the parties.

The Green List

The Green List is a non-exhaustive list of specific situations where no appearance and no actual conflict of interest exist from an objective point of view. Thus, the arbitrator has no duty to disclose situations falling within the Green List. A common Green List example is when the arbitrator had previously expressed legal opinion on an issue raised in the arbitration.

For the situations covered in each of the three lists, *see* Annex 1 to this chapter.

[b] New ICC Guidance Note for the Disclosure of Conflicts by Arbitrators

The ICC International Court of Arbitration has adopted a Guidance Note for the disclosure of conflicts by arbitrators (ICC Guidance Note).[118] The aim is to ensure that arbitrators are forthcoming and transparent in their disclosure of potential conflicts in ICC arbitrations.

The Guidance Note, as the IBA Guidelines, 'rests on the fundamental principle that parties to an arbitration have a legitimate interest in being fully informed of all facts or circumstances that may be relevant in their view in order to be satisfied that a prospective arbitrator or sitting arbitrator is and remains independent and impartial or, if they so wish, to explore the matter further and take the possible courses of action contemplated by the ICC Rules'.[119]

The ICC Guidance Note states the general principles of disclosure, which include the subjective assessment by the arbitrator, the ongoing nature of the duty to disclose and the fact that the lack of disclosure does not automatically mean that there is a conflict.

118. The Note was adopted unanimously by the Bureau of the Court on 12 Feb. 2016.
119. ICC Press Release, *ICC Court adopts Guidance Note on conflict disclosures by arbitrators* (23 Feb. 2016), https://iccwbo.org/media-wall/news-speeches/icc-court-adopts-guidance-note-on-conflict-disclosures-by-arbitrators (accessed 1 Jun. 2018). *See also* ICC Note to Parties and Arbitral Tribunals on the Conduct of the Arbitration Under the ICC Rules of Arbitration (30 Oct. 2017), https://cdn.iccwbo.org/content/uploads/sites/3/2017/03/icc-note-to-parties-and-arbitral-tribunals-on-the-conduct-of-arbitration.pdf (accessed 29 May 2018), paras 17–24.

The Note's most notable contribution, perhaps, is that of an additional procedural safeguard for transparency. For arbitrations commenced on or after 1 January 2016, the ICC will publish certain information regarding the tribunal, such as the names and nationalities of arbitrators.[120] It is certainly a welcome development, since the ICC arbitration has been generally known for its confidentiality, which has been questioned by multiple commentators.[121] Unlike ICSID awards, most of which are published on their own website as well as on italaw, ICC awards are confidential and when made public, are only done so in redacted form. The lack of non-disclosure has raised issues of fairness and transparency.[122] Publishing the names of the arbitrators, while still protecting the confidentiality of the proceedings, will certainly facilitate the finding and resolution of potential conflicts of interest.

[4] Institutional Disclosure Procedures

Different institutions adopt different procedures for disclosure. For example, Article 6(2) of ICSID Arbitration Rules establishes a declaration to be signed by each member of the tribunal before the first session, in which they declare the following:[123]

> To the best of my knowledge there is no reason why I should not serve on the Arbitral Tribunal constituted by the International Centre for Settlement of Investment Disputes with respect to a dispute between ________________ and ________________.
>
> ... Attached is a statement of (a) my past and present professional, business and other relationships (if any) with the parties and (b) any other circumstance that might cause my reliability for independent judgment to be questioned by a party. I acknowledge that by signing this declaration, I assume a continuing obligation promptly to notify the Secretary-General of the Centre of any such relationship or circumstance that subsequently arises during this proceeding.

Under the ICC Rules, an arbitrator must disclose in writing to the Secretariat 'any facts or circumstances which might be of such a nature as to call into question the arbitrator's independence in the eyes of the parties, as well as any circumstances that could give rise to reasonable doubts as to the arbitrator's impartiality',[124] or what is called a Statement of Independence.

The Statement of Independence provides that, in deciding what to disclose, the prospective arbitrator should consider, *inter alia*, whether there exists any past or present relationship, direct or indirect, with any of the parties or their counsel, whether financial, professional or of another kind.

120. ICC Note to Parties and Arbitral Tribunals on the Conduct of the Arbitration Under the ICC Rules of Arbitration (30 Oct. 2017), https://cdn.iccwbo.org/content/uploads/sites/3/2017/03/icc-note-to-parties-and-arbitral-tribunals-on-the-conduct-of-arbitration.pdf (accessed 29 May 2018), para. 28.
121. Andrea Carlevaris & Rocio Digón, *Arbitrator Challenges under the ICC Rules and Practice* 1 ICC Dis. Res. Bull. 30 (2016).
122. *Ibid.*
123. ICSID Arbitration Rules, Rule 6(2).
124. ICC Arbitration Rules, Art. 11(2).

The nominee must decide whether to file an unqualified or qualified Statement of Independence. In the case of an unqualified Statement of Independence, the nominee is required to declare as follows:

> I am independent of each of the parties and intend to remain so; to the best of my knowledge, there are no facts or circumstances, past or present, that I should disclose because they might be of such nature as to call into question my independence in the eyes of any of the parties.

If the Statement of Independence is qualified, the prospective arbitrator declares as follows:

> I am independent of each of the parties and intend to remain so; however, in consideration of ICC Rules of Arbitration, I wish to call your attention to the following facts or circumstances which I hereafter disclose because they might be of such a nature as to call into question my independence in the eyes of any of the parties.

When the parties have proposed an arbitrator or the co-arbitrators, the arbitrator's Statement of Independence and curriculum vitae are sent by the Secretariat to the parties prior to confirmation. If the Statement of Independence is qualified, the parties are given a time limit in which to provide their comments or objections. If it is unqualified, then no time limit is given. If the prospective arbitrator has submitted an unqualified Statement of Independence or a qualified Statement of Independence that has not given rise to any objection, the Secretary General of the Court may confirm him or her. If the Secretary General considers that an arbitrator should not be confirmed, the matter is submitted to the Court.

In the event that the Court appoints an arbitrator, the appointment is generally made upon the proposal of an ICC National Committee. The Court will not normally accept a qualified Statement of Independence from an arbitrator proposed by a National Committee, since the Court seeks to ensure absolute independence for all appointments that it makes. Also, when the Court makes an appointment, the parties are not sent the arbitrator's Statement of Independence and curriculum vitae before the appointment, so, from a practical viewpoint, no time limit can be granted to the parties for possible objections, as is required with qualified Statements of Independence.

When an objection is made on the basis of a qualified or unqualified Statement of Independence prior to confirmation, the Secretariat will invite the other side to provide its comments. Generally, the nominee is not informed of the objection, so as to preserve the prospective arbitrator's neutrality. The Court uses its discretion in determining whether the objection has been raised in good faith, or whether it is dilatory and frivolous.

Traditionally, the Court has preferred not to confirm an arbitrator if there seems to be a reasonable basis for the objection. This is in keeping with the Court's wish to maximize confidence in the arbitral tribunal from the outset. In deciding whether to confirm an arbitrator, the Court will also consider possible difficulties that may be encountered during the procedure or at the time of an award if the arbitrator is confirmed.[125]

[5] Flexibility after Disclosure

The fact that the parties can waive the conflict, such as the ones in the mentioned IBA red waivable list, shows the importance of the party's autonomy in arbitration. And, after disclosure, it is up to the parties to determine the flexibility they want to have with the prospective arbitrator. This is why disclosure is so important. The purpose of the disclosure is to inform the parties of a situation that they may wish to explore further in order to determine, whether objectively there are justifiable doubts as to the arbitrator's impartiality or independence. But as mentioned above, disclosure does not mean or imply the existence of a conflict of interest. The parties will decide and have the final word on the subject.

[C] Challenges to Arbitrators

Parties can play an active role in the impartiality and independence of the arbitrator. Either party may propose the disqualification of a tribunal member once the tribunal has been constituted. A proposal to disqualify an arbitrator must be made promptly and, in any event, before the proceeding is declared closed. Failure to object promptly will result in the rejection of the proposal. The challenge must be done in good faith and not with a dilatory or frivolous purpose.

It may also occur that when potential conflicts of interest arise, arbitrators may decide to tender their resignation immediately. Sometimes the arbitrator informs the parties of the situation and offers to resign if any party so requests. At other times, the arbitrator is challenged and then decides to step down before the challenge is examined. The sections below provide a useful illustration of provisions on arbitrator challenges under the ICSID Convention (1) and the ICC Arbitration Rules (2).

[1] ICSID Grounds for Disqualification

An arbitrator may be disqualified on the ground of incapacity, 'manifest lack of the qualities required' or ineligibility for appointment.[126] Regarding the required qualities, they must possess 'high moral character, recognized competence in the fields of law, commerce, industry or finance, and reliability to exercise independent judgment'.[127] Candidates appointed from outside the Panel must also meet these qualities.[128]

125. Anne Marie Whitesell, *Independence in ICC Arbitration: ICC Court Practice concerning the Appointment, Confirmation, Challenge and Replacement of Arbitrators*, ICC Intl. Ct. Arb. Bull., Special Supplement 2007, Independence of Arbitrators, 7, 19 (2008).
126. ICSID Convention, Art. 57.
127. *Ibid.*, Art. 14(1).
128. *See Ibid.*

Lack of the ICSID nationality requirements applicable to members of a Tribunal should also be mentioned; a majority of arbitrators on a tribunal must be nationals of States other than the State party to the dispute and the State whose national is a party to the dispute.[129] Non-compliance with these nationality requirements constitutes a ground for disqualification under Article 57 of the ICSID Convention.

[a] Procedure

The ICSID challenge procedure starts with the submission by a party of a proposal to disqualify one or more members of the tribunal. The proposal is filed with the ICSID Secretary General. A proposal to disqualify suspends the proceeding.[130] Once received, the proposal is transmitted to the tribunal or to the Chairman of the ICSID Administrative Council if the challenge is to a sole arbitrator or the majority of the tribunal.[131] The proposal is also transmitted to the other party, and a schedule for submissions is established. The schedule will provide an opportunity for the challenged arbitrator to furnish explanations and for the other party to make observations on the proposal.

The other members of the tribunal usually make the decision on the proposal. However, the Chairman of the ICSID Administrative Council (when the other members are equally divided or where the proposal refers to a sole arbitrator or to a majority of the tribunal) will make the decision. The President of the World Bank serves as the Chairman of the Administrative Council ex officio, and it is currently Dr. Jim Yong Kim. The competence and objectiveness of the decision-maker give rise to serious doubts as to the appropriateness of this system, since a single person who has little to do with arbitration decides whether or not to replace an arbitrator.

The decision will either reject or uphold the proposal for disqualification. There is a two-part test, which is applied: first, the request for disqualification must have been brought in a timely manner,[132] and, second, it must establish the 'manifest lack' of the required qualifications on the merits.[133]

If the proposal is rejected, the proceeding will resume immediately with the same tribunal. A proposal that is upheld results in the disqualification of the challenged arbitrator and, consequently, a vacancy on the tribunal. A vacancy resulting from the disqualification of an arbitrator is filled using the same method by which the disqualified arbitrator had been appointed. If no new appointment is made and accepted within forty-five days of the notification of the vacancy, the appointment will be made by the Chairman of the ICSID Administrative Council at the request of a party. As soon as the vacancy has been filled, the proceeding will resume from the point when the proposal was submitted.

129. *Ibid.*, Art. 38 and Art. 39.
130. ICSID Arbitration Rules, Art. 9(6).
131. ICSID Convention, Art. 58.
132. ICSID Arbitration Rules, Rule 9(1).
133. ICSID Convention, Art. 14(1) and Art. 57.

[b] Applicable Legal Standard

The recent decisions on proposals for disqualifications demonstrate the development of a uniform legal standard for disqualifying arbitrators under ICSID.[134] Historically, the grounds for disqualification under ICSID have been interpreted more restrictively than under other institutional rules or the UNCITRAL Model Law.[135] If UNCITRAL allows challenges in case of 'justifiable doubts' that can be harbored by the parties,[136] Article 57 of the ICSID Convention requires 'manifest lack' of arbitrator qualifications, thus placing a higher burden on the party challenging the nomination.

The phrase 'manifest lack' has been interpreted as an objective test of arbitrators' qualities.[137] The subjective opinion of the party requesting disqualification is not enough to justify it.[138] As the most recent of the *ConocoPhillips* disqualification decision succinctly puts it:

> The standard to be applied to Respondent's Proposal is whether a reasonable third person, with knowledge of all the facts, would conclude, on an objective basis, that the challenged arbitrator is manifestly lacking in the ability to act impartially (Article 14 read with Article 57 of the ICSID Convention).[139]

Recently, *Blue Bank International v. Venezuela*[140] seems to have become the golden standard for ICSID arbitrator challenges, and it has been referred to or quoted verbatim by multiple decisions on disqualification since.[141] Albeit there is no rule of

134. *See*, generally, *Blue Bank International & Trust (Barbados) Ltd. v. Bolivarian Republic of Venezuela*, ICSID Case No. ARB 12/20, Decision on the Parties' Proposals to Disqualify a Majority of the Tribunal (12 Nov. 2013); *Burlington Resources Inc. v. Republic of Ecuador*, ICSID Case No. ARB/08/5, Decision on the Proposal for Disqualification of Professor Francisco Orrego Vicuña (13 Dec. 2013); *Conoco-Phillips Petrozuata B.V., ConocoPhillips Hamaca B.V. and ConocoPhillips Gulf of Paria B.V. v. Bolivarian Republic of Venezuela*, ICSID Case No. ARB/07/30, Decisions on the Proposals to Disqualify L. Yves Fortier, Q.C., Arbitrator (27 Feb. 2012; 15 Dec. 2015; 15 Mar. 2016; 26 Jul. 2016), etc.
135. *See*, for example, Christoph H. Schreuer, *The ICSID Convention: A Commentary*, 1200 (Cambridge University Press 2001); Nathalie Bernasconi-Osterwalder, Lise Johnson & Fiona Marshall, *Arbitrator Independence and Impartiality: Examining the Dual Role of Arbitrator and Counsel*, IV Annual Forum for Developing Country Investment Negotiators Background Papers (27-29 Oct. 2010), p. 11.
136. *See*, for example, UNCITRAL Arbitration Rules, Art. 12.
137. Nathalie Bernasconi-Osterwalder, Lise Johnson & Fiona Marshall, *Arbitrator Independence and Impartiality: Examining the Dual Role of Arbitrator and Counsel*, IV Annual Forum for Developing Country Investment Negotiators Background Papers (27-29 Oct. 2010), p. 11.
138. *Suez, Sociedad General de Aguas de Barcelona S.A. and Interagua Servicios Integrales de Agua S.A. v. Argentine Republic*, ICSID Case No. ARB/03/17, and *Suez, Sociedad General de Aguas de Barcelona S.A. and Vivendi Universal S.A v. Argentine Republic*, ICSID Case No. ARB/03/19, Decision on the Proposal for the Disqualification of a Member of the Arbitral Tribunal (22 Oct. 2007).
139. *ConocoPhillips Petrozuata B.V., ConocoPhillips Hamaca B.V. and ConocoPhillips Gulf of Paria B.V. v. Bolivarian Republic of Venezuela*, ICSID Case No. ARB/07/30, Decision on the Proposal to Disqualify L. Yves Fortier, Q.C., Arbitrator (26 Jul. 2016), p. 10.
140. *Blue Bank International & Trust (Barbados) Ltd. v. Bolivarian Republic of Venezuela*, ICSID Case No. ARB 12/20, Decision on the Parties' Proposals to Disqualify a Majority of the Tribunal (12 Nov. 2013).
141. *Blue Bank* itself refers to *Suez, Sociedad General de Aguas de Barcelona S.A. and Interagua Servicios Integrales de Agua S.A. v. Argentine Republic*, ICSID Case No. ARB/03/17, and *Suez*,

binding precedent in arbitration, it is useful to consider these decisions given their similarity and ostensible uniformity. Moreover, in many cases it is the Chairman of the Administrative Council who will decide on disqualification and he or she is, therefore, very likely to apply the same methodology to the different cases brought before him or her.

First of all, *Blue Bank International* clarifies that both independence and impartiality are required of the arbitrators even though the latter is not explicitly mentioned by the Convention.[142] With regard to the burden of proof, it is stated that 'it is sufficient to establish the appearance of dependence or bias'[143] without demonstrating that the challenged arbitrator is actually dependent or biased.[144] *Caratube Oil* explicitly upheld that as the applicable burden of proof standard when questioned by the parties,[145] and there seems to be a concurrence among the subsequent decisions. This clarification attenuates the high burden placed on the party requesting disqualification by the objective test.

The word 'manifest' is meant to refer to 'evident' or 'obvious',[146] and 'it relates to the ease with which the alleged lack of the required qualities can be perceived'.[147] Both in *Blue Bank* and *Burlington*, the Chairman qualifies the above as the standard required by the ICSID Convention and specifically indicates that it overrides the IBA Guidelines, which are merely informative for the parties.[148]

In practice, *Blue Bank* illustrates the effect of complex structures of law firms on the appearance of independence. In this case, a partner from the Madrid office of Baker & McKenzie was appointed as the arbitrator in an arbitration against Venezuela. It later became known that there is a parallel case against the same State, in which the New York and Caracas offices of Baker & McKenzie are representing the investor, also brought under ICSID. The Chairman upheld the challenge against this arbitrator brought by Venezuela, because he considered that the arbitrator would be in a position to decide on the same legal issues as would be at stake in a proceeding involving his firm acting as counsel, which gives an objective appearance of dependence. It is interesting to highlight that the firm's offices are independent and the disqualified

Sociedad General de Aguas de Barcelona S.A. and Vivendi Universal S.A v. Argentine Republic, ICSID Case No. ARB/03/19, Decision on the Proposal for the Disqualification of a Member of the Arbitral Tribunal (22 Oct. 2007).

142. *Blue Bank International & Trust (Barbados) Ltd. v. Bolivarian Republic of Venezuela*, ICSID Case No. ARB 12/20, Decision on the Parties' Proposals to Disqualify a Majority of the Tribunal (12 Nov. 2013), p. 10: '[T]he Spanish version of the ICSID Convention refers to "imparcialidad de juicio" (impartiality of judgment). Given that both versions are equally authentic, it is accepted that arbitrators must be both impartial and independent.'
143. *Ibid.*, p. 11.
144. *Ibid.*
145. *Caratube International Oil Company LLP and Devincci Salah Hourani v. Republic of Kazakhstan*, ICSID Case No. ARB/13/13, Decision on the Proposal for Disqualification of Bruno Boesch (20 Mar. 2014), p. 18.
146. *Blue Bank International & Trust (Barbados) Ltd. v. Bolivarian Republic of Venezuela*, ICSID Case No. ARB 12/20, Decision on the Parties' Proposals to Disqualify a Majority of the Tribunal (12 Nov. 2013).
147. *Ibid.*; *Burlington Resources Inc. v. Republic of Ecuador*, ICSID Case No. ARB/08/5, Decision on the Proposal for Disqualification of Professor Francisco Orrego Vicuña (13 Dec. 2013).
148. *Ibid.*

arbitrator's remuneration depends primarily on the performance of the Madrid office. However, these facts did not suffice to disprove the apparent lack of independence.[149]

In another case, an arbitrator was disqualified due to his personal comments on the ethics and responsibility of one of the party's legal counsel.[150] This case is particularly curious, since these admonishing comments were included in the arbitrator's response to proposal for disqualification. In fact, the original basis for the challenge, which was the fact that this arbitrator has been appointed eight times by the same law firm in the course of six years, was dismissed due to its untimeliness. A decision on whether multiple appointments by the same counsel constitutes grounds for disqualification and, if so, how many appointments are numerous enough, would have been a welcomed decision. Yet, this case gives a useful illustration of the type of conduct the arbitrator may not want to give in to if he or she wants to avoid being challenged.

Abaclat provides a helpful illustration of the refusal to disqualify the majority of the arbitral tribunal.[151] In this case, Argentina challenged two of the members of the tribunal after they made a ruling, which gave significantly more time for the other party to prepare their Reply Memorial than it did to Argentina for its Rejoinder Memorial. The Chairman firmly affirmed that an adverse ruling does not constitute 'manifest lack' of impartiality and is not grounds for disqualification.[152]

[2] Confirmation and Challenge of an Arbitrator under the ICC Arbitration Rules

Under ICC Arbitration Rules, the terminology for replacing an arbitrator is slightly different from other institutions. The parties may *nominate* an arbitrator, whereas it is the Court that *appoints* or *confirms* an arbitrator.[153] Once a party or the parties (or the two arbitrators, who have the power to select the president) *nominate* an arbitrator, the Court or the Secretary General may *confirm* the nomination. Absent nomination by the parties, the Court shall *appoint* the arbitrator upon *proposal* from one of the ICC's National Committees.[154]

There are several stages, at which an arbitrator may be confirmed or challenged. First of all, when an arbitrator is nominated, the Court can choose not to confirm her or him if one of the parties or the Secretary General has objected to the nomination.[155]

149. *Blue Bank International & Trust (Barbados) Ltd. v. Bolivarian Republic of Venezuela*, ICSID Case No. ARB 12/20, Decision on the Parties' Proposals to Disqualify a Majority of the Tribunal (12 Nov. 2013).
150. *Burlington Resources Inc. v. Republic of Ecuador*, ICSID Case No. ARB/08/5, Decision on the Proposal for Disqualification of Professor Francisco Orrego Vicuña (13 Dec. 2013).
151. *Abaclat and Others v. Argentine Republic*, ICSID Case No. ARB/07/5 (formerly *Giovanna a Beccara and Others v. The Argentine Republic*), Decision on the Proposal to Disqualify a Majority of the Tribunal (21 Dec. 2011).
152. *Ibid.*
153. Jason Fry & Simon Greenberg, *The Arbitral Tribunal: Applications of Articles 7-12 of the ICC Rules in Recent Cases*, 20(2) ICC Intl. Ct. Arb. Bull. 12 (2009).
154. *Ibid.*
155. *Ibid.*

The same applies to appointed arbitrators. Once an arbitrator has been confirmed, the parties may bring *challenges* on the basis of Article 14 for an alleged lack of impartiality or independence. Finally, Article 15(2) allows the Court to replace an arbitrator of its own initiative 'when it decides that the arbitrator is prevented de jure or de facto from fulfilling the arbitrator's functions, or that the arbitrator is not fulfilling those functions in accordance with the Rules or within the prescribed time limits'.[156] These three scenarios for replacing an arbitrator shall be discussed below.

[a] Confirmation

When an arbitrator is nominated or appointed, he is required to sign a statement of independence, in which a prospective arbitrator must disclose 'any facts or circumstances which might be of such a nature as to call into question the arbitrator's independence in the eyes of the parties'.[157] The statement of disclosure is communicated to the parties and they have an opportunity to express their objections to the nomination. The Court will consider these objections when deciding to confirm or not to confirm an arbitrator. However, even in the absence of party objections, the Secretary General may also suggest that an arbitrator should not be confirmed, which the Court will examine. In the absence of disclosure, the parties may still object to the nomination if they are aware of any conflicts of interest.

At this early juncture in the proceedings, the Court has wide discretion to appoint or not a prospective arbitrator, since it is early in the arbitration and will not be particularly disruptive.[158] Given the fact that it is a party-driven form of dispute resolution, the Court is likely to give more weight to any objections at this stage. Satisfying the parties at the beginning of the arbitration will prevent challenges at more advanced stages and will decrease the risk of contesting the final award. Until recently, the arbitrators were not even informed of the parties' objections, nor were they given an opportunity to comment.[159] However, this practice was criticized since it was suggested that the prospective arbitrator is best placed to comment on the request for his disqualification.[160] Under the new Rules, the prospective arbitrator will be provided with information on the objection and will have a possibility to provide comments.[161]

The Court does not communicate the reasons for its decision to confirm or not to confirm an arbitrator.[162] However, some examples may be informative in better understanding this practice.

---

156. ICC Arbitration Rules, Art. 15(2).
157. *See* above§4.04[B][4].
158. Andrea Carlevaris & Rocio Digón, *Arbitrator Challenges under the ICC Rules and Practice,* (1) ICC Disp. Res. Bull. 23, 31 (2016).
159. *Ibid.*
160. *Ibid.*
161. *Ibid.*
162. Andrea Carlevaris, *The Bounds of Party Autonomy in Institutional Arbitration* Intl. Arb. under Rev.: Essays in Honour of John Beechey 121–122 (2015): 'The Paris Court of First Instance held that the arbitral institution is under no obligation to give reasons for its decisions on challenges, which are administrative in nature, and added that not giving reasons does not amount to a

Table 1 Cases Where an Arbitrator Was Confirmed[163]

	Statement of Independence with Disclosure	*No Disclosure*
Parties Objected	- Respondent-nominated arbitrator disclosed that he had participated in several professional organizations with the respondent's counsel, and that they had been co-arbitrators in two prior cases.[164] - The counsel of one the parties and an arbitrator had been classmates at school, but had no other relationship at the time of the dispute.[165] - The nominee disclosed that she had served as arbitrator in two previous ICC arbitrations involving the same parties (both times nominated by the claimant). The claims in these cases were not identical, and both parties had the same counsel in all three proceedings, so there was no problem of "unequal access to information."[166]	- The claimant objected to the nomination of an arbitrator, claiming that he had had prior direct contact with the respondent. It transpired that the latter had simply approached the prospective arbitrator in order to enquire as to his availability to serve on the tribunal.[167] - One of the parties put forward an objection based on the fact that a prospective arbitrator had co-authored a law treatise with the counsel of the other party, and that the two men had worked at the same law firm. According to the other party, the professional relationship between the counsel and the prospective arbitrator had ended nine years prior to nomination.[168] - Objection to an arbitrator who was the member of the same parliament as the counsel for a period of time, as well as of the same political party.[169]

violation of due process and is not otherwise contrary to public policy.' (Referring to *Fairplus Holding et La Valaisanne v. CCI*, Judgment (19 Dec. 2012) 2 The Paris Journal of International Arbitration 455 (2013).).

163. For more examples *see*, generally, Anne Marie Whitesell, *Independence in ICC Arbitration: ICC Court Practice concerning the Appointment, Confirmation, Challenge and Replacement of Arbitrators*, 7 ICC Intl. Ct. Arb. Bull., Special Supplement 2007, Independence of Arbitrators (2008).
164. *Ibid.*, pp. 17–18.
165. *Ibid.*, p. 18.
166. *Ibid.*
167. *Ibid.*, p. 14.
168. *Ibid.*, p. 15.
169. *Ibid.*

	Statement of Independence with Disclosure	*No Disclosure*
Parties Did Not Object	- The arbitrator indicated that he had advised the subsidiary of the claimant in the past.[170] - The arbitrator nominated by the respondent indicated that he and his law firm had in the past provided advice to a company, in which the respondent held a majority interest.[171]	- A party, which was a State, nominated an officer of that State to serve as an arbitrator, indicating that he held 'the appropriate office for appointment as an arbitrator by the State'.[172] The counsel of the other party expressly stated that it does not object to the nomination, and the Court deferred to the party's judgment in confirming the arbitrator.[173]

Table 2 Cases Where an Arbitrator Was Not Confirmed

	Statement of Independence with Disclosure	*No Disclosure*
Parties Objected	- The nominee indicated that his law firm had previously acted against the other party on three different occasions.[174] - The respondents jointly nominated an arbitrator, who disclosed that he had provided legal advice to the claimant and that his partner was at the time advising a subsidiary of one of the respondents. The claimant objected to the nomination.[175]	- The arbitrator was an acting director of a company, which was the largest shareholder in another company, which was, itself, the largest shareholder of the respondent.[176] - Respondent nominated an arbitrator working at a law firm, which was part of an alliance with the firm of the respondent's counsel.[177] - The nominee had a professional relationship with the law firm of the respondent's counsel. Moreover, the address and the phone number he had provided were the same as that firm's.[178]

170. *Ibid.*, p. 16.
171. *Ibid.*
172. Jason Fry & Simon Greenberg, *The Arbitral Tribunal: Applications of Articles 7-12 of the ICC Rules in Recent Cases*, 20(2) ICC Intl. Ct. Arb. Bull. 12, 19 (2009).
173. *Ibid.*
174. Anne Marie Whitesell, *Independence in ICC Arbitration: ICC Court Practice concerning the Appointment, Confirmation, Challenge and Replacement of Arbitrators*, ICC Intl. Ct. Arb. Bull., Special Supplement 2007, Independence of Arbitrators 7, 22 (2008).
175. *Ibid.*, p. 23.
176. *Ibid.*, p. 19.
177. *Ibid.*
178. *Ibid.*

	Statement of Independence with Disclosure	*No Disclosure*
Parties Did Not Object	- The nominee indicated that some of his partners were representing the nominating party in several matters. [179] - The arbitrator disclosed that he was acting as counsel for the nominating party in several unrelated matters.[180] - The arbitrator had been previously asked to act as a mediator in the same dispute.[181]	- The Court decided not to confirm an arbitrator after the Secretary indicated that he had caused considerable delays in a previous arbitration.[182] - The same party, represented by the same counsel, had nominated the arbitrator in three other ICC cases. When contacted by the Secretariat, the nominee refused to make a disclosure.[183]

Tables 1 and 2 clearly demonstrate that disclosure made by an arbitrator does not automatically lead to a party objection or non-confirmation by the Court. It should, however, be noted that there is a clear trend of non-confirmation in cases of disclosure and objections by the parties. From 1998 to 2006, 124 out of 169 non-confirmations were preceded by an objection further to the nominee disclosing a potential conflict of interest.[184]

[b] Challenges

After the arbitrator has been confirmed, the procedure to remove him or her is referred to as 'challenge' and is regulated by Article 14 of the ICC Rules.[185] In order to bring a challenge, a party must notify the Secretariat in writing, specifying its reasons and the facts that form the basis for the challenge.[186] In the same manner as ICSID, the ICC Rules impose a timeliness requirement: the parties have thirty days from the notification of the confirmation or appointment of the arbitrator, or from the time when it becomes aware of the circumstances that raise doubts as to the independence or impartiality of the person challenged.[187]

179. *Ibid.*, p. 21.
180. *Ibid.*, p. 22.
181. *Ibid.*
182. Jason Fry & Simon Greenberg, *The Arbitral Tribunal: Applications of Articles 7-12 of the ICC Rules in Recent Cases*, 20(2) ICC Intl. Ct. Arb. Bull. 12, 19 (2009).
183. Anne Marie Whitesell, *Independence in ICC Arbitration: ICC Court Practice Concerning the Appointment, Confirmation, Challenge and Replacement of Arbitrators*, ICC Intl. Ct. Arb. Bull., Special Supplement 2007, Independence of Arbitrators, 7, 19 (2008).
184. *Ibid.*, p. 22.
185. ICC Arbitration Rules, Art. 14.
186. *Ibid.*
187. *Ibid.*

Another requirement for a challenge to be admissible is that it has to be brought before the final award is rendered by the tribunal.[188] At that point, the tribunal is *functus officio* – its purpose has been exhausted, and the arbitrators can no longer be challenged since they no longer serve in that quality. The only exception to the general rule of inadmissibility is bringing a concurrent challenge against the award.[189] In this case, the tribunal is reconstituted for this limited purpose and its members can, therefore, be challenged.

The ICC Court generally does not communicate the reasons for accepting or rejecting a challenge.[190] In response to users growing demand, this practice has recently evolved in a number of ways. In 2012, a task force of the ICC Commission on Arbitration and ADR produced a report inviting the States, when drafting investment protection treaties, to include 'appropriate wording requiring the Court to provide reasons for decisions on challenges'.[191] It answers the concerns about greater transparency in arbitration involving States, but the relevant investor protection instruments will have to be modified before this development can have a practical effect. Since 2015, the Court also allows private parties to request the communication of reasons for its decisions. However, the parties have to submit a joint request before the decision, for which the reasons are sought,[192] which is problematic in cases where one of the parties does not participate.

The applicable standard for challenges under ICC differs from ICSID in its scope. Article 14 states that a challenge may be brought for 'an alleged lack of impartiality or independence, or otherwise'.[193] It is more difficult to ascertain the outer limits of this standard because the ICC does not publish the reasons for its decisions. Moreover, it is due to the fact that in the ICC system, the challenges are decided during the Plenary Sessions of the Court. This means that a variety of legal professionals coming from different backgrounds have the opportunity to assess the issue. They generally reach a consensus, but providing uniform reasons might be more problematic.[194] It is, therefore, informative to consider some examples where challenges have been accepted or rejected (Table 3).

188. Andrea Carlevaris & Rocio Digón, *Arbitrator Challenges under the ICC Rules and Practice,* (1) ICC Disp. Res. Bull. 23, 32 (2016).
189. *Ibid.*
190. ICC Arbitration Rules, Art. 11(4).
191. Andrea Carlevaris & Rocio Digón, *Arbitrator Challenges under the ICC Rules and Practice,* (1) ICC Disp. Res. Bull. 23, 30 (2016).
192. *Ibid.*
193. ICC Arbitration Rules, Art. 14(1).
194. The ICC system seems preferable to the ICSID procedure with regard to challenges, where it is either the two other arbitrators or the President of the World Bank make the decision. The former will understandably feel uncomfortable deciding the fate of a fellow member of the tribunal, whereas the latter is not an arbitration specialist. Moreover, a decision made at the Plenary Session will appear more objective and fair, than that made by a single person, member of a financial institution.

Table 3 ICC Challenges

Challenge Accepted	*Challenge Rejected*
- A co-arbitrator had rendered an expert opinion on the matter in arbitration in the preceding judicial proceedings without disclosing it in the Statement of independence.[195] - After the confirmation, an arbitrator disclosed that he had previously advised the nominating party and, as such, had taken part in the project, which led to the dispute.[196] - A foreign office of the chair's law firm represented a client in a lawsuit against the parent company of the party, which brought a challenge.[197] - A State and a State entity, respondents in the proceedings, challenged an arbitrator because he had acted in matters brought against them, some of which were still ongoing.[198] - The respondent challenged an arbitrator appointed on its behalf by the Court, because of his participation as a chairman in a non-ICC case concerning the same construction project. The challenged arbitrator had not disclosed his participation in the previous matter.[199]	- The claimant challenged an arbitrator for communicating to the respondent's representatives at a conference sometime before the hearing, alleging that his objective had been to promote himself seeking a business relationship with the respondent. The arbitrator replied indicating that he took no part in the organization of the said conference, and that he had no information about the invitees. Moreover, his contact with the respondents had been very limited and not substantial. [200] - One of the parties challenged an arbitrator alleging that he lacked independence, because he had lived and worked in the same country as the other party for more than twelve years. However, the arbitrator did not share a nationality with the other party, and had simply studied in that country for two years, working in various international law firms thereafter.[201] - An arbitrator was challenged for having a relationship with the lawyer of one of the parties. He had supervised the latter's thesis and did not contribute to its publication financially.[202]

[c] Replacement

The ICC Rules allow the Court to replace an arbitrator, on its own initiative, 'when it decides that the arbitrator is prevented de jure or de facto from fulfilling the arbitrator's functions, or that the arbitrator is not fulfilling those functions in accordance with the

195. Anne Marie Whitesell, *Independence in ICC Arbitration: ICC Court Practice Concerning the Appointment, Confirmation, Challenge and Replacement of Arbitrators*, ICC Intl. Ct. Arb. Bull., Special Supplement 2007, Independence of Arbitrators, 7, 27 (2008).
196. *Ibid.*, p. 28.
197. *Ibid.*
198. *Ibid.*, p. 29.
199. *Ibid.*
200. *Ibid.*, p. 30.
201. *Ibid.*
202. *Ibid.*

Rules or within the prescribed time limits'.[203] This is a particular feature of the ICC, which allows the institution to intervene even after confirmation in order to continue monitoring the conduct of arbitrators. The procedure followed is similar to that of a challenge: the Court will give all the parties concerned an opportunity for a comment before making a decision during the Plenary Session.

The authority under Article 15(2) is generally used by the Court as a policing power. For example, the president of the tribunal was replaced in a situation where the arbitrators could not agree with one another, which significantly delayed the preparation of the award.[204] In another case, the replacement proceedings were initiated when a sole arbitrator was not able to attend any of the hearing times requested by the parties. The arbitrator resigned promptly upon notification of the replacement procedure initiated against him.[205] The Court may also initiate replacement proceedings when it is aware of certain facts that may give rise to doubts as to the independence and impartiality of the arbitrator, but that were not disclosed. This scenario does not represent the current practice, however.[206]

§4.05 CONCLUSION

The analysis on choice of forum, applicable law and appointment and challenges of arbitrators in this chapter is by no means comprehensive. It is meant to enunciate the differences between ICSID and non-ICSID arbitrations, as well as elicit and engage the reader into potential benefits and drawbacks in the choices available for resolving investor-State disputes. In that same vein, the following questions are intended to ponder further into the issues articulated.

Questions

(1) What is the extent to which international law applies in investor-State arbitration? Should it be more or less important?
(2) What is a conflict issue?
(3) What is the legal effect of the IBA Guidelines? Do the arbitrators have to follow them? Should they?
(4) Is an independent arbitrator necessarily impartial and vice versa?

203. ICC Arbitration Rules, Art. 15(2).
204. Jason Fry & Simon Greenberg, *The Arbitral Tribunal: Applications of Articles 7-12 of the ICC Rules in Recent Cases*, 20(2) ICC Intl. Ct. of Arbitration Bulletin 12, 29 (2009).
205. *Ibid.*
206. Anne Marie Whitesell, *Independence in ICC Arbitration: ICC Court Practice Concerning the Appointment, Confirmation, Challenge and Replacement of Arbitrators*, ICC Intl. Ct. Arb. Bull., Special Supplement 2007, Independence of Arbitrators, 7, 33 (2008).

CHAPTER 5

Expropriation

Treaty clauses and customary international law on expropriation clearly state that sovereigns have a right to expropriate. However, this right is not without limits. To be legitimate, the taking has to be for a public purpose, of a non-discriminatory nature, respectful of due process, and on payment of prompt and adequate compensation. These conditions seek to protect foreign investors' property against arbitrary expropriation and are omnipresent in modern public international law.

International law distinguishes direct expropriation from indirect expropriation. In the first case, the investor is dispossessed of its property; in the second, the investor keeps its property, but the value of the investment is severely affected by measures adopted attributable to the State.

While investors may legitimately expect that the State will not deprive them of the value of their investment, those expectations have to evaluate States' fundamental right to regulate for a public purpose. The tension between indirect expropriation, and the exercise of regulatory power is at the forefront of legal debate. The distinction between the two is not straightforward, and arbitral tribunals, as well as academic commentators, proceed on a case-by-case basis.

Different criteria have been put forward as helpful when distinguishing indirect expropriation and non-compensable regulation. This chapter will discuss these criteria, which include the effects of the measure on the value of investment, investors' legitimate expectations, the purpose of the measure, and proportionality of the regulation to its objectives. Generally, a variety of the aforementioned factors is pondered, but the ultimate goal is to distinguish whether the government took a measure that specifically targeted the investor who claims to have been expropriated, or whether it was a regulation of general application, which has negatively affected the investment.

§5.01 INTRODUCTION

Investing in any industry or sector can be a bet against the unknown. There are many risks associated with allocation of funds, especially concerning foreign investments. Indeed, many investors[1] seek to maximize the value of their investments and their assets by taking risks in their business decision-making. When dealing with foreign investment, that is, the investment of capital from a source which is not originated in the host State receiving the capital injection through investment, the risk of losing private property or part of its value due to measures taken by the State may be even greater than it is for domestic investments.

The need for international economic cooperation and the importance of free capital flow in the economy is requisite to increase foreign investment worldwide. Thus, investment treaties, whether bilateral or multilateral, seek to provide investors with security, confidence and market transparency while leveraging the economic interests of the signatory countries. However, one of the risks faced by foreign investment is the risk of expropriation of tangible and intangible rights through the adoption of one or more governmental measures. Matters such as environmental and health issues, control of the markets, and the investments' impact on the country's culture are some of the factors which may drive States to interfere with the investors' freedom.

Certainly, countries have an imperative to regulate for the general welfare of their citizens. Moreover, certain State actions may be driven by the political and financial environment of the country. However, host States are called to respect and honor the legal protections provided in investment treaties and relied upon by foreign investors.

The widespread phenomenon of privatization of certain industries in the twentieth century went hand in hand with the conclusion of new BITs.[2] In addition to selling off publicly owned or managed companies, States recognized a need to create a stable regulatory environment for the development of the private industry.[3] As a consequence, the drafters included among other protections, clauses that prohibit expropriation, or the taking of the investor's property by the State, without prompt and adequate compensation. In the modern world, it was rare for a State to nationalize a whole industry or directly appropriate an asset that belonged to a private business. As it will be analyzed later in this chapter, Venezuela is the exception. Under the Chavez regime, Venezuela nationalized many industries which prompted investor-State disputes under ICSID.

This chapter will begin by giving a definition of expropriation (§5.02). It will then examine the different types of expropriatory measures (§5.03) and the calculation of compensation when State breaches its obligation (§5.04).

1. As used in this Chapter, the term 'investor' refers to the person who can be either an individual or a legal entity.
2. Michael W. Reisman & Robert D. Sloane, *Indirect Expropriation and Its Valuation in the BIT Generation*, Faculty Scholarship Series. Paper 1002, 117 (2004).
3. *Ibid.*

§5.02 DEFINITION OF EXPROPRIATION

The protection of foreigners has been incorporated into the law of nations since the nineteenth century.[4] The minimum standard of treatment of aliens has two essential elements: the protection of the person and of his or her property. The fundamental right to property is widely recognized and protected by such instruments as the European Convention on Human Rights.[5] It is no surprise that public international law has also sought to protect more specifically the right of foreigners not to have their property taken or expropriated by the State where they have decided to invest.[6]

One of the defining elements of investment may be risk, but investors may not want to invest in a country where the government arbitrarily decides at a given moment to appropriate their assets. Hence, all States generally include a provision regulating expropriation in the bilateral and multilateral treaties they have signed. The treaty clauses on expropriation coexist with customary international law, and arbitral awards all seeking to clarify when precisely a taking occurs, such that it gives rise to a claim for compensation.

At the other end of the spectrum is the State's right to regulate in the public interest. Many developing States have signed treaties guaranteeing investors protection from expropriation to attract foreign investment for economic development purposes. However, some of these countries are also attractive to foreign investors, because their legislation is less stringent and allows the investors more liberties with their business. Yet, an important part of the economic development is sustainability; therefore, the States have been increasingly aware of the environmental issues, public health, etc. When States enact legislation aiming to improve the state of the environment and social welfare, often the investor's rights are affected in a negative manner. This is due to the fact that it may be more costly to comply with the new, more stringent legislation.

When addressing issues germane to expropriation, there is a tension between a government's right to regulate for a public purpose and the investor's legitimate expectations that its investment will not suffer from governmental measures. When deciding whether a governmental measure amounts to a taking which would give rise to compensation, tribunals have to weigh these competing interests to determine on a case-by-case basis the relevant outcome.

What is Expropriation?

Expropriation is a taking by the host State of an investor's rights or properties. Some expropriations may be clear and imminent; others are achieved by depriving the investor of rights which result in the investor's loss of control, use, enjoyment or value of its property.

4. Sebastián López Escarcena, *Indirect Expropriation in International Law*, 2 (Edward Elgar 2014).
5. Council of Europe, *European Convention for the Protection of Human Rights and Fundamental Freedoms, as amended by Protocols Nos. 11 and 14*, 4 November 1950, ETS 5, http://www.refworld.org/docid/3ae6b3b04.html (accessed 23 May 2018).
6. *See* OECD Draft Convention on the Protection of Foreign Property.

Important terminological clarifications must be made regarding the distinction between expropriation and nationalization (A). Moreover, direct expropriation should be distinguished from indirect or creeping expropriation (B).

[A] Nationalization

Although many investment treaties would define the terms 'expropriation or nationalization' under the 'Expropriation' article or chapter, these two are different terms and should not be used interchangeably. While nationalization does involve losing proprietary rights of individual owners, the object behind the action is to provide for the domestication of the expropriated activity as a whole, without exceptions. As UNCTAD put it: '[n]ationalization usually refers to massive or large-scale takings of private property in all economic sectors or on an industry – or sector-specific basis.'[7] Expropriation, by contrast, has a narrower scope, and tends in most cases to be more directed towards one specific investor's interests.

One of the most famous cases of nationalization took place in Libya in 1973–1974, when the el-Qaddafi government took over the interests and properties in oil business located on its territory, owned by private companies.[8] Politically motivated, the acts of nationalization were carried out, first, in response to the UK's lack of action when Iran occupied three islands in the Persian Gulf, which were nominally under British patronage.[9] The second wave of takings was in retaliation to the US supporting Israel in the Arab-Israeli conflict.[10]

These actions by the Libyan Government led to three arbitrations, in which some of the most important principles of customary international law on nationalization were enounced.[11] In the *Texaco/Calasiatic* case, the sole arbitrator Jean-René Dupuy declared that the UN Resolution 1803 of December 1962 reflects the state of the customary international law in the field.[12] This conclusion has generally been accepted

7. UNCTAD, *Expropriation*, UNCTAD Series on Issues in International Invesment Agreements II, 5 (United Nations 2012), http://unctad.org/en/Docs/unctaddiaeia2011d7_en.pdf (accessed 30 May 2018).
8. Robert B. von Mehren & P. Nicholas Kourides, *International Arbitrations Between States And Foreign Private Parties: The Libyan Nationalization Cases*, 75 Am. J. Intl. L. 476–477 (1981).
9. *Ibid.*, pp. 484–485.
10. *Ibid.*, p. 485.
11. *BP Exploration Co. (Libya) Ltd. v. The Government of the Libyan Arab Republic,* Award on the Merits, 53 ILR 297 (1979); *Texaco Overseas Petroleum Co./California Asiatic Oil Co. v. The Government of the Libyan Arab Republic,* Award on the Merits, 53 ILR 389 (1979); *Libyan American Oil Co. v. The Government of the Libyan Arab Republic* 20 ILM 1 (1981).
12. Professor Jean-René Dupuy stated: 'Resolution 1803 (XVII) seems to this Tribunal to reflect the state of customary law existing in this field. Indeed, on the occasion of the vote on a resolution finding the existence of a customary rule, the States concerned clearly express their views. The consensus by a majority of States belonging to the various representative groups indicates without the slightest doubt universal recognition of the rules therein incorporated, i.e., with respect to nationalization and compensation the use of the rules in force in the nationalizing State, but all this in conformity with international law.' *Texaco Overseas Petroleum Co./California Asiatic Oil Co. v. The Government of the Libyan Arab Republic,* Award on the Merits, 53 ILR 389 (1979), para. 87.

by other academics since.[13] Resolution 1803 confirmed the States' right of permanent sovereignty over natural resources, and its corollary, the sovereign right to nationalize.[14] However, it also set out the bounds for nationalization, which should be based on public interest and provide for prompt and adequate compensation.[15]

All three arbitrators agreed that, while nationalization is a sovereign right, it is by no means an absolute right.[16] More specifically, all three arbitrators separately concluded that a sovereign could bind itself when making commitments in international law.[17] They restated another basic principle of international law, *pacta sunt servanda* – agreements must be complied with. This principle also found support in Libyan law.[18] Libya had included stabilization clauses that limited its recourse to nationalization in all concession contracts entered into with the foreign oil companies.[19] The arbitrators held that by nationalizing in spite of those commitments, Libya breached its international obligations and had to pay compensation to the oil companies.[20]

In the more recent years, Venezuela carried out multiple nationalizations, taking over the steel and oil industries. This led to numerous ICSID arbitrations fueling the law on expropriation.[21]

[B] Direct and Indirect Expropriation

[1] Direct Expropriation

Direct expropriation or taking of property by a State occurs when it takes a measure, which aims to deprive the investor of the value of its investment.[22] Direct expropriation may come in the form of a decree or by physical force. The 2012 US Model BIT refers to interference 'with a tangible or intangible property right or property interest in an

13. Robert B. von Mehren & P. Nicholas Kourides, *International Arbitrations Between States And Foreign Private Parties: The Libyan Nationalization Cases*, 75 Am. J. Intl. L. 476, 526 (1981).
14. *Ibid.*, p. 522.
15. *Ibid.*
16. *Ibid.*, pp. 516–518.
17. *Ibid.*, pp. 520–521.
18. *Ibid.*, pp. 517–518.
19. *Ibid.*, pp. 519–520.
20. *Ibid.*, p. 513.
21. *See*, for example, *Venezuela Holdings, B.V., et al (case formerly known as Mobil Corporation, Venezuela Holdings, B.V., et al.) v. Bolivarian Republic of Venezuela*, ICSID Case No. ARB/07/27, Award (9 Oct. 2014); *Tidewater Inc., Tidewater Investment SRL, Tidewater Caribe, C.A., et al. v. The Bolivarian Republic of Venezuela*, ICSID Case No. ARB/10/5, Award (13 Mar. 2015); *Tenaris S.A. and Talta – Trading e Marketing Sociedade Unipessoal Lda. v. Bolivarian Republic of Venezuela*, ICSID Case No. ARB/11/26, Award (29 Jan. 2016).
22. *Copper Mesa Mining Corporation v. Republic of Ecuador*, PCA No. 2012-2, Award (15 Mar. 2016), paras 6.58–6.59.

investment'.[23] There is also a general consensus among tribunals that revocation of a permit or concession constitutes direct expropriation.[24]

While distinguishing it from indirect expropriation, the arbitral tribunal in *Metalclad Corp. v. Mexico* described certain characteristics of direct expropriation, such as the 'open, deliberate, and acknowledged takings of property, such as outright seizure or formal or obligatory transfer of title in favour of the host State'.[25] The most classic example of direct expropriation would be the government sending military to take over a factory owned by the foreign investor. This notion is also referred to as expropriation de jure. In the *Feldman v. Mexico* case, the tribunal stated: '[r]ecognizing direct expropriation is relatively easy: governmental authorities take over a mine or factory, depriving the investor of all meaningful benefits of ownership or control.'[26]

Direct expropriations are not as common in the modern times, but there are some examples following nationalizations carried out by some Latin American countries, such as Venezuela. For example, in *Tidewater v. Venezuela*, the government promulgated a law (Reserve Law) that reserved hydrocarbon activities to the State.[27] Pursuant to this law, the day it was published, a State-owned company called PDVSA (Petróleos de Venezuela, S.A.) took over the operations and assets of a number of companies, among which was Tidewater. The investor's vessels were physically seized as well.[28] In another case, *Venezuela Holdings v. Venezuela*, Mobil's interests in Venezuela were automatically transferred to an affiliate of PDVSA following a failure to reach an agreement with regard to creation of new mixed companies, where PDVSA or one of its affiliates would hold at least a 60% interest.[29]

In both of these cases, there was no dispute that direct expropriation had occurred. The issues raised in arbitration concerned the lawfulness requirement and the compensation to which investors should be entitled to in such a situation.

[2] Indirect Expropriation

Most treaties in the expropriation clause also make a reference to indirect expropriation, or measures tantamount to expropriation.[30] This type of expropriation may be defined as 'covert or incidental interference with the use of property which has the

23. 2012 US Model BIT, Annex B Expropriation, https://ustr.gov/sites/default/files/BIT%20text%20for%20ACIEP%20Meeting.pdf (accessed 23 May 2018).
24. *See Antoine Goetz et consorts v. République du Burundi*, ICSID Case No. ARB/95/3, Award (10 Feb. 1999).
25. *Metalclad Corporation v. United Mexican* States, ICSID Case No. ARB(AF)/97/1, Award (30 Aug. 2000).
26. *Marvin Roy Feldman Karpa v. United Mexican States*, ICSID Case No. ARB(AF)/99/1 (also known as *Marvin Feldman v. Mexico*), Award (16 Dec. 2002), p. 36.
27. *Tidewater Inc., Tidewater Investment SRL, Tidewater Caribe, C.A., et al. v. The Bolivarian Republic of Venezuela*, ICSID Case No. ARB/10/5, Award (13 Mar. 2015), p. 33.
28. *Ibid.*, pp. 34–35.
29. *Venezuela Holdings, B.V., et al. (case formerly known as Mobil Corporation, Venezuela Holdings, B.V., et al.) v. Bolivarian Republic of Venezuela*, ICSID Case No. ARB/07/27, Award (9 Oct. 2014), pp. 45–47.
30. *See*, for example, US Model BIT 2012, Art. 6; France Model BIT 2006, Art. 6; Energy Charter Treaty 34 ILM 360 (1995), Art. 13.

effect of depriving the owner, in whole or in significant part, of the use or reasonably-to-be-expected economic benefit of property even if not necessarily to the obvious benefit of the host State'.[31] This concept includes de facto expropriation, where the main or ostensible aim of the measure is to regulate a certain sector in the public interest. For example, in *Metalclad*, the government revoked a permit to operate a hazardous waste plant ostensibly for reasons of environmental protection, but the arbitral tribunal, nevertheless, found that there was expropriation.[32]

Treaties and arbitral tribunals also refer to 'creeping expropriation', or a 'measure tantamount to expropriation',[33] which is a sub-category of indirect expropriation.[34] What sets creeping expropriation apart is that it consists of multiple actions carried out over a period of time.[35] While the first act does not violate the investor's rights, the cumulative effect of the measures taken by the State leads to the deprivation of the investment's value.[36] As clarified by the Iran-US Claims tribunal, 'the Tribunal prefers the term "deprivation" to the term "taking", although they are largely synonymous, because the latter may be understood to imply that the Government has acquired something of value, which is not required'.[37] The *Starrett v. Iran* tribunal went further to clarify that: 'it is recognized in international law that measures taken by a State can interfere with property rights to such an extent that these rights are rendered so useless that they must be deemed to have been expropriated, even though the State does not purport to have expropriated then and the legal title remains in with the original owner'.[38]

The 2012 US Model BIT defines indirect expropriation as one of the two types of situations that give rise to valid expropriation claims. In this case, 'an action or series of actions by a Party has an effect equivalent to indirect expropriation without formal transfer of title or outright seizure'.[39] Although this determination is to be made on a case-by-case basis, some of the factors that must be taken into account, as per the 2012 US Model BIT, Annex B, are: (1) the economic impact of the government action; (2) the

31. *Metalclad Corporation v. The United Mexican States*, ICSID Case No. ARB(AF)/97/1, Award (30 Aug. 2000), p. 28.
32. *Ibid.*, p. 29.
33. NAFTA Art. 1110(1). *See also* NAFTA, Art. 1110(8): 'For purposes of this Article and for greater certainty, a non-discriminatory measure of general application shall not be considered a measure tantamount to an expropriation of a debt security or loan covered by this Chapter solely on the ground that the measure imposes costs on the debtor that cause it to default on the debt.'
34. The tribunal in Waste Management noted that NAFTA Art. 1110 seems to make a distinction between direct or indirect expropriation and measures tantamount to expropriation. However, other tribunals appear to support the view that such measures are subsumed under the definition of indirect expropriation.
35. *See Generation Ukraine, Inc. v. Ukraine*, ICSID Case No. ARB/00/9, Award (16 Sep. 2003), pp. 87–88.
36. *Ibid.*: 'Creeping expropriation is a form of indirect expropriation with a distinctive temporal quality in the sense that it encapsulates the situation whereby a series of acts attributable to the State over a period of time culminate in the expropriatory taking of such property.' *See also* Art. 15 of ILC Draft Convention on State responsibility: Breach consisting of a composite act.
37. Iran-US Claims Tribunal, *Tippetts, Abbett, McCarthy, Stratton v. TAMS-AFFA*, 6 Iran–US CTR 219, 225.
38. Iran-US Claims Tribunal, *Starrett Housing Corp. v. Iran* (Interlocutory Award dated 19 Dec. 1983), 4 Iran–US CTR 122 (1983).
39. 2012 US Model BIT, Annex B.

extent to which the government action interferes with distinct, reasonable investment-backed expectations; and (3) the character of the actions by the government.[40]

Generally speaking, when States act, they do so through the adoption of regulatory decisions by government agencies or by the adoption of laws from the legislative power. Many times, State action can be drafted and executed in a way that will not have an automatic direct effect on investment, but rather will start creating situations such that will make it more onerous or costly for an investor to keep or sell its investment. As will be further explained below, regulatory measures that are discriminatory and directed at specific investments or investors, may be an expropriation.

The US-Egypt BIT of 1986, which entered into force in June 1992, provides a series of examples of what actions may constitute expropriation, such as:

> the levying of taxation, the compulsory sale of all or part of such investment, or impairment or deprivation of management, control or economic value of such an investment by the national or company concerned...[41]

Often, certain measures could potentially constitute both expropriation and denial of equal protection under the law or a violation of national treatment clauses.

Special Issues Relating to Indirect Expropriation

The line between indirect expropriation and non-compensable regulation has not been clearly defined and will be determined on a case-by-case basis, depending on the pertinent facts and circumstances. States are sovereigns and as such have the right and duty to regulate within their territories. Thus, not all measures constitute indirect expropriation and therefore subject to compensation.

Basically, all treaties address indirect expropriation, but are silent on non-compensable regulatory measures. Only a limited few actually address non-compensable regulatory measures, including the European Convention on Human Rights, US-Free Trade Agreements, and US and Canada Model BITs.[42] Arbitral tribunals have not been consistent in applying the criteria to determine which measures qualify as expropriation requiring compensation and which emanate from a non-discriminatory regulatory measure of the State that does not require compensation. Many doctrines, standards or theories have been developed for dissecting the indirect expropriation non-compensable regulation conundrum. The principal theories that have been developed in this area include the 'sole effects' doctrine (a), the legitimate expectations of the investor (b), the police powers doctrine (c), substantial deprivation test (d), and proportionality (e).

40. *Ibid.*
41. Treaty Between the United States of America and the Arab Republic of Egypt Concerning the Reciprocal Encouragement and Protection of Investments (as modified) (11 Mar. 1986), Art. III.
42. Other texts that address non-compensable expropriation based on regulatory measures are the Harvard Draft Convention on International Responsibility and the Third Restatement of Foreign Relations of the United States. This is a body of work produced by scholars that is considered influential doctrine, even if it does not rise to the level of State practice.

[a] 'Sole Effects' Doctrine

The 'sole effects' doctrine focuses on 'the effect on the owner'[43] as its main criterion. The doctrine is sometimes attributed to the *Metalclad v. Mexico* tribunal, which held that it need not 'consider the motivation or intent of the adoption' of the government measure and that deprivation effect on the investor was sufficient to characterize expropriation.[44] In other words, intent is less important than the effect, as clearly stated in the *Tippetts* case: '[t]he intent of the government is less important than the effects of the measure on the owner, and the form of the measures of control or interference is less important than the reality of their impact.'[45]

In the same vein, the *Santa Elena v. Costa Rica* tribunal refused to hear the State's submissions on its international obligations to preserve the unique ecological land in question when considering the State's obligation to compensate.[46] According to the arbitral panel, 'the purpose of protecting the environment for which the property was taken does not alter the legal character of the taking for which adequate compensation must be paid'.[47] Other tribunals have also demonstrated their support for the sole effects doctrine, such as *Tokios Tokelès v. Ukraine* and *Telenor Communications v. Hungary*.[48]

The importance of the effect on the owner as a criterion for finding expropriation does not appear to be controversial.[49] However, the question of whether it should be the sole factor has raised debates over the years. More specifically, States and academics have vindicated the sovereign right to regulate in the public interest.[50] A case on point is *Saluka* where the tribunal stated that State intent will be considered: '[i]t is now established in international law that States are not liable to pay compensation to a foreign investor when, in the normal exercise of their regulatory powers, they adopt in a non-discriminatory manner bona fide regulations that are aimed at the general welfare.'[51]

43. Sebastián López Escarcena, *Indirect Expropriation in International Law*, 79 (Edward Elgar 2014).
44. *See Metalclad Corporation v. The United Mexican States*, ICSID Case No. ARB(AF)/97/1, Award (30 Aug. 2000), p. 30.
45. *See* Iran-US Claims Tribunal, *Starrett Housing Corp. v. Iran* (Interlocutory Award dated 19 Dec. 1983), 4 Iran–US CTR 122, 225–226 (1983).
46. *Compañia del Desarrollo de Santa Elena S.A. v. Republic of Costa Rica*, ICSID Case No. ARB/96/1, Award (17 Feb. 2000), p. 192.
47. *Ibid.*
48. *See Tokios Tokelès v. Ukraine* (2005) 20 ICSID Review-FILJ 205, para. 120; *Vivendi Universal SA v. Argentina*, ICSID Case No. ARB/97/3, Award (20 Aug. 2007), para. 7.5.20; *Telenor Mobile Communications AS v. Hungary*, ICSID Case No. ARB/04/15, Award (13 Sep. 2006), paras 67, 70: '[T]he test the Tribunal has to apply is whether, viewed as a whole, the investment has suffered substantial erosion of value.'
49. *See* Sebastián López Escarcena, *Indirect Expropriation in International Law*, 79 (Edward Elgar 2014).
50. *See*, for example, *Renée Rose Levy de Levi v. Republic of Peru*, ICSID Case No. ARB/10/17, Award (26 Feb. 2014).
51. *Saluka Investments B.V. v. The Czech Republic*, UNCITRAL, Partial Award (17 Mar. 2006), p. 52.

[b] Investor's Legitimate Expectations

The purpose of investment treaties is to encourage investment while countries provide minimum guarantees of security to prospective investors. Thus, the treaty is the first source to determine what the expectations of the investors are.

Investors' expectations are not only limited to the end result of their businesses, these also include, among other things, the host States' compliance with minimal protections granted by the international agreement. Such protections are FET, FPS, NT, MFN and, for our purposes, protection from expropriation.

Multiple BITs include compliance with investors' legitimate expectations as one of the factors to be taken into account when determining whether there has been indirect expropriation.[52] Investors' expectations must be based on reasonable and concrete facts to yield a reasonable expectation.[53] One of the aspects to consider when determining whether the investor has reasonable expectations is the negotiation with the government, as well as the factors that played a role as a basis for the written contract among the parties under which the investment was made. As Professor Schreuer noted in the context of FET, 'the investor's legitimate expectations [are] based on [a] clearly perceptible legal framework and on any undertakings and representations made explicitly or implicitly by the host State'.[54]

Some arbitral tribunals have explicitly stated that treaties should not be used to protect the investor from bad business decisions.[55] In *Methanex v. USA*, the panel highlighted the fact that the investor had entered a market notorious for monitoring 'the use and impact of chemical compounds and commonly prohibit[ing] or restrict[ing] the use of some of those compounds for environmental and/or health reasons'.[56] Methanex itself had participated in these processes by hiring lobbyists to represent its interests. As such, the investor could not have legitimately expected the government not to intervene with its use of certain chemicals.

However, the *Methanex* tribunal reserves the hypothesis, in which the host State would have offered 'specific commitments' to induce the investment.[57] It does seem logical that an investor's expectations would be legitimate if he relies on express assurances given by the government.[58] It should be noted that legitimate expectations

52. For example, 2012 US Model BIT: 'The determination of whether an action or series of actions by a Party, in a specific fact situation, constitutes an indirect expropriation, requires a case-by-case, fact-based inquiry that considers, among other factors: ... the extent to which the government action interferes with distinct, reasonable investment-backed expectations.'
53. *See Consortium RFCC v. Royaume du Maroc*, ICSID Case No. ARB/00/6, Award (22 Dec. 2003), p. 45.
54. Christoph Schreuer, *Fair and Equitable Treatment in Arbitral Practice*, 6(3) J. World Inv. & Trade 357, 374 (2005).
55. *See Saluka Investments B.V. v. The Czech Republic*, UNCITRAL, Partial Award (17 Mar. 2006), p. 172: '[N]o investment treaty is an insurance or guarantee of investment success, especially when the investor makes bad business decisions.'
56. *Methanex Corporation v. United States of America*, UNCITRAL, Final Award on Jurisdiction and Merits (3 Aug. 2005), Part IV, Ch. D, p. 5.
57. *Ibid.*
58. *See Revere Copper & Brass, Inc. v. OPIC*, 17 ILM 1321, 1340 (1978); *see also Waste Management, Inc. v. United Mexican States*, ICSID Case No. ARB(AF)/98/2, Award (2 Jun. 2000).

alone do not justify compensation by the State, and it merely constitutes one of the factors that an arbitral tribunal will take into account when determining whether indirect expropriation occurred. However, in the absence of expropriation, the breach of legitimate expectation may justify compensation when it held to amount to breach of the FET due to the investor.

[c] Police Powers Doctrine

Academic commentators and arbitrators alike have remarked on the harsh impact of the sole effects doctrine on the ability of States to regulate. The arbitral practice seems to have moved away from this theory by adopting the police powers doctrine.[59] Initially developed in the US, this theory has particularly influenced NAFTA tribunals. According to this doctrine, when the State is acting in the interests of public policy, measures taken in furtherance of such goals or interests will not necessarily constitute expropriation and thus, do not require compensation.

At first, the public purpose criterion was merely accepted as one of the factors to be considered when establishing indirect expropriation. The *Azurix* tribunal referred to and criticized the *S.D. Myers v. Canada* award for holding that 'Parties [to the Bilateral Treaty] are not liable for economic injury that is the consequence of bona fide regulation within the accepted police powers of the State.'[60] The arbitrators pointed out that public purpose is one of the requirements for the expropriation to be lawful, which does not obviate the need for the prompt, adequate and effective compensation. As such, it cannot be the sole distinguishing criterion for whether there is indirect expropriation and may only be contemplated among other factors, including the effects of the measure and the investor's expectations.[61]

However, multiple other tribunals have since then given the full effect to the police powers theory, which is clearly established today.[62] The first award to formally rely on the doctrine was rendered in the *Methanex v. USA* case.[63] The tribunal stated that, 'as a matter of general international law, a non-discriminatory regulation for a public purpose, which is enacted in accordance with due process and, which affects, *inter alios*, a foreign investor or investment is not deemed expropriatory and compensable unless specific commitments had been given by the regulating government to the then putative foreign investor contemplating investment that the government would refrain from such regulation'.[64]

59. *See*, generally, *Methanex Corporation v. United States of America*, UNCITRAL, Final Award on Jurisdiction and Merits (3 Aug. 2005).
60. *Azurix Corp. v. The Argentine Republic*, ICSID Case No. ARB/01/12, Award (14 Jul. 2006), p. 110.
61. *Ibid.*
62. For example, *see Tidewater Inc., Tidewater Investment SRL, Tidewater Caribe, C.A., et al. v. The Bolivarian Republic of Venezuela*, ICSID Case No. ARB/10/5, Award (13 Mar. 2015).
63. *See Methanex Corporation v. United States of America*, UNCITRAL, Final Award on Jurisdiction and Merits (3 Aug. 2005).
64. *Ibid.*, Part IV, Ch. D, p. 4.

As seen in the above excerpt from the *Methanex* award and other arbitral practice, tribunals consider that the police powers doctrine is part of customary international law and, hence, rely on it even if the BIT in question does not refer to it.[65] Note, however, that treaties are expressly including the language of the police powers exception. For example, the 2012 Model US BIT provides that:

> An uncompensated taking of an alien property or a deprivation of the use or enjoyment of property of an alien which results from the execution of tax laws; from a general change in the value of currency; from the action of the competent authorities of the State in the maintenance of public order, health or morality; or from the valid exercise of belligerent rights or otherwise incidental to the normal operation of the laws of the State shall not be considered wrongful.[66]

One would surmise that, in light of general acceptance of the measures exercised on the basis of the States' police powers not requiring compensation, that the arbitral practice has abandoned the *Santa Elena v. Costa Rica* and *Azurix* positions.

[d] Substantial Deprivation Test

As mentioned above, the sole effects doctrine is no longer a stand-alone method used to determine whether an indirect expropriation has occurred. The effects on the investor will of course play an important role in finding a compensable taking, but the definition of indirect expropriation would be too broad if it included any situation where a State measure had a negative impact on the value of the investment. As such, many tribunals have adopted a 'substantial deprivation test' to limit meritless claims.

Pope & Talbot v. Canada is often credited with the first application of the substantial deprivation test, where the arbitral tribunal suggested that there must be a deprivation of the investor's control over the day-to-day operations of its investment: 'the test is whether that interference is sufficiently restrictive to support a conclusion that the property has been "taken" from the owner'.[67] The arbitrators in *PSEG v. Turkey* further elaborated that 'there must be some form of deprivation of the investor in the control of the investment, the management of day-to-day operations of the company, interfering in the administration, impeding the distribution of dividends, interfering in

65. *See also Compañia del Desarrollo de Santa Elena S.A. v. Republic of Costa Rica*, ICSID Case No. ARB/96/1, Award (17 Feb. 2000), p. 52; *Suez, Sociedad General de Aguas de Barcelona S.A., and InterAguas Servicios Integrales del Agua S.A. v. The Argentine Republic*, ICSID Case No. ARB/03/17, Decision on Liability (30 Jul. 2010); Harvard Draft Convention on the International Responsibility of States for Injuries to Aliens: 'An uncompensated taking of an alien property or a deprivation of the use or enjoyment of property of an alien which results from the execution of tax laws; from a general change in the value of currency; from the action of the competent authorities of the State in the maintenance of public order, health or morality; or from the valid exercise of belligerent rights or otherwise incidental to the normal operation of the laws of the State shall not be considered wrongful.'
66. 2012 US Model BIT, Annex B Expropriation; *see also* 205 Norway Model BIT; Canada Model BIT.
67. *Pope & Talbot Inc. v. The Government of Canada*, UNCITRAL, Interim Award (26 Jun. 2000), p. 35.

the appointment of officials and managers, or depriving the company of its property or control in total or in part'.[68]

Numerous other tribunals have relied on the substantial deprivation test and used similar terms to describe it.[69] The result is that a regulatory measure has to deprive the investment of almost all of its value, or the investor of control, in order to be equivalent to expropriation, and not merely diminish the profits. For example, in *CMS v. Argentina*, the investor's revenues decreased by almost 75%, but it was not sufficient to constitute substantial deprivation.[70] The tribunal in *Vivendi v. Argentina* suggested that there has to be a 'complete or near complete deprivation of value'.[71]

[e] Proportionality

Despite the ubiquity of the use of police powers theory, several commentators have noted that a more nuanced approach should be adopted. The public purpose justification is criticized for giving the States a *carte blanche* to freely take the investors' property as long as they can find a public interest for such taking. It is suggested that, in determining whether there has been compensable expropriation, the tribunals should adopt a more balanced approach.[72] Not only should the effect on the investor and the purpose of the measure be examined, but also the legitimate expectations of the investor and proportionality of the State actions.[73]

Applying the proportionality analysis to indirect expropriation would limit the acceptable measures to those taken pursuant to legitimate public interest objectives and exercised in a manner proportionate to those objectives.[74] The idea of assessing the proportionality of a State's measures, which have necessarily adverse effect on a party, is not new. It has notably been done by the European Court of Human Rights (ECHR)

68. *PSEG Global, Inc., The North American Coal Corporation, and Konya Ingin Electrik Üretim ve Ticaret Limited Sirketi v. Republic of Turkey*, ICSID Case No. ARB/02/5, Award (19 Jan. 2007), p. 72.
69. *See*, generally, *CMS Gas Transmission Company v. The Republic of Argentina*, ICSID Case No. ARB/01/8, Award (12 May 2005); *Enron Corporation and Ponderosa Assets, L.P. v. Argentine Republic*, ICSID Case No. ARB/01/3 (also known as: *Enron Creditors Recovery Corp. and Ponderosa Assets, L.P. v. The Argentine Republic*), Award (22 May 2007); *LG&E Energy Corp., LG&E Capital Corp., and LG&E International, Inc.v. Argentine Republic*, ICSID Case No. ARB/02/1, Award (25 Jul. 2007); *Azurix Corp. v. The Argentine Republic*, ICSID Case No. ARB/01/12, Award (14 Jul. 2006); *Suez, Sociedad General de Aguas de Barcelona S.A., and InterAguas Servicios Integrales del Agua S.A. v. The Argentine Republic*, ICSID Case No. ARB/03/17, Decision on Liability (30 Jul. 2010).
70. *CMS Gas Transmission Company v. The Republic of Argentina*, ICSID Case No. ARB/01/8, Award (12 May 2005), pp. 22, 76–77.
71. *Compañiá de Aguas del Aconquija S.A. and Vivendi Universal S.A. v. Argentine Republic, ICSID Case No. ARB/97/3*, Award (20 Aug. 2007), p. 225.
72. Stephen Olynyck, *A Balanced Approach to Distinguishing Between Legitimate Regulation and Indirect Expropriation in Investor-State Arbitration*, 15 Intl. Trade & Bus. L. Rev. 254, 279 (2012).
73. *Ibid.*, p. 279.
74. Caroline Henckels, *Indirect Expropriation And The Right To Regulate: Revisiting Proportionality Analysis And The Standard Of Review In Investor-State Arbitration*, 15(1) J. Intl. Econ. L. 223, 228 (2012).

in the context of human rights violations, one of the rights being the right to property. The proportionality test is traditionally seen as having three prongs:[75]

(1) Is the measure suitable to attain its ostensible objective?
(2) Is the measure necessary (are there less onerous ways to achieve the same goal)?
(3) Is the measure reasonable in view of the competing interests (strict proportionality test)?

The most well-known example of proportionality analysis carried out in determining whether there is expropriation is found in the *Tecmed v. Mexico* award.[76] Beginning by emphasizing the deference that the tribunal owes to the State to define its own public policy, the arbitral panel continues to accept the mission of examining the State's actions, stating that 'there must be a reasonable relationship of proportionality between the charge or weight imposed to the foreign investor and the aim sought to be realized by any expropriatory measure'.[77] The tribunal in this case cited several ECHR decisions and adopted its definition of proportionality, such as reproduced above. Some commentators, however, have criticized the application of the analysis to Mexico's actions. The tribunal considered that Mexico denied the renewal of permit based primarily on political unrest in the country and not the environment protection. As such, it examined the proportionality of this denial against the suitability, necessity and reasonableness of the political circumstances and not environmental concerns.[78]

The tribunal in *Tecmed* concluded that public pressure on the government did not constitute a situation of necessity or crisis, which would have legitimized Mexico's actions.[79] Albeit some have commended this decision as going beyond the ostensible aim offered by a State to justify its actions and assessing the true purpose behind it, other commentators have expressed their reservations.[80]

§5.03 LAWFULNESS OF EXPROPRIATION

As mentioned previously, the State has the right to expropriate provided the expropriation satisfies the conditions of the customary international law or the applicable treaty. When the measures in question do not satisfy these conditions, the expropriation is considered unlawful and gives rise to a compensation obligation for the State (*see* below §5.04).

The protection treaty will define the lawfulness conditions, and it is always important to look at the precise language of the treaty. In general, most BITs refer to the

75. *Ibid.*, p. 227.
76. *Técnicas Medioambientales Tecmed, S.A. v. The United Mexican States*, ICSID Case No. ARB (AF)/00/2, Award (29 May 2003).
77. *Ibid.*, p. 47.
78. *Ibid.* pp. 50–51.
79. *See* Caroline Henckels, *Indirect Expropriation and the Right to Regulate: Revisiting Proportionality Analysis and the Standard of Review in Investor-State Arbitration*, 15(1) JIEL 223, 232 (2012).
80. *Ibid.*

following requirements, which will now be examined in more detail: public purpose or interest (A), due process (B), non-discriminatory nature (C) and compensation (D).

[A] Public Purpose or Interest

The notion of public purpose or interest has already been discussed in the context of defining indirect expropriation. Given that it is examined at the stage of verifying the existence of indirect taking when using the police powers test, the tribunals will generally not consider it for the second time when examining lawfulness. However, this requirement will still be examined in the context of direct expropriation.

Tribunals have noted that there has to be an actual public purpose behind the measure, which is to be demonstrated by the State. According to *ADC Affiliate Limited v. Hungary*, 'if mere reference to "public interest" can magically put such interest into existence and therefore satisfy this requirement, then this requirement would be rendered meaningless since the Tribunal can imagine no situation where this requirement would not have been met'.[81]

[B] Due Process

Most treaties indicate the necessity to respect the due process of law when expropriating.[82] This notion is familiar to American lawyers, who have seen the Due Process clause in the US Constitution.[83] It refers to a minimum level of procedural fairness, which should be followed in carrying out the expropriation.

The condition of due process was analyzed in the *Venezuela Holdings v. Venezuela* case.[84] The investor had alleged that its property had been expropriated by coercion and without following 'any established legal procedure'.[85] Venezuela had reserved the oil production activities in its territory to the State, and private companies were only allowed to participate in those activities through mixed enterprises, in which the State would hold a majority interest. The Orinoco Oil Belt, where Claimants operated, was an exception to this legal regime. However, in 2007 Venezuela decided to subject the Orinoco Oil Belt to the same framework as all other oil production. The State enacted a law requiring private companies to change their structure and become mixed enterprises by a certain date, after which the State would nationalize their holdings. In particular, the law provided for a four-month negotiation period, during

81. *ADC Affiliate Limited and ADC & ADMC Management Limited v. The Republic of Hungary*, ICSID Case No. ARB/03/16, Award (2 Oct. 2006), p. 79.
82. *See*, for example, 2012 US Model BIT, Art. 6: 'Neither Party may expropriate or nationalize a covered investment either directly or indirectly through measures equivalent to expropriation or nationalization ("expropriation"), except: ... in accordance with due process of law and Article 5 [Minimum Standard of Treatment] (1) through (3)'; Norway Model BIT.
83. US Constitution, Amend. V and XIV.
84. *See Venezuela Holdings, B.V., et al. (case formerly known as Mobil Corporation, Venezuela Holdings, B.V., et al.) v. Bolivarian Republic of Venezuela*, ICSID Case No. ARB/07/27, Award (9 Oct. 2014).
85. *Ibid.*, p. 98.

which companies could change their structure to comply with the oil production regime. The tribunal held that the negotiation provision, which was successfully used by other oil companies, was sufficient to comply with the due process requirement, making the nationalization carried out at the end of the four months lawful.[86]

[C] Non-discriminatory Nature

The condition that the expropriatory measure cannot discriminate against a specific investor seems relatively straightforward. It means that the measure is applied in the same way to the investor in question and other investors. 'Discriminatory taking is one that singles out a particular person or group of people without a reasonable basis.'[87]

The tribunal in *LIAMCO v. Libya* considered that a political motive does not itself 'constitute sufficient proof of a purely discriminatory measure'.[88] Noting that LIAMCO was not the first company to be nationalized, neither the only oil nor American company, the arbitral panel held that Libya's actions were not discriminatory.[89]

[D] Compensation

Countries signatories to investment treaties vow to provide the nationals of the other contracting party with minimum substantive protection, which have been agreed to under the treaty. One of the most common protections, which comes, as recognition of the right to property is that the foreign national has a right to be compensated for expropriation in a fair way.[90] Countries can expropriate inasmuch as adequate compensation, as defined by the treaty in question, is given.

Under the CAFTA-DR, the expropriation must be accompanied by the payment of 'prompt, adequate and effective compensation', which is also referred to as the Hull formula and is widely used in protection treaties.[91] The CAFTA-DR also sets forth four minimum requirements of a prompt, adequate and effective compensation. Therefore, compensation shall:

(a) be paid without delay;
(b) be equivalent to the fair market value (FMV) of the expropriated investment immediately before the expropriation took place ('the date of expropriation');
(c) not reflect any change in value occurring because the intended expropriation had become known earlier; and

86. *Ibid.* pp. 101–102.
87. Noah Rubins & N. Stephan Kinsella, *International Investment, Political Risk and Dispute Resolution. A Practitioner's Guide*, 177 (Oceana 2005).
88. *Libyan American Oil Co. (LIAMCO) v. Libya*, 20 ILM 1, 60 (1981).
89. *Ibid.*
90. *See* Lucy Reed, Jan Paulsson & Nigel Blackaby, *Guide to ICSID Arbitration*, 88 (Kluwer Law International 2011).
91. For example, 2012 US Model BIT 2012, Canada Model BIT, ECT.

(d) be fully realizable and freely transferable.[92]

Compensation is awarded on the basis of public international law principles, not according to national law.[93] In this context, the question is what constitutes FMV. Pursuant to the International Glossary of Business Valuation Terms of the American Society of Appraisers, FMV is:

> The price, expressed in terms of cash equivalents, at which property would change hands between a hypothetical willing and able buyer and a hypothetical willing and able seller, acting at arms length in an open and unrestricted market, when neither is under compulsion to buy or sell and when both have reasonable knowledge of the relevant facts.[94]

The above definition, which some arbitral tribunals have echoed, indicates that a payment of the compensation at a FMV must be agreed on based on negotiations at arms' length and free of coercion from the paying State, which is in a more powerful position. The *Vivendi v. Argentina* tribunal held that words 'actual value' in a protection treaty may be interpreted as FMV.[95]

Other methods of valuation of FMV, including replacement value, book value, discounted cash flow (DCF) analysis will be dealt with in Chapter 9 on Damages and Costs more thoroughly. Suffice it to say that the DCF analysis is most used now by arbitral tribunal when dealing with a going concern for which there is no comparable market. As such, the DCF analysis evaluates a company based on its future earnings and not the value of its assets.

Compensation, however, is not without limits. At the core of investor-State arbitration is the protection of investors' interests when dealing with a country as counterparty, which by definition is politically and financially stronger than the investor. Thus, while evaluating the measure of compensation, the arbitral tribunal's goal is also to avoid a double repayment in the favor of the investor, among other potential inequalities, while mitigating the losses and damages to which it can be exposed. Compensation for lawful and unlawful expropriation is discussed in detail in Chapter 9.

---

92. Dominican Republic–Central America Free Trade Agreement, https://ustr.gov/sites/default/files/uploads/agreements/cafta/asset_upload_file328_4718.pdf (accessed 23 May 2018), Ch. 10.
93. Markham Ball, *Assessing Damages in Claims by Investors Against States*, 16(2) ICSID Rev-.-F.I.L.J. 408–411. (2001).
94. American Society of Appraisers, International Glossary of Business Valuation Terms [cited in] American Institute of Certified Public Accountants, Inc., Statement on Standards for Valuations Services No. 1, Appendix B, June 2007, http://www.aicpa.org/InterestAreas/ForensicAndValuation/Membership/DownloadableDocuments/Intl%20Glossary%20of%20BV%20Terms.pdf (accessed 23 May 2018).
95. *See Compañiá de Aguas del Aconquija S.A. and Vivendi Universal S.A. v. Argentine Republic, ICSID Case No. ARB/97/3*, Award (20 Aug. 2007), p. 246.

§5.04 CONCLUSION

This chapter builds on the premise that investment treaty clauses and customary international law on expropriation recognize the sovereigns' right to expropriate. Nevertheless, the right to expropriate is subject to the requirement that it be for a public purpose, of a non-discriminatory nature, respectful of due process, and on payment of prompt and adequate compensation.

Customary international law distinguishes direct expropriation from indirect expropriation. When a host State takes the investor's property title, it directly expropriates. When a host State adopt measures that do not directly affect the investor's property title but severely affect the value of the investment.

The tension between indirect expropriation and the legitimate exercise of regulatory power is clear. Because distinction between the two is not straightforward, different criteria have been put forward to help distinguishing indirect expropriation and non-compensable regulation. These criteria include the effects of the measure on the value of investment, investors' legitimate expectations, the purpose of the measure, and proportionality of the regulation to its objectives.

Questions

(1) What are the differences between NAFTA Article 1110 and the expropriation provision in the 2012 US Model BIT?
(2) What criteria should be used to tell the difference between a regulatory action that does not give rise to expropriation and one that does?
(3) What role, if any, should the government's purpose in enacting a measure play in a tribunal's decision?
(4) Are some public purposes permissible, whereas others are not?
(5) Should the measure of compensation differ if the purpose of the expropriation is to meet a public purpose, or if the expropriation is wrongful?
(6) When/where is the line between a regulatory act that diminishes the value of an investment and an expropriation?
(7) How much deprivation is 'substantial deprivation'? How can it be measured?

CHAPTER 6

Standards of Protection

Investment treaties provide a wide range of protections to investors. These include fair and equitable treatment (FET), full protection and security (FPS), most-favored-nation (MFN), and national treatment (NT). Each of these protections has been the subject of many debates and controversies focusing on investor protection on the one hand, and the role of a State in regulating its affairs on the other.

The interpretation of each of the clauses would depend on the actual language used in the investment treaty. There is a wide range of formulations that exists and the differences in interpretation in some cases could be attributed to the precise language in the investment treaty.

The FET clause is the most frequently invoked treaty provision and is also the most controversial one. First, there is controversy based the precise scope of the FET clause. Commentators and tribunals have shed some light in this regard and have explained the various elements in the FET clause, there is still room for inconsistent application because the terms are malleable and fact dependent. The legitimate expectations of an investor, in particular, have assumed specific significance although some critics point out that it is subjective and one-sided. Thus, there is a growing trend to focus on 'reasonably backed investor expectations'. Second, there is also debate on the precise scope of FET clause and on whether it is restricted to the customary international law minimum standard of treatment as famously expounded in the *Neer v. Mexico* case. Further, there is also a debate as to whether the customary international law minimum standard applies or whether it would be the standard as expounded in the Neer case or whether the standard has evolved. Finally, there appear to be two strands of analysis when it comes to the FET clause: a broad interpretation and a narrow interpretation. The difference often boils down to the extent to which deference must be accorded to a State's regulatory powers.

The FPS clause protects the integrity of the investment. Almost all tribunals would agree that it extends to the physical integrity of the investment. Several arbitral tribunals following the ICJ's ruling in the *ELSI* case have noted that the obligation would be on of due diligence and would not impose a strict liability on the host State (*see*, e.g., the *AAPL v. Sri Lanka* case). However, some tribunals such as the *Azurix v. Argentina* have gone further and have ruled that the clause would not merely extend to physical security of an investment but would also cover legal security.

The MFN and NT clauses are both examples of non-discrimination clauses: the MFN clause prohibiting discrimination between foreign investors while the NT prohibiting discrimination between foreign investors and national investors.

The MFN clause permits an investor to rely on the clause to 'import' a more favorable provision from another BIT. This has posed no problem when it comes to 'substantive' protections in a treaty but has led to considerable debates when it comes to procedural or jurisdictional matters. The question here is whether an MFN clause can permit an investor to overcome jurisdictional or procedural prerequisites such as waiting periods, cooling-off periods, or selection of particular arbitral forums. The jurisprudence is famously split in this regard with the *Maffezini v. Spain* case seemingly permitting a broader interpretation on the one hand, while the *Plama v. Bulgaria* case adopting a more narrow formulation. The Argentinean cases present an interesting case study in this regard because the jurisprudence has been wholly inconsistent.

A breach of the NT clause involves a three-prong analysis: (1) determining whether a domestic and foreign investor that are in 'like circumstances', (2) determining whether the treatment to the foreign investor is at least as favorable as the treatment accorded to domestic investors, and (3) if the treatment was less favorable, determining whether less favorable treatment was justified.

§6.01 INTRODUCTION

Standards of protection are substantive obligations that bind States toward investors, usually under BITs or MITs such as NAFTA or the ECT. Those standards are usually the same in every treaty, but the wording used may change.

To implement and enforce those protections, investors must prove that a State infringed them under the applicable treaty in order to have a valid claim before an arbitral tribunal. The difficulty comes from the different possible interpretations of those standards of protection and their diverse application by arbitral tribunals. Therefore, the precise content and scope of a given protection is decided on a case-by-case basis when an issue arises. The protections due to foreign direct investment by host countries are of two kinds: (1) absolute and non-contingent standard of treatment, i.e., the treatment – or breach thereof of the standard of treatment – to be accorded is to be determined by reference to specific circumstances of application; FET is an absolute standard of protection[1] and (2) relative standard of treatment, i.e., the treatment to be accorded is to be defined by reference to the treatment accorded to other investments.[2] National treatment and MFN are relative standards of protection.

This chapter intends to provide an overview of some of the key protections offered and will focus on FET (§6.02), FPS (§6.03), MFN (§6.04), and NT (§6.05).

A few preliminary remarks are important in this regard. First, the wording of the clause in any instrument might be of some special significance and may result in different treatment. Second, in some instances, even where the clauses might be similar, there may be different outcomes that could be attributed either to the facts in the case or to the views of the particular arbitrators. The latter is troubling because it results in an inconsistent jurisprudence. Finally, it must be borne in mind that arbitral awards do not have binding precedential value and therefore the cases used herein as for illustrative purposes and gauging relevant jurisprudence.

§6.02 FAIR AND EQUITABLE TREATMENT

The FET standard is one of the most, invoked standard by investors. There is no precise definition of FET. If the words composing the standard have to be defined, it would be suggested that 'fair' brings to mind words such as 'just', 'unbiased', and, 'in accordance with rules or laws'. If the word 'equitable' is considered, it evokes terms such 'balanced', 'impartial', 'egalitarian'. Accordingly, anything that is not fair and equitable violates the FET standard accorded to a foreign investor. Not surprisingly, the violation of the FET standard is centered on the facts of the pertinent case.

Investment treaties vary in their drafting of FET clauses. Some expressly define the standard by reference to international law, e.g., treaties concluded by France, US and Canada. Others do not refer to it, e.g., treaties concluded by the Netherlands, Sweden, Switzerland and Germany.[3]

[A] Examples of FET Clauses

- Article 2(2) of the German Model BIT 2008 provides that '[e]ach contracting State shall in its territory in every case accord investments by investors of the other contracting State Fair and Equitable Treatment as well as full protection under this Treaty.'
- Article 10(1) of the ECT provides that '[e]ach contracting Party shall, in accordance with the provisions of this Treaty, encourage and create stable, equitable, favorable and transparent conditions for Investors of other contracting Parties to make Investment in its Area. Such conditions shall include a

1. *See* Arghyrios A. Fatouros, *Government Guarantees to Foreign Investors*, 135–141, 214–215 (Columbia University Press 1962).
2. *Ibid.*
3. UNCTAD, *Bilateral Investment Treaties 1995-2006: Trends in Investment Rulemaking* (United Nations Publication 2007).

commitment to accord at all times to Investments of Investors of other contracting Parties fair and equitable treatment.'

- Article 1105 of the NAFTA provides that '[e]ach Party shall accord to investments of investors of another Party treatment in accordance with international law, including fair and equitable treatment and FPS. 2. Without prejudice to paragraph 1 and notwithstanding Article 1108(7)(b), each Party shall accord to investors of another Party, and to investments of investors of another Party, non-discriminatory treatment with respect to measures it adopts or maintains relating to losses suffered by investments in its territory owing to armed conflict or civil strife.'

Some States have attempted to establish an exhaustive definition of the content of the FET standard as demonstrated by Article 9, Chapter 10 of the CETA between Canada and the European Union:

> Section 4: Investment Protection
>
> Article X.9: Treatment of Investors and of Covered Investments
>
> 1. Each Party shall accord in its territory to covered investments of the other Party and to investors with respect to their covered investments fair and equitable treatment and Full Protection and Security in accordance with paragraphs 2 to 6.
> 2. A Party breaches the obligation of fair and equitable treatment references in paragraph 1 where a measure or series of measures constitutes:
>   a. Denial of justice in criminal, civil or administrative proceedings;
>   b. Fundamental breach of due process, including a fundamental breach of transparency, in judicial and administrative proceedings.
>   c. Manifest arbitrariness;
>   d. Targeted discrimination on manifestly wrongful grounds, such as gender, race or religious belief;
>   e. Abusive treatment of investors, such as coercion, duress and harassment; or
>   f. A breach of any further elements of the fair and equitable treatment obligation adopted by the Parties in accordance with paragraph 3 of this Article.
> 3. The Parties shall regularly, or upon request of a Party, review the content of the obligation to provide fair and equitable treatment. The Committee on Services and Investment may develop recommendations in his regard and submit them to the Trade Committee for decision.
> 4. When applying the above fair and equitable treatment obligation, a tribunal may take into account whether a Party made a specific representation to an investor to induce a covered investment, that created a legitimate expectation, and upon which the investor relied in deciding to make or maintain the covered investment, but that the Party subsequently frustrated. ...[4]

FET is meant to protect investors against serious instances of arbitrary, discriminatory or abusive conduct by States. They can result in arbitrary cancellation of

4. CETA, http://trade.ec.europa.eu/doclib/docs/2014/september/tradoc_152806.pdf (accessed 30 May 2018), Art. X.9. It must be noted that CETA has replaced the traditional investor-State system by a new permanent investment court system.

licenses, harassment of investor through unjustified fines and penalties, denial of justice, among others. In turn, the host State may feel these measures justified in some circumstances such as when a new government accuse their predecessors of selling 'national assets' at a discount and want to get them back or renegotiate agreements, or when the host State feels that the investor is getting a 'windfall' in profits due to significant increases in market prices, or even more when an economic crisis hit the country and so on.

The obligation to provide investments FET has been given various interpretations by government officials, arbitrators and scholars, depending on whether the standard of treatment is measured against the customary international law minimum standard, a broader international law standard, i.e., including other sources such as investment protection obligations found in treaties and general principles, or whether the standard is 'an autonomous self-contained concept in treaties which do not explicitly link it to international law'.[5]

The precise meaning and content of the FET standard is therefore determinative of what will constitute a violation.

[B] FET as Developed by Reference to the Minimum Standard of Treatment

The international minimum standard of treatment is commonly defined as a norm of customary international law:

> which governs the treatment of aliens, by providing for a minimum set of principles which States, regardless of their domestic legislation and practices, must respect when dealing with foreign nationals and their property. While the principle of national treatment foresees that aliens can only expect equality of treatment with nationals, the international minimum standard sets a number of basic rights established by international law that States must grant to aliens, independent of the treatment accorded to their own citizens. Violation of this norm engenders the international responsibility of the host State and may open the way for international action on behalf of the injured alien provided that the alien has exhausted local remedies.[6]

Although this definition has been challenged by arbitral tribunals, especially regarding rights to be accorded to aliens even if such treatment would be denied to nationals, it is now a generally recognized interpretation of the standard.[7]

5. OECD, *Fair and Equitable Treatment Standard in International Investment Law*, OECD Working Papers on International Investment 2004/03 (OECD Publishing 2004), http://dx.doi.org/10.1787/675702255435 (accessed 30 May 2018), p. 2.
6. OECD, *Fair and Equitable Treatment Standard in International Investment Law*, OECD Working Papers on International Investment 2004/03 (OECD Publishing 2004), http://dx.doi.org/10.1787/675702255435 (accessed 30 May 2018), p. 8, note 32.
7. *See* Ian Brownlie, *Principles of Public International Law*, 514 (8th ed., Oxford University Press 2012); Charles Rousseau, *Droit International Public*, 46 (Sirey 1970).

The *Neer Claim*[8] is the landmark case on minimum standard of treatment. In this case, the US Mexico Claim Commission held that:

> the propriety of governmental acts should be put to the test of international standards ... The treatment of an alien, in order to constitute an international delinquency should amount to an outrage, to bad faith, to willful neglect of duty, or to an insufficiency of governmental action so far short of international standards that every reasonable and impartial man would readily recognized its insufficiency. Whether the insufficiency proceeds from the deficient execution of a reasonable law or from the fact that the laws of the country do not empower the authorities to measure up to international standards is immaterial.[9]

The NAFTA Free Trade Commission (FTC) decided to remedy the level of uncertainty surrounding the FET standard and issued in 2001 a binding determination of the content of FET. It considered that Article 1105(1) of the NAFTA prescribes the customary international law minimum standard of treatment of aliens as:

> the minimum standard of treatment to be afforded to investments of investors of another Party. The concepts of 'fair and equitable treatment' ... do not require treatment in addition to or beyond that which is required by the customary international law minimum standard of treatment of aliens.[10]

However, the NAFTA Tribunal in the *Mondev* case considered that FET needed to be interpreted according to 'current international law'.[11] As such, one can surmise that that FET standard has evolved since the *Neer* decision.

The main influences in the development of the content of the FET standard are investment treaties and arbitral tribunals' decisions. The FET notion is continuously developing and thrives through arbitral tribunals' tendency to refer to, and discuss earlier awards, although under no obligation to do so or in any way bound by them.

Over time, arbitral tribunals have identified recurrent elements that are acknowledged as constituting the normative content of the FET standard, on a case-by-case basis. Treaties are the basis of the interpretation, but normally contain little indication as to the substantive content of the standard.

In early decisions, FET and FPS standards were examined together by tribunals because many treaties included FET and FSP under the same clause. FPS is now included in most treaties as a separate obligation and considered a separate issue from FET by arbitral tribunals.

---

8. *L. F. H. Neer and Pauline Neer (U.S.A.) v. United Mexican States*, Award (15 Oct. 1926), IV Reports of International Arbitral Awards 60 (2006).
9. *Ibid.*
10. NAFTA Trade Commission, *Interpretation of Article 1105(1)* (31 Jul. 2001). NAFTA Art. 2001 establishes the Free Trade Commission (FTC). Among other things, the FTC has the power to supervise the implementation of NAFTA and to resolve disputes that arise regarding its interpretation or application. Interpretations by the FTC are issued in the form of an interpretative note and are binding on NAFTA arbitral tribunals pursuant to Art. 1131(2).
11. *Mondev International Ltd. v. United States of America*, ICSID Case No. ARB/AF/99/2, Award (11 Oct. 2002), para. 125.

[C] Examples of Minimum Standard of Treatment Clauses

NAFTA

Article 1105: Minimum Standard of Treatment

1. Each Party shall accord to investments of investors of another Party treatment in accordance with international law, including fair and equitable treatment and FPS.

NAFTA Interpretative Note issued on 21 July 2011

Having reviewed the operation of proceedings conducted under Chapter Eleven of the North American Free Trade Agreement, the Free Trade Commission hereby adopts the following interpretations of Chapter Eleven in order to clarify and reaffirm the meaning of certain of its provisions: ...

2. Minimum Standard of Treatment in Accordance with International Law

1. Article 1105(1) prescribes the customary international law minimum standard of treatment of aliens as the minimum standard of treatment to be afforded to investments of investors of another Party.

2. The concepts of 'fair and equitable treatment' and 'FPS' do not require treatment in addition to or beyond that which is required by the customary international law minimum standard of treatment of aliens.

3. A determination that there has been a breach of another provision of the NAFTA, or of a separate international agreement, does not establish that there has been a breach of Article 1105(1).

DR-CAFTA

Article 10.5: Minimum Standard of Treatment

1. Each Party shall accord to covered investments treatment in accordance with customary international law, including fair and equitable treatment and FPS.

2. For greater certainty, paragraph 1 prescribes the customary international law minimum standard of treatment of aliens as the minimum standard of treatment to be afforded to covered investments. The concepts of 'fair and equitable treatment' and 'FPS' do not require treatment in addition to or beyond that which is required by that standard, and do not create additional substantive rights. The obligation in paragraph 1 to provide:

(a) 'fair and equitable treatment' includes the obligation not to deny justice in criminal, civil, or administrative adjudicatory proceedings in accordance with the principle of due process embodied in the principal legal systems of the world; and ...

3. A determination that there has been a breach of another provision of this Agreement, or of a separate international agreement, does not establish that there has been a breach of this Article.

2015 India Model BIT

Article 3 Treatment of investments

3.1 No Party shall subject investments made by investors of the other Party to measures which constitute a violation of customary international law through:

(i) Denial of justice in any judicial or administrative proceedings; or
(ii) fundamental breach of due process; or
(iii) targeted discrimination on manifestly unjustified grounds, such as gender, race or religious belief; or

(iv) manifestly abusive treatment, such as coercion, duress and harassment.

[D] FET as Developed by Arbitral Tribunals

[1] Denial of Justice and Due Process

Compliance with the most basic due process requirements is necessary to avoid a denial of justice. In principle, host States are under the obligation to establish a judicial system that allows the effective exercise of the substantive rights granted to foreign investors.

The violation of FET for 'miscarriage of justice' has been upheld by arbitral tribunals in numerous cases, one of the most emblematic being the *Loewen* case[12] where the trial process, the verdict, the denial of an appeal and what Loewen refers to in its pleadings as the 'coerced settlement' all amounted to a denial of substantive and procedural justice, contrary to applicable requirements of NAFTA Chapter 11 and international law protecting FET.

The principle of denial of justice encompasses both procedural and substantive wrongdoings by the courts, i.e., improper procedural irregularities and deficiencies as well as unjust decisions and defects in the substances of judgments.[13]

Only gross or manifest instances of injustice are usually considered a denial of justice and denial of justice is very difficult to establish in practice. Simple error, misinterpretation or misapplication of domestic law is not per se a denial of justice.[14]

The following instances are likely to be considered a denial of justice:[15]

- Denial of access to justice and the refusal of courts to decide.
- Unreasonable delay in proceedings.[16]
- Lack of a court's independence from the legislative and the executive branch of the State.[17]
- Failure to execute final judgments or arbitral awards.[18]
- Corruption of a judge.
- Discrimination against the foreign litigant.[19]

---

12. *The Loewen Group Inc. and Raymond L. Loewen v. the United States of America*, Final Award (26 Jun. 2003), para. 132; *see also Mondev v. USA*, para. 96; *Waste Management v. Mexico*, para. 98.
13. Alwyn V. Freeman, *The International Responsibility of States for Denial of Justice*, 309 (Kraus Reprint Co. 1970) (1938).
14. *See* the 1929 Harvard draft codification, Responsibility of States for damage done in their territory to the person or property of foreigners, in 23 American Journal of International Law, Special Supplement 131 (1929), Art. 9.
15. For a general description of denial of justice, *see Robert Azinian, Kenneth Davitian, & Ellen Baca v. The United Mexican States*, ICSID Case No. ARB (AF)/97/2, Award (1 Nov. 1999), 39 ILM (2000) 537, paras 102–103.
16. The length of delay required to characterize a denial of justice is unclear.
17. For instance, in *Petrobart v. Kyrgyz Republic*, the tribunal held that the collusion between the executive and the court constituted 'a clear breach of the prohibition of denial of justice under international law', *see Petrobart Limited v. The Kyrgyz Republic*, Award (29 Mar. 2005), p. 28.
18. *Petrobart Limited v. The Kyrgyz Republic*, Award (29 Mar. 2005).
19. *Loewen v. United States*, ICSID Case No. ARB(AF)98/3, Award (26 Jun. 2003), para. 135.

- Breach of fundamental due process guarantees, such as failure to give notice of the proceedings and failure to provide an opportunity to be heard.[20,21]

The 2012 US Model Treaty in Article 5(2)(a) clearly States that the FET standard includes the obligation 'not to deny justice in criminal, civil, or administrative adjudicatory proceedings in accordance with the principle of due process embodied in the principal legal systems of the world', illustrating the broader definition of denial of justice.

[2] Manifest Arbitrariness in Decision-Making and Discrimination

Arbitrary conduct has been defined as 'founded on prejudice or preference rather than on reason or fact'[22] or where 'prejudice, preference or bias is substituted for the rule of law'.[23] Thus, a measure that inflicts damage on the investor without serving any legitimate purpose and without a rational explanation, but that instead rests on prejudice or bias, would be considered arbitrary.[24]

In *CMS v. Argentina*, the tribunal found violations of the FET as 'any measure that might involve arbitrariness or discrimination is in itself contrary to the Fair and Equitable Treatment'.[25] In the case of NAFTA tribunals, arbitrary treatments are considered as violation of the FET standard, even though NAFTA does not contain any explicit prohibition of arbitrary treatment.[26]

In a comprehensive definition of arbitrariness, the *LG&E* tribunal[27] defined arbitrary measures as "measures that affect the investments of nationals of the other Party without engaging in a rational decision-making process. Such process would include a consideration of the effect of a measure on foreign investments and a balance of the interests of the State with any burden imposed on such investments."[28] Establishing some rational relationship to the alleged objective of a measure should be sufficient for a measure to be considered non-arbitrary, even if it is "unwise, inefficient or not he best course of action in the circumstances."[29]

20. *TECMED v. Mexico*, Award (29 May 2003), 43 ILM (2004) 133.
21. UNCTAD, *Fair and Equitable Treatment*, UNCTAD Series on Issues in International Investment Agreements II (United Nations Publication 2012), p. 80.
22. *Lauder v. Czech Republic*, UNCITRAL, Award (3 Sep. 2001), para. 221; *Plama Consortium Limited v. Bulgaria*, ICSID Case No. ARB/03/24, Award (27 Aug. 2008), para. 184.
23. *Joseph C. Lemire v. Ukraine*, ICSID Case No. ARB/06/18, Decision on Jurisdiction and Liability (21 Jan. 2010), para. 385.
24. *Ibid.*
25. *CMS Gas Transmission Company v. the Argentine Republic*, ICSID Case No. ARB/01/8, Award, 12 May 2005, para. 290; *see also*, *Eureko B.V. v. Republic of Poland*, Partial Award under UNCITRAL Rules (19 Aug. 2005), paras 248–253.
26. *SD Myers v. Canada*, First Partial Award (13 Nov. 2000), 40 ILM (2001) 1408, para. 263; *Mondev v. USA*, Award (11 Oct. 2002), 42 ILM (2003) 85, para. 127; *Waste Management v. Mexico*, Final Award (30 Apr. 2004), 43 ILM (2004), 967, para. 98.
27. *LG&E v. Argentina*, Decision on Liability (3 Oct. 2006).
28. *Ibid.*, para. 158.
29. UNCTAD, *Fair and Equitable Treatment*, UNCTAD Series on Issues in International Investment Agreements II (United Nations Publication 2012), p. 78.

In treaty practice, the rule against arbitrariness is often combined with the prohibition of discrimination: 'shall not impair investments by arbitrary or discriminatory measures'. The ICJ in the *ELSI* case had to apply this standard and found that '[a]rbitrariness is not so much something opposed to a rule of law ... It is a willful disregard of due process of law, an act which shocks, or at least surprises, a sense of judicial propriety.'[30]

Discrimination can take a number of forms but in the context of the treatment of foreign investment, the most frequent problem is discrimination based on nationality. Two standards specifically address those types of issues: NT and MFN. Those standards will be addressed later on in this chapter.

[3] Abusive Treatment of Investors, Including Coercion, Duress and Harassment

Some arbitral tribunals have recognized abusive conducts in the form of coercion,[31] duress[32] and harassment[33] involving unwarranted and improper pressure, abuse of power, persecution, threats, intimidation and use of force as FET violations. Many different situations can be considered as abusive conduct on the part of the host State: arresting or jailing of executives or personnel; threats of or initiation of criminal proceedings; deliberate imposition of unfunded tax assessments, criminal or other fines; arresting or seizing of physical assets, bank accounts and equity; interfering with, obstructing or preventing daily business operations; and deportation from the host State or refusal to extend documents that allow a foreigner to live and work in the host State.[34]

FET violations are all the more likely to be found if instances of harassment and coercion are 'repeated and sustained',[35] amount to a 'deliberate conspiracy ... to destroy or frustrate the investment'[36] or a 'conspiracy to take away legitimately acquired rights'.[37]

[4] Investors' Legitimate Expectations

The notion of legitimate expectations means that the legal and business framework in which the investment was made should not change to investor's disadvantage.

30. *Case Concerning Elettronica Sicula (ELSI)*, Judgment (20 Jul. 1989), ICJ Reports 15, 76 (1989); *Asylum Case*, Judgment (20 Nov. 1950), ICJ Reports 266, 284 (1950).
31. *TECMED v. Mexico*, Award (29 May 2003), 43 ILM (2004) 133.
32. *Desert Line Projects LLC v. Yemen*, ICSID Case No. ARB/05/17, Award (6 Feb. 2008), paras 179, 185–187, 190 and 193.
33. *Pope & Talbot v. Canada*, Award on Damages (31 May 2002), 41 ILM 1347 (2002), paras 156–181.
34. UNCTAD, *Fair and Equitable Treatment*, UNCTAD Series on Issues in International Investment Agreements II (United Nations Publication 2012), p. 82.
35. *Eureko v. Poland*, Partial Award (19 Aug. 2005), para. 237.
36. *Waste Management v. Mexico*, Final Award (30 Apr. 2004), para. 138.
37. *PSEG v. Turkey*, Award (19 Jan. 2007), para. 245.

Investors' legitimate expectations are based on the host State's legal framework and, at times, may be based on specific undertakings and representations made explicitly by the host State, i.e., legislation and treaties, assurances contained in decrees, licenses and similar executive assurances as well as contractual undertakings. Arbitral decisions suggest that an investor may derive legitimate expectations either from specific commitments addressed to it personally, e.g., in the form of a stabilization clause, or rules that are not specifically addressed to a particular investor, but which are put in place with a specific aim to induce foreign investments and on which the investor relied in making his investment.[38]

Thus, key qualifying elements identified by arbitral tribunals are the following:

- 'Legitimate expectations may arise only from a State's specific representations or commitments made to the investor, on which the latter has relied.
- The investor must be aware of the general regulatory environment of the host country.
- Investors' expectations must be balanced against legitimate regulatory activities of host countries.'[39]

Context and experience are factors taken into consideration as well as the fact that investors' expectations must be grounded in reality rather than frivolous and unrealistic. Therefore, some have considered that '[t]he assessment of the reasonableness or legitimacy [of investors' expectations] must take into account all circumstances, including not only the facts surrounding the investment, but also the political, socioeconomic, cultural and historical conditions prevailing in the host State.' Moreover, 'such expectations must arise from the conditions that the State offered the investor and the latter must have relied upon them when deciding to invest'.[40]

Although not typically considered a customary international law standard, some arbitral tribunals have identified transparency as a concept encompassed by the FET standard.[41] Transparency involves some level of stability of the host State's legal framework for the investor's operations and predictability of decisions affecting the investor based on that regulatory framework. These concepts can be joined together as being part of the legitimate expectations of the investors. These concepts focus on stability and predictability of the host State's legal and business framework but are also related to the good faith principle.

38. *See Glamis Gold, Ltd. v. United States*, UNCITRAL (NAFTA), Award (8 Jun. 2009), para. 627.
39. UNCTAD, *Fair and Equitable Treatment*, UNCTAD Series on Issues in International Investment Agreements II (United Nations Publication 2012), p. 68.
40. *Duke Energy v. Ecuador*, ICSID Case No. ARB/04/19, Award (18 Aug. 2008), para. 340.
41. OECD, *Fair and Equitable Treatment Standard in International Investment Law*, OECD Working Papers on International Investment 2004/03 (OECD Publishing 2004), http://dx.doi.org/10.1787/675702255435 (accessed 30 May 2018), p. 37.

Transparency is clearly interconnected to investors' legitimate expectations, especially in the way it has been defined by arbitral tribunal. In *Metalclad Corporation v. United Mexican States,*[42] the tribunal defined the obligation of transparency as the idea that 'all relevant legal requirements for the purpose of investing should be capable of being readily known to all investors'. In addition, in the event a Party would become aware of 'confusion or misunderstanding' concerning the legal requirements to be fulfilled by investors, the Party would have 'the duty to ensure that the correct position [would be] promptly determined and clearly Stated so that the investors can proceed with all appropriate expedition in the confident belief they are action in accordance with all relevant laws'.[43]

[5] Balance Between Investors' Legitimate Expectations and Reasonable Regulatory Actions of the Host State

The FET obligation does not have as its aim to prevent host States from acting in the public interest or to develop its legal, administrative and business frameworks. Therefore, some actions, even if they adversely affect investments, will not be considered a breach of the FET standard.[44] Indeed, arbitral tribunals recognized the need for host States to make legitimate changes to their legislation and to take actions for public interest purposes. In *Saluka Investments BV (The Netherlands) v. Czech Republic*, the tribunal held that:

> No investor may reasonably expect that the circumstances prevailing at the time the investment is made remain totally unchanged. In order to determine whether frustration of the foreign investor's expectations was justified and reasonable, the host State's legitimate right subsequently to regulate domestic matters in the public interest must be taken into consideration as well...[45]

A similar approach has been adopted in many other cases and is now considered a requirement to the characterization of a breach of legitimate expectations.[46]

---

42. *Metalclad Corporation v. The United Mexican States*, ICSID Case No. ARB(AF)/97/1, Award (30 Aug. 2000).
43. *Ibid.*, para. 76.
44. *Joseph C. Lemire v. Ukraine*, ICSID Case No. ARB/06/18, Decision on Jurisdiction and Liability (21 Jan. 2010).
45. *Saluka Investments BV (The Netherlands) v. Czech Republic*, UNCITRAL, Partial Award (17 Mar. 2006), para. 305.
46. *Parkerings-Compagniet AS v. Lithuania*, ICSID Case No. ARB/05/8, Award (11 Sep. 2007), para. 332. *Continental Casualty v. Argentina*, ICSID Case No. ARB/03/9, Award (5 Sep. 2008), para. 258; *Vivendi v. Argentina II*, ICSID Case No. ARB/97/3, Award (20 Aug. 2007), para. 7.4.31; *EDF v. Romania*, ICSID Case No. ARB/05/13, Award (8 Oct. 2009).

Several forces are therefore to be balanced by tribunals when identifying a breach of the FET standard based on legitimate expectations of the investors. Some cases are essential in this regard: *Saluka v. Czech Republic*,[47] *Tecmed v. United Mexican States*, [48] *Rompetrol v. Romania*,[49] and *Bayindir v. Pakistan*.[50]

§6.03 FULL PROTECTION AND SECURITY

States are not mandated nor obliged to allow foreign capital in their countries. However, if they provide the platform for foreign investments, they must also provide foreigners with at least the same protections they give to their nationals, not only in terms of the treatment of their investments, but more so with regards to their own physical protection.

The principles of international law seek to provide foreigners with certain standards of protection when dealing with sovereign States. The origin of this protection stems from older bilateral treaties of friendship, commerce and navigation, and is part of the developing history of international business, trade and investment.

47. *Saluka Investments BV (The Netherlands) v. Czech Republic*, UNCITRAL, Partial Award (17 Mar. 2006), paras 306–308: 'The determination of a breach of [the FET obligation] requires a weighing of the Claimant's legitimate and reasonable expectations on the one hand and the Respondent's legitimate regulatory interests on the other ... A foreign investor ... may in any case properly expect that the [host State] implements its policies bona fide by conduct that is, as it affects the investors' investment, reasonably justifiable by public policies and that such conduct does not manifestly violate the requirements of consistency, transparency, even-handedness and non-discrimination....The host State must never disregard the principles of procedural propriety and due process and must grant the investor freedom from coercion or harassment by its own regulatory authorities.'
48. *Técnicas Medioambientales Tecmed, S.A. v. The United Mexican States*, ICSID Case No. ARB (AF)/00/2, Award (29 May 2003) 43 ILM 133, 137 (2004), para. 154: Legitimate expectations was defined as the entitlement of investors that a host State will 'act in a consistent manner, free from ambiguity and totally transparently in its relations with the foreign investor, so that it may know beforehand any and all rules and regulations that will govern its investment, as well as the goals of the relevant policies and administrative practices or directives, to be able to plan its investment and comply with such regulations. Any and all State actions conforming to such criteria should relate not only to the guidelines, directives or requirements issued, or the resolutions approved thereunder, but also to the goals underlying such regulations. The foreign investor also expects the host State to act consistently, i.e., without arbitrarily revoking any pre-existing decisions or permits issued by the State that were relied upon by the investor to assume its commitments as well as to plan and launch its commercial and business activities. The investor also expects the State to use the legal instruments that govern the actions of the investor or the investment in conformity with the function usually assigned to such instruments, and not to deprive the investor of its investments without the required compensation...'
49. *The Rompetrol Group N.V. v. Romania*, ICSID Case No. ARB/06/3, Award (6 May 2013), para. 278 (The tribunal noted that the legitimate expectations of a protected investor include the expectation that the State authorities will seek means to avoid unnecessary damage or at least to minimize or mitigate the adverse effects on the investment.).
50. *Bayindir Insaat Turizm Ticaret Ve Sanayi A.S. v. Islamic Republic of Pakistan*, ICSID Case No. ARB/03/29, Award (27 Aug. 2009). (The tribunal found that the claimant's reasonable expectations as to the treatment it would be afforded had not been frustrated since 'it could not reasonably have ignored the volatility of the political conditions prevailing in Pakistan' at the time that it entered into the contract (there having been a preceding period of four years during which the contract had been negotiated, terminated and then revived by reason of changes in government.).

Prior to establishing the provision of FPS, at the core of diplomatic protection was States' liability for the injuries to foreigners and their assets.[51] This meant that the acts of one host State which caused harm to a national of another State were dealt with by diplomatic intervention, whereby the home State of the foreign national would espouse the claim of the person. In many instances, actions of this kind also led to hostile relations between the intervening States, which was at times referred to as 'gunboat diplomacy'.

Article 2 of the ILC Articles on Responsibility of States for Internationally Wrongful Acts[52] (ILC Articles on State Responsibility or ILC Articles) prescribes that in order for an internationally wrongful act to be attributable to a State, it must pass a two-prong test: (a) the actions must be attributable to a State under international law and (b) the act must constitute a breach of an international obligation of that State.

Although it is understood that public riots, insurrects, civil unrest, strikes and other types of public disorders can and do happen without government incitement, the host State has the obligation of providing investors with the minimum standard of FPS. However, despite violence being the most common pattern, this standard of protection is also triggered with non-violent situations. FPS seeks to ensure that host States take 'active and reasonable measures to protect a foreign investment from adverse effects or actions (of a physical or legal nature) of the host State, its organs, or third parties'.[53]

In the *Biwater v. Tanzania* case, the arbitral tribunal alluded to a definition of the duty of due diligence, where it said that 'a substantive failure to take reasonable, precautionary and preventive action is sufficient to engage the international responsibility of a State for damage to public and private property in that area'.[54]

FPS guarantees that the host State must provide investors with adequate protection to preserve its investments as well as the physical integrity of investors. Liability for the host State is triggered when the investors face losses or damages that could have been prevented if the government had provided adequate and timely protection for the investment or persons. This protection may be provided by the government, its legal authorities, or by means of law enforcement officials. Accordingly, the government's failure to act promptly to prevent losses or damages to the investment would trigger the application of the standard.

[A] The Extent of the FPS Provision

Article 10 on Promotion, Protection, and Treatment of Investments of the ECT establishes that:

---

51. James Crawford, *The International Law Commission's Article on State Responsibility: Introduction, Text and Commentaries* (Cambridge University Press 2002), cited R. Doak Bishop, James Crawford & W. Michael Reisman, *Foreign Investment Disputes. Cases, Materials and Commentary*, 787 (Kluwer Law International 2005).
52. ILC Articles on Responsibility of States for Internationally Wrongful Acts (2001), Art. 2.
53. Girsberger, Daniel & Nathalie Voser, *International Arbitration: Comparative and Swiss Perspectives*, 475 (3rd ed., Schulthess Juristiche Medien AG 2016).
54. *Biwater Gauff (Tanzania) Ltd. v. United Republic of Tanzania*. ICSID Case No. ARB/05/22, Award (24 Jul. 2008), para. 725, reference to Professor Ian Brownlie.

> [e]ach Contracting Party shall, in accordance with the provisions of this Treaty, encourage and create stable, equitable, favourable, and transparent conditions for investors of other Contracting Parties to make Investments in its Area ...Such Investments shall also enjoy the most constant protection and security and no Contracting Party shall in any way impair by unreasonable or discriminatory measures their management, maintenance, use, enjoyment or disposal. In no case shall such Investments be accorded treatment less favourable than that required by international law, including treaty obligations...[55]

FPS imposes a two-tier obligation on host States. On the one hand, they are required to provide actively protection on foreign investments, and on the other one, they are also obliged to refrain from adopting any measure, whether direct or indirect, with consent or by assent, detrimental to foreign investments. The limits of this protection, however, have to be reasonable. Thus, a State is not obliged to provide protection against harm or threats of which it is not aware. Yet, when a host State becomes aware of potential threats directed exactly at foreign nationals or their investments, the duty to act is triggered and effective police protection within reasonable means must be provided.

Thus, in light of the ILC Articles on State Responsibility, '[t]here is a breach of an international obligation ... when an act of that State is not in conformity with what I required of it by that obligation, regardless of its origin or character.'[56] Generally speaking, this principle has always tied State responsibility to the preservation and care of investors' property, whether tangible or intangible.

The 2012 US Model BIT establishes that covered investments shall be given a treatment including FPS in accordance with the treatment as per customary international law, without creating 'additional substantive rights'.[57] In expanding the definition, FPS, under the 2012 US Model BIT requires 'each [host State] to provide the level of police protection required under customary international law'.[58]

There are several risks faced by foreign investments. One of them is the potential of local hostility by civilians in the host country geared towards the investors' physical security and their assets. FPS requires that the host State exercise a proper level of due diligence and care in preventing civil unrests that harm foreign investors' physical integrity and their properties. Host States thus have an obligation to adopt reasonable measures that fairly protect investors' interests. This means that they have the obligation to exercise police power in diligently procuring the safeguard and protection of investors' properties. This protection also extends to those direct or indirect foreign investments, such as in cases of recapitalization of already existing operations. Some of the general aspects that will be evaluated by the tribunal are the actions or inactions of the host State aimed at protecting the foreign investment, as well as the efforts and due diligence conducted by the host State to preserve and prevent actual damages to the

55. ECT, Part III – Investment Promotion and Protection, Art. 10.
56. ILC Articles on Responsibility of States for Internationally Wrongful Acts (2001), Art. 12.
57. 2012 US Model BIT, Art. 5(2).
58. *Ibid.*, Art. 5(2)(b).

investment property of the foreign investor.[59] FPS requires that host States adopt reasonable measures to prevent the 'physical destruction of an investor's property'.[60]

In the *Saluka* case, the arbitral tribunal emphasized that the standard of FPS is not one of strict liability on the host State.[61] This means that the host State's liability may be shielded by proving that it took reasonable precautionary measures in preserving and protecting the investors' physical and economic interests in the territory against attacks that threaten or may threaten foreigners in its territory.[62]

Additionally, the *AAPL v. Sri Lanka* case dealt in part with an investor's claims that the Sri Lanka government owed it strict liability to guarantee its FPS. The arbitral tribunal found that the duty was not of a strict liability but rather an obligation of means, thus requiring a link between the damages suffered and the causal responsibility of the State or its dependency for acting without due diligence. Thus, the principle is read to establish a reasonable duty of care to act with due diligence in protecting both the investor's physical integrity, as well as its corporeal or intangible investment property.[63]

§6.04 MOST-FAVORED-NATION

The MFN clause affords an investor from Country A investing in Country B the assurance that it will not be treated less favorably than an investor from a third country by Country B. UNCTAD has specified that in the international investment law context, the purpose of the MFN clause is '[to give] investors a guarantee against a certain forms of discrimination by host countries, and [to establish] equality of competitive opportunities between investors from different foreign countries'.[64]

Most investment agreements contain MFN clauses, although the wording, context and scope may differ. Despite its essentialness, the MFN clause brings debate as to its relation to the different provisions in treaties. While the general consensus is that the MFN clause can be applied to substantive rights, it is 'highly controversial as to whether the clause should equally apply to procedural rights'.[65]

59. *See Wena Hotels Ltd v. Arab Republic of Egypt,* ICSID Case No. ARB/98/4, Award on Merits (8 Dec. 2000).
60. Gary Born, *International Arbitration: Law and Practice,* 431 (Kluwer Law International 2012).
61. *See also Asian Agricultural Products Ltd v. Sri Lanka, ICSID Case No. ARB/87/3,* Final Award (27 Jun. 1990).
62. *Saluka Investments BV (The Netherlands) v. The Czech Republic,* UNCITRAL, 2006 (This dispute was based on the Netherlands-Czech Republic BIT.).
63. *Asian Agricultural Products v. Sri Lanka,* ICSID Case No. ARB/87/3, Final Award (27 Jun. 1990).
64. UNCTAD, *Most-Favored-Nation Treatment,* UNCTAD Series on Issues in International Investment Agreements, UN Doc. UNCTAD/ITE/IIT/10 (Vol. III), 1 (United Nations 1999), http://unctad.org/en/Docs/psiteiitd10v3.en.pdf (accessed 30 May 2018).
65. Nartnirun Junngam, *An MFN Clause and BIT Dispute Settlement: A Host State's Implied Consent to Arbitration by Reference,* 15 UCLA Journal of International Law & Foreign Affairs 399 (2010).

[A] Historical Background of the Development of the MFN Clause and Its Current Relevance

The MFN clause originated from the practices of international trade law. The clause first began as a unilateral form in which powerful nation states, predominantly European, would make the less powerful States promise to MFN treatment.[66]

Later in history, another form emerged (though no longer in use today): the conditional MFN clause. The clause was conditional because an economic concession was only granted if some compensation was promised and the benefitting State had also to grant the same compensation to the other State.[67] The conditional MFN clause was based on the idea of reciprocity.[68]

MFN treatment is defined in Article 5 of the ILC Draft Articles on MFN Clauses as 'treatment accorded by the granting State to the beneficiary State, or to persons or things in a determined relationship with that State, not less favourable than treatment extended by the granting State to a third State or to persons or things in the same relationship with that third State'.[69]

MFN and NT go hand in hand to constitute the non-discrimination principle under international. While analyzing the MFN clause a few things should be borne in mind. First, the obligation to grant MFN treatment is a treaty obligation, and it does not arise from customary international law. Second, the MFN clause is a contingent or relative obligation as it will depend on what is granted to investors of other nationalities and their investments in the host state. Third, the MFN clause may only be pleaded when arising from the same sphere of relationship. In accordance with the *ejusdem generis* principle, the MFN clause can only apply to matters belonging the same subject matter of the clause.

[B] Examples of MFN Clauses

2012 US Model BIT

Article 4: Most-Favored-Nation Treatment

Each Party shall accord to investors of the other Party treatment no less favorable than that it accords, in like circumstances, to investors of any non-Party with respect to the establishment, acquisition, expansion, management, conduct, operation, and sale or other disposition of investments in its territory.

Each Party shall accord to covered investments treatment no less favorable than that it accords, in like circumstances, to investments in its territory of investors of any non-Party with respect to the establishment, acquisition, expansion, management, conduct, operation, and sale or other disposition of investments.

66. *Ibid.*
67. *Ibid.*
68. *Ibid.*
69. ILC Draft Articles on Most-Favoured Nation Clauses with Commentaries (1978).

Bulgaria-Cyprus BIT, Article 3[70]

1. Each Contracting Party shall apply to the investments in its territory by investors of the other Contracting Party a treatment which is not less favourable than that accorded to investments by investors of third States.

2. This treatment shall not be applied to the privileges which either Contracting Party accords to investors from third countries in virtue of their participation in economic communities and unions, a customs union or a free trade area.

Argentina-Spain BIT, Article IV(2)[71]

In all matters subject to this Agreement, this treatment shall not be less favorable than that extended by each Party to the investments made in its territory by investors of a third country.

[C] A Few Cases Dealing with MFN Clauses

Although there are no binding precedents in international arbitrational (commercial or investor-State), it is useful to see how arbitral tribunals have dealt with the application of the MFN clause. There are a number of cases where tribunals have struggled through the MFN legal quagmire, but only a few will be focused.

As stated in the beginning of this chapter, the application of the MFN clause has not given rise to much debate as to importing a more favorable provision in a BIT to 'substantive' protections but has brought about debate and much criticism as to its application with respect to procedural or jurisdictional matter. Thus, the question is whether an investor is allowed to use the MFN provision in the BIT that is applicable to its dispute for purposes of establishing jurisdiction in a more favorable way to the investor. An example of such an instance is where the investor does not want to comply with a requirement in the dispute resolution provisions of its applicable treaty – such as to refer a dispute to domestic procedures before commencing international arbitration – that does not exist under the host State's BIT with a third State. As will be addressed below, the *Maffezini* case grappled with this issue.

[1] Maffezini v. Spain[72]

This case involved a dispute between an Argentine claimant and the Kingdom of Spain as respondent. The claim was brought under the Argentina-Spain BIT. The BIT included an eighteenth-month condition precedent, which required that the dispute be submitted to domestic litigation in Spain and, only if the matter was not resolved on the

70. Agreement between the Government of the People's Republic of Bulgaria and the Government of the Republic of Cyprus on Mutual Encouragement and Protection of Investments (12 Nov. 1987).
71. Acuerdo para la Promoción y la Protección Recíproca de Inversiones entre el Reino de España y la República Argentina (3 Oct. 1991) (Free translation from the Spanish original).
72. *Emilio Agustin Maffezini v. Kingdom of Spain*, ICSID Case No. ARB/97/7, Decision on Jurisdiction (25 Jan. 2000).

merits by the domestic courts or no decision had been rendered within the eighteen-month period, would the investor be able to bring his claim under ICSID as a forum.[73] Maffezini resorted directly to international arbitration and argued, invoking the MFN clause in the Argentina-Spain BIT, that the Spain-Chile BIT did not have a similar provision requiring to resort to the local courts and allowed Chilean investors in Spain to go straight to arbitration. As such, Maffezini argued that he was receiving less favorable treatment than the Chilean investors were.[74]

Despite the fact that the Argentine-Spain BIT did not expressly state that the MFN clause covered dispute settlement, the tribunal ruled that dispute settlement mechanisms are 'inextricably related to the protection of the rights of the investors since they are related to the fair and equitable treatment promised by the MFN clause'.[75] The tribunal followed the *Ambatielos*[76] case regarding the relation of dispute settlement provisions to the category of matters encompassed by the MFN clause. It stated, 'if a third-party treaty contains provisions for the settlement of disputes that are more favorable to the protection of the investor's rights and interests than those in the basic treaty, such provisions may be extended to the beneficiary of the most-favored-nation clause as they are fully compatible with the *ejusdem generis* principle'.[77] Agreeing with the investor, the tribunal stated that if the situation had been such that the host State made the exhaustion of domestic remedies a condition for its consent to arbitration, the investor would not have been able to invoke a third party treaty that eliminated the waiting period.[78] Thus, if there were a specific provision laying out the contours of consent, the parties would not be able to refer to another treaty to bypass it.

The *Maffezini* tribunal basically agreed with the practice of importing dispute settlement provisions from a third-party treaty, but also highlighted four public policy considerations that would be exceptions to this practice.[79] First, if one country made its consent to arbitration only upon the exhaustion of local remedies, this condition cannot be bypassed by the MFN clause.[80] Second, if the treaty contained a 'fork-in-the-road' provision requiring an absolute choice between settling of disputes through the domestic court system or international arbitration, the MFN clause cannot help bypass this provision.[81] Third, if the treaty set forth a specific forum of arbitration, such as ICSID, the MFN clause would not be allowed to be invoked to argue for an entirely different system of arbitration.[82] The last scenario in which the tribunal would not allow the invocation of the MFN clause is when the parties have agreed to a 'highly institutionalized system of arbitration that incorporates precise rules of procedure'.[83] It

73. *Ibid.*, para. 24.
74. *Ibid.*, paras 29–31.
75. *Ibid.*, paras 38, 54.
76. *Ambiatelos Case* (*Greece v. United Kingdom*), Judgment (1 Jul. 1952), ICJ Reports 28 (1952).
77. *Emilio Agustin Maffezini v. Kingdom of Spain*, ICSID Case No. ARB/97/7, Decision on Jurisdiction (25 Jan. 2000), para. 56.
78. *Ibid.*, para. 63.
79. *Ibid.*, para. 56.
80. *Ibid.*, para. 63.
81. *Ibid.*
82. *Ibid.*
83. *Ibid.*

seems that the tribunal pointed out to these public policy considerations out of the concern of potential treaty shopping. It is important to note that the tribunal found that none of these four situations applied to Maffezini and thus, resulted in a liberal ruling allowing the claimant to invoke a different dispute mechanism.

[2] Siemens v. Argentina[84]

Like in *Maffezini*, this case involved the provision of a requirement to resort to domestic litigation in Argentina under the Argentina-Germany BIT. The tribunal reached the same conclusion as the one in Maffezini and concluded that the MFN clause encompassed dispute settlement provisions. The *Siemens* tribunal had a more thorough explanation of its reasoning than in Maffezini and relied on the purpose of the Treaty – 'to protect' and 'to promote' investments.[85] Thus, the Tribunal interpreted the Treaty as to 'create favorable conditions for investments and to stimulate private initiative'.[86]

The *Siemens* tribunal also considered the issue of whether a claimant invoking the MFN clause had to import the allegedly more favorable third party treaty's provisions as a whole or only the provisions deemed beneficial to the claimant's situation. The tribunal concluded that parties can indeed select provisions that are favorable to them; if this practice was not allowed, according to the tribunal, the 'MFN clause would be of limited use'.[87] The arbitrators in this case did not think the holding would be that problematic since the BIT works in both ways: just as an Argentinean investor can receive benefits through an Argentinean BIT, a Chilean investor will be able to do the same through his own country's BIT.[88] The tribunal further asserted that 'claiming a benefit by the operation of an MFN clause does not carry with it the acceptance of all the terms of the treaty which provides for such benefit whether or not they are considered beneficial to the party making the claim; neither does it entail that the claiming party has access to all benefits under such treaty' and that it would be a case-by-case scenario based on the terms of the disputed MFN clause.[89]

[3] Salini v. Jordan[90]

Salini rejected the liberal interpretation and application of MFN clauses to dispute settlements set forth by *Siemens* and *Maffezini*. In this case, the Jordan-Italy BIT

84. *Siemens A.G. v. The Argentine Republic*, ICSID Case No. ARB/02/8, Decision on Jurisdiction (3 Aug. 2004).
85. *Ibid.*
86. *Ibid.*, para. 81.
87. *Ibid.*, para. 108.
88. *Ibid.*
89. *Ibid.*, para. 109.
90. *Salini Costruttori S.p.A. and Italstrade S.p.A. v. The Hashemite Kingdom of Jordan*, ICSID Case No. ARB/02/13, Decision on Jurisdiction (9 Nov. 2004), 44 ILM 573 (2004). This case must not be confused with the famous *Salini* case discussed in Ch. 2 (*Salini Costruttori S.p.A. and Italstrade S.p.A. v. Kingdom of Morocco*, ICSID Case No. ARB/00/4).

contained a provision laying out a specific dispute settlement procedure: ICSID arbitration for disputes arising from treaty violations and contractual dispute settlement procedures for investment contract disputes.[91] The case concerned a conflict over the final payment of the construction of a dam. Thus, the parties had to settle their dispute domestically in Jordanian courts, unless the parties had agreed to arbitrate instead.[92] Notwithstanding, the Italian investors attempted to bring their claim to ICSID on the theory that Jordan's BITs with other countries allowed contractual claims to be arbitrated and that the claimants were entitled to the same treatment.[93]

The *Salini* tribunal reached its decision on jurisdiction only around three months after the decision in *Siemens*. The tribunal first distinguished this case from *Maffezini* and the *Ambatielos* cases; it observed that Article 3 of the Jordan-Italy BIT did not provide for its application over dispute settlement and did not 'envisage all rights or all matters covered by the agreement'.[94] The tribunal further reasoned that Article 9(2) of the BIT was clear in that it wanted contractual disputes to be settled according to the terms of the particular investment agreement and thus, ICSID arbitration was not an available procedure.[95] Thus, unlike the *Maffezini* tribunal, the *Salini* arbitrators narrowed the scope of the application of the MFN clause to dispute settlements and deferred to the express condition set forth in the BIT.

[4] Plama v. Bulgaria[96]

Plama is a case that favors a narrower interpretation of MFN clauses. There, the claimant, a Cyprus corporation, brought the claim due to the Bulgarian government's treatment of its oil refinery.[97] *Plama* wanted to resolve the dispute through international arbitration rather than through Bulgarian courts through the operation of the MFN clause and resorted to the more generous Bulgaria-Finland BIT, as the Bulgaria-Cyprus BIT, provides for 'the possibility of ICSID arbitration'.[98]

The tribunal ruled, however, that the MFN clause cannot be applied to replace the dispute settlement system that had already been agreed to.[99] It endorsed the doctrine that, as a matter of domestic and international law, an agreement to arbitrate must be clear and unambiguous.[100] The Tribunal explained, '[i]n the framework of a BIT, the agreement to arbitrate is arrived at by the consent to arbitration that a state gives in advance in respect of investment disputes falling under the BIT, and the acceptance thereof by an investor if the latter so desires.'[101] According to the Tribunal, without the

91. *Ibid.*, para. 66.
92. *Ibid.*, para. 71.
93. *Ibid.*, para. 21.
94. *Ibid.*, paras 117–118.
95. *Ibid.*, para. 118.
96. *Plama Consortium Limited v. Republic of Bulgaria*, ICSID Case No. ARB/03/24, Decision on Jurisdiction (8 Feb. 2005), 44 ILM 721 (2005).
97. *Ibid.*, para. 21.
98. *Ibid.*, para. 79.
99. *Ibid.*, para. 240(C).
100. *Ibid.*, para. 198.
101. *Ibid.*

specific language granting such forum, it cannot be understood that the MFN clause is to be read broadly as to import broad languages from other BITs.[102] The *Plama* Tribunal expressly rejected the interpretation held by the Siemens Tribunal that the phrase 'with respect to all matters' allows the MFN clause to be interpreted and applied broadly.[103]

§6.05 NATIONAL TREATMENT

According to UNCTAD, the NT standard can be defined as a principle whereby a host country extends to foreigners' treatment that is at least as favorable as the treatment that it accords to national investors in like circumstances. [104] NT is said to be a 'relative' standard of protection, which is comparable or dependent on the treatment accorded to domestic investors. As such, if the foreign and the domestic investor are both in like circumstances, both must be treated equally and no national or domestic investor shall be afforded privileges and protections denied to the foreign investor just on the basis of nationality.

In international law, the NT standard has been invoked in two different settings. First, under the Calvo Doctrine,[105] supported in the past by most Latin American countries, where the treatment of aliens and their property are entitled only to the same treatment accorded to nationals of the host country under its national laws. And, second, in opposition to the Calvo Doctrine, the doctrine of State responsibility for injuries to aliens and their property, which has been supported by developed countries, asserts that customary international law establishes a minimum international standard of treatment to which aliens are entitled, allowing for treatment more favorable than that accorded to nationals where this falls below the international minimum standard.

[A] Examples of NT Clauses

France Model BIT

Article 4: National treatment and most favored Nation treatment

Each Contracting Party shall apply on its territory and in its maritime area to the nationals and companies of the other Party, with respect to their investments and activities related to the investments, a treatment not less favorable than that granted to its nationals or companies, or the treatment granted to the nationals or companies of the most favored nation, if the latter is more favorable. In this respect, nationals authorized to work on the territory and in the maritime area of

102. *Ibid.*, para. 206.
103. *Ibid.*, para. 205.
104. *See* UNCTAD, *National Treatment*, UNCTAD Series on Issues in International Investment Agreements, UN Doc. No. UNCTAD/ITE/IIT/11 (Vol. IV), (United Nations 1999), http://unctad.org/en/Docs/psiteiitd11v4.en.pdf (accessed 30 May 2018).
105. The Calvo Doctrine was first proposed by Carlos Calvo, an Argentine diplomat and legal scholar. Among other things, the doctrine stated that foreigners who held property in Latin American States and had claims against such States should seek redress in the courts of such States and not through diplomatic means. Thus, a Calvo clause in a contract between a Latin American State and a foreign investor stipulates that the investor agrees to have any disputes between it and the State adjudicated in the courts of the host State.

one Contracting Party shall enjoy the material facilities relevant to the exercise of their professional activities.

This treatment shall not include the privileges granted by one Contracting Party to nationals or companies of a third party State by virtue of its participation or association in a free trade zone, customs union, common market or any other form of regional economic organization.

The provisions of this article do not apply to tax matters.

2012 US Model BIT:

Article 3: National Treatment

Each Party shall accord to investors of the other Party treatment no less favorable than that it accords, in like circumstances, to its own investors with respect to the establishment, acquisition, expansion, management, conduct, operation, and sale or other disposition of investments in its territory.

Each Party shall accord to covered investments treatment no less favorable than that it accords, in like circumstances, to investments in its territory of its own investors with respect to the establishment, acquisition, expansion, management, conduct, operation, and sale or other disposition of investments.

The treatment to be accorded by a Party under paragraphs 1 and 2 means, with respect to a regional level of government, treatment no less favorable than the treatment accorded, in like circumstances, by that regional level of government to natural persons resident in and enterprises constituted under the laws of other regional levels of government of the Party of which it forms a part, and to their respective investments."

2007 Colombia Model BIT[106]

Article IV, Treatment of Investments

1. Each Contracting Party shall grant to the investments of investors of the other Contracting Party made in its territory, a not less favourable treatment than that accorded, in like circumstances, to investments of its own investors or to investors of any other third State, whichever is more favorable to the investor.

2. The most favourable treatment to be granted in like circumstances referred to in this Agreement does not encompass mechanisms for the settlement of investment disputes, such as those contained in Articles IX and X of this Agreement, which are provided for in treaties or international investment agreements.

3. The provisions of this Agreement concerning the granting of a no less favourable treatment than that accorded to investments of investors of any of the Contracting Parties or of any third state shall not be construed so as to bind a Contracting Party to extend to investments of investors of the other Contracting Party the benefit of any treatment, preference or privilege resulting from: Any existing or future free trade area, customs union, common market, economic union or any other kind of economic or regional organization or any international agreement intended at facilitating border trade, which a Contracting Party is or becomes a Party to.

In deciding whether a host State has discriminated against an investor for the purposes of the NT standard, the tribunal must compare the State's treatment of the

106. 2007 Colombia Model BIT, https://www.italaw.com/documents/inv_model_bit_colombia.pdf (accessed 30 May 2018).

investor with its treatment of others in like circumstances. The tribunal's interpretation of 'like circumstances' is thus critical.

Rudolf Dolzer indicates that in order to find breach of NT, a tribunal must determine whether the investors are in like circumstances (A), then determine whether the treatment accorded to a foreign investor is less favorable than the one enjoyed by domestic investors (B). And, lastly, it must determine the host State's intent and whether there was a justification for this differentiation (C).[107]

[B] 'Like Circumstances'

Different tribunals have taken different approaches. The tribunal in *S.D. Myers v. Canada Myers v. Canada*, a case brought under NAFTA where the issue was whether Canada breached the NT protection accorded to Myers when it established that the disposal of the PCBs shall be done in Canada and by Canadians. The Tribunal said that:

> [t]he Tribunal considers that the interpretation of the phrase 'like circumstances' in Article 1102 must take into account the general principles that emerge from the legal context of the NAFTA, including both its concern with the environment and the need to avoid trade distortions that are not justified by environmental concerns. The assessment of 'like circumstances' must also take into account circumstances that would justify governmental regulations that treat them differently in order to protect the public interest. The concept of 'like circumstances' invites an examination of whether a non-national investor complaining of less favourable treatment is in the same 'sector' as the national investor. The Tribunal takes the view that the word 'sector' has a wide connotation that includes the concepts of 'economic sector' and 'business sector'.[108]

[C] 'Comparable'

The *Methanex v. United States* tribunal focused on whether the economic activities of the foreign investor were 'comparable' to those in the domestic sphere.[109]

[D] 'Like Situation'

In *Occidental v. Ecuador*, Occidental brought an action for breach of NT under the US-Ecuador BIT. The tribunal decided in favor of the petitioner holding thereby, in fact, 'in like situations' cannot be interpreted in the narrow sense advanced by Ecuador as the purpose of NT is to protect investors as compared to local producers, and this

---

107. Rudolf Dolzer, *National Treatment: New Developments*, in OECD Symposium, *Making the Most of International Investment Agreements: A Common Agenda* (12 Dec. 2005), https://www.oecd.org/investment/internationalinvestmentagreements/35805957.pdf (accessed 30 May 2018).
108. *S.D. Myers, Inc. v. Government of Canada*, UNCITRAL, Partial Award (13 Nov. 2000), para. 250.
109. *Methanex Corporation v. United States of America*, UNCITRAL, Final Award (3 Aug. 2005).

cannot be done by addressing exclusively the sector in which the particular activity is undertaken.

In *Bayindir Insaat Turizm Ticaret Ve Sanayi A.S. v. Islamic Republic of Pakistan*,[110] Bayindir was contracted to build a six-lane motorway between Islamabad and Peshawar by the National Highway Authority (NHA), an agency of the Pakistani government. The project was damaged by disagreements over delays in the construction schedule for a period of eight years. Bayindir, among other things, blamed the delays on factors outside of its control, including arguing the breach of NT. As such, Bayindir argued that it was expelled so that the highway project could be handed to local contractors on more favorable terms.

The tribunal decided whether Bayindir's investment was in a 'similar situation'. If so, Bayindir's investment was accorded less favorable treatment than the local contractor, PMC-JV, and the tribunal had to decide whether the difference in treatment was justified. In its Decision, the Tribunal did not rule out that the contracts with PMC-JV and Bayindir may be similar, as they both related to the same project, but the tribunal found that the terms and circumstances of the contractual relationships between, on the one hand, NHA and Bayindir, and, on the other hand, NHA and PMC-JV were different. Such differences were in the financial terms, the constitution of the two entities, their level of experience and expertise, the scope of work. As a result, the tribunal concluded that 'the two contractual relationships are too different for Bayindir and the local contractors to be deemed in 'similar situations'. Therefore, it found no breach of the NT clause.

[E] Discriminatory

Another important aspect that tribunals consider is whether the measure is discriminatory on its face and whether the interest of the State in protecting the public interest is actually at issue. This point was raised by the tribunal in both, *S.D. Myers Inc. v. Canada* and in *Total S.A. v. Argentine Republic*. In *Total S.A. v. Argentine Republic*, the tribunal said that:

> [t]o determine whether treatment is discriminatory, it is necessary to compare the treatment challenged with the treatment of persons or things in a comparable situation. In economic matters the criterion of 'like situation' or 'similarly-situated' is widely followed because it requires the existence of some competitive relation between those situations compared that should not be distorted by the State's intervention against the protected foreigner. This is inherent in the very definition of the term 'discrimination' under general international law that:
>
> Mere differences of treatment do not necessarily constitute discrimination... discrimination may in general be said to arise where those who are in all material

110. *Bayindir Insaat Turizm Ticaret Ve Sanayi A.S. v. Islamic Republic of Pakistan*, ICSID Case No. ARB/03/29, Award (27 Aug. 2009).

respects the same are treated differently, or where those who are in material respects different are treated in the same way.[111]

Therefore a claimant complaining of a breach by the host State of the BIT's NT clause: (a) has to identify the local subject for comparison, (b) has to prove that the claimant-investor is in like circumstances with the identified preferred national comparator(s), and (c) must demonstrate that it received less favorable treatment in respect of its investment, as compared to the treatment granted to the specific local investor or the specific class of national comparators.[112]

§6.06 CONCLUSION

Investment treaties provide a wide range of protections to investors. These include FET, FPS, MFN and NT. Each of these protections has been the subject of many debates and controversies focusing on investor protection on the one hand, and the role of a State in regulating its affairs on the other. Standards of protection are substantive obligations that bind States toward investors, usually BITs or MITs. Those standards are usually the same in every treaty, but the wording used may change. Thus, the interpretation of each of the clauses will depend on the actual language used in the investment treaty.

There is a wide range of formulations and the differences in interpretation in some cases could be attributed to the precise language in the investment treaty. To implement and enforce those protections, investors must prove that a State infringed them under the applicable treaty in order to have a valid claim before an arbitral tribunal. Awards issued by international arbitrators against States have in numerous cases incorporated expansive interpretations of the language in investment treaties. This is especially evident in the approach adopted by many arbitration tribunals to investment treaty concepts of MFN, non-discrimination and FET. The difficulty arises from the different possible interpretations of those standards of protection and their heterogeneous application by arbitral tribunals. Therefore, the precise content and scope of a given protection is decided on a case-by-case basis when an issue arises. The cases cited and many more that were not covered in this chapter reflect the different ways in which investment tribunals have applied treatment standards. Ideally, future international investment tribunals will be more consistent so as to create a balanced jurisprudence on the different standards.

Questions

(1) Why is FET considered controversial when it is analyzed by international arbitral tribunals?

111. *Total S.A. v. Argentine Republic*, ICSID Case No. ARB/04/01, Decision on Liability (27 Dec. 2010), para. 210.
112. *Ibid.*, (27 Dec. 2010).

(2) What is the 'denial of justice' standard of protection with respect to international investments?
(3) How does 'denial of justice' compare with the standard of FPS?
(4) The 'international minimum standard' refers to States' minimum obligations to provide protections as set forth by customary international law. Do you think this offers a strong means of protection, or do you see any shortcomings in this standard?
(5) In several cases regarding MFN treatment, parties have compared provisions in multiple BITs negotiated by a certain country (e.g., the Maffezini case compared dispute settlement provisions in two of Spain's BITs: the Argentine-Spain BIT and the Chile-Spain BIT). Given that States negotiate different treaties as they see fit, do you think it is reasonable for a party to compare different BITs in order to support its MFN claim?
(6) When an NT violation is alleged by an investor against a Host State, how should a tribunal go about deciding who is 'in like circumstances' with whom?
(7) Does a finding that there is a difference in the treatment of an investor versus a national 'in like circumstances' mean there is automatically a finding that the host State violated the BIT?

CHAPTER 7
General Defenses on the Merits

Are States bound to fulfil the obligations and commitments they undertake under a BIT or MIT? Pursuant to *pacta sunt servanda*, they are. This Latin phrase, which may be translated, as 'agreements must be kept', expresses a general principle of international law – one that is fundamental to treaties and relations between States. This principle – the duty to perform one's commitments – is not unique to international law and the law of treaties. Similar principles may be found in the contract law of many domestic legal traditions throughout the world.

Pacta sunt servanda has been recognized and applied as an international law principle for centuries, and was codified in the Vienna Convention on the Law of Treaties (VCLT) of 1969. Article 26 of the VCLT states, '[e]very treaty in force is binding upon the parties to it and must be performed by them in good faith.' Thus, a State cannot avoid its obligations under a treaty. Every wrongful act of a State calls for State responsibility.

There are, however, exceptions to this rule or principle of *pacta sunt servanda*. International law gives the States a possibility to invoke certain defenses that would absolve them of responsibility. These defenses include necessity and force majeure, as the most important. Both concepts were incorporated in Articles 25 and 23 of the ILC Articles on State Responsibility as circumstances precluding wrongfulness. More recently, it is seen that States invoke bribery and corruption as a defense. Exceptions are defenses that excuse the wrongful actions thus making thus the respondent State not liable.

§7.01 DEFENSES

Under international law, States are responsible for the wrongful acts and breaches they commit to their international obligations. The ILC codified a number of the customary rules concerning State responsibility. The ILC Articles on State Responsibility, among other things, address the requirement of an international wrongful act and the legal consequences of such act. Similar to domestic contract laws, international law allows States to assert defenses against the claims for breach of contract or the applicable treaty protection. In investment arbitration, a defense is usually raised by the respondent State, which, accordingly, has to bear the burden of proof of its allegations, once the investor has to prove the prima facie breach the State's obligation. These legal justifications represent grounds either constituting a defense to a claim under an investment contract, like force majeure or necessity, or for challenging the continued existence of an investment contract or obligation. These defenses can also be classified as legal justifications for breach of international obligations.

In investor-State arbitration, if the arbitration is based on a foreign investment law or treaty, the investor is the only party that can start a procedure challenging an action of the host State. The State can reply affirming that its conduct does not constitute a violation of international law or national law. Given the distinction between contract and treaty claims, defenses can be derived from the applicable law of the contract, and under general principles of international law.[1]

Concerning the defenses under a contract, it is necessary to refer to the applicable law of the contract, which is generally the law of the host State. With regard to international law defenses, the ILC has recognized six circumstances that preclude wrongfulness: consent, self-defense, countermeasures, force majeure, distress and necessity.[2]

The ILC classifies the aforementioned defenses as 'circumstances precluding wrongfulness',[3] which should be distinguished from the 'termination of the obligation itself'.[4] Defenses do not obviate the existence of an obligation under international law; they simply provide an excuse for the prima facie breach of that obligation under particular circumstances.[5] The most important aspect of defenses in international investment arbitration is to deem the State not liable for the breach of a particular obligation under a contract or treaty, as a circumstance precluding wrongfulness. In other words, defenses represent exceptions to international responsibility, thus relieving States from responsibility for implementing measures necessary to safeguard, preserve and protect interests like national peace, stability, security and environment. In practice, these defenses 'are more in the nature of excuses which may defeat a claim only for a certain period of time, or may nonetheless require the party relying on them to pay compensation for actual loss suffered'.[6]

1. The law of contract only applies when the investor may invoke the contract, for example if there is an umbrella clause in the BIT.
2. International Law Commission, Commentary to the Articles on Responsibility of States for Internationally Wrongful Acts, 141 (2012).
3. *Ibid.*
4. *Ibid.*
5. *Ibid.*
6. R. Doak Bishop, James Crawford & W. Michael Reisman, *Foreign Investment Disputes: Cases, Materials and Commentary*, 1171 (Kluwer Law International 2005).

The defenses that have been most invoked by host States and thus on which we will focus are: force majeure, necessity and, more recently, although not technically a defense listed by the ILC, corruption.

§7.02 FORCE MAJEURE

Unforeseeable occurrences sometimes arise in domestic and international contracts, thus affecting international trade. Acts of God, natural disasters and political and economic changes may influence the parties' relationship and basis upon which they initially negotiated the bargained-for exchange.

The most natural corollary to *pacta sunt servanda* is the principle of *impossibilium nulla est obligatio*, loosely translated from Latin, as 'the impossible is not an obligation' or, paraphrased as, 'there is no obligation to perform impossible things'. Similar principles apply in the realm of international conventions: *rebus sic stantibus* ('things thus standing' in Latin) is the legal doctrine that allows treaties to become inapplicable in the event of a fundamental change in circumstances. The doctrines of impossibility and force majeure have become common grounds used in all legal systems as an exception to the performance of obligations.

The concept of force majeure is recognized as a general principle of international law.[7] Many legal systems have codified it in some form or another.[8] In international law, the term alludes to a situation where an unforeseen event takes place that makes the performance of the international obligation under a treaty impossible. In other words, under a force majeure event, the respondent is compelled by an external action, to act or not act in such a manner, which prevents the respondent from being deemed to have acted wrongfully. Force majeure qualifies as an exception to performance, and the party alleging it has the burden of proof.

For a State to be able to argue successfully that it cannot fulfil its obligations under a treaty due to changed circumstances, certain requirements must be met:

- The circumstances at the time of the contract negotiation were essential to the contract itself.
- The change in circumstances has a radical effect on the obligations of the contract.

---

7. ILC, Commentary to the Articles on Responsibility of States for Internationally Wrongful Acts, 157 (2012).
8. *See*, generally, Ilya Kokorin & Jeroen Van Der Weide, *Force Majeure and Unforeseen Change of Circumstances. The Case of Embargoes and Currency Fluctuations (Russian, German and French Approaches)* 3 Russian L. J. 46 (2015). Under Russian law, there is strict liability for non-performance or defective performance of contractual obligations unless such lack of performance was due to 'irresistible force, i.e., extraordinary circumstances, which were impossible to avert under the given conditions'. Force majeure is often confused with impossibility of performance as well as change of circumstances, even though the Russian Civil Code contains separate provisions for each of these defences. German law, on the other hand, does not distinguish between objective and subjective impossibility, and it does not take into account whether impossibility was caused by the debtor. The French definition of force majeure may be the closest to international law, as it requires unforeseeability, irresistibility and exteriority (or non-attributability), the standard for foreseeability being very high.

- The changed circumstances were never contemplated by the parties when the contract was negotiated; in other words, the changed circumstances were not foreseeable.

Force majeure should be distinguished from other similar concepts. The VCLT has adopted the defense of 'Fundamental change of circumstances' under its Article 62.[9] Such a change would justify termination or suspension of a treaty if those circumstances constituted an essential element of the parties' consent to the treaty, and the effect of the change is so dramatic that it transforms the obligations to be performed under the treaty. Fundamental change of circumstances may not be invoked if it was caused by the State's breach of its international obligations. It should be noted that there is no requirement that change of circumstances not be due to the State's actions; merely that it should not be caused by a breach of the State's obligations.

The main characteristic of force majeure is that it entails legal or physical impossibility:

> by *force majeure* we mean social and economic forces beyond the power of the state to control through the exercise of due diligence. Injuries caused by the operation at such forces are therefore not attributable to the State for purposes of its responding for damages. Similarly, as between private parties, one party cannot claim against the other for injuries suffered as a result of delays in or cessation of performance during the time force majeure conditions prevail, unless the existence of these conditions is attributable to the fault of the Respondent party.[10]

Under Article 23 of the ILC Articles, Force majeure is defined as follows:

> Force Majeure
> 1. The wrongfulness of an act of a State not in conformity with an international obligation of that State is precluded if the act is due to force majeure, that is the occurrence of an irresistible force or of an unforeseen event, beyond the control of the State, making it materially impossible in the circumstances to perform the obligation.
> 2. Paragraph 1 does not apply if:
>   (a) the situation of force majeure is due, either alone or in combination with other factors, to the conduct of the State invoking it; or
>   (b) the State has assumed the risk of that situation occurring.[11]

From the Commentary on the ILC Articles, it is also understood that 'force majeure differs from a situation of distress or necessity because the conduct of the State which would otherwise be internationally wrongful is involuntary or at least involves no element of free choice ... [And] the wrongfulness of the State's conduct is precluded for so long as the situation of force majeure subsists'.[12]

9. Vienna Convention on the Law of Treaties (1969), 1155 UNTS 331, Arts 62, 23.
10. *Gould Marketing, Inc. v. Ministry of National Defense of Iran*, Interlocutory Award No. 24-49-2 of 27 Jul. 1983, 3 Iran-US Cl. Trib. Rep. 147.
11. International Law Commission, Articles on Responsibility of States for Internationally Wrongful Acts (2001).
12. UN Legislative Series, Materials on the Responsibility of States for Internationally Wrongful Acts, UN Doc. No. ST/LEG/SER.B/25, 154 (United Nations 2012), http://legal.un.org/legislativeseries/documents/Book25/Book25.pdf (accessed 30 May 2018).

The Commentary goes on to set forth the three elements that must be met for a situation of *force majeure* precluding wrongfulness to arise. Those conditions are: (a) the act must be an unforeseen event and an irresistible force, (b) beyond the control of the State and (c) makes the performance of the obligation materially impossible.[13] From the three elements cited, one surmises that force majeure does not include circumstances where performance is just more difficult or more expensive. It does not cover situations where the State's actions or lack thereof was due to its own failure or omission.

Moreover, '*force majeure* should be presumed not to exist where the state act is an individual one which affects a specific contract or specific contracts. Where the state act is of a general character and is based on general considerations, which would affect private enterprises in the same manner as a state enterprise, the plea of force majeure may be available ... For a plea of force majeure to be accepted the act of state must be a political decision involving the exercise of national sovereignty; it must not have been taken to favour the personal interests of the state or contracting party ...'[14]

Force majeure makes the performance of duties and obligations under a treaty temporarily or permanently impossible; thus, suspending such duties and obligations. It is therefore necessary to analyze the particular facts of the case and the circumstances around those facts; it is a case-by-case analysis and *decision* for the arbitrators. Force majeure may then have the power of terminating a contract or obligation when the performance becomes permanently impossible or at least impossible for a long period.

It is worth noting that arbitral tribunals have rendered inconsistent decisions regarding the defense of force majeure. For most arbitrators, when the requirements or the definition of force majeure is met, the defense excuses non-performance of an obligation. Given that to date there are no examples of an investment tribunal accepting a defense of force majeure, it is difficult to appreciate these doctrinal differences. There does seem to be a consensus with regard to one notion – that of foreseeability – which is most often the condition not satisfied by the State, thus precluding the operation of force majeure.

Some of the earliest decisions of international tribunals on force majeure date back to 1912. The PCA had the opportunity to interpret this defense in the context of the Ottoman wars that took place at the end of the nineteenth century. The Russian Empire brought claims against Turkey for interest on indemnities for Russians harmed during the war. The arbitral tribunal rejected the defense of force majeure argued by Turkey because the payment of indemnity would not 'imperil the existence of the Ottoman Empire or seriously compromise its internal or external *situation*'.[15] From the start, arbitral tribunals set a very high standard for force majeure: the defense would only be accepted if the performance had imperiled the State's very existence.

13. *Ibid.*
14. R. Doak Bishop, James Crawford & W. Michael Reisman, *Foreign Investment Disputes: Cases, Materials and Commentary*, 1190–1191 (Kluwer Law International 2005).
15. *Russian Claim for Interest on Indemnities (Damages Claimed by Russia for Delay in Payment of Compensation Owed to Russians Injured During the War of 1877-1878)*, *Russian Federation v. Turkey*, Award (11 Nov. 1912), 13 (PCA 1912).

Subsequent interstate cases also concentrated on the 'absolute and material impossibility'.[16] In the *Rainbow Warrior* case, the government of New Zealand commenced arbitration against France after two officers of the latter sank a New Zealand civilian vessel. France stated that the officers were acting on its command and offered to make reparations, requesting the return of the officers who would be set to freedom. New Zealand, where the officers had been arrested for their crimes, contended that the two officers should not be released to France unless they would be in custody. Unable to reach a diplomatic solution, the two countries approached the UN Secretary General. The Secretary General decided that the two officers would be sent to an isolated island of Hao in the French Polynesia for a period of three years without permission to leave the island for any reason. Before the end of this term, one of the officers, Major Mafart, was diagnosed with serious health problems that could not be adequately treated on the island, according to France. Claiming force majeure, France brought Major Mafart to Paris for treatment, which was contested by New Zealand in arbitration.

The arbitral tribunal rejected the force majeure excuse invoked by France, because it did not make the actions of the French government materially impossible.[17] The tribunal considered that in this case France's obligation merely became more burdensome, but not impossible to perform. The tribunal did accept the defense of distress, which will be discussed below, with regard to the removal of Major Mafart from the island, but not with regard to his continued presence in mainland France.[18]

The ICJ in *Gabčíkovo-Nagymaros* case clarified the distinction between force majeure as contained in Article 23 of the ILC and supervening impossibility of performance, which was codified in VCLT Article 61.[19] The case concerned a treaty signed in 1977 between Hungary and then Czechoslovakia for construction of a barrage system on the river Danube. In 1989, the government of Hungary decided to suspend the works because of environmental concerns. Initially, a temporary suspension became permanent, which was contested by Czechoslovakia in an arbitration before the ICJ after the two governments could not reach an agreement by diplomatic means. Hungary claimed the existence of a state of 'environmental necessity', which justified its non-performance while also accusing Slovakia (now responsible for the project following political changes) of violating the 1977 Treaty with regard to its environmental obligations.[20]

Hungary relied on the supervening impossibility of performance and fundamental change of circumstances to justify the suspension of works on the *Gabčíkovo-Nagymaros* project. It led the Court to clarify that the standard for supervening impossibility is even higher than for force majeure, because it excuses the termination

16. *Case concerning the difference between New Zealand and France concerning the interpretation or application of two agreements concluded on 9 July 1986 between the two States and which related to the problems arising from the Rainbow Warrior Affair, New Zealand v. France*, Award (30 Apr. 1990) XX UN Report of International Arbitral Awards 215, 253 (2006).
17. *Ibid.*
18. *Ibid.* pp. 258–59.
19. *Gabčíkovo-Nagymaros Project* (Hungary/Slovakia), Judgment, ICJ Reports 7 (1997).
20. *Ibid.* pp. 30–35.

of a treaty and not just non-performance of an obligation. Citing the deliberations of the Diplomatic Conference, which adopted the VCLT, the court clarifies that 'impossibility to make certain payments because of serious financial difficulties' could be a circumstance precluding wrongfulness of non-performance, but would not rise to the level of Article 61 justifying termination of a treaty.[21] The ICJ rejected both defenses, because it considered that there had been no dramatic shift in the circumstances or the scientific knowledge to justify the abandonment of the works because of environmental concerns.[22]

Investor-State arbitral tribunals have concentrated more on the requirement that force majeure be unforeseeable, which is extremely difficult to satisfy in practice. In *Autopista v. Venezuela*, an ICSID tribunal considered that violent protests due to increase in costs of transportation were not unforeseeable, since there had been similar protests eight years earlier.[23] In that case, Venezuela entered into a concession agreement for the operation of a highway by *Autopista*. The investor was to be remunerated in part from toll collection on the road, which was to be increased following an agreed schedule. The State refused to increase the tolls because of social unrest and attempted to claim force majeure, which was not accepted by the tribunal.

In *Niko Resources v. Bangladesh*, another ICSID case, the State of Bangladesh also attempted to raise the defense of force majeure without success.[24] The investor entered into a joint venture with a State-controlled company, BAPEX, for the exploration of abandoned gas fields, which was to be sold on the internal market. *Niko Resources* started producing and delivering gas before finalizing the contract for sale and purchase with another State-controlled company, Petrobangla. Petrobangla and the State of Bangladesh, respondents in this case, encouraged and demanded continued deliveries of gas even before the signing of the contract for sale and purchase while refusing to make payments. In the meantime, the Supreme Court of Bangladesh issued an order restraining the State companies from making any payments in respect of any gas fields. The agreement for sale and purchase of gas was finally executed after the issuance of the restraining order. The respondents sought to rely on the Court order as constituting an unforeseeable force majeure event with regard to the gas payments. However, the Tribunal rejected this argument for the simple reason that the agreement was concluded after the Court order had already been issued and, as such, the interdiction to make payments was known by the respondents when they entered into the agreement.[25]

21. *Ibid.* p. 63.
22. *Ibid.* p. 65.
23. ICSID, *Autopista Concesionada de Venezuela, C A ('Aucoven') v. Bolivarian Republic of Venezuela*, Case No ARB/00/5, Award (23 Sep. 2003), pp. 34–35.
24. *Niko Resources (Bangladesh) Ltd. v. Bangladesh Petroleum Exploration & Production Company Limited ('Bapex') and Bangladesh Oil Gas and Mineral Corporation ('Petrobangla')*, ICSID Case No. ARB/10/18, Decision on the Payment Claim (11 Sep. 2014), paras 228–230.
25. *Ibid.*, paras 199–205.

§7.03 THE STATE OF NECESSITY

The state of necessity is a defence precluding wrongfulness that a State may invoke under exceptional circumstances. Necessity arises when a State, under a grave and imminent peril, adopts measures not in conformity with its obligations because it is its only means to protect an essential security interest of the State.

State of necessity represents an exemption from State responsibility for the protection of foreign investments when necessary to preserve essential interests. On the one hand, it reasonably mitigates the legal force of international legal obligations in those exceptional circumstances in which compliance with the law would put an essential interest of the State under grave and imminent peril. On the other hand, the rule in point has evolved and has been codified in sufficiently restrictive terms to avoid lending itself to abuses on the part of the States invoking it. Such abuses could undermine the legal force of any international obligation whenever a State found that compliance with it would be in contrast with its own immediate interests.[26]

Similar to force majeure, necessity bears a very high standard and arbitral tribunals diligently look at the specific circumstances of every case to determine whether the requirements of such a defence are satisfied in order to prevent abuse. Necessity should be considered as one of the customary international law defenses (A) and as an exception contained in a treaty clause (B). Further to that, the jurisprudence rendered under ICSID concerning necessity will be discussed (C).

[A] Necessity under Customary International Law

The concept of 'necessity' has been historically related to the notion of self-preservation, which later developed into the doctrine of essential interests. That is to say, when a threat to self-preservation arose, it was considered justified to take any steps necessary to preserve one's existence, even if such steps would have been unlawful had they been taken in the absence of a threat to self-preservation.[27] During most of the twentieth century, a State's 'essential interests' were confined to those necessary to maintain its existence in context of a military threat.[28] However, the concept has broadened starting with the ICJ in *Gabčíkovo-Nagymaros* case; environmental protection was also accepted as a potential essential interest.[29]

It is crucial to distinguish essential interests from the defence of 'necessity' itself. The concept of 'essential interests' is intended to circumscribe the cases in which a State can invoke necessity. First of all, an objective has to be classified as 'essential' by a tribunal for the State's protective measures to be justified. Second, it must not impair

26. Attila Tanzi, *Necessity, State of* (Max Planck Encyclopedia of Public International Law 2013).
27. Roman Boed, *State of Necessity as a Justification for Internationally Wrongful Conduct*, 3 Yale Hum. Rights & Dev. J. 1, 4 (2000).
28. Jonathan Bellish, *In Principle but Not in Practice: The Expansion of Essential State Interests in the Doctrine of Necessity under Customary International Law*, 41 Denv. J. Intl. L. & Policy 127 viii (2012).
29. *Gabčíkovo-Nagymaros Project*, (*Hungary v. Slovakia*), Judgment, ICJ Reports 7 (1997).

an essential interest of another State or a peremptory norm of international law.[30] In addition to these two basic premises, there are other conditions to be satisfied to claim successfully the necessity defence, such as imminent danger and impossibility of safeguarding the interest by other measures, which will be discussed in more detail below. Necessity encompasses more that is more than essential interests. One may say that the protection of an essential interest is a rung in the ladder of necessity.

Necessity is used to denote exceptional cases whereby the only means a State has to safeguard an essential interest from a grave and imminent peril is not to perform an international obligation of lesser urgency or weight. Notwithstanding the fact that the necessity defense is more often used by States than by investors, States still feel uncertainty about this defense because, as shown later, necessity is a subjective concept, with no clear and objective requirements to be fulfilled to constitute a state of necessity. In other words, it is a defense that poses a high threshold for States.

As compared to force majeure, where the State has no control of the intervening act, under necessity, the host State has complete control of the wrongful act or conduct not in conformity with its obligations, but it is alleging necessity to safeguard an essential interest of the State to preclude wrongfulness:

> In the case of the state of necessity, on the other hand, the deliberate nature of the conduct, the intentional aspect of its failure to conform with the international obligation are not only undeniable but in some sense logically inherent in the justification alleged; invoking a state of necessity implies perfect awareness of having deliberately chosen to act in a manner not in conformity with an international obligation.[31]

The application of necessity is usually evaluated under customary international law according to the criteria established in Article 25 of ILC Articles on State Responsibility for precluding the wrongfulness of an act not in conformity with an international obligation. The main objective of Article 25 is to adopt strict conditions that need to be cumulatively satisfied in order for a State to allege the Necessity defense only in exceptional circumstances. The stringent requirements of Necessity are to protect against its abuse.[32]

> Article 25 – Necessity
> 1. Necessity may not be invoked by a State as a ground for precluding the wrongfulness of an act not in conformity with an international obligation of that State unless the act:
>   (a) is the only means for the State to safeguard an essential interest against a grave and imminent peril; and

30. Jonathan Bellish, *In Principle but Not in Practice: The Expansion of Essential State Interests in the Doctrine of Necessity under Customary International Law*, 41 Denv. J. Intl. L. & Policy 127, 134–135 (2012).
31. Marie Christine Hoelck Thjoernelund, *State of Necessity as an Exemption from State Responsibility for Investments*, 13 Max Planck Y.B. U.N. L. 423, 433 (2009).
32. The most famous case of abusing the defence of necessity is Germany when it occupied Belgium and Luxembourg during World War. Germany claimed necessity because Belgium and Luxembourg would have otherwise been invaded by France.

(b) does not seriously impair an essential interest of the State or States towards which the obligation exists, or of the international community as a whole.

2. In any case, necessity may not be invoked by a State as a ground for precluding wrongfulness if:
   (a) the international obligation in question excludes the possibility of invoking necessity; or
   (b) the State has contributed to the situation of necessity.[33]

Paragraph 1 of Article 25 sets forth two conditions that must be met in order to be able to invoke the necessity defense, whereas paragraph 2 establishes two situations that exclude the applicability of this defense. A State invoking necessity has to satisfy paragraphs 1 and 2.

The Commentary to Article 25 assists in clarifying the key words and requirements set forth for the Necessity defense. It explains that the state of necessity:

> has been invoked to protect a wide variety of interests, including safeguarding the environment, preserving the very existence of the State and its people in time of public emergency, or ensuring the safety of a civilian population ... The extent to which a given interest is 'essential' depends on all the circumstances ... The peril has to be objectively established and not merely apprehended as possible ...The plea is excluded if there are other . . . means available, even if they may be more costly or less convenient ... Any conduct going beyond what is strictly necessary for the purpose will not be covered ... For a plea of necessity to be precluded under paragraph (2) (b), the contribution to the situation of necessity must be sufficiently substantial and not merely incidental or peripheral.[34]

The balancing test provided in Article 25(1)(b) means that the essential interest on which the breaching State is relying must outweigh the interest of the other State or of the international community that is being violated. This defense essentially involves sacrificing the interests of one State, because of the vital interests of another. Arbitral tribunals will have to balance the interests of the State with the interests of the other State and the foreign investor.

Furthermore, it is important to keep in mind that necessity is not grounds for the termination of a treaty. It may suspend the treaty for the period of time during which the state of necessity exists. However, as soon as necessity is over, the treaty would have to be given its full effect again.[35]

[B] State of Necessity under Treaty Clauses

The state of necessity defense became more relevant in investment arbitration with the social, economic, and political crisis in Argentina. In order to react to the internal economic crisis between 1999 and 2002, Argentina took some emergency measures affecting foreign investors and their investments. Argentina invoked this defense

33. ILC, Articles on Responsibility of States for Internationally Wrongful Acts (2001).
34. *Ibid.*
35. R. Doak Bishop, James Crawford & W. Michael Reisman, *Foreign Investment Disputes: Cases, Materials and Commentary*, 1209 (Kluwer Law International 2005).

before ICSID arbitral tribunals by arguing that, during the crisis, Argentina was faced with a state of necessity. Moreover, Argentina took the position that, while the measures were in breach of the BIT obligations, it had to adopt actions harming the investors to face the particular circumstances of the crisis in 2001 and 2002.[36]

As discussed above, Article 25 requirements represent the recognized customary international law for necessity. Although not common, a few BITs contain 'exception clauses', which allow States to adopt certain emergency measures in order to deal with particular circumstances. For example, Article XI in the US-Argentina BIT reads:

> This treaty shall not preclude the application by either party of measures necessary for the maintenance of public order, the fulfillment of its obligations with respect to the maintenance or restoration of international peace or security, or the protection of its own essential security interests.[37]

Tribunals have not been consistent in their interpretation and application of necessity and arbitral awards have reflected this lack of uniformity. A few cases will be highlighted before ICSID on the issue of necessity and how tribunals decided them. The tribunals in *CMS*, *Enron*, *Sempra*, and *Impregilo*, among others, have rejected the state of necessity as argued by Argentina. In the *LG&E* and *Continental Casualty*, the necessity argument was accepted.[38] There are other decisions also dealing with the interpretation and relationship between necessity under customary international law and bilateral treaties, including the annulment decisions in *CMS*, *Sempra* and *Enron*.[39]

36. For more information on the Argentine crisis, *see* Elizabeth A. Martinez, *Understanding the Debate over Necessity: Unanswered Questions and Future Implications of Annulments in the Argentine Gas Cases*, 23 Duke J. Comp. & Intl. L. 149 (2012). In early 1990s, Argentina created a favorable regime for international investors by taking such measures as pegging the value of peso to the US dollar one-to-one, which was meant to guarantee security for investments. It also gave assurances to investors with regard to continuing their licenses. Due to constricted exchange rate and relaxed fiscal regime, towards the end of 1990s, the Argentine economic situation began to worsen at a rapid rate. In 2001, the stock market went down and Argentina lost its credit ratings. The government responded by enacting a tighter budget and cutting salaries, which prompted public unrest. Fearing government freezing bank accounts, account holders began withdrawing all their savings, which led to liquidity problems. Economic and social problems led to political instability and virtual collapse of the Argentine economy.
37. Treaty Between the United States of America and the Argentine Republic Concerning the Reciprocal Encouragement and Protection of Investment (14 Nov. 1991).
38. *See also*, *Total S.A. v. The Argentine Republic*, ICSID Case No. ARB/04/01, Award (27 Nov. 2013), *EDF International S.A.*, *SAUR International S.A. and León Participaciones Argentinas S.A. v. Argentine Republic*, ICSID Case No. ARB/03/23, Award (11 Jun. 2012).
39. It is important to highlight that, although (a) the facts of the Argentine gas cases (*CMS*, *Sempra*, *Enron* and *LG&E*) were identical, (b) the claims brought against Argentina were the same, and, (c) the defenses invoked by Argentina were the same in all cases, the arbitral awards diverged on a few points. The tribunals diverged on: (a) the governing law, (b) the treatment of the defense of necessity: whether under the BIT or under the doctrine of necessity of CIL, (c) whether 'essential security interest' included economic crisis, and, (d) the result of a successful necessity plea, in terms of damages. The one thing all tribunals did agree on was that the NPM clause was not self-judging.

[C] ICSID Jurisprudence on Necessity

In *CMS v. Argentina*, the claimant CMS, a company incorporated in the US, brought the case against the respondent Argentina, alleging breach of the Argentina-US BIT based on the emergency measures adopted by Argentina during the crisis. Argentina argued that even if there was a breach of the BIT, responsibility should be precluded and wrongfulness excluded because of the existing circumstances of necessity caused by the severe crisis. Argentina also stated that the requirements for necessity of Article 25 of the ILC Articles were satisfied and that the measures adopted were the only means available to protect the essential interests of the State.

In this case, the tribunal held that some elements of the doctrine of necessity were present, the crisis qualifying as 'difficult enough to justify the government taking action to prevent a worsening of the situation and the danger of total economic collapse', but the cumulative test was not satisfied.[40] In particular, the tribunal reached its decision by looking first at the necessity defence under customary international law reflected in Article 25 of the ILC Articles.

On the matter of essential interests, the tribunal held that the need to avoid a major crisis could constitute an essential interest of the State. In *CMS*, the panel concluded that the crisis was severe, but nevertheless the severity should not automatically preclude wrongfulness.[41] With respect to 'serious and imminent peril', the tribunal concluded that, while the situation was serious enough to justify the measures taken to safeguard the economy of the State, the circumstances of the crisis did not satisfy the exceptional character allowing for an exemption of responsibility or preclusion of wrongfulness.

The tribunal went on to say that the measures adopted by Argentina were not the only means available to safeguard the essential interests of the State. The tribunal arrived at this conclusion after having considered that there were a variety of alternatives to remedy the financial crisis. The tribunal did address the issue concerning the possibility of invoking necessity in times of economic difficulties and held that the Argentina-US BIT was specifically designed to protect investments in times of economic difficulties. Finally, in deciding whether Argentina contributed to the situation of necessity, the tribunal recognized that the events leading to the crisis could not be qualified as entirely internal or external. According to the tribunal, there was an international dimension to the crisis, but Argentina itself had made a significant contribution to the crisis by applying inapt policies, which were further fueled by the external factors.[42] In conclusion, under customary international law, the tribunal held that the cumulative requirements for a finding of necessity were not met in the *CMS* case to preclude wrongfulness and responsibility.

---

40. *CMS Gas Transmission Company v. Argentine Republic*, ICSID Case No. ARB/01/8, Award (12 May 2005).
41. Marie Christine Hoelck Thjoernelund, *State of Necessity as an Exemption from State Responsibility for Investments*, 13 Max Planck Y.B. U.N. L. 423, 433 (2009). *See also CMS Gas Transmission Company v. Argentine Republic*, ICSID Case No. ARB/01/8, Award (12 May 2005).
42. *Ibid.*, pp. 448–449.

The tribunal then proceeded with the analysis of necessity under the clauses of the Argentina-US BIT, referring in particular to Article XI of the BIT:

> This treaty shall not preclude the application by either Party of measures necessary for the maintenance of public order, the fulfillment of its obligations with respect to the maintenance or restoration of international peace or security, or the protection of its own essential security interests.[43]

The objective of this clause is to provide a way for States to exercise domestic powers, rights and measures in times of national emergency. These clauses are also known as non-precluded measures (NPM) clauses, and the effect of such clauses is not to prevent the treaty from operating. NPM clauses provide for temporary conduct necessary to maintain public order, but they do not cancel the underlying obligations. As soon as the State's essential interests are no longer under threat, the treaty goes back into full force.

The tribunal found that, even if not expressly envisaged in Article XI, it is consistent with international law and the object of the BIT to include major economic crisis or economic emergencies in the scope of the article, without limiting the definition of essential security interests to political or national security interests. 'When a state's economy fails, the preservation of its own country and its efforts to ensure the preservation of public order and a stable government, rather than ensuring the financial security of its investors and creditors must be its main priority.'[44] The tribunal concluded also that Article XI is not self-judging;[45] thus, the tribunal has to decide on the legitimacy of the measures involved. In addition, when a State invokes the necessity defense to avoid the obligations under the treaty, it must also prove that there is a nexus between the measures taken and the resolution of the crisis.

The *CMS* annulment committee criticized the reasoning applied by the tribunal in CMS.[46] The committee stated that in a case where the BIT contains an NPM clause, a tribunal should first analyze whether the NPM clause excludes responsibility. If the conditions laid down in the NPM clause are fulfilled, the State's conduct cannot prima facie constitute a breach of the treaty. Therefore, the enquiry into the applicability of customary international law should only be carried out if it is held that there has been an actual breach not precluded by an NPM clause.

---

43. Treaty Between the United States of America and the Argentine Republic Concerning the Reciprocal Encouragement and Protection of Investment (14 Nov. 1991).
44. Oludotun Ogunfolu, *The Necessity Exception to State Liability in International Investment Arbitration: The ICSID Approach*, 44 Inst. Advanced Leg. Stud. (2013).
45. A self-judging clause is a clause declaring that the State should be deemed the sole judge of whether measures could be taken under that clause that would otherwise be a derogation from a treaty obligation. The Treaty between the United States of America and the Republic of Mozambique Concerning the Encouragement ad Reciprocal Protection of Investment (1 Dec. 1998) in its Art. XIV provides language that is used to draft a self-judging clause: '1. This Treaty shall not preclude a Party from applying measures that it considers necessary for the fulfillment of its obligations with respect to the maintenance or restoration of international peace or security, or the protection of its own essential security interests.'
46. *CMS Gas Transmission Co. v. Argentine Republic*, ICSID Case No. ARB/01/8, Decision of the Ad Hoc Committee on the Application for Annulment of the Argentine Republic (25 Sep. 2007).

LG&E v. Argentina gives an instructive comparison, as the tribunal followed reasoning more similar to that of the CMS annulment committee. The tribunal stated that, in deciding about the necessity defence, it 'shall apply first, the Treaty, second, general international law to the extent that it is necessary, and third, the Argentine domestic law'.[47] The tribunal agreed with the *CMS* award in deciding that Article XI of the BIT is not self-judging. However, the tribunal concluded that Argentina was dealing with devastating conditions and a crisis 'during which it was necessary to enact measures to maintain public order and protect its essential security interests'.[48] Such crisis commenced on 1 December 2001 and ended on 26 April 2003. Therefore, Argentina was excused from its obligations under the BIT under Article XI during the stated period because the measures were legitimate to protect the social and economic system. In particular, the tribunal considered that the measures adopted by Argentina as economic recovery were the only means to respond to the crisis.

The tribunal went on to analyze necessity under customary international law. It stated that the BIT clause alone was sufficient to excuse Argentina and that the necessity defence, as recognized in international law, supports the finding of the tribunal. The tribunal confirmed that an essential interest includes economic or other financial interests, that Article XI of the Argentina-US BIT allows the invocation of necessity and added that Argentina has not contributed to the severe crisis but it was instead trying to remedy it by adopting the only means available.

The tribunals also diverged on the question of compensation in the context of necessity defence. The *CMS* panel considered that, in accordance with Article 27(b) of the ILC, it was up to the State to carry the financial burden created by the state of necessity. Hence, the State should compensate the investor. The tribunal in *LG&E* based its interpretation on Article XI of the BIT, which does not explicitly address the question of compensation. It allowed the panel to shift the burden of consequences to the investor and hold that the State does not have to pay compensation for the acts covered by Article XI.[49]

In the *Enron*,[50] and *Sempra*[51] cases, the tribunals reach practically the same decisions as the CMS panel regarding the different requirements for a finding of state of necessity as applied to the crisis in Argentina, concluding that the State did not fully meet such requirements. However, the *Sempra* case follows the tribunal in the *LG&E* case in applying the BIT first as prevailing over international law and then turning to international law for interpretation and definitions. Like the *CMS* case, the *Enron* and *Sempra* awards were subject to annulment proceedings on the question of necessity. The CMS award was eventually upheld in spite of the criticisms of the tribunal's analysis; the *Enron* and *Sempra* awards were annulled with regard to Argentina's

47. *LG&E Energy Corp., LG&E Capital Corp. and LG&E International, Inc. v. Argentine Republic*, ICSID Case No. ARB/02/1, Decision on Liability (2006), para. 206.
48. *Ibid.*, para. 226.
49. Atipo Ambrose Peter, *The International Investment Arbitration System and How the Doctrine of Necessity Exposed Its Weakness*, 13 CEPMLP Annual Review 11-12 (2010).
50. *Enron Corp. & Ponderosa Assets, L.P. v. Argentine Republic*, ICSID Case No. ARB/01/3, Award (22 May 2007).
51. *Sempra Energy Int'l v. Argentine Republic*, ICSID Case No. ARB/02/16, Award (28 Sep. 2007).

necessity defense.[52] The annulment committees followed the logic of the *CMS* annulment, but found that the misapplication of reasoning was so serious as to amount to 'manifest excess of powers'.[53] The CMS and Enron committees agreed that Article XI of the BIT absolved the State of liability for damages, so that Argentina should pay no compensation to the investors for actions taken during the economic crisis.[54]

While *CMS*, *Enron* and *Sempra* tribunals found Argentina responsible, another panel agreed with *LG&E* in *Continental Casualty*.[55] The tribunal took into consideration the analytical considerations expressed by the CMS annulment committee, and began by applying Article XI as *lex specialis*.[56] The panel concluded that Argentina satisfied the requirements of necessity as contained in Article XI, which were not as strict as in case of the customary international law defence.[57]

The investors of countries other than the US were also affected by the Argentine crisis. Other arbitral awards, such as *Total*,[58] *Impregilo*[59] and *EDF*,[60] allowed the arbitrators to interpret the customary international law defence of necessity in cases where the BIT contained no NPM clause. All of these awards agree with the *CMS* interpretation of the customary international law defence of necessity as applied to the Argentine crisis. It seems that absent the more broad necessity exception of NPM type, tribunals concur in rejecting Argentina's defence.

It is possible to conclude that the Argentine cases highlighted the state of uncertainty and perplexity that exists around the necessity defence. Different tribunals reached contradictory conclusions by applying conflicting legal and factual analyses to the same set of facts and provisions. ICSID tribunals have not interpreted the doctrine of necessity uniformly, and therefore, both States and foreign investors cannot have a clear prospect when pursuing and arguing this defence in international arbitration.

52. Elizabeth A. Martinez, *Understanding the Debate over Necessity: Unanswered Questions and Future Implications of Annulments in the Argentine Gas Cases*, 23 Duke J. Comp. & Intl. L. 149, 162 (2012).
53. *Ibid.* p. 169.
54. *Ibid.* pp. 174–175.
55. *Continental Casualty Co. v. Argentine Republic*, ICSID Case No. ARB/03/9, Award (5 Sep. 2008).
56. *Ibid.*, p. 74.
57. *Ibid.*
58. *Total S.A. v. The Argentine Republic*, ICSID Case No. ARB/04/01, Award (27 Nov. 2013). The award was later annulled with regard to the necessity defence in *Total S.A. v. The Argentine Republic*, ICSID Case No. ARB/04/01, Decision on annulment (1 Feb. 2016). It should be noted that the annulment concerned the fact that the tribunal had not elaborated on the legal standards of 'essential interests' and 'only way', thus manifestly exceeding its powers in failing to apply the law. The conclusion that the crisis in Argentina did not constitute a state of necessity was not directly addressed by the Annulment Committee.
59. *Impregilo S.p.A. v. Argentine Republic*, ICSID Case No. ARB/07/17, Award (21 Jun. 2011). The Annulment Committee upheld the reasoning of the tribunal.
60. *EDF International S.A., SAUR International S.A. and León Participaciones Argentinas S.A. v. Argentine Republic*, ICSID Case No. ARB/03/23, Award (11 Jun. 2012). The Annulment Committee upheld the tribunal's interpretation of necessity.

§7.04 SELF-DEFENSE OR NATIONAL SECURITY DEFENSE

The national security defense in international law usually refers to military threats involving a State. The national security defence is an implied exception to international obligations in treaties. 'The Oxford English Dictionary defines the term as the "safety of a nation and its people, institutions, etc., especially from military threat or from espionage, terrorism, etc."'[61] Similar to necessity, it is possible to argue that national security encompasses the nation's health and environment, as well as political and economic vitality of the country.

Customary international law encompasses exceptional reasons for derogation from international obligations, including 'particularly acute security threats that could undermine a country's very existence or make compliance impossible or extremely costly. Many treaties contain explicit national security exceptions, and these take various forms tailored to the particular subject at issue'.[62] The exceptions identified in customary international law usually apply implicitly to all treaties. Many treaties exempt States from compliance with all or parts of their treaty obligations in situations where an investment poses a threat to the essential security interests of such State. The test for States is to find an equilibrium that serves to protect its national security interests and the foreign investor's investment.

States have used different language in drafting a national security defense clause. Terms such as 'national security', 'essential security interests', 'international peace and security', or 'public order' have been used to define it. Two important issues have emerged in recent years related to national security concerns in respect of foreign investment. One has to do with the relationship between economic crisis and national security. As seen, when discussing the Argentina cases above, a number of recent investment disputes has addressed the question of whether Argentina's economic crisis amounted to a threat to the country's national security and whether this could be a valid defense. This is very important development as it included economic threat as a basis for a national security defense and not only military and political threats.

The national security defence is invoked in relation to four exceptions, some of which have already been discussed before. Not surprisingly, change of circumstances and necessity are invoked when the national security of the State is at stake. Moreover, the law of reprisal allows a country to suspend or terminate a treaty in retaliation to the other party's breach. [63] However, there are limits to this exception: 'reprisals (1) can only be executed by agencies or instrumentalities of a State; (2) must be proportionate; and (3) must follow a failed attempt to resolve the violation by peaceful negotiation'.[64] Finally, self-defense, listed in Article 21 of the ILC Articles, is a general principle of law

61. UNCTAD, *The Protection of National Security in IIAs*, UNCTAD Series on International Investment Policies for Development, 7 (United Nations 2009).
62. Susan Rose-Ackerman & Benjamin Billa, *Treaties and National Security*, 40 Intl. L. & Politics 437, 441 (2008).
63. *Ibid.* pp. 443–444.
64. *Ibid.*, pp. 437, 446.

recognized by Article 51 of the UN Charter allowing the States to defend themselves from an armed attack.[65]

The language of treaties usually provides that the parties can take measures necessary for the protection of public order and security. The cited exceptions, however, are not always self-judging.[66] This means that the arbitral tribunal will review the legality of the measures taken to determine whether such measures are justified on national security grounds, with less deference to the State's assessment. The self-defense exception must usually be in response to an armed attack, but like the other exceptions, the State is not the only judge in determining compliance with the exceptions.

Some protection treaties contain specific national security provisions different from the customary international law defenses. NAFTA Article 2102 contains an explicit national security exception, which is considered self-judging in nature, leaving prerogative and discretion to the State to assess whether there is a threat to national security and how to react to it, but subject to the principle and requirement of good faith, to limit the government's discretion. When taking actions inconsistent with the NAFTA provisions in order to protect national security interests, the government still has to act with bona fide intentions and there must be a rational basis for invoking national security.[67]

Here is a typical formulation of the national security exception in NAFTA Chapter XXI, Article 2102:

> 1. Subject to Articles 607 (Energy – National Security Measures) and 1018 (Government Procurement Exceptions), nothing in this Agreement shall be construed:
>
> (a) to require any Party to furnish or allow access to any information the disclosure of which it determines to be contrary to its essential security interests;
> (b) to prevent any Party from taking any actions that it considers necessary for the protection of its essential security interests
>   (i) relating to the traffic in arms, ammunition and implements of war and to such traffic and transactions in other goods, materials, services and technology undertaken directly or indirectly for the purpose of supplying a military or other security establishment,
>   (ii) taken in time of war or other emergency in international relations, or
>   (iii) relating to the implementation of national policies or international agreements respecting the non-proliferation of nuclear weapons or other nuclear explosive devices; or
> (c) to prevent any Party from taking action in pursuance of its obligations under the United Nations Charter for the maintenance of international peace and security.

65. ILC, Commentary to the Articles on Responsibility of States for Internationally Wrongful Acts, 148 (2012).
66. Self-judging clauses are provisions whereby states reserve the right of non-compliance with international legal obligations under certain circumstances, mainly if the State considers that compliance would harm an essential security interest.
67. UNCTAD, *The Protection of National Security in IIAs*, UNCTAD Series on International Investment Policies for Development, 40 (United Nations 2009).

Compare the above to the language in the 2004 US Model Treaty under Article 18:

Article 18: Essential Security

Nothing in this Treaty shall be construed:

1. to require a Party to furnish or allow access to any information the disclosure of which it determines to be contrary to its essential security interests; or
2. to preclude a Party from applying measures that it considers necessary for the fulfillment of its obligations with respect to the maintenance or restoration of international peace or security, or the protection of its own essential security interests.

It is possible to find similar provisions in the ECT (Article 24) and in model BITs, like the 2004 Canada Model BIT (Article 10), and the 2015 India Model BIT (Article 33), with just slight differences in content and scope. There are open-ended provisions and precisely defined provisions, self-judging or non-self-judging provisions, exempting from all obligations or only specific treaty provisions, and these provisions must usually not be applied arbitrarily or in a discriminatory way. Other national security provisions can be found in the Australia-India BIT (Article 15), the Czech Republic-United States BIT (Article X), the Estonia-United States BIT (Article IX), the Japan-China BIT (Protocol) and many others.[68]

In general, this defence allows States to determine, within the limits of the language of the treaty or of international law, what is necessary to protect the national security interests of the State and thus an exception to compliance with its obligations under the treaty. Since national security and self-defense are generally more concerned with threats to the nation and the very existence of the State, case law in investment law context is rather scarce.

§7.05 DISTRESS

Distress is a state of emergency, concerning the safety of individuals in the immediate circumstances, and is included in Article 24 of the ILC Articles.[69] Contrary to force majeure, the individual whose acts are imputable to the State is acting in violation of the State's international obligations of his own free will. Unlike necessity, there is no essential interest of the State that is at stake. This defense has most often been invoked when a foreign ship or aircraft enters into the territory of a State without permission to safeguard the lives of their crews.

It is difficult to imagine circumstances in which distress may be invoked in the context of investor-State arbitration, since it is concerned purely with serious danger to a person's life. The most prominent case where distress was invoked in the context of arbitration is the *Rainbow Warrior* case, already discussed above with regard to force

68. For further reading *see* Katia Yannaca-Small, *Essential Security Interests under International Investment Law*, in *International Investment Perspectives: Freedom of Investment in a Changing World*, 93, Annex 5.A2, 112 (OECD 2007).
69. International Law Commission, Commentary to the Articles on Responsibility of States for Internationally Wrongful Acts, 161 (2012).

majeure.[70] The tribunal accepted a broad definition of distress as including a 'serious health risk' in addition to life-threatening circumstances.[71] However, the defense was not accepted with regard to routine medical concerns, such as examination during pregnancy, absent facts demonstrating that the life of the baby was in grave danger.[72]

In the context of investor-State arbitration, the defense of necessity is usually more relevant than distress, since the interests concerned are of economic and political nature as opposed to individual lives. However, it is possible to imagine a State claiming distress to preclude wrongfulness of an expropriation of investor facilities, which put the lives of workers in immediate danger by not complying with health regulations.

§7.06 CORRUPTION

Although the ILC does not expressly include corruption as a defense, corruption is nonetheless invoked more and more by host States. Bribery, as a form of corruption, comes in many forms and colors and, over time changes and morphs into entirely new forms. Such an explanation may be the reason why OECD Anti-Bribery Convention, does not contain a definition of corruption at all.[73] The same holds true for the UN Office on Drugs and Crime, when it states that 'there is no single, comprehensive, universally accepted definition of corruption and that attempts to develop such a definition invariably encounter legal, criminological and, in many countries, political problems'.[74] It further refers to different modalities under which corruption may appear, including, 'bribery, embezzlement, theft and fraud, extortion, abuse of discretion, favoritism, nepotism and clientelism, conduct creating or exploiting conflicting interests, and improper political contributions'.[75]

Bribery is a phenomenon that has been tied to human existence for thousands of years. It asserts itself in all forms of human relationships and activity. A relevant verse of the Book of Exodus states: '[a]nd you shall take no bribe, for a bribe blinds the discerning and perverts the words of the righteous.'[76] Many efforts are underway to uproot bribery, including implementing anti-corruption measures. It is, however, quite ingenious and naive to assume that corruption can be eradicated.

Notwithstanding, proper regulation can lead to the prevention of situations where a party to a dispute bases its defense claims on its own, or the opposing party's corrupt acts, while at the same time it is involved in unlawful behavior.

Corruption has been at the forefront in international investor arbitration in recent years, sparking changes in policy and international law, as well as transparency and

70. *See* above §7.02.
71. ILC, Commentary to the Articles on Responsibility of States for Internationally Wrongful Acts, 163 (2012).
72. *Ibid.*
73. OECD Convention on Combating Bribery of Foreign Public Officials in International Business Transactions (adopted 21 Nov. 1997, in force since 15 Feb.1999).
74. *Ibid.*
75. *Ibid.*
76. Exodus, 23:8 NKJV.

rule of law debates. All of this ultimately resulting in international organizations pronouncing themselves on the subject by means of conventions against corruption from the 1997 OECD Anti-Bribery Convention,[77] the 1996 OAS Inter-American Convention against Corruption,[78] the 1997 EU Convention against Corruption Involving Officials,[79] the 2003 African Convention on Preventing and Combating Corruption,[80] to the 2003 UN Convention against Corruption.[81]

Corruption refers to any action of transferring something of value, including money, to a public official, for his or her own benefit, in order that the official act or refrain from acting in the exercise of his or her official duties. The State generally argues this defence when the foreign investor was involved in corruption practices with a State entity to procure the contract. Unfortunately, it is not infrequent in international arbitration that the transaction or contract in question has been obtained by bribery or corruption of government officials. While an agreement that is obtained or induced by corruption or bribery is generally void *ab initio*, it is also very difficult to prove corruption. When successfully proven, the foreign investor may lose substantial investments.

The fight against corruption is ongoing and, in addition to international conventions to fight corruption, States have also jumped on the bandwagon, enacting legislation to that end. The most cited and, perhaps, well-enforced example is the Foreign Corrupt Practices Act (FCPA) enacted by the US in 1977.[82] The FCPA prohibits bribery, but carves out an exception for routine governmental action. It is important to note that the amount of money involved in the action is relevant. This Act is of broad application, as it covers not only the US companies but also covers any individual who is a citizen, national or resident in the US. The FCPA sets forth the following:

> § 78dd-2. Prohibited foreign trade practices by domestic concerns
>
> (a) Prohibition
>
> It shall be unlawful for any domestic concern, other than an issuer which is subject to section 78dd-1 of this title, or for any officer, director, employee, or agent of such domestic concern or any stockholder thereof acting on behalf of such domestic concern, to make use of the mails or any means or instrumentality of interstate commerce corruptly in furtherance of an offer, payment, promise to pay, or authorization of the payment of any money, or offer, gift, promise to give, or authorization of the giving of anything of value to
>
> (1) any foreign official for purposes of
>
> (a) Influencing any act or decision of such foreign official in his official capacity, (ii) inducing such foreign official to do or omit to do any act in violation of the lawful duty of such official, or (iii) securing any improper advantage; or

77. OECD Convention on Combating Bribery of Foreign Public Officials in International Business Transactions (17 Dec. 1997) 38 ILM 505 (1999).
78. Inter-American Convention Against Corruption (29 Mar. 1996).
79. EU Convention Against Corruption Involving Officials (26 May 1997) 37 ILM 12 (1998).
80. African Union Convention on Preventing and Combating Corruption (1 Jul. 2003) 43 ILM 5 (2004).
81. UN Convention Against Corruption (31 Oct. 2003), Doc. No. A/58/422.
82. Foreign Corrupt Practices Act (1977) (FCPA) (15 USC §§78 dd-1 et seq.).

(b) inducing such foreign official to use his influence with a foreign government or instrumentality thereof to affect or influence any act or decision of such government or instrumentality, in order to assist such domestic concern in obtaining or retaining business for or with, or directing business to, any person;

(2) any foreign political party or official thereof or any candidate for foreign political office for purposes of

(a) influencing any act or decision of such party, official, or candidate in its or his official capacity, (ii) inducing such party, official, or candidate to do or omit to do an act in violation of the lawful duty of such party, official, or candidate, or (iii) securing any improper advantage; or

(b) inducing such party, official, or candidate to use its or his influence with a foreign government or instrumentality thereof to affect or influence any act or decision of such government or instrumentality, in order to assist such domestic concern in obtaining or retaining business for or with, or directing business to, any person;

(3) any person, while knowing that all or a portion of such money or thing of value will be offered, given, or promised, directly or indirectly, to any foreign official, to any foreign political party or official thereof, or to any candidate for foreign political office, for purposes of

(a) influencing any act or decision of such foreign official, political party, party official, or candidate in his or its official capacity, (ii) inducing such foreign official, political party, party official, or candidate to do or omit to do any act in violation of the lawful duty of such foreign official, political party, party official, or candidate, or (iii) securing any improper advantage; or

(b) inducing such foreign official, political party, party official, or candidate to use his or its influence with a foreign government or instrumentality thereof to affect or influence any act or decision of such government or instrumentality, in order to assist such domestic concern in obtaining or retaining business for or with, or directing business to, any person.

(b) Exception for routine governmental action

Subsections (a) and (i) of this section shall not apply to any facilitating or expediting payment to a foreign official, political party, or party official the purpose of which is to expedite or to secure the performance of a routine governmental action by a foreign official, political party, or party official.[83]

As stated in the Preamble of the OECD Convention on Combating Bribery, 'bribery is a widespread phenomenon in international business transactions, including trade and investment, which raises serious moral and political concerns, undermines good governance and economic development, and distorts international competitive conditions ... All countries share a responsibility to combat bribery in international business transactions'.[84]

Corruption was accepted as a defense in arbitration for the first time in the *ICC Case No. 1110* from 1963, in which sole arbitrator, Mr Lagergren, famously maintained

83. FCPA, § 78dd-2.
84. OECD Convention on Combating Bribery of Foreign Public Officials in International Business Transactions (17 Dec. 1997) 38 ILM 505 (1999).

that 'parties who had entered into an "agency agreement" by which one party paid bribes to government officials on behalf of the other, have forfeited any right to ask for assistance of the machinery of justice (national courts or arbitral tribunals) in settling their disputes'.[85] In that case, the claimant asked the arbitrator to enforce an agency agreement, the main object of which was payment of bribes by the agent on behalf of the principal. After the principal did not remunerate the agent, the latter tried to get the enforcement of the contract through arbitration. It was one of the rare cases where the parties themselves submitted a dispute arising out of an agreement for corruption to arbitration, which is almost never invoked in modern investment dispute resolution.[86]

There is a variety of ways in which corruption may affect investor-State arbitration. In most cases, the respondent State claims that the investment agreement was procured by corruption and, as such, should not be enforced. Since corruption is not listed as one of affirmative defenses summarized by the ILC, the introduction of such claims is surrounded by debate and inconsistency. Generally, there are three approaches to address corruption. First, corruption may act to preclude jurisdiction *ratione materiae* in cases where the applicable treaty mentions that investment has to be brought 'in accordance' with the laws of the host State.[87] Second, some tribunals have declined jurisdiction on the basis that a contract procured by bribes is contrary to the *ordre public international* or public policy.[88] Third, a last category encompasses general principles of law, which are invoked to dismiss claims of a corrupt investor, such as unclean hands and lack good faith.

There are two different approaches as to how the tribunal may tackle corruption allegations. The first approach is treating investor's misconduct as a jurisdictional issue. Another approach would be to employ separability principle[89] and undertake the finding of corruption as the issues of admissibility and the merits. In any event, the approach of the tribunal would depend on the timing, type, and the degree of severity of the corruption itself.

The arbitrators and commentators conflict on the question of whether corruption should be accepted as a defense precluding jurisdiction or decided on the merits. In cases where the BIT defines investment as one made according to the laws of the host State and the claim is brought on the basis of the treaty, it seems straightforward that an investment procured by corruption in violation of anti-corruption laws would not

---

85. Joe Tirado, Matthew Page & Daniel Meagher, *Corruption Investigations by Governmental Authorities and Investment Arbitration: An Uneasy Relationship*, 29(2) ICSID Rev. 493–513 (2014).
86. Another modern example of an investor admitting to corruption himself is *World Duty Free Company Limited v. Republic of Kenya*, ICSID Case No. ARB/00/7, Award (4 Oct. 2006).
87. Joe Tirado, Matthew Page & Daniel Meagher, *Corruption Investigations by Governmental Authorities and Investment Arbitration: An Uneasy Relationship*, 29(2) ICSID Rev. 495 (2014).
88. *Ibid.*, p. 495, citing *World Duty Free Company Limited v. Republic of Kenya*, ICSID Case No. ARB/00/7, Award (4 Oct. 2006).
89. In *Fiona Trust Holding Corporation v. Privalov (HofL)*, DMC/Arbn/07/04, the tribunal described the separability principle as follows: 'The principle of separability … means that the invalidity or rescission of the main contract does not necessarily entail the invalidity or rescission of the arbitration agreement. The arbitration agreement must be treated as a – distinct agreement and can be void or voidable only on grounds that relate directly to the arbitration agreement.'

satisfy the definition of the protection instrument.[90] However, it should be noted that there has to be a specific law enacted by the host State that would be breached by the corrupt investor in order for the defence to be successful.

In *Fraport AG Frankfurt Airport Services Worldwide,*[91] Philippines successfully demonstrated that the investor had breached its criminal law. In that case, the State law enforcement agency brought an internal investigation concurrently to the arbitral proceedings. It later found that no violation of criminal law had occurred. The tribunal requested that the State disclose the agency's case file to assist the panel with the determination of jurisdiction. After analyzing the documents supplied by the agency as well as other information disclosed during the arbitration, the tribunal concluded that the investor had indeed breached the State law and declined jurisdiction. Later the award was annulled, but not with regard to the finding of criminal law violation where the domestic law enforcement agency found none.[92]

An ICSID tribunal also declined jurisdiction in *World Duty Free*, this time based on considerations of *ordre public international.*[93] This case is particularly curious because the investor himself submitted the evidence to the tribunal that he had bribed the President of Kenya to procure the contract.[94] Claiming that it was standard practice in Kenya, the investor described in detail all the circumstances surrounding the bribe, which proved to be successful in procuring the investment contract. However, the tribunal rejected this argument and found that it had no jurisdiction based on both transnational law and English or Kenyan public policy.[95]

A claimant admitted to bribery in another case, where the parties settled before the tribunal had a chance to make its decision.[96] The tribunal in *EDF (Services)* established the 'clear and convincing evidence' standard for demonstrating corruption in investor-State arbitration.[97] In that case, it was the claimant who was alleging that the government officials had requested bribes, and the panel considered that the proffered evidence was insufficient.[98]

However, there are also examples of awards where the tribunal did not accept the proof of corruption adduced by the State, such as the prominent *Wena Hotels*

---

90. But *see* Joe Tirado, Matthew Page & Daniel Meagher, *Corruption Investigations by Governmental Authorities and Investment Arbitration: An Uneasy Relationship*, 29(2) ICSID Rev. 496 (2014). '[I]n some instances such challenges to the tribunal's jurisdiction failed.' *See*, for example, *Salini Construttori SpA and Italstrade SpA v. Kingdom of Morocco*, ICSID Case No ARB/00/4, Decision on Jurisdiction (23 Jul. 2001), paras 38 and 46; *Tokios Tokelès v. Ukraine*, ICSID Case No ARB/02/18, Decision on Jurisdiction (29 Apr. 2004), paras 83–86.
91. This case was not concerned with the defence of corruption, but it is useful when corruption is invoked as a breach of the host State's law.
92. *Ibid.*, pp. 503–504.
93. *World Duty Free Company Limited v. Republic of Kenya*, ICSID Case No. ARB/00/7, Award (4 Oct. 2006).
94. Joe Tirado, Matthew Page & Daniel Meagher, *Corruption Investigations by Governmental Authorities and Investment Arbitration: An Uneasy Relationship*, 29(2) ICSID Rev. 510 (2014).
95. *Ibid.*
96. *Ibid.*, p. 510, citing *Azpetrol International Holdings BV, Azpetrol Group BV, Azpetrol Oil Services Group BV v. Republic of Azerbaijan*, ICSID Case No. ARB/06/15, Award (8 Sep. 2009).
97. *EDF (Services) Limited v. Romania*, ICSID Case No. ARB/05/13, Award (8 Oct. 2009), para. 5.
98. Joe Tirado, Matthew Page & Daniel Meagher, *Corruption Investigations by Governmental Authorities and Investment Arbitration: An Uneasy Relationship*, 29(2) ICSID Rev. 497 (2014).

decision.[99] Egypt sought to dismiss the investor's claims in relation to leases of hotels claiming that those leases had been obtained through corrupt means. The Tribunal dismissed the claim of corruption, because Egypt had not satisfied its burden of proof. The allegation that an agent hired to advise the investor with regard to doing business in Egypt had improperly influenced government officials was only evidenced by the coincidence of payments to the agent, which came after acquisition of each lease. The agent had not been convicted under Egyptian law, and the respondent had not adduced any further proof of improper influence of the government officials.[100] This case is a perfect illustration of the difficulties States incur in proving corruption, which is most often not documented and sometimes very similar to agency or consultancy services.

§7.07 LACK OF GOOD FAITH

Although good faith is not listed as a defense, it is a principle that applies to all parties at all stages of the arbitration. Good faith is the cord that binds honest and trusting relationships colored by goodwill intentions. While good faith is required by law in many countries, it is not the case in all of them. Good faith is a term that falls within the spheres of morality and ethics. The word evokes a sense of fairness, sincerity and goodness. Good faith is required in an array of situations in everyday life. In many countries it is required in business dealings, contracts, business law, fiduciary duties as well as arbitration.

The concept of good faith is a very well-accepted principle in international arbitration, even if the definition and the application of the term are not so clear. The term 'good faith', though referenced by different international documents, has long escaped precise definition. The difficulty in providing a precise definition of the term is related to the fact that the legal concept of good faith is based upon the moral concept of fairness; which varies depending on one's perception. To analyze this principle, it is necessary to consider general principles of law, contract law, international law and international arbitration rules.

In the area of investment dispute arbitration, the obligation of the parties to arbitrate in good faith is reflected in different legal documents and decisions of tribunals. This duty to arbitrate in good faith can be inferred from the preamble as well as VCLT Article 26, which states: '[e]very treaty in force is binding upon the parties to it and must be performed in good faith.' Accordingly, the performance of an investment treaty, including its dispute settlement provision, must be in good faith. This obligation is also reflected in the 1958 ILC Model Rules on Arbitral Procedure, which under its first paragraph of the preamble states: '[a]ny undertaking to have a recourse to arbitration ... constitutes a legal obligation which must be carried out in good faith.'

99. *Wena Hotels Limited v. Arab Republic of Egypt*, ICSID Case No. ARB/98/4, Award (8 Dec. 2000).
100. *Ibid.*, paras 111–117.

Article 23 of the ICSID Conciliation Rules establishes an express duty to resolve disputes in good faith[101] while Article 11 of the 1996 PCA Optional Conciliation Rules holds states engaging in arbitration proceedings to cooperate in good faith.

Under contract law, every contract must generally be performed in good faith. In international law, the introduction of the principle of good faith is very recent, but it has become a general principle of law, which should be taken into consideration by arbitrators. VCLT Article 31 states that treaties should be interpreted in good faith and there is no reason why arbitration treaties and agreements would be covered by this provision.[102]

In international arbitration, good faith is relevant both for commercial disputes and for investment disputes. The tribunal in *Inceysa Vallisoletana* put it clearly: 'good faith is a supreme principle, which governs legal relations in all of their aspects and content'.[103] Thus, the principle of good faith precludes the tribunals from granting relief to investors who had obtained their investment through fraud or corrupt means.

This principle also affects the arbitrators and the parties, who should conduct the proceedings in good faith in performance of their arbitration contract. The *Methanex v. United States* tribunal stated 'the Disputing Parties each owed in this arbitration a general legal duty to the other and to the Tribunal to conduct themselves in good faith during these arbitration proceedings and to respect the equality of arms between them, the principles of 'equal treatment' and procedural fairness'.[104] The duty to conduct the arbitration in good faith is disrespected when one of the parties intervenes with the proper running of the proceedings, such as by offering illegally obtained evidence or the arbitrators are challenged simply to delay the process.[105]

When a foreign investor violates the principle of good faith during the relationship with the host State, the host State may be able to raise the defense of lack of good faith. 'Respondent states can rely on good faith to deny the right of claimants to seize the tribunal ... to challenge the jurisdiction of the tribunal or admissibility, to contest the right of the claimant to have a decision in its favor, or to challenge the right to compensation.'[106] Moreover, the States have relied on good faith and abuse of procedure to defend themselves against the claims that abuse the direct access that the investors have to arbitrate against a sovereign. By removing the case from the start, the

---

101. ICSID Conciliation Rules, Art. 23(1): 'The parties shall cooperate in good faith with the Commission and, in particular, at its request furnish all relevant documents, information and explanations as well as use the means at their disposal to enable the Commission to hear witnesses and experts whom it desires to call...'
102. Bernardo M. Cremades, *Good Faith in International Arbitration*, 27 Am. U. Intl. L. Rev. 761, 781 (2012).
103. *Inceysa Vallisoletana S.L. v. Republic of El Salvador*, ICSID Case No. ARB/03/26, Award (2 Aug. 2006), para. 230, 28 ICSID Review – Foreign Investment Law Journal 311 (2008).
104. *Methanex Corp. v. United States*, Final Award of the Tribunal on Jurisdiction and Merits, para. 54 (NAFTA Ch. 11 Trib. 3 Aug. 2005).
105. *Ibid.*, at 787.
106. Sanja Đajić, *Mapping the Good Faith Principle in International Investment Arbitration: Assessment of its Substantive and Procedural Value*, Зборник радова Правног факултета у Новом Саду 207, 207 (2012).

good faith argument offers a considerable advantage to the respondent State as it saves the time and costs of arbitration.[107]

The principle of good faith is also used by respondent States to raise preliminary objections to jurisdiction of the arbitral tribunal or admissibility of the claim. In particular, there are some grounds that are usually accompanied by the breach of good faith argument. The first ground is the legality of investment requirement. 'The breach of good faith is easily associated with the unlawful acquisition of the investment, so the accusation of corruptive practices or fraudulent behaviour, if proven correct will deny the protection and thereby jurisdiction of the investment tribunal.'[108]

Lack of good faith may also be alleged as a defense at the investment restructuring stage. Restructuring foreign investment is not uncommon, but it may also be done in view of benefitting from the protection of particular investment treaties. The tribunals have to strike a careful balance between controlling forum shopping through the application of good faith and allowing the investors to structure their ventures in the most efficient way.[109] The underlying idea is to deny access to international arbitration to investments that are made uniquely to benefit from the jurisdiction of a tribunal as opposed the variety of benefits that may be offered by the BIT.[110]

Another instance where lack of good faith may be asserted is complying with the nationality requirement. Here, the good faith principle becomes relevant because the investment protection system is supposed to guarantee protections only to foreign investors. The issue arises when an investor abuses the legal personality of a company to access the investment protection system, acting in bad faith. Arbitral tribunals will have to pierce the corporate veil to establish the real and effective control of the foreign investor.

The tribunal refused to pierce the corporate veil and accepted its jurisdiction in *Tokios Tokelès*.[111] In that case, a company incorporated in Lithuania was actually owned by Ukrainian nationals, who brought a claim under ICSID against Ukraine. Stating that the investor satisfied the definition of the BIT, the tribunal refused to pierce the corporate veil. Moreover, it refuted the good faith argument, because the company had been established six years before the entry into force of the BIT, so there was no abuse of process.[112] The president of the tribunal penned a strong dissent in this case highlighting that the dispute at hand was actually between the Ukrainian state and

107. *Ibid.*, pp. 218–219.
108. *Ibid.*, p. 220.
109. *Ibid.*, p. 223.
110. *Ibid.*, pp. 224–225. *See also Pac Rim Cayman LLC v. Republic of El Salvador*, ICSID Case No. ARB/09/12, Decision on the Respondent's jurisdictional objections (1 Jun. 2012).
111. *Tokios Tokelès v. Ukraine*, ICSID Case No. ARB/02/18, Decision on Jurisdiction (29 Apr. 2004).
112. Sanja Đajić, *Mapping the Good Faith Principle in International Investment Arbitration: Assessment of Its Substantive and Procedural Value*, Зборник радова Правног факултета у Новом Саду 207, 226 (2012).

Ukrainian nationals, who should not have access to ICSID arbitration, no matter the entry into force of the BIT.[113]

An ICSID tribunal rejected jurisdiction in a case with similar facts in *TSA Spectrum*. Although the principle of good faith was not mentioned, the panel considered the objectives of the investment protection treaties to find that the investor had abused it. By piercing the corporate veil, the tribunal concluded that the claimant was national of the respondent State and could not benefit from the protection of the ICSID Convention.[114]

Finally, lack of good faith may be raised by the respondent State at the merits of the case stage, arguing misrepresentation of the investor or unconscionable or unlawful conduct in conducting the investment should preclude the investor from the BIT protection. For example, in *Plama v. Bulgaria*, the tribunal refused to accept the good faith argument at the jurisdiction stage of the arbitration.[115] However, on the merits it found that the misrepresentation perpetrated by the investor breached the principle of good faith. Hence, the investor could not benefit from the protection of the ECT.[116]

§7.08 CONCLUSION

In conclusion, it should be noted that there are different defenses available to respondent States in international investment arbitration to avoid and excuse their obligations under treaties. For most or all of these defenses, it is difficult to find precise, unique, and agreed-upon definitions to be used and applied by international arbitral tribunals. Indeed, it is often the case that these definitions become fact-specific, and the meaning of every defense is construed by looking at the specific facts of a case.

Of course, as the specific facts of a case may be different or interpreted differently by the arbitrators, and because of the absence of the doctrine of stare decisis in international arbitration, it is possible to see different definitions and applications of the same defense in different cases. Arbitrators may embrace narrower or broader interpretations.

However, it is important to keep in mind that arbitrators, when interpreting and applying a specific defense to a case, should always balance the rights of respondent States with the protections guaranteed to foreign investors in the international arena. Arbitrators tend to avoid a broad interpretation because that would create too much discretion for the States in determining when they can legitimately comply or not with international obligations. On the other hand, arbitral tribunals also avoid overly strict

113. *Ibid. See also The Rompetrol Group N.TV. v. Romania*, ICSID Case No. ARB/06/3, Decision on Jurisdiction and Admissibility (18 Apr. 2008). In a case similar to *Tokios Tokelès*, the tribunal accepted that the claimant satisfied the definition of investor contained in the BIT and retained jurisdiction.
114. *Ibid.*, p. 227.
115. *Plama Consortium Limited v. Republic of Bulgaria*, ICSID Case No. ARB/03/24, Award (27 Aug. 2008).
116. Sanja Đajić, *Mapping the Good Faith Principle in International Investment Arbitration: Assessment of Its Substantive and Procedural Value*, Зборник радова Правног факултета у Новом Саду 207, 230 (2012).

and narrow interpretations to accommodate the needs of the States by maintaining reasonable means to derogate from their obligations when dictated by the circumstances.

Finally, a balanced and restrictive interpretation is also necessary and desirable not only to avoid abuse and the eluding of international obligations but also for the stability and predictability of the law, cardinal points of international law and treaties. They need to 'distinguish between legitimate regulatory choices and illegitimate excuses for protectionism'.[117] And, since not all jurisdictions have provisions encompassing these defenses (or maybe the standards are subject to particular interpretations), the parties to international investment agreements have the freedom to draft and adapt clauses based on the purpose and objectives of the agreement and on the needs of the parties.

International agreements and BITs 'therefore need to fulfil a dual purpose: on the one hand, they need to give appropriate protection to foreign investors so that they feel attracted to the host country, and on the other hand, they must give sufficient comfort to the [States] that they remain able to regulate foreign investment for ... security reasons'.[118]

Questions

(1) To raise a defense of necessity under customary international law, a State cannot have contributed to the situation of emergency. This was one of the hurdles that Argentina had a hard time overcoming in its plea of economic distress. Does this requirement mean that necessity should not be available in claims of economic distress? Or should the requirement be interpreted with some leeway to permit at least theoretically a claim to move forward?

(2) The defense of 'necessity' under customary international law is seen as very stringent. Is it too stringent to be of any practical use?

(3) How would you interpret the requirement that a measure be the 'only means' available to respond to a sudden and imminent crisis?

(4) Should the treaty provision that referring to nothing in the treaty prevents a State from taking acts in accordance with its essential security interests be read as incorporating the customary international law of necessity, or as a separate standard? If it is separate, what is the standard? How do you measure what is necessary?

(5) Should States make treaty exceptions 'self-judging'?

(6) Are self-judging treaty exceptions still subject to principles of 'good faith'?

(7) What effect should a successful necessity defense have? Should it exculpate the State from any monetary liability? Should there be only partial exculpation?

117. Cynthia C. Galvez, *'Necessity', Investor Rights, and State Sovereignty for NAFTA Investment Arbitration*, 46 Cornell Intl. L. J. 143, 147 (2013).

118. UNCTAD, *The Protection of National Security in IIAs*, UNCTAD Series on International Investment Policies for Development, 25 (United Nations 2009).

(8) Does your answer to the previous question change if the defense is found as a treaty standard independent from customary international law?
(9) If the treaty standard is separate from customary international law, how does one assess whether measures are 'necessary'?

CHAPTER 8

Evidence, Burden of Proof and Document Production

Most arbitral rules do not provide detailed guidance on evidentiary matters leaving it to a tribunal's discretion. However, a standard international arbitration procedure that borrows from both the common law and the civil law traditions has been progressively devised. Yet, arbitrators' legal backgrounds and cultures may affect the tribunal's disposition and create tension arising from the common law and civil law approaches to evidence.

The IBA Rules on the Taking of Evidence in International Arbitration (IBA Rules) on Taking of Evidence were amended in 2010 to provide guidelines in investor-State arbitration and serve as a compromise between the civil and common law traditions differences in dealing with evidentiary matters.

The general rule in international law as to burden of proof is *actori incumbit onus probatio*. This means that the party who makes an allegation has the burden of proving it. This rule applies to investor-State arbitration as well. Based on this rule, the investor must prove its factual and legal allegations and the host State has to prove its defenses or any allegations it makes.

The burden of proof refers to who bears the burden of proving what he or she alleges; the standard of proof indicates how much evidence has to be produced by the party who bears the burden of proof.

The most common standard of proof that is applied is the balance of probabilities or preponderance of evidence. For allegations that might touch on criminal law matters (such as allegations of corruption) some tribunals have insisted on a heightened standard of proof.

§8.01 INTRODUCTION

Evidence plays a crucial role in the outcome of all cases because disputes are determined by the application of the law to factual data. In investor-State arbitration, this is also true. Its particularity comes from the fact that arbitrators and counsel often bring the 'bag and baggage'[1] of their respective legal cultures, as well as their own timetables, into the process of bridging gaps between practices rooted in national procedural traditions. In civil law systems, the emphasis is traditionally on substantive rights. Common law systems, on the other hand, remain under the influence of the old 'remedies precede rights' principle – now largely abandoned – whereby the emphasis is placed on the proceedings through which the rights will be established and protected.[2] Because international arbitration encompasses disputes between parties of different legal systems, divergence in evidentiary issues in a common law country versus a civil law country should be expected. Variances may range from, the accessibility of documentary evidence, the standard of proof, to who can be witnesses and how expert evidence is presented. Yet, in many ways, evidentiary issues in arbitration have taken on an integrated hybrid form of the two.

Even if it is so, the current practice on evidence taking in international arbitration leaves itself open to many questions. Some may be asking: What is the stand on hearsay? Are leading questions allowed on direct examination? Which privileges will be recognized to deny the presentation of evidence? What about the confidentiality of documents, especially for sovereign State parties in investment disputes? Many of these questions can only be answered on a case-by-case basis by the arbitral tribunal. Accordingly, one common critique of the evidence taking process in international arbitration surrounds arbitrator discretion. The result of a lack of any kind of robust, expounded evidentiary framework is the inevitable reliance on arbitrator decision-making.[3]

§8.02 GENERAL DIFFERENCES BETWEEN THE COMMON LAW AND CIVIL LAW APPROACH ON EVIDENCE

For the civil law lawyer, it is essential that the legal problem in dispute be clearly defined so that the judge can solve it. Facts are relevant and have to be proved only insofar as they help in defining the legal problem. The common law lawyer generally takes the opposite approach, the chief concern being that all parties have equal and full knowledge of the facts. It is on this basis that they will then be able to express precise legal claims, often presented as alternatives.

1. *See* Guillermo Aguilar Alvarez, *To What Extent Do Arbitrators in International Cases Disregard the Bag and Baggage of National Systems?*, ICCA Seoul Conference, 10–12 Oct. 1996, ICCA Congress Series No. 8, 139 (Kluwer Law International 1998).
2. *See* René David, *L'arbitrage dans le commerce international*, 149 (Economica 1982).
3. Karl Pornbacher &Alexander Dolgorukow, *Reconciling Due Process and Efficiency in International Arbitration – The Arbitrator's Task of Achieving the One Without Sacrificing the Other*, 3 The Annals of the Faculty of Law in Belgrade – Belgrade L. Rev. 50, 51 (2013).

The common law system is a party-driven system. Parties have complete autonomy to collect evidence and decide how the evidence will be presented to prove their respective case. Most of the fact-finding or discovery process is done pretrial and out of court and many documents so produced will never be submitted to it. Accordingly, the parties' lawyer has a very important role. The judge in this system has no investigative role. Its function is to listen to the evidence presented and decide the case upon the evidence presented. Under the common law system, the judge acts as an administrator and overseer of justice. He or she monitors the process to ensure the law is correctly and fairly applied.

In the civil law system, the judge has the task of making an inquiry. In this system, the judge plays a very active role. The judge questions witnesses and examines all relevant evidence. Since the witnesses are considered as witnesses of the court, it is the judge who obtains most of the evidence through the process of questioning these witnesses. A civil law judge will not hesitate to invite discussion on legal issues that have not been raised by any of the parties or to appoint one or more experts if he or she feels that it is the best way of establishing relevant facts.

[A] Oral or Documentary Evidence?

Under the common law legal system, oral testimony of the parties and their respective witnesses carry the greatest weight and importance. In oral testimony, cross-examination of the witness is regarded as an invaluable tool for obtaining the truth. Because the witness' credibility is at stake, cross-examination of the witness is crucial. Documentary evidence is generally regarded as being inferior to oral evidence. The physical presence of the witness also gives the accused the opportunity to rebut his testimony and confront the accusers. This is considered one of the factors of a fair trial.

Under the civil law system, emphasis is on written or documentary evidence. The notion is that documents do not lie and that, in case of witness testimony, recollection of events is not always accurate, either because time has passed after the event, the witnessed event was over in a matter of seconds or the state of mind of the witness under the event's circumstances.

[B] Who Can Be Witnesses?

In common law legal systems, anyone can be a witness, including the parties themselves. However, in the civil law system, a witness has to be a disinterested third party. No one is a witness in his or her own case. The notion is that parties view disputes from their own angle and they are interested in the outcome; thus, this often clouds their view. For this reason, a party testifying as to events will naturally be skewed in his or her favor. This exclusion extends to third parties, whose testimony may not be neutral under the circumstances, such as employees, commercial partners and other closely related persons.

Another difference between legal systems is the issue of witness preparation. Witness preparation under the US common law system is standard whereas under other common law systems such as English law it is strictly limited, while it is not allowed under most civil law systems.

[C] Is Hearsay Evidence Admissible?

As stated earlier, in the common law system great emphasis is placed on oral evidence. Oral evidence has to be direct in common law legal systems. This means that if the witness is referring to a fact that could be seen, it must be the evidence of the witness who actually saw it. Direct evidence excludes hearsay evidence. This is so because in hearsay evidence there is no way the opposing party can discern or check whether the witness is speaking the truth about what has happened. His or her knowledge is limited to what was said about it. However, in the civil law legal system, since documentary evidence carries the most weight, a judge has discretion to determine the admissibility of other the evidence by applying his or her own personal evaluation. Thus, in the civil law legal system there is no rule that excludes 'hearsay' evidence. Rather, it is left for the court to decide the value of what has been said and is reported by the witness.

It is sometimes argued that the common law – civil law differences are overstated and that in practice the two dominant systems are more alike than not. Notwithstanding, the differences may pose a problem where the parties need to agree and reach a harmonized approach to determine the limits and boundaries of evidence and fact-finding. In investor-State arbitration, the arbitrators use the relevant institutional or ad hoc rules that the parties have agreed to in addition to the option of using the IBA Rules[4] to handle evidentiary questions that arise.

Bearing in mind that parties, pursuant to the arbitration agreement, can agree on the procedures of their arbitration, many procedural rules give the arbitral tribunal discretion to determine 'admissibility, relevance, materiality, and weight of the evidence'.[5]

Yet, the arbitrator(s) nationality, legal background and experience may be a factor in the way the arbitrator conducts the arbitral proceeding and the procedural rules he or she uses, as well as his or her position on evidence and document production. This should be a consideration when selecting arbitrators.

§8.03 GUIDING PROVISIONS ON EVIDENCE AND THEIR APPLICATION BY INTERNATIONAL TRIBUNALS

[A] Party Autonomy

Because party autonomy in arbitration is paramount, it is important to start the evidentiary process pursuant to the terms of the parties' agreement – the rules of law they have chosen to the proceedings,[6] if any, as well as the lex arbitri. However,

4. *See* IBA Rules on the Taking of Evidence in International Arbitration (2010).
5. *Ibid.*, Art. 9(1); ICSID Arbitration Rules, Art. 34(1); UNCITRAL Arbitration Rules Art. 27(4).
6. In most cases, parties fail to agree on the law applicable to the proceedings.

procedural laws applicable to arbitration rarely include any procedures for evidence gathering. The institutional or ad hoc rules chosen by the parties may provide general evidence taking guidelines, but it will be up to the parties and the arbitral tribunal to decide on more specific rules of evidence.

[B] 2010 IBA Rules on the Taking of Evidence

The principal institutional and ad hoc rules do not require that every arbitration be conducted in the same manner, which therefore allows parties flexibility in devising the evidence procedures best suited for each arbitration.[7] Because party autonomy and flexibility are among the significant advantages of international arbitration, the IBA introduced the IBA Rules to establish some consistency in international arbitral proceedings.[8] The Foreword to the IBA Rules makes clear that the parties can adopt its procedures through explicit agreement beforehand or at the commencement of the arbitration, as well as adopting a part or the entirety of the rules after commencement.[9] It also makes clear that these Rules are *in addition* to otherwise agreed upon standards and that it acts as gap fillers and does not replace agreed upon institutional or ad hoc rules or chosen laws,[10] unless the parties have agreed otherwise.

The IBA Rules reflect a compromise between the civil and common law traditions. For instance, Article 3(3) on requesting of documents of the 2010 IBA Rules offers a solid example of this compromise in which the Rules allow for document production of relevant and material documents (acceptable to civil law) but limit grandiose document production by allowing only a request for specific documents of a narrow category (favored by common law), yet.[11] The IBA Rules are applied when the parties wish so. However, arbitral tribunals prefer to use them as non-binding guidelines because they do not want to be bound by them and run the risk to see their awards subject to annulment for breach of the parties agreed procedural rules in case a party challenges the interpretation they have given to them. [12] Investor-State arbitrations have benefitted from the IBA Rules, as many arbitral tribunals have utilized their provisions.

---

7. *Commentary on the revised text of the 2010 IBA Rules on the Taking of Evidence in International Arbitration*, 1999 IBA Working Party and 2010 IBA Rules of Evidence Review Subcommittee, 5 Dispute Resolution International 45 (2011).
8. *See Ibid.*; IBA Rules.
9. Foreword, IBA Rules on the Taking of Evidence in International Arbitration (2010); *See Cambodia Power Company v. Kingdom of Cambodia*, ICSID Case No. ARB/09/18, Amended Decision on the Claimant's Application to Exclude Mr Lobit's Witness Statement and Derivative Evidence (14 Feb. 2012) (Stating that the Tribunal considers that it may be guided, as agreed by the Parties and by the IBA Rules on the Taking of Evidence in International Commercial Arbitration.).
10. *See* IBA Rules, Preamble 1 (Stating that the Rules are meant to 'supplement the legal provisions and the institutional, ad hoc or other rules that apply to the conduct of the arbitration'.).
11. *See* IBA Rules, Art. 3.3; *see also Commentary on the revised text of the 2010 IBA Rules on the Taking of Evidence in International Arbitration*, 1999 IRA Working Party and 2010 IBA Rules of Evidence Review Subcommittee.
12. *Ibid.*

[C] Additional Guidelines: ICSID, UNCITRAL, ICC, LCIA and ICDR

Although the IBA Rules on the Taking of Evidence have become the common and accepted form of procedural guidelines for evidence taking in international arbitration, the parties are not under any obligation to adopt them. It may be the case that the parties have only agreed to a certain set of institutional or ad hoc rules in their arbitral agreement and do not agree on adopting the IBA Rules or on the arbitrators using them as guidelines. In that case, the institutional or ad hoc rules offer guidance on the taking of evidence which may differ depending on the rules. Institutional rules include ICSID for investor-State disputes, ICC, LCIA, ICDR and UNCITRAL. In general, each set of rules confers broad power over the procedural process regarding evidence taking to the arbitral tribunal.[13]

For example, the ICC Arbitration Rules state that the arbitral tribunal may summon the parties to produce additional evidence at any time; the UNCITRAL Arbitration Rules give the authority to the arbitral tribunal to determine admissibility, relevance, and weight of the evidence as well as requiring parties to produce evidence at any time; additionally, the ICSID Arbitration Rules contain similar language, giving the arbitral tribunal the power to demand additional evidence or documents if it deems necessary and act as the judge of admissibility for any evidence presented.[14] The ICDR Arbitration Rules allow for even broader discretion conferring wide discretion to the tribunal to 'conduct the arbitration in whatever manner it considers appropriate' (provided the proceeding is equal and fair).[15] The LCIA Arbitration Rules permits the tribunal to apply rules of evidence and decide as the time, manner and form that the evidence should be exchanged between the parties and the tribunal.[16] Overall, the arbitral rules surrounding evidence taking provide for wide flexibility to the arbitral tribunal to decide if and when more evidence is needed and the weight such evidence will be given on a case-by-case basis.

[D] Obligation to Act in Good Faith

Balancing efficiency, due process concerns and procedural fairness may differ across the cultural gamut; nonetheless, the duty to act in good faith is an omnipresent principle guiding all proceedings in investor-State arbitration.

The duty of parties to act in good faith is present in many legal systems. The term good faith not only appears in several institutional rules' provisions, but it is often cited

13. ICSID Convention Art. 43; ICSID Arbitration Rules Art. 34; 2010 UNCITRAL Arbitration Rules Art. 27; 2017 ICC Arbitration Rules, Art. 22 and Art. 25; 2014 LCIA Arbitration Rules, Art. 15 and Art. 22; ICDR Arbitration Rules, Art. 20 and Art. 21.
14. ICSID Convention, Art. 43; ICSID Arbitration Rules, Art. 34; 2010 UNCITRAL Arbitration Rules, Art. 27; 2017 ICC Arbitration Rules, Art. 22 and Art. 27.
15. ICDR Arbitration Rules, Art. 20 and Art. 21.
16. 2014 LCIA Arbitration Rules, Art. 15 and Art. 22.

by arbitral tribunals as a point of analysis.[17] The IBA Rules provide in the Preamble that the rules were 'intended to provide an efficient, economical and fair process for the taking of evidence in international arbitrations'. Article 3 of the Preamble calls for good faith by the parties in their conduct throughout the arbitral proceedings. Moreover, the IBA Rules call for adverse inferences and additional costs if parties are found not to have acted in good faith in the taking of evidence.[18] ICSID Arbitration Rule 34 requires that the parties 'cooperate with the Tribunal in the production of the evidence ...'[19]

§8.04 BURDEN AND STANDARD OF PROOF

Idem est non esse et non probari. This Latin maxim of Roman law in a literal translation means *it is the same not to exist and not prove.* Thus, because evidence is the procedure by which the parties seek to convince the arbitral tribunal of the veracity of a fact, the lack of proof may suggest that the assertion is untrue. The question as to who must produce evidence and how much evidence needs to be produced will certainly arise during the arbitral proceeding.

[A] Burden of Proof: Who Must Produce Evidence?

The basic rule in international law as to who has the burden of proof rests on a rule that comes from Roman law, *actori incumbit onus probation* – the party who makes an assertion has the burden of proof. Accordingly, the party seeking to rely on facts has the burden to prove that they are true. The burden of proof essentially addresses who is responsible to produce the evidence, which normally is the party with a claim or defense or counterclaim. The initial burden rests on the claimant to establish the claim, and respondent has to prove its defenses and counterclaims. But if the claimant does not discharge its burden of proof, its claim fails.

In investor-State arbitration, burden of proof is not something that the institutional rules generally specify or define. However, Article 27(1) of the UNCITRAL Arbitration Rules and Article 24 of the Iran-US Claims Tribunal Rules of Procedure prescribe that '[e]ach party shall have the burden of proving the facts relied on to support its claim or defence.' The IBA Rules implicitly refer to the burden of proof in Article 3(1) for the production of documents where the parties must submit all

17. ICSID Convention, Art. 34; ICSID Arbitration Rules, Rule 34(3); LCIA Arbitration Rules, Art. 14.5 and Art. 32.2; ICDR Arbitration Rules, Art. 20.7 (Stating that the arbitral tribunal may take the necessary steps to protect the integrity of the arbitration); IBA Rules, Preamble, 1, 3.
18. IBA Rules, Preamble, Art. 9; *see also Iran-United States Claims Tribunal* (stating i.e., an accepted principle that an adverse inference be drawn from failure to comply with evidentiary requests); *Inceysa Vallisoletana S.L. v. Republic of El Salvador*, ICSID Case No. ARB/03/26, Award, ¶ 230 (2 Aug. 2006), 28 ICSID Rep. 311 (2008) (Stating that good faith is a supreme principle, which governs legal relations in all of their aspects and content) (Citing Bernardo M. Cremades, *Good Faith in International Arbitration*, 27 Am. U. Intl. L. Rev. 761, 785 (2012)); *Methanex Corporation v. United States of America*, UNCITRAL, Final Award on Jurisdiction and Merits (3 Aug. 2005), para. 54 (Reiterating that the parties have a duty to act in good faith towards each other and the Tribunal.).
19. ICSID Arbitration Rules, Art. 34(3).

available documents on which they will rely, showing that there is a burden on parties to offer the supporting evidence that they have to prove their case.[20] The other institutional rules do not specifically address the burden of proof.

The ICSID Arbitration Rules do not specifically provide for the burden of proof; however, arbitral tribunals commonly cite the generally accepted principle that the burden of proof is with the claimant.[21] The Tribunal in *Windstream Energy v. Canada* held that it is for each Party to support its position as to the content of the rule with appropriate legal authorities and evidence.[22] The Tribunal in *Rompetrol v. Romania* reiterated the principle when it stated that, '[t]he Tribunal finds that it can safely rest, so far as the burden of proof is concerned, on the widely accepted international principle that a party in litigation bears the burden of proving the facts relied on to support its claim or defence.'[23]

Moreover, the burden to prove one's assertions has been accepted to apply to all stages of the arbitration process, including the jurisdictional, merits, and damages phases. However, in investor-State arbitration, at the jurisdictional phase, many tribunals have followed what is known as the Higgins test requiring the claimant to show first that the facts it is alleging are capable of falling under the appropriate treaty.[24] In other words, a party must prove it has an investment under the BIT and a tribunal will provisionally accept the allegations of fact as true and then assess whether those alleged facts, if proved, would lead to a violation of the relevant treaty.[25]

---

20. IBA Rules, Art. 3; *Commentary on the revised text of the 2010 IBA Rules on the Taking of Evidence in International Arbitration*, 1999 IBA Working Party & 2010 IBA Rules of Evidence Review Subcommittee, 6.
21. *See Libananco Holdings Co. Limited v. Republic of Turkey* ICSID Case (2011) (It is now common ground between the Parties that the Claimant has the burden of proof); *see also Asian Agricultural Products Limited v. Sri Lanka*, ICSID Case (1990) ('There exists a general principle of law placing the burden of proof upon the claimant'); Art. 24(1) Iran-United States Claims Tribunal ('Each party shall have the burden of proving the facts relied on to support his claim or defense.').
22. *Windstream Energy LLC v. The Government of Canada* (PCA Case No. 2013-22), Award (27 Sep. 2016).
23. *Rompetrol Group NV v. Romania*, ICSID Case No. ARB/06/3, Award (6 May 2013), para. 179.
24. *Oil Platforms* (*Islamic Republic of Iran v. United States of America*), Preliminary Objection, Judgment, Separate Opinion of Judge Higgins ICJ Reports 803, 847 (1996).
25. *Ibid.*, 803, 856 ('The only way in which, in the present case, it can be determined whether the claims of Iran are sufficiently plausibly based upon the 1955 Treaty is to accept pro tem the facts as alleged by Iran to be true and in that light to interpret Articles 1, IV and X for jurisdictional purposes – i.e., to say, to see if on the basis of Iran's claims of fact there could occur a violation of one or more of them.'); *See Phoenix Action, Ltd. v. Czech Republic*, ICSID Case No. ARB/06/5, Award (15 Apr. 2009) ('If jurisdiction rests on the existence of certain facts, they have to be proven at the jurisdictional stage. In addition, if the alleged facts are facts that, if proven, would constitute a violation of the relevant BIT, they have indeed to be accepted as such at the jurisdictional stage, until their existence is ascertained or not at the merits level.'). But *see PSEG Global Inc and Konya Ilgin Elektrik Uretim ve Ticaret Limited Sirketi v. Republic of Turkey*, ICSID Case No. ARB/02/5, Decision on Jurisdiction (4 Jun. 2004) (Noting however, that the prima facie test in the *Phoenix Action* is always case-specific and will only be utilized when appropriate; it is not appropriate when the parties disagree strongly about the facts.).

Once the claimant or party seeking to rely on certain facts has satisfied its burden, the burden is then shifted onto the other party to defend with its own evidence.[26] For example, one tribunal stated that there is a point when the claimant can be determined to have provided sufficient evidence to shift the burden to the respondent.[27] A failure to meet the burden of proof can result in the arbitral tribunal refusing to rely or recognize certain evidence, potentially drawing adverse inferences, or even dismissing a claim or an entire case.[28]

Some questions inevitably arise when it comes to the burden of proof: What should the Tribunal do if producing the evidence is too burdensome on a party? How should arbitrators determine when the burden has been satisfied? As to the first question, the IBA Rules permit the exclusion of evidence based on an "unreasonable burden to produce."[29] This does not mean a party can escape document production because the evidence is 'voluminous', rather the difficulties in producing the evidence must be of 'sufficient magnitude to deny the requesting party the document production it seeks', as well as weighing it against its potential relevance and use to the case.[30] As to the latter question, tribunals have the discretion to determine the standard of proof that will satisfy a party's burden to prove a claim.

[B] Standard of Proof: How Much Evidence Must Be Produced?

Whereas the burden of proof surrounds who has an obligation to produce evidence, the standard of proof deals with the level of proof required. This refers to the amount of evidence that a party needs to produce in order to satisfy and establish its claim or defense. Common law systems and civil law systems differ on the standard of proof. For example, the US places standards of proof into several categories including 'preponderance of the evidence', 'clear and convincing evidence', and 'beyond a

26. *See Marvin Feldman v. Mexico*, ICSID Case No. Arb(AF)/99/01, Award (Dec. 2002) ('Also, it is a generally accepted canon of evidence in civil law, common law and, in fact, most jurisdictions, that the burden of proof rests upon the party, whether complaining or defending, who asserts the affirmative of a claim or defence. If that party adduces evidence sufficient to raise a presumption that what is claimed is true, the burden then shifts to the other party, who will fail unless it adduces sufficient evidence to rebut the presumption.'); *see also Pac Rim Cayman LLC v. Republic of El Salvador*, ICSID Case No. ARB/09/12 ('Once the claimant has established a prima facie case of jurisdiction, the burden of proof then shifts to the respondent.').
27. Some scholars hold an opposite view and hold the position that the burden never shifts. In *Reza Said Malek v. Iran* (1992) Iran-USCTR Award No. 534-193-3 [111]; *But see United Parcel Service of America v. Canada*, UNCITRAL/NAFTA, Award on the Merits (24 May 2007), para. 84 (Expressing that the legal burden rests squarely with the Claimant and that burden never shifts.).
28. *See* Ali Z. Marossi, *Shifting the Burden of Proof in the Practice of the Iran-United State Claims Tribunal*, 28 J. Intl. Arb. 427, 431 (2011) ('Where a claimant fails to meet its burden of proof, the Tribunal normally dismisses the claim.'); *see also* Simon Greenberg and Felix Lautenschlager, *Adverse Inferences in International Arbitral Practice*, 22 ICC Intl. Ct. Arb. Bull. 43, 45–47 (2011).
29. IBA Rules, Art. 9(2)(c).
30. Nathan D. O'Malley, *Rules of Evidence in International Arbitration: An Annotated Guide*, 294 (Informa Law from Routledge 2012) (Citing *INA Corp. v. The Islamic Republic of Iran*, Award No. 184-161-1 (1985); *Noble Ventures Inc. v. Romania*, ICSID Case No. ARB/01/11, Award (12 Oct. 2005).).

reasonable doubt'. On the other hand, there are no developed set standards of proof in civil law. The standard in civil law is the '*intime conviction*' of the judge.[31]

Much like in civil law, rules that define or discuss the standard of proof that should be applied by an arbitral tribunal are wanting. Accordingly, tribunals possess wide discretion in the fact-finding process and will handle evidentiary matters pursuant to their discretion and approval. This can also be seen in the IBA Rules under Article 9(1), which grants wide authority to the arbitral tribunal to determine evidence admissibility, relevance, materiality and weight.[32] Overall, the institutional and ad hoc rules do not offer significant guidance as to the degree of proof required to satisfy the arbitral tribunal. Again, the arbitral tribunal holds the cards in determining when a party has satisfied its burden.

[1] Standards of Proof as Applied by Arbitral Tribunals

Although tribunals have wide authority, this authority is not absolute. There are certain standards that a tribunal will apply to determine the level of proof required.

In international arbitral practice, some scholars suggest that the 'preponderance of the evidence' or 'balance of probabilities' standard matches the ordinary standard of proof in practice because the arbitral tribunal is looking for the party whose evidence 'outweighs' the others.[33] The preponderance of the evidence or balance of probabilities is most commonly applied in situations that are not seen as warranting a heightened standard of proof (i.e., for fraud or corruption allegations), breach of contract. This standard of proof 'calls for a claim to be upheld if the tribunal is convinced by the evidence that the claim is more likely than not true'.[34] In other words, the tribunal will evaluate all the evidence from both parties and determine which party's evidence is more likely than not true. Some instances where a tribunal will use the balance of probabilities standard include: allegations of breach of contract, claims for damages, interpretation of contractual clauses, and 'claims based on breach of international treaties regulating the treatment afforded to investors'.[35]

As for allegations of corruption, fraud, bribery or other serious issues that could concern criminal law, arbitral tribunals often use a heightened standard of proof. Their

31. The '*intime conviction*' of the judge standard in Civil law is akin to or may be compared to the 'beyond a reasonable doubt' standard in common law as it is a mental state where the judge is free of doubt as to his or her stance on an issue.
32. IBA Rules, Art. 9(1).
33. *See* Jeff Waincymer, *Procedure and Evidence in International Arbitration, Part II: The Process of an Arbitration, Chapter 10: Approaches to Evidence and Fact Finding*, 765 (Kluwer Law International 2012) (Citing David D. Caron, Lee Caplan & Matti Pellonpä, *The UNCITRAL Arbitration Rules: A Commentary*, 572 (Oxford University Press 2006).
34. Nathan D. O'Malley, *Rules of Evidence in International Arbitration: An Annotated Guide*, 208 (Informa Law from Routledge 2012) (Citing *Ioannis Kardassopoulos v. The Republic of Georgia*, ICSID Case No. ARB/05/18 and ARB/07/15, Award (3 Mar. 2010): 'The Tribunal finds that the principle articulated by the vast majority of arbitral tribunals in respect of the burden of proof in international arbitration proceedings applies in these concurrent proceedings and does not impose on the Parties any burden of proof beyond a balance of probabilities.').
35. Nathan D O'Malley, *Rules of Evidence in International Arbitration: An Annotated Guide*, 208 (Informa Law from Routledge 2012).

view is that a heightened standard and ample evidence is needed in these situations because these are serious allegations and necessary to deter any disgruntled party from easily claiming and succeeding in a corruption or fraud allegation. However, there is no single elevated standard of proof, as arbitral tribunals take on standards including 'clear preponderance of the evidence', 'evidence beyond doubt',[36] 'clear and convincing proof/evidence',[37] or 'further and direct evidence', among others.[38]

When direct evidence is not available or difficult or impossible to procure, the arbitral tribunal may permit circumstantial evidence. Several tribunals have used the reasoning found in *Corfu Channel* that it is accepted practice to allow in circumstantial evidence where a party is unable to prove an allegation directly.[39]

§8.05 FORMS OF EVIDENCE ADMISSIBLE IN INVESTOR-STATE ARBITRATION

Evidence in international arbitral proceedings can mainly be classified into two categories: oral and written. This includes the production of documents and witness testimony (fact and expert witnesses). The arbitral tribunal will decide which methods of presentation of evidence to use as well as the weight accorded to the evidence. The admissibility of any evidence depends on the discretion of the arbitral tribunal, provided the parties are given a reasonable chance to present their case. International arbitration does not follow the rigors of common law exclusionary rules, and thus, arbitrators will decide on the relevancy of evidence to determine its admissibility. Admissibility, however, is not without its exceptions, including confidentiality, privilege, illegally obtained evidence, etc., which shall be delved into later in this chapter.

[A] Documentary Evidence

'[T]he best evidence that can be presented in relation to any issue of fact is almost invariably contained in the documents which came into existence at the time of the events giving rise to the dispute.'[40] The IBA Rules define 'document' broadly, as 'a writing, communication, picture, drawing, program or data of any kind, whether

36. *Hilmarton v. Omnium*, ICC Case No. 5622 (1988).
37. *Westinghouse and Burns & Roe (USA) v. National Power Company and the Republic of Philippines*, ICC Case No. 6401, Award (19 Dec. 1991).
38. *See* Peter Muchlinski et. al, *The Oxford Handbook of International Investment Law*, 604 (Oxford University Press 2008); *see also Libananco Holdings Co. Limited v. Republic of Turkey*, ICSID Case (2011) (noting that for fraud, '[t]he applicable standard of proof is greater than the balance of probabilities but less than beyond reasonable doubt. The term favoured by Claimants is "clear and convincing evidence".').
39. *Corfu Channel (UK v Alb)*, 1949 ICJ 4 (9 Apr. 1949); *see* Lucy Reed, *Confronting Complexities in Fact-Finding and the Nature of Investor-State Arbitration Fact-Finding in Interstate Disputes*, 106 Am. Socy. Intl. L. Procs. 233, 235 (2012) (Citing *Corfu Channel* (*U.K. v. Albania*), Judgment on the Merits (25 Mar. 1948) ICJ Reports 4 (1949).).
40. Alan Redfern & Martin Hunter et.al., *Law and Practice of International Commercial Arbitration* 298 (4th ed., Thomson Professional Publication 2004).

recorded or maintained on paper or by electronic, audio, visual or any other means'.[41] As noted earlier, common law systems tend to rely on oral testimony as the main method of evidence gathering, whereas civil law systems rely on contemporaneous, written documentary evidence. The divergence in the evidentiary process mainly shows its face in how discovery 'should be allowed and how the procedure should be managed'.[42] One of the most substantial differences between common law and civil law is the scope of document production. In the US wide document production is expected and mandatory disclosures are required, whereas civil law countries view these kind of wide reaching 'fishing expeditions' as abhorrent.

[B] Document Production

It has been suggested that to be efficient, document production must serve the purpose of bringing to the arbitral tribunal's knowledge not any documents relevant and material to the outcome of the dispute, but only documentary evidence without which a party would not be able to discharge the burden of proof lying upon it. On the other hand, when a document production request is disputed, the arbitrators have the responsibility of determining whether the requesting party actually needs the documents to discharge the burden of proof. If not, the request should be denied. When assessing requests, arbitrators must carefully check that the burden of proof actually lies on the requesting party.[43] This approach is not accepted by all arbitrators, some of them consider that a party is entitled to have access to documents that are in the hand of the other party to be able to show that the other side has not proved its case.

Document production in international arbitration is not as expansive and wide-ranging as US discovery in litigation; it takes on a more limited approach. The document requests that can be made by parties in international arbitration must be tailored to specific, relevant documents that are believed to exist or a narrow category of documents assumed to be in the control of the other party. One of the most common means of obtaining documentary evidence in international arbitration is using the 'Redfern Schedule'. The Redfern Schedule was created by Alan Redfern, a prominent British arbitration practitioner. It is essentially a spreadsheet that contains four columns outlining the method to handle document requests. The first column contains the requesting parties' request, which should be furnished with enough detail to identify what the document being requested is or what the narrow category of documents being requested is. The second column outlines how the requesting party believes the document(s) is relevant to the case and material to its outcome. The third column then allows the requested party to interject and object to the request or detail how much it is going to accede to the request. The fourth and last column is left to the

41. IBA Rules, Definitions.
42. Pierre Tercier & Tetiana Bersheda, *Document Production in Arbitration: A Civil Law Viewpoint*, in *The Search for 'Truth' in Arbitration: Is Finding the Truth what Dispute Resolution is About?*, 35, 77 (Markus Wirth, Christina Rouvinez & Joachim Knoll, ASA Special Series, Juris 2011).
43. Yves Derains, *Towards Greater Efficiency in Document Production Before Arbitral Tribunals, A Continental Viewpoint*, Bulletin of the ICC International Court of Arbitration, Special Supplement, Document Production in International Arbitration, 83 (ICC 2006).

arbitral tribunal's decision on the matter.[44] A number of arbitral tribunals have utilized the Redfern Schedule to facilitate their decision on the production of documents.

[1] IBA Rules Concerning Document Requests

Article 3 of the IBA Rules[45] calls for each party involved to submit all documents upon which it will rely to the arbitral tribunal according to the arbitral tribunal's deadlines.[46] In addition, parties may initiate a 'Request to Produce' documents to the arbitral tribunal and/or the other party.[47] This 'Request to Produce', which appears in the two first columns of the Redfern Schedule is used, must contain five components: (a)(i) a description of the requested document so it can be identified; (a)(ii) a specific request for a narrow category of documents that are believed to exist and must be described with sufficient detail; (b) a statement showing that the document(s) is relevant to the case and material to the outcome; (c)(i) a statement showing the documents are not in the control of the requesting party or why it would be unreasonably burdensome for the requesting party to submit such documents; and (c)(ii) a statement delineating why the requesting party believes the document(s) is in the control of the other party.[48] The party that the 'Request to Produce' is addressed to must hand over the documents described in the request within the timeline the arbitral tribunal sets, if no objection is made.[49] A party may refuse to produce documents, but it must formally do so in writing to the tribunal under the guidelines of Article 9(2) and Article 3(3).[50] This is usually done in the third column of the Redfern Schedule. The arbitral tribunal may then ask the parties to consult one another if agreement about document production cannot be reached.[51] If consultation between the parties fails, then the arbitral tribunal will decide to order or not the production of the documents. The arbitral tribunal may also request to inspect the documents before deciding on the objections or in exceptional circumstances, appoint an impartial third party to inform it on the content of the document(s).[52]

[2] IBA Rules, Article 9 on Admissibility and Assessment of Evidence

Article 9 of the IBA Rules affirms the arbitral tribunals authority over the evidence, regarding its 'admissibility, relevance, materiality and weight' according to the arbitrator's discretion.[53] The Commentary on the Revised Text of the 2010 IBA Rules states

44. Nigel Blackaby et. al., *Redfern and Hunter on International Arbitration: Student Version*, 396 (5th ed., Oxford University Press 2009).
45. IBA Rules, Art. 3.
46. *Ibid.*, Art. 3(1).
47. *Ibid.*, Art. 3(2).
48. *Ibid.*, Art. 3(3)(a)–(c).
49. *Ibid.*, Art. 3(4).
50. *Ibid.*, Arts 3(3), 3(5), 9(2).
51. *Ibid.*, Art. 3(6).
52. *Ibid.*, Arts 3(7), 3(8), 3(10).
53. *Ibid.*, Art. 9(1).

that the purpose of Article 9 is to assist the arbitral tribunal in determining 'what evidence it should properly consider and how it should assess the evidence that is properly before it'.[54] There are seven different bases included in Article 9(2) under which the arbitral tribunal can/will choose to limit the admittance of oral or written evidence, based (of course) on its own discretion.

Article 9(2)(a) states simply that the arbitral tribunal will deny the admittance of evidence or deny a document production request that is neither relevant nor material to the outcome of the dispute.[55] Article 9(2)(b) deals with the matter of privilege in international arbitration, which will be discussed further below. Article 9(2)(c) can be invoked when it is unreasonably burdensome to produce the requested evidence, whether it is due to the quantity of the evidence or the difficulty in physically finding and producing the document.[56] This article can be interpreted broadly according to the discretion of the arbitral tribunal. The loss or destruction of documents is another basis upon which evidence may be excluded.[57] Articles 9(2)(e) and (f) deal with confidentiality concerns in producing particular evidence based on the arbitral tribunal's discretion. Article 9(2)(e) concerns evidence that has a 'commercial or technical confidentiality' while Article 9(2)(f) goes even further to establish confidentiality based on 'special political or institutional sensitivity' grounds that are considered to be 'compelling', including evidence that is deemed secret by a government or public institution.[58] The last ground acts as a catch-all provision, where evidence can be excluded if the arbitral tribunal finds its admittance to be counter to 'procedural economy, proportionality, fairness or equality' and those considerations are compelling.[59]

[3] Article 9(2)(b), (3): Privilege

One of the more notable and potentially more expansive limitations in Article 9(2)(b) is left for a more detailed discussion. This article will be familiar to common law trained students, as it deals with the potential privileges that can be invoked as privileges in US litigation in courts. Article 9(2)(b) states that documentary or oral evidence can be denied admittance based on the arbitral tribunal's recognition of a 'legal impediment or privilege' under applicable 'legal or ethical rules'.[60] It is important to note that the manner in which privileges are utilized in US litigation is not the same for international

54. *Commentary on the revised text of the 2010 IBA Rules on the Taking of Evidence in International Arbitration*, 1999 IBA Working Party & 2010 IBA Rules of Evidence Review Subcommittee, 25.
55. *See* IBA Rules, Art. 9(2)(a) (The inverse can be seen in Art. 3(b), where relevance and materiality are required for document requests/production).
56. *See* IBA Rules, Art. 9(2)(c); *see also* Nathan D. O'Malley, *Rules of Evidence in International Arbitration: An Annotated Guide*, 294 (Informa Law from Routledge 2012) (Citing *INA Corporation, Claimant v. The Government of the Islamic Republic of Iran)*, Award No. 184-161-1 (1985); *Noble Ventures, Inc. v. Romania*, ICSID Case No. ARB/01/11, Award (12 Oct. 2005).).
57. *See* IBA Rules, Art. 9(2)(d).
58. *Ibid.*, Art. 9(2)(e), (f); *see also* IBA Rules, Art. 9(4) (providing for an agreement or arrangement where the arbitral tribunal will consider certain evidence as confidential).
59. *See Ibid.*, Art. 9(2)(g).
60. *Ibid.*, Art. 9(2)(b).

arbitration, where the rules are not so strict. Complications can arise in international arbitration over the very definition and scope of privilege, as different legal systems protect different people under the same legal concept. Common law systems interpret privilege very broadly, which is also distinguished from confidentiality. Civil law systems do not have a concept of privilege, but rather have the duty of confidentiality or professional secrecy. Under US law, communications with in-house counsel are protected by attorney-client privilege, whereas under some civil law systems such communications are not. In a civil law country such as France, a lawyer may decide not to share information even though the client has consented to its production,[61] whereas under U.S. common law, and under certain circumstances, the client has the full power to waive attorney-client privilege. These two divergent viewpoints, along with many others in the evidentiary process, may cause confusion and conflict when deciding the best course of action to take in international arbitration. The Commentary on Article 9(2)(b) on the IBA Rules notes that privilege is important to recognize in international arbitration and that protection of documents can be founded on the basis of 'attorney-client privilege, professional secrecy, or the without prejudice privilege'. Some of the most common privileges invoked in international arbitration include attorney-client privilege, privilege for settlement negotiations or without prejudice privilege, and professional secrecy. Article 9(3) outlines these aforementioned applicable privileges. According to the Commentary on the IBA Rules, Article 9(3)(a) attempts to converge the common law's doctrine of attorney-client privilege with the civil law's duty of professional secrecy.[62]

The attorney-client privilege is the most frequently invoked basis for excluding evidence in international arbitration. The institutional and ad hoc rules governing the arbitration offer little to no guidance on the attorney-client privilege, leaving it up to the parties' agreement or ultimately the arbitral tribunal to decide the applicability of the privilege and its scope. This particular privilege deals with the communications between an attorney and their client. More specifically, the *Vito Gallo v. Canada* tribunal set out to define the scope of the privilege by establishing that there must be an attorney acting as an attorney (not in some other capacity), there must be a relationship of trust between the client and attorney, the information or document must have been made in the pursuit of seeking or giving legal advice, and that this information had an expectation of confidentiality when given and would be kept confidential in a contentious situation.[63] This language acts to constrain the privilege to be construed narrowly for fear of abusing the privilege in international arbitral proceedings.

61. Tom Ginsburg & Richard Mosk, *Evidentiary Privileges in International Arbitration*, 50 Intl. & Comp. L.Q. 345, 346 (2013).
62. *Commentary on the revised text of the 2010 IBA Rules on the Taking of Evidence in International Arbitration*, 1999 IBA Working Party & 2010 IBA Rules of Evidence Review Subcommittee, 25.
63. *Vito G. Gallo v. Government of Canada*, NAFTA/UNCITRAL/PCA, Procedural Order No. 3, para. 47.

In investor-State arbitration, many times the investor will not have access to internal government documents that are deemed confidential by the host State.[64] Because the sovereign State is always a party to the dispute, document production in investor-State arbitrations usually must be narrowly tailored and specific. These disputes many times center around actions that the State has undertaken in its sovereign right over its own territory, therefore, document production can touch upon very sensitive issues which inevitably can then lead to challenges in producing documents.[65] Thus, States will prefer to include in their BIT a provision to exclude from production any and all privileged, confidential, private, or secret information, communications, etc. For example, the 2012 US Model BIT includes provisions for the Tribunal to abide by certain procedures to prevent the disclosure of what is defined as 'protected information'.[66]

[4] Additional Institutional and Ad Hoc Rules Concerning Evidence Production

The institutional and ad hoc rules offer some guidance on the role of documentary and oral evidence in international investor-State arbitration. The ICSID Arbitration Rules give broad power to the tribunal to request documents and the appearance of witnesses at any time during the proceedings with a requirement that the parties cooperate with the tribunal in the production of evidence.[67] ICC Arbitration Rules make it clear that the arbitral tribunal may decide the case solely on the documents submitted by the parties, as well as the ability to decide whether to hear from witnesses and the power to summon any party to submit additional evidence.[68] The UNCITRAL Arbitration Rules establish the arbitral tribunal's power, similar to the ICSID and ICC Rules, by providing that it may require the parties to produce evidence at any time during the proceedings as it sees fit.[69] The ICDR Arbitration Rules offer the same language as the other rules regarding the wide-ranging authority over evidence production given to the arbitral tribunal, with additional language of its authority to control how the proceedings are directed.[70]

64. *See* Nathan D. O'Malley, *Rules of Evidence in International Arbitration: An Annotated Guide*, 47 (Informa 2012).
65. Mayer Brown, *Discovery in Investor-State Disputes: A Different Matter Altogether* (2011), https://www.mayerbrown.com/pt/publications/detailprint.aspx?publication = 1172 (accessed 30 May 2018); *Giovanna A Beccara and Others v. The Argentine Republic*, ICSID Case No. ARB/07/5, Procedural Order No. 3 (Confidentiality Order) (27 Jan. 2010).
66. 2012 US Model BIT (Defining 'protected information' as 'confidential business information or information that is privileged or otherwise protected from disclosure under a Party's law'.).
67. ICSID Arbitration Rules, Rule 34; *see also* ICSID Convention, Art. 43 ('Except as the parties otherwise agree, the Tribunal may, if it deems it necessary at any stage of the proceedings, (a) call upon the parties to produce documents or other evidence...').
68. ICC Arbitration Rules, Article 25, Establishing the Facts of the Case.
69. UNCITRAL Arbitration Rules, Art. 27(4).
70. ICDR Arbitration Rules, Art. 20(3), (4).

[5] Failure to Disclose

Arbitration does not contemplate mandatory disclosures. However, a failure to disclose evidence once the arbitral tribunal has requested it can have severe consequences. The IBA Rules provide that a failure to produce a document without satisfactory explanation will result in that document being considered adverse to the non-producing party.[71] The ICSID Arbitration Rules state that 'The Tribunal shall take formal note of the failure to comply with its obligations under this paragraph and of any reasons given for such failure.'[72] The UNCITRAL Rules provide authority to the arbitral tribunal to make an award based on the evidence that was submitted if a party fails to disclose evidence that was requested.[73] Thus, the arbitral tribunal has the power to draw adverse inferences from a party's failure to comply with an order of production without reasonable excuse. An adverse inference is not a punitive action; it is a way to outweigh the non-produced evidence in favor with the evidence submitted.[74]

Here again, care must be taken to note the differences in common law and civil law traditions in this area. US common law lawyers submit all information relevant to the case, save privileged documents, whether favorable or unfavorable to their case. Lawyers from civil law systems do not submit and are not expected to submit documents or information that is unfavorable to their case. In that same vein, taking negative inferences must be approached with caution. In this regard, it has been stressed that:

> Arbitrators must also take into account a party's particular cultural environment before drawing inferences from its behavior, for practices vary when it comes to drawing up and conserving documents. In common law countries companies anticipate discovery procedures and go to great lengths to keep all kinds of documents, official or otherwise, and at the same time are very cautious in their drafting. As there is a strong tradition of litigation, businessmen expect at some point to be called as witnesses in proceedings and, with this in mind, take detailed notes of meetings and telephone conversations, which they keep carefully. This is not necessarily the case in civil law countries, where there is no discovery and the risk of being called as a witness in court proceedings is very remote. For these reasons there are limits to the practice of drawing negative inferences when a party resists a document production order.[75]

71. IBA Rules, Art. 9(5).
72. ICSID Arbitration Rules, Rule 34(3).
73. UNCITRAL Arbitration Rules, Art. 30(3).
74. Jeffrey Waincymer, *Procedure and Evidence in International Arbitration, Part II: The Process of an Arbitration, Chapter 10: Approaches to Evidence and Fact Finding*, 774–775 (Kluwer Law International 2012).
75. Yves Derains, *Towards Greater Efficiency in Document Production Before Arbitral tribunals, A Continental Viewpoint*, Bulletin of the ICC International Court of Arbitration, Special Supplement, Document Production in International Arbitration 83 (2006).

[6] Illegally Obtained Evidence and Evidence from Non-parties

Students trained in US common law are all too familiar with the principle that evidence obtained in violation of the Fourth Amendment is generally inadmissible in a court of law. However, this same standard does not apply to international arbitration. Because of the arbitral tribunal's broad discretion in the area and the absence of any binding rules on the matter, there is no precise rule that prevents the admission of illegally obtained evidence. The arbitral tribunal will decide what evidence is relevant and material in a case, which may or may not, depending upon the circumstances and the arbitrators, include unlawfully obtained evidence. This can be seen very clearly in a recent ICSID case award known as *Caratube International Oil Company and Mr. Devincci Saleh Hourani v. Kazakhstan*, where the tribunal allowed the admittance of and reliance on certain non-privileged evidence that was hacked from Kazakhstan's government computer systems and published on a public website.[76] This case sheds light on the fact that the IBA Rules may be insufficient to deal with the potential issues that arise with the introduction of illegally obtained evidence. The rules leave it wide open to the arbitrators to not only decide the admissibility of illegally obtained evidence, but what weight to give it when analyzing the dispute. Notwithstanding this, the arbitral tribunal will likely refuse to admit evidence that either results in procedural unfairness or was obtained in bad faith, thus violating the parties' obligations to act in good faith.

Unlike illegally obtained evidence, international arbitral rules do offer some guidance on obtaining evidence from non-parties. For instance, IBA Rule 3(9) provides that a party to a dispute may ask the arbitral tribunal 'to take whatever steps are legally available to obtain the requested Documents or seek leave from the arbitral tribunal to take such steps itself'.[77] Moreover, under ICSID Arbitration Rules, a non-party may submit a written request to the arbitral tribunal after the tribunal consults with both parties to the dispute.[78] In determining whether this request will be granted, the Tribunal will take into account: (a) whether the submission is different from what the parties have to offer and whether it will help decide any factual or legal questions, (b) whether the submission will address an issue within the scope of the dispute; and (c) whether or not the non-party has a significant interest in the dispute.[79] The tribunal in *Methanex* was the first tribunal to permit amicus briefs pursuant to Article 15 of the UNCITRAL Arbitration Rules explaining that the parties' rights remained unchanged by third-party submissions citing this practice in the Iran-US Claims tribunal as support.[80] Thus, tribunals may request and accept evidence from non-parties. It is important to

76. *See Caratube International Oil Company LLP and Devincci Salah Hourani v. Republic of* Kazakhstan, ICSID Case No. ARB/13/13, Award (27 Sep. 2017); *see also Corfu Channel Case, United Kingdom of Great Britain v. People's Republic of Albania* (Merits), 1949 ICJ 4 (9 Apr. 1949) (Admitting evidence from an illegal sweep of mines in Albanian territory.).
77. IBA Rules, Art. 3(9); *see also* IBA Rules, Art. 4(9) (Concerning testimony from non-parties.).
78. ICSID Arbitration Rules, Rule 37(2).
79. *Ibid.*, Rule 37(2)(a)-(c).
80. *Methanex Corporation v. United States of America*, Decision of the Tribunal on Petitions from Third Persons to intervene as 'Amici Curiae' (15 Jan. 2001).

note, the modern effort to promote transparency within ICSID arbitrations (and international arbitration in general) is evident in the introduction of non-party involvement in the arbitral proceeding.

[C] Witness Testimony

International arbitration uses witnesses in the fact-finding process often, whether they are fact witnesses or expert witnesses. As discussed earlier, the civil law tradition favors documentary evidence over witness testimony in the evidentiary process. In the common law tradition, witness testimony is commonplace in which witnesses are examined directly, cross-examined, or questioned under oath in depositions, all of which are used in the proceeding.

In international arbitration, oral evidence is typically presented and submitted in the form of written witness statements. Generally, any person can submit witness statements, including parties and their employees, legal representatives, or officers.[81] One notable similarity to common law is the opportunity for cross-examination during the evidentiary hearing where the witnesses pre-submitted written statements are presented, and the opposing party can cross-examine and question the witness on those prior filed statements.[82]

[1] Factual Witnesses

Just as in the admissibility of documentary evidence, without the prior agreement of the parties or silence in the chosen institutional rules, the arbitral tribunal has wide discretion to determine the manner of witness testimony. The tribunal can decide what witness statements to admit, the terms and conditions of the testimony, as well as the order in which witnesses are heard.

The IBA Rules outline the procedure to be followed for witnesses of fact under Article 4.[83] Article 4(1)–(4) delineate the requirement of identifying the witnesses that will be used pursuant to the arbitral tribunal's timeline, the permission of any person to present evidence as a witness, counsel's ability to prepare witnesses, as well as the timely submission of Witness Statements.[84] According to the IBA Rules, a Witness Statement is a 'written statement of testimony by a witness of fact'.[85] Article 4(5) specifically delineates what each witness statement must contain.[86]

81. *See* IBA Rules, Art. 4(2); Julian D. M. Lew QC et. al, *Comparative International Commercial Arbitration*, 571 (Kluwer Law International 2003).
82. Lawrence W. Newman & Ben H. Sheppard, Jr., *Take the Witness: Cross Examination in International Arbitration*, XXIX (JurisNet, LLC. 2010).
83. IBA Rules, Art. 4.
84. *Ibid.*, Art. 4(1)–(4).
85. *Ibid.*, Definitions.
86. *Ibid.*, Art. 4(5) (Stating that a witness statement must include: '(a) the full name and address of the witness, a statement regarding his or her present and past relationship (if any) with any of the Parties, and a description of his or her background, qualifications, training and experience, if such a description may be relevant to the dispute or to the contents of the statement; (b) a full

[2] Expert Witnesses

For parties in international arbitration it may be advantageous or even necessary to rely on expert witnesses to defend one's case, especially in matters that deal with scientific or technical matters, quantum of damages or complicated legal matters. The IBA Rules provide guidelines for expert witnesses divided between party-appointed expert witnesses and tribunal-appointed expert witnesses (IBA Rules Articles 5 and 6). For common law trained lawyers, the party-appointed experts are commonplace in one's claim or defense, whereas tribunal-appointed experts are unfamiliar territory and somewhat more akin to civil law procedure where the judge acts as the fact finder. Therefore, international arbitration has adopted somewhat of a hybrid system, where convergence of common law and civil law practices comes together in party-appointed and tribunal-appointed experts. However, tribunal-appointed experts are of exceptional use in practice. Similar provisions for expert witnesses can be found in the institutional rules, as well.[87]

Party-Appointed Expert

Article 5 of the IBA Rules outlines the rules for appointing a witness made by a party to the dispute. Article 5(1) provides that a party may appoint an expert witness to provide evidence on specific issues. The identity of the expert, the subject matter on which the expert will testify, and an expert report must be submitted. In addition, the party must notify the other party of its potential expert.[88] Article 5(2) sets forth the requirements that the expert's report must contain. One of the more important requirements includes the experts "opinions and conclusions, including a description of the methods, evidence and information used in arriving at the conclusions."[89] There is also a requirement that the expert takes responsibility for his/her opinions.[90] Other requirements include the disclosure of any relationships the expert has with the parties, their legal advisors, and the arbitral tribunal, as well as a statement by the expert of his/her independence, showing that the expert is neutral in evaluating the specific issue he/she was asked to comment on.

---

and detailed description of the facts, and the source of the witness's information as to those facts, sufficient to serve as that witness's evidence in the matter in dispute. Documents on which the witness relies that have not already been submitted shall be provided; (c) a statement as to the language in which the Witness Statement was originally prepared and the language in which the witness anticipates giving testimony at the Evidentiary Hearing; (d) an affirmation of the truth of the Witness Statement; and (e) the signature of the witness and its date and place'. *See Methanex Corp v. United States, 7 Aug 2002 Partial Award* (Factual witness must provide a full and detailed account of all the facts to which that witness will testify, capable of standing as that witness' examination-in-chief at an oral hearing, expressed in that witness's own words, and identifying the specific source of the witness's information, whether it be from that witness's own knowledge or derived from another person or document.).

87. ICC Arbitration Rules, Art. 20(3); ICDR Arbitration Rules, Art. 22(4); LCIA Arbitration Rules, Art. 21(2); UNCITRAL Arbitration Rules, Art. 27(4).
88. IBA Rules, Art. 5(1).
89. *Ibid.*, Art. 5(1)(e).
90. *Ibid.*, Art. 5(1)(g).

The Chartered Institute of Arbitrators' Protocol for the Use of Party-Appointed Expert Witnesses in International Arbitration expands upon the IBA Rules and is offered as further guidance for issues dealing with party-appointed experts.

Tribunal-Appointed Expert

Unfamiliar to common law trained lawyers, is the ability of the Tribunal in international arbitration to appoint experts. However, even though the arbitral tribunal has the power to appoint experts, the parties are involved in the process. For example, Article 6(1) of the IBA Rules makes clear that the arbitral tribunal will consult with the parties before appointing an expert. In addition, Article 6(2) allows the parties to object to any tribunal-appointed expert for reasons including lack of qualifications or independence, potentially due to relationships with the parties, legal advisors or the tribunal, either personally or financially, etc. The arbitral tribunal has the final say on whether to deny or accept any objections. The parties have the right to receive any information that is obtained by the tribunal-appointed expert, as well as to examine any documents the expert has examined and to inspect any correspondence between the expert and the tribunal.[91] Article 6(4) sets forth the requirements of what must be contained in the expert report. These requirements are almost identical to the party-appointed requirements in Article 5(2), except for the statement of independence, which is required beforehand, when the expert is appointed. The rules make certain that it is the duty of the arbitral tribunal, not the tribunal-appointed expert, to decide on the issues of the case.[92]

§8.06 CONCLUSION

Despite cultural and legal differences, many scholars see a trend toward standardization of evidentiary procedures that favor a more harmonized, yet still flexible method of convergence. A new trend toward increasing transparency in the evidentiary process may also be catching steam, as States are increasingly pressured to divulge information that they traditionally would have tried to protect. Investor-State arbitration and international arbitration as a whole will have to face what has become known as "due process paranoia", which can be described as a reluctance by Tribunals to act decisively in certain situations for fear of the arbitral award being challenged on the basis of a party not having had the chance to present its case fully.[93] Partnered with the lack of speed and increased cost of international arbitration, practitioners are facing new challenges to what has consistently been a favored form of resolving disputes. Nonetheless, the evidence taking procedures offer many advantages because of their flexibility and relative simplicity.

91. *Ibid.*, Art. 6(3), (5).
92. *Ibid.*, Art. 6(7).
93. White & Case and School of International Arbitration at Queen Mary University of London, *International Arbitration Survey: Improvements and Innovations in International Arbitration* (White & Case LLP 2015).

Questions

(1) Tribunals have broad discretion regarding evidentiary matters. Should standards be set to serve as a guide for tribunals to exercise this discretion? If so, provide reasons for setting such a standard or criteria.

(2) Do you think the IBA Rules is an appropriate guideline to deal with evidentiary and document production issues?

(3) What suggestions would you recommend to bolster the IBA Rules in light of the common law civil law differences?

(4) Do you think that the IBA Rules harmonize and balance the international framework dealing with document production and examination of witnesses?

(5) The most common standard of proof is a balance of probabilities or preponderance of evidence for matters excluding fraud and corruption. Should it be a 'heightened standard' for matters such as fraud and corruption and if so which one?

CHAPTER 9

Damages and Costs

Investment treaties sometimes provide for compensation or reparation requirements after lawful acts of the State, such as lawful expropriation. Yet, these treaties often fail to provide for attribution and compensation conditions; hence, arbitral tribunals seek guidance in customary international law rules when ruling on attribution of conduct to the State and fixing reparation.

For instance, the ILC Articles on State Responsibility enshrine customary rules attributing to the State certain conduct by State organs and State entities. These Articles also indicate that a causal analysis between injury and internationally wrongful conduct is relevant for reparation.

The interface between investment treaties and customary international law is crucial when quantifying damages for internationally wrongful conduct. While investment treaties usually provide for the fair market value compensation rule for lawful expropriation, they often fail to provide for reparation rules for investment treaty breaches. Thus, customary rules of international law providing for the 'full reparation' principle come into play when tribunals determine reparation for unlawful expropriation, breaches of fair and equitable treatment, full protection and security, national treatment and most-favored-nation treatment, among other breaches.

Moreover, some arbitration rules governing investment treaty arbitration provide for substantive criteria on the arbitration costs' allocation, such as the 'loser pays' maxim, although other rules do not. Tribunals have taken different approaches when allocating arbitration costs, these costs sometimes reaching millions or ten millions of dollars.

§9.01 INTRODUCTION

This chapter considers certain conditions for host State responsibility for wrongful acts, and the legal consequences flowing from these acts. As discussed in Chapter 6, investment treaties provide for standards of treatment to foreign investors and investments. These treaty standards enshrine primary rules[1] of international law whose breach may culminate in wrongful acts and thus to State responsibility.[2]

Investment treaties sometimes provide for compensation or restoration requirements after lawful acts of the State, such as lawful expropriation. These treaty requirements contain primary obligations whose breach could engage the international responsibility of the State concerned. For instance, the host State's failure to compensate or restore may lead to a wrongful act contrary to international law.[3]

Treaty-based primary rules are often silent on the conditions for State responsibility, such as attribution and compensation conditions. Thus, investment tribunals may seek guidance in the secondary rules of the ILC Articles on State Responsibility.[4] Article 2 of the ILC Articles on State Responsibility sets forth two conditions for an internationally wrongful act, requiring that State conduct be (a) 'attributable to the State in international law'; and (b) breaching a State's international obligation.

These two conditions were cited by the Permanent Court of International Justice (PCIJ) in the *Phosphates in Morocco* case.[5] When discussing jurisdiction *ratione temporis*, the PCIJ considered an application by an Italian national seeking recognition as a discoverer of phosphate deposits in the capacity of transferee of existing phosphate prospecting licenses in Morocco. The PCIJ referred to the Department of Mines of Morocco's decision rejecting this application, as follows:

> [T]he Italian Government has represented the decision of the Department of Mines as an unlawful international act, because that decision was inspired by the will to get rid of the foreign holding and because it therefore constituted a violation of the vested rights placed under the protection of the international conventions. That being so, it is in this decision that we should look for the violation of international law – a definitive act which would, by itself, directly involve international responsibility. This act being attributable to the State and described as contrary to the treaty right of another State, international responsibility would be established immediately as between the two States.

1. Primary rules are a source of international obligations, and secondary norms, a source of international responsibility. *See* ILC, Draft Articles on Responsibility of States for Internationally Wrongful Acts With Commentaries, adopted by the International Law Commission at its fifty-third session (2001), p. 31, para. 1.
2. Article 1 of the ILC Articles on Responsibility of States for Internationally Wrongful Acts ('ILC Articles on State Responsibility') provides that '[e]very internationally wrongful act of a State entails the international responsibility of that State.'
3. ILC, Draft Articles on Responsibility of States for Internationally Wrongful Acts With Commentaries, adopted by the International Law Commission at its fifty-third session (2001), pp. 31–32, para. 4(c).
4. ILC, Articles on Responsibility of States for Internationally Wrongful Acts (2001).
5. *Phosphates in Morocco (Judgment)*, 1938 PCIJ Series A/B No. 74 10, 28. *See also* ILC, Draft Articles on Responsibility of States for Internationally Wrongful Acts With Commentaries, adopted by the International Law Commission at its fifty-third session (2001), p. 34, para. 2.

Attribution appears in *Phosphates in Morocco* as a condition for States' international responsibility. Attribution is also a condition for States' responsibility in investor-State arbitration.

Investment treaties seldom address attribution, this chapter will discuss arbitral tribunals' reliance on secondary rules on attribution under the ILC Articles on State Responsibility (§9.02). State responsibility leading to the reparation obligation, this chapter will look at the role of the causation principle in reparation to foreign investors (§9.03). Except for lawful expropriation, investment treaties are also silent on reparation standards and quantification for treaty breaches. This chapter will then look at standards of reparation and quantification of damages (§9.04) and applicable interest (§9.05). Finally, this chapter will discuss the rules on the allocation of arbitration costs (§9.06).

§9.02 ATTRIBUTION

Attribution is a condition for States' international responsibility under Article 2 of the ILC Articles on State Responsibility. Attribution is 'when conduct consisting of an act or omission or a series of acts or omissions is to be considered as the conduct of the State'.[6]

Conduct attributable to the State in international law is, as a rule, conduct 'of its organs of government, or of others who have acted under the direction, instigation or control of those organs, i.e., as agents of the State'.[7] With or without legal personality, State organs, instrumentalities and officials form part of the State and act in this capacity.[8] Seeking to limit responsibility to conduct that engages the State, international law generally acknowledges, however, the autonomy of persons; private conduct is not attributable to the State.

As stated earlier, since investment treaties do not provide attribution rules, arbitral tribunals have often relied on international law attributing to the State conduct by State organs (A) and State entities (B).

[A] State Organs

Article 4 of the ILC Articles on State Responsibility attributes to the State conduct of its organs, as follows:

> 1. The conduct of any State organ shall be considered an act of that State under international law, whether the organ exercises legislative, executive, judicial or any other functions, whatever position it holds in the organization of the State, and whatever its character as an organ of the central government or of a territorial unit of the State.

6. ILC, Draft Articles on Responsibility of States for Internationally Wrongful Acts With Commentaries, adopted by the International Law Commission at its fifty-third session (2001), p. 38, para. 1.
7. *Ibid.*, para. 2.
8. *Ibid.*, p. 39, para. 7.

> 2. An organ includes any person or entity which has that status in accordance with the internal law of the State.

Under Article 4, whether exercising legislative, executive, judicial or any other functions, a State organ's act or omission will be attributable to the State. This recognizes that the principle of separation of powers has no uniform application and that State organs sometimes combine different public powers.[9] The expression 'or any other functions' provides for flexibility.

It is irrelevant whether the State organs' acts are commercial (*acta iure gestionis* as opposed to *acta iure imperii*).[10] Neither is the expression 'State organs' limited to the meaning ascribed to it by internal law. The term 'includes' in Article 4(2) should be presumed to convey this.

Therefore, even if a State organ's act or omission exercising governmental authority (and acting in this capacity) 'exceeds its authority or contravenes instructions', this act or omission will remain attributable to the State under Article 7 of the ILC Articles on State Responsibility.

Applying the international law principle of responsibility for State organs, the *CMS v. Argentina* tribunal stated that:

> In so far as the international liability of Argentina under the Treaty is concerned, it also does not matter whether some actions were taken by the judiciary and others by an administrative agency, the executive or the legislative branch of the State. Article 4 of the Articles on State Responsibility adopted by the International Law Commission is abundantly clear on this point. Unless a specific reservation is made in accordance with Articles 19, 20 and 23 of the Vienna Convention on the Law of Treaties, the responsibility of the State can be engaged and the fact that some actions were taken by the judiciary and others by other state institutions does not necessarily make them separate disputes. No such reservation took place in connection with the BIT.[11]

In contrast to most investment treaties providing for investor-State arbitration, the ECT[12] expressly attributes conduct by regional and local governments and authorities to its Contracting Parties. Article 23(1) ECT on 'Observance by Sub-National Authorities' provides that:

> [e]ach Contracting Party is fully responsible under this Treaty for the observance of all provisions of the Treaty, and shall take such reasonable measures as may be available to it to ensure such observance by regional and local governments and authorities within its Area.

9. *Ibid.*, p. 41, para. 6.
10. *See* James R. Crawford, *Revising the Draft Articles on State Responsibility*, 10 Eur. J. Intl. L. 435, 440 (1999): '[T]he rules of responsibility do not, generally speaking, rest on a distinction between conduct *iure imperii* and conduct *iure gestionis*; if the state acts or fails to act, its responsibility is potentially engaged and remaining questions are left to be resolved by the interpretation and application of the relevant primary rules'; ILC, Draft Articles on Responsibility of States for Internationally Wrongful Acts With Commentaries, adopted by the International Law Commission at its fifty-third session (2001), p. 41, para. 6.
11. *CMC Gas Transmission Company v. The Republic of Argentina*, ICSID Case No. ARB/01/8, Decision of the Tribunal on Objections to Jurisdiction of 17 Jul. 2003, para. 108.
12. Energy Charter Treaty (entered into force on 16 Apr. 1998).

By stating that each Contracting Party will be fully responsible and take reasonable measures to make regional and local governments and authorities observe the ECT, this Treaty provides for an attribution rule. Pursuant to Article 23(2), this attribution rule applies in ECT investor-State arbitration under Article 26 ECT. Thus, qualifying investors may claim reparation in relation to conduct by regional and local governments and authorities affecting ECT's observance.

[B] State Entities

Article 5 of the ILC Articles on State Responsibility 'covers the exercise of governmental authority by entities that do not fall into the category "organs of state"'.[13] Therefore, conduct by persons or entities exercising elements of governmental authority – and authorized to do so – are also attributable to the State in certain cases under Article 5.

By the expressions 'persons or entities' Article 5 seeks to cover parastatal entities exercising elements of governmental authority and privatized former State companies retaining public or regulatory functions.[14] The expression 'entities' may also include State-owned corporations, mixed-capital entities, agencies, including private companies legally authorized to exercise public authority functions, as long as their conduct relates to these functions.[15] Classification under domestic law of public and private entities based on asset ownership or control is not decisive for qualifying under Article 5; rather, Article 5 expressly requires empowerment to exercise elements of governmental authority.[16]

For instance, the *Noble Ventures v. Romania* tribunal examined whether two Romanian entities qualified as State entities whose conduct could be attributable to Romania. As they were separate entities, they were not State organs under Article 4 of the ILC Articles on State Responsibility. Rather, these Romanian entities exercised governmental authority under Article 5, being legally empowered to do so:

> The Tribunal deduces from the foregoing that it was not only within the competence of SOF – and APAPS which replaced SOF at the end of 2000 – when acting as the empowered public institution under the Privatization Law, to conclude agreements with investors but also, acting as a governmental agency, to manage the whole legal relationship with them, including all acts concerned with the implementation of a specific investment. In the judgment of the Tribunal, no relevant legal distinction is to be drawn between SOF/APAPS, on the one hand, and a government ministry, on the other hand, when the one or the other acted as the empowered public institution under the Privatization Law.[17]

13. Christoph H. Schreuer, *Principles of International Investment Law*, 221 (2nd ed., Oxford University Press 2012).
14. ILC, Draft Articles on Responsibility of States for Internationally Wrongful Acts With Commentaries, adopted by the International Law Commission at its fifty-third session (2001), p. 42, para. 1.
15. *Ibid.*, p. 43, para. 2.
16. *Ibid.*, p. 43, para. 3.
17. *Noble Ventures, Inc. v. Romania*, ICSID Case No. ARB/01/11, Award (12 Oct. 2005), para. 79.

Diverging from the *Maffezini v. Spain* tribunal,[18] the *Noble Ventures v. Romania* tribunal noted that the distinction between *acta iure imperii* and *acta iure gestionis* was irrelevant for attribution purposes.[19]

§9.03 CAUSATION

As discussed in §9.02 above, international responsibility requires attributable conduct and breach of an international legal obligation by the State.[20] As a rule, international responsibility is established regardless of a causal analysis under the ILC Articles on State Responsibility; however, causation may be required by primary rules creating international legal obligations.

Causation between injury and the internationally wrongful conduct is relevant for quantifying damages in reparation cases.[21] The Black's Law Dictionary defines 'causation' as '[t]he causing or producing of an effect',[22] the Cambridge Dictionary's definition being 'the process of causing something to happen or exist'.[23] 'Causation' in the law is the link between the wrongful act or omission and the injury leading to the reparation obligation.

Causation appears in primary rules of international legal obligations, in secondary rules enshrined in the ILC Articles on State Responsibility, or as 'a feature of judicial

18. The *Maffezini* tribunal discussed whether the acts of a Spanish private corporation 'Sociedad para el Desarrollo Industrial de Galicia' (SODIGA) were attributable to Spain. *See* Emilio *Agustín Maffezini v. The Kingdom of Spain*, ICSID Case No. ARB/97/7, Decision of the Tribunal on Objections to Jurisdiction (25 Jan. 2000), para. 89: 'In view of the fact that SODIGA meets both the structural test of State creation and capital ownership and the functional test of performing activities of a public nature, the Tribunal concludes that the Claimant has made out a prima facie case that SODIGA is a State entity acting on behalf of the Kingdom of Spain. Whether SODIGA is responsible for the specific acts and omissions complained of, whether they are wrongful, whether all these acts or omissions always were governmental rather than commercial in character, and, hence, whether they can be attributed to the Spanish State, are questions to be decided during the proceedings on the merits of the case.'
19. Rather, the *Noble Ventures* tribunal noted that the distinction between *acta iure imperii* and *acta iure gestionis* was relevant for sovereign immunity, referring to ILC discussions. *See Noble Ventures, Inc. v. Romania*, ICSID Case No. ARB/01/11, Award (12 Oct. 2005), para. 82.
20. Differently from domestic law systems, damage (or injury) and fault are irrelevant for determining international responsibility. But if the primary rule requires damage or fault then these will be relevant. *See* James Crawford, *Revising the Draft Articles on State Responsibility*, 10 Eur. J. Intl. L. 435, 438 (1999): '[T]he essential point is this, that different primary rules of international law impose different standards, ranging from "due diligence" to strict liability, and that all of those standards are capable of giving rise to responsibility in the event of a breach … Responsibility is "objective" in the sense that it is governed by international law, but the requirements for responsibility vary from one primary rule to another. If the primary rule requires fault (of a particular character) or damage (of a particular kind) then they do; if not, then not.'
21. *See* León Castellanos-Jankiewicz, *Causation and International State Responsibility*, ACIL Research Paper No. 2012-07 (SHARES Series), 1, 11 (3 Apr. 2012).
22. Black's Law Dictionary, 106 (5th ed., pocket edition, Thomson Reuters 2016).
23. Cambridge Dictionary (online version), https://dictionary.cambridge.org/pt/dicionario/ingles/causation (accessed 7 Mar. 2018).

reasoning'.[24] Article 31(1) of the ILC Articles on State Responsibility sets for the full reparation rule for injury 'caused' by internationally wrongful acts. This is reproduced in Article 31(2), providing for reparation of injury including damage – material or moral – 'caused' by the State's wrongful act or omission. According to the ILC, a 'sufficient', 'not too remote' causal link between the wrongful act or omission and the injury leads to the reparation obligation:

> The notion of a sufficient causal link which is not too remote is embodied in the general requirement in article 31 that the injury should be in consequence of the wrongful act, but without the addition of any particular qualifying phrase.[25]

Injury 'resulting from and ascribable to the wrongful act, rather than any and all consequences flowing from an internationally wrongful act'[26] is thus subject to reparation under Article 31(1).

It is, however, uncertain whether the qualifiers 'sufficiency' and 'remoteness' to causality are customary international law. This is because Article 31 refers to causality but does not define it. Some scholars regret the absence of a 'causation' standard under the ILC Articles on State Responsibility, arguing that primary rules often fail to provide for causation of injury.[27]

International practice illustrates different causation standards, including the direct causation standard as opposed to the proximate causation standard.[28] The strict, objective, 'direct' causation standard requires an unbroken sequence between the internationally wrongful conduct and injury. For instance, the *Alabama Claims* arbitrators required 'direct' causation therefore excluding 'indirect' injury from the quantum finding.

The US in the *Alabama Claims* arbitration against Great Britain claimed losses caused by the destruction of vessels and their cargos by insurgent cruisers built in British shipyards, breaching Britain's neutrality obligation during the American civil war. The *Alabama Claims* tribunal found, among other things, that 'prospective earnings cannot properly be made the subject of compensation, inasmuch as they depend in their nature upon future and uncertain contingencies'.[29]

---

24. On 'causation' as a 'feature of judicial reasoning', *see* Ilias Plakokefalos, *Causation in the Law of State Responsibility and the Problem of Overdetermination: In Search of Clarity*, 26(2) Eur. J. Intl. L. 471,474.
25. ILC, Draft Articles on Responsibility of States for Internationally Wrongful Acts With Commentaries, adopted by the International Law Commission at its fifty-third session (2001), p. 93, para. 10.
26. *Ibid.*, p. 92, para. 9.
27. Professor Brigitte Stern states that 'even if in certain cases the primary rule gives rise to some causal link problems, it cannot be the same causation as the one which arises when the primary rule is breached'. Causes of internationally wrongful acts or omissions (causes of action) differ from causes leading to injury. *See* Brigitte Stern, *The Obligation to Make Reparation*, in *The Law of International Responsibility*, 563, 570 (James R. Crawford, Alain Pellet & Simon Olleson, Oxford University Press 2010); León Castellanos-Jankiewicz, *Causation and International State Responsibility*, ACIL Research Paper No. 2012-07 (SHARES Series), 1, 45 (3 Apr. 2012).
28. León Castellanos-Jankiewicz, *Causation and International State Responsibility*, ACIL Research Paper No. 2012-07 (SHARES Series), 1, 52 (3 Apr. 2012).
29. *Alabama Claims of the United States of America against Great Britain*, Award of 14 Sep. 1872, XXIX Reports of International Arbitral Awards 125, 133.

Conversely, the mixed (objective and subjective), 'proximate' causation standard, used in common law, combines the objective notion of 'natural sequence' between conduct and harm, and the subjective notion of foreseeability. Decision No. 7 of the *Eritrea-Ethiopia Claims Commission* discussed proximate causation in relation to injury in regard to Eritrea's purported violation of the *jus ad bellum*. Ethiopia's claims included reparation for loss caused by shelling, persons' internal displacement, deaths and injuries attributable to landmines, among others. The Commission adopted the proximate causation standard, as follows:

> Given this ambiguous terrain, the Commission concludes that the necessary connection is best characterized through the commonly used nomenclature of 'proximate cause'. In assessing whether this test is met, and whether the chain of causation is sufficiently close in a particular situation, the Commission will give weight to whether particular damage reasonably should have been foreseeable to an actor committing the international delict in question. The element of foreseeability, although not without its own difficulties, provides some discipline and predictability in assessing proximity. Accordingly, it will be given considerable weight in assessing whether particular damages are compensable.[30]

Investment treaties rarely define the causation required in investment arbitration, but several investment tribunals have dealt with this matter.[31] According to the *Biwater Gauff v. Tanzania* tribunal, 'causation' required a sufficient link between injury and the wrongful act, and 'a threshold beyond which damage, albeit linked to the wrongful act, is considered too indirect or remote'.[32] The *Biwater Gauff v. Tanzania* tribunal concluded that the claimant's loss was caused by other factors because the investment no longer had value at the time of the treaty breach.[33] It found that 'factual' causality was missing,[34] refusing to award damages because of a broken causal chain of injury.

In turn, in *Micula v. Romania* the arbitral tribunal noted that in certain cases contributory fault as a 'compelling' intervening event could break or interrupt the causal chain, making the initial event too remote.[35] Nevertheless, it found that this was not the case because all treaty violations had their origin in the same fact: 'the premature revocation of incentives or in direct connection with that premature revocation'.[36]

The *SD Myers v. Canada* tribunal held that 'damages may only be awarded to the extent that there is a sufficient causal link between the breach of a specific NAFTA

30. *Eritrea-Ethiopia Claims Commission*, Preliminary Decision No. 7 (27 Jul. 2007), XXVI Reports of International Arbitral Awards 1, 15, para. 13.
31. Christian Tietje & Emily Sipiorski, *Offset of Benefits in Damages Calculation in International Investment Arbitration*, 29(5) J. Intl. Arb. 545, 553 (2012).
32. *Biwater Gauff (Tanzania) Ltd. v. United Republic of Tanzania*, ICSID Case No. ARB/05/22, Award (24 Jul. 2008), para. 785.
33. *Ibid.*, paras 789–792, 805.
34. *Ibid.*, para. 786: 'The key issue in this case is the factual link between the wrongful acts and the damage in question, as opposed to any issue as to remoteness or indirect loss.'
35. *Ioan Micula, Viorel Micula, S.C. European Food S.A., S.C. Starmill S.R.L. and S.C. Multipack S.R.L. v. Romania*, ICSID Case No. ARB/05/20, Award (11 Dec. 2013), para. 927.
36. *Ibid.*, para. 928. The tribunal further clarified that contributory fault could play a role in reducing damages (para. 926).

provisions and the loss sustained by the investor' and to the extent that 'the breach of the specific NAFTA provision be the *proximate* cause of the harm'.[37] The *SD Myers* tribunal noted that subjective foreseeability as understood in contract law was irrelevant; rather, foreseeability as a causation element had to be limited to what was anticipated and realistic, remoteness being the key to causation.[38] For this reason, the tribunal in *SD Myers* held that whether damages were direct or indirect was irrelevant.[39]

Dissimilarly from *SD Myers*, the *Lemire v. Ukraine* tribunal integrated into the causation standard subjective 'foreseeability'. In addition to objective proximity (injury as a 'natural consequence' of the wrongful act), causation requires that 'the wrongdoer could have foreseen that through successive links the irregular acts finally would lead to the damage'.[40]

The *Lemire* tribunal further distinguished between 'pure' and 'transitive' causal links, noting that '[t]ransitive causal links do not exclude the responsibility of the wrongdoer – even in cases where a *lucrum cessans* is claimed.'[41] It then concluded that there was a causal link between Ukraine' wrongful acts denying broadcasting licences to Claimant's company, as follows:

> [T]he Tribunal finds that Claimant has been able to prove that the initial cause (Ukraine's wrongful acts) and the final effect (Claimant's frustration to fulfil his plans and operate a nationwide FM channel plus an AM informational channel) are linked through a chain of causation. And this chain of causation is proximate and foreseeable: Ukraine was aware of Claimant's business plans, Ukraine could foresee that irregularities in the tender procedures would result in the rejection of Gala Radio' applications thwarting Gala's expansion and eventually leading to a reduction in the value of the company and to a loss for its investor.[42]

To be sure, causality is a necessary but not a sufficient condition for reparation. §9.04[D] below dealing with grounds for reducing damages will discuss this point.

§9.04 REPARATION AND QUANTIFICATION OF DAMAGES

Like the notion of responsibility under domestic law, State responsibility in international law 'implies the substitution of a primary obligation by a secondary or subsidiary obligation, which is to make reparation'.[43] Harm leading to the reparation obligation seems to be inherent to international law breaches in investment treaty arbitration. The *Merrill v. Canada* tribunal made a useful remark in this regard:

37. *S.D. Myers, Inc. v. Government of Canada*, NAFTA Second Partial Award (21 Oct. 2002), para. 140.
38. *Ibid.*, paras 158–159.
39. *Ibid.*, para. 160.
40. *Joseph Charles Lemire and others v. Ukraine*, ICSID Case No. ARB/06/18, Award (28 Mar. 2011), para. 170.
41. *Ibid.*, paras 164–166.
42. *Ibid.*, para. 208.
43. Brigitte Stern, *The Obligation to Make Reparation*, in *The Law of International Responsibility*, 563 (James R. Crawford, Alain Pellet & Simon Olleson, Oxford University Press 2010).

> While, for specific purposes, responsibility has occasionally been de-linked from the occurrence of damages, so as to enlarge the scope of its application ... Valid as that conclusion may be as far as state responsibility is concerned, in the case of conduct that is said to constitute a breach of the standards applicable to investment protection, the primary obligation is quite clearly inseparable from the existence of damage. Indeed, a finding of liability without a finding of damage would be difficult to explain in the context of investment law arbitration and would indeed be contrary to some of its fundamental tenets.[44]

As discussed in Chapter 5 on Expropriation, most investment treaties expressly provide for the FMV compensation rule for lawful expropriation. But they fail to provide for reparation rules for investment treaty breaches, including for unlawful expropriation. Unlawful expropriation and breaches of FET, FPS, NT and MFN, among others, are subject to reparation rules of customary international law (A). This section will also discuss calculation methods (B), grounds for reducing damages (C) and valuation dates (D).

[A] Reparation Standards

Many investment treaties stipulate FMV compensation for lawful expropriation. For instance, Article 6(2) of the 2012 US Model BIT provides that compensation for lawful expropriation, done for a public purpose, in a non-discriminatory manner, on payment of 'prompt, adequate and effective' compensation, pursuant to due process and the minimum standard of treatment shall:

> (a) be paid without delay;
> (b) be equivalent to the fair market value of the expropriated investment immediately before the expropriation took place ("the date of expropriation");
> (c) not reflect any change in value occurring because the intended expropriation had become known earlier; and
> (d) be fully realizable and freely transferable ... .

The primary rule under Article 6(2) of the 2012 US Model BIT provides for compensation using the 'FMV' standard. The International Glossary of Business Valuation Terms defines 'FMV' as:

> [T]he price, expressed in terms of cash equivalents, at which property would change hands between a hypothetical willing and able buyer and a hypothetical willing and able seller, acting at arm's length in an open and unrestricted market, when neither is under compulsion to buy or sell and when both have reasonable knowledge of the relevant facts.[45]

44. *Merrill & Ring Forestry L. P. v. Government of Canada*, UNCITRAL, ICSID Administrated, Award (31 Mar. 2010), paras 244–245.
45. National Association of Certified Valuators and Analysts, International Glossary of Business Valuation Terms, http://www.nacva.com/content.asp?contentid=166 (accessed 12 Mar. 2018). The *CMS v. Argentina* tribunal relied on this definition; *see CMS Gas Transmission Company v. The Argentine Republic*, ICSID Case No. ARB/01/8, Award (12 May 2005), para. 402.

The host State's breach of the primary rule under Article 6(2) above on lawful expropriation, including the obligation to provide 'FMV' compensation, could lead to unlawful expropriation. However, the model treaty fails to stipulate a primary rule on reparation for unlawful compensation.

As noted, investment treaties generally fail to provide rules on reparation for treaty breaches such as unlawful expropriation,[46] failure to provide FET, FPS, NT and MFN treatment. Breach of these primary rules of international law leads to application of customary, secondary rules on reparation of the ILC Articles on State Responsibility. Article 31 of the ILC Articles on State Responsibility provides for the full reparation obligation for internationally wrongful conduct by the State, in the following terms:

> 1. The responsible State is under an obligation to make full reparation for the injury caused by the internationally wrongful act.
> 2. Injury includes any damage, whether material or moral, caused by the internationally wrongful act of a State.

As discussed in Chapter 5 on Expropriation, the ILC Articles on State Responsibility codify the customary international rule on full reparation adopted by the PCIJ in the *Chorzów Factory* case.[47]

Article 34 sets forth that full reparation 'shall take the form of restitution, compensation and satisfaction, either singly or in combination'. Restitution under Article 35 is re-establishing the situation existing before the breach if restitution is 'not materially impossible' or disproportionately burdensome compared to compensation. Compensation features as an alternative remedy when restitution does not make good damage, covering 'any financially assessable damage including loss of profits' under Article 36. Finally, satisfaction as 'an acknowledgement of the breach, an expression of regret, [or] a formal apology' is an alternative to restitution and compensation under Article 37.

In investment disputes, restitution is often impracticable leading thus to tribunals' awarding compensation (damages).[48] Having found breaches of treaty provisions

46. On the difference between lawful and unlawful expropriation for reparation purposes, *see* Mark W. Friedman & Floriane Lavaud, *Damages Principles in Investment Arbitration*, in *The Guide to Damages in International Arbitration*, 93, 99 (2nd ed., John A. Trenor, Global Arbitration Review 2018).
47. Sergey Ripinsky & Kevin Williams, *Damages in International Investment Law* 89 BIICL (2015). *See The Factory at Chorzów (Germany v. Poland)* (Claim for Indemnity) (Merits) (1928) PCIJ Rep. Series A No. 17, 47: 'Reparation must, as far as possible, wipe out all consequences of the illegal act and re-establish the situation which would, in all probability, have existed if that act had not been committed. Restitution in kind, or, if this is not possible, payment of a sum corresponding to the value which a restitution in kind would bear; the award, if need be, of damages for loss sustained which would not be covered by restitution in kind or payment in place of it – such as the principles which should serve to determine the amount of compensation due for an act contrary to international law.'
48. Abby Cohen, *Principles of Compensation in Investment Arbitration*, 22 ICSID Rev. 1, 5 (2007); H. Perezcano Díaz, *Damages in Investor-State Arbitration*, in *Evaluation of Damages in International Arbitration*, 113, 115 (Yves Derains, Richard H. Kreindler, ICC 2006). *See* ILC, Draft Articles on Responsibility of States for Internationally Wrongful Acts With Commentaries, adopted by the International Law Commission at its fifty-third session (2001), p. 99, para. 3: 'Restitution, despite its primacy as a matter of legal principle, is frequently unavailable or

on fair equitable treatment, full protection and expropriation, the *Siag v. Egypt* tribunal held that restitution was no longer possible because property was conveyed to a third party, 'the only relief … practically available [being] an award of damages'.[49]

Investment claims sometimes relate to investment contracts (even if most investment claims are treaty-based). In *Sapphire v. NIOC*, the arbitrator applied the principle of 'full compensation' as a general principle of law requiring that the aggrieved party be placed 'in the same pecuniary position as [it] would have been in if the contract had been performed in the manner provided for by the parties at the time of its conclusion'.[50] According to the *Sapphire* arbitrator, the 'full reparation' principle is:

> a direct deduction from the principle *pacta sunt servanda*, since its only effect is to substitute a pecuniary obligation for the obligation which was promised but not performed. It is therefore natural that the creditor should thereby be given full compensation. This compensation includes the loss suffered (*damnum emergens*), for example the expenses incurred in performing the contract, and the profit lost (*lucrum cessans*), for example the net profit which the contract would have produced.[51]

Moreover, umbrella clause claims[52] founded on breaches of specific contractual commitments undertaken by the host State may have their basis on contract and thus be subject to the contract's governing law and respective reparation rules. Reparation for umbrella clause breaches of contractual basis is highly complex because contractual breaches, through the umbrella clause, rise to the level of treaty breaches. Besides relying on the contract's governing law, parties may sometimes seek to rely on customary international law on full reparation in its 'corrective' function.[53] But the customary international law standard of full reparation 'does not determine valuation methodology'[54] let alone calculation methods, which will be discussed below.

[B] Calculation Methods

The distinction between lawful and unlawful expropriation plays an important role for calculation purposes. 'FMV' compensation for lawful expropriation should not be

inadequate. It may be partially or entirely ruled out either based on the exceptions expressed in article 35, or because the injured State prefers compensation or for other reasons.'

49. *Waguih Elie George Siag & Clorinda Vecchi v. Arab Republic of Egypt*, ICSID Case No. ARB/05/15, Award (1 Jun. 2009), paras 532–534.
50. *Sapphire International Petroleums Ltd. v. National Iranian Oil Company (NIOC)*, Award (15 Mar. 1963), 35 ILR 136, 185–186.
51. *Sapphire International Petroleums Ltd. v. NIOC*, Award (15 Mar. 1963), 35 ILR 136, 186.
52. For a definition and a jurisdictional aspects of umbrella clauses, *see* Ch. 3 on Jurisdiction.
53. On the 'corrective' or 'complementary' function of international law provided in Art. 42(1) ICSID Convention, *see* Sergey Ripinsky & KevinWilliams, *Damages in International Investment Law* 104 BIICL (2015).
54. *See Murphy Exploration and Production Company International v. Republic of Ecuador [II]*, PCA Case No. 2012-16 (formerly AA 434), Partial Final Award (6 May 2016), para. 481.

higher or lower than the property's value at the date of compensation.[55] Reparation calculation for unlawful expropriation, however, should consider a possible increase in the property's value between the expropriation date and the date of the award pursuant to the 'full reparation' principle of *Chorzów Factory*.[56]

The same rational of 'full reparation' applies to other international wrongful conduct breaching other investment treaty standards such as FET, FPS and NT and MFN treatment. In *Gemplus v. Mexico*, the tribunal held that the *Chorzów Factory*'s 'full reparation' standard applying to unlawful expropriation was indistinguishable from the one applying to FET breaches.[57]

Calculating methods of compensation or reparation taken from economics and/or accounting, are more complex for intangible property (e.g., company shares and concession contract rights) than for tangible property.[58] These calculation methods can be objective or subjective.

The market value is an objective method relying on market data, such as stock prices, prior sales and offerings, to calculate property value. According to the International Valuation Standards (IVS):

> Market Value is the estimated amount for which an asset or liability should exchange on the valuation date between a willing buyer and a willing seller in an arm's length transaction, after proper marketing and where the parties had each acted knowledgeably, prudently and without compulsion.[59]

For instance, the tribunal in *Crystallex v. Venezuela* calculated an average value combining the stock market method ('Crystallex's stock was actively and heavily traded on two main stock exchanges for mining companies') and the market multiples method (using data on 'market valuation of companies holding properties of similar characteristics').[60]

For instance, the tribunal in *Crystallex v. Venezuela* calculated an average value combining the stock market method ('Crystallex's stock was actively and heavily traded on two main stock exchanges for mining companies') and the market multiples method (using data on 'market valuation of companies holding properties of similar characteristics').[61]

Nevertheless, a disadvantage of the market value method is its presumption that property's price is negotiated in an open and competitive market with actors acting freely, which is not always realistic in valuation cases. Foreign investment often relates

---

55. Irmgard Marboe, *Calculation of Compensation and Damages in International Investment Law*, 3.102 (Oxford University Press 2012).
56. *Ibid.*
57. *Gemplus, S.A., SLP, S.A. and Gemplus Industrial, S.A. de C.V. v. United Mexican States*, ICSID Case No. ARB(AF)/04/3 & ARB(AF)/04/4, Award (16 Jun. 2010), paras 12–52.
58. Abby Cohen, *Principles of Compensation in Investment Arbitration*, 22 ICSID Rev. 1, 11 (2007).
59. International Valuation Standards (IVS), available at http://www.cas.org.cn/docs/2017-01/20170120142445588690.pdf (accessed 13 Mar. 2018), IVS 104 Bases of Value, 30.1.
60. *Crystallex International Corporation v. Bolivarian Republic of Venezuela*, ICSID Case No. ARB(AF)/11/2, Award (4 Apr. 2016), paras 890, 901–905, 916–917.
61. *Ibid.*

to large and unique projects with no comparable projects on which to base market value.[62]

Variables of the market value method are the comparable sales and comparable multiples methods. The comparable sales method uses data about sales of comparable property with adjustments on a case-by-case basis.[63] Moreover, the comparable multiples method uses data measuring other comparable company's performance, such as cash flow, earnings, profits, Earnings before Interest and Taxes (EBIT), Earnings before Interest, Taxes, Depreciation and Amortisation (EBITDA) multiplied by a factor calculated with sales' data of comparable companies.[64] Distinct from the comparable sales method, the comparable multiples method combines elements of the market value method and of the income method.

The income method includes the DCF method, often relied on in investment arbitration for valuation of income-producing property.[65] Under a simplistic approach, the value of a cow pursuant to the DCF method is the income generated by her milk during her lifetime.[66] According to the more sophisticated presentation of the International Valuation Standard:

> The income approach provides an indication of value by converting future cash flow to a single current value. Under the income approach, the value of an asset is determined by reference to the value of income, cash flow or cost savings generated by the asset.[67]

The DCF method consists of forecasting cash flow subject to a discount rate bringing valuation to its present value at the valuation date. The discount rate will consider 'the time value of money, but also the risks associated with the type of cash flow and the future operations of the asset'.[68] In *CMS v. Argentina*, the tribunal discussed two DCF calculating ways, adopting the second one:[69]

> There are two recognized ways of computing the value of a firm and it DCF basis. One can start computations with the cash flows to the firm debt repayments, discount such flows at the weighted average cost of capital (the 'WACC') and add the discounted cash flows to the firm to establish its value; then, the value of debt is subtracted and the residual value is the value of equity ('the indirect equity value'). Alternatively, one can compute first the cash flows to equity (cash flows

62. I. Marboe, *Calculation of Compensation and Damages in International Investment Law*, 5.13 (Oxford University Press 2012).
63. *Ibid.*, paras 5.53–5.56.
64. *Ibid.*, para. 5.59.
65. *See ADC Affiliate Limited and ADC & ADMC Management Limited v. The Republic of Hungary*, ICSID Case No. ARB/03/16, Award (2 Oct. 2006), para. 502: 'Like many other tribunals in cases such as the present one, the Tribunal prefers to apply the DCF method, although it is mindful of the Respondent's admonishment that:

    '"[I]nternational tribunals have exercised great caution in using the [DCF] method due to its inherently speculative nature".'

66. This very telling explanation is from the Spanish arbitrator Manuel Conthe.
67. International Valuation Standards (IVS), available at http://www.cas.org.cn/docs/2017-01/20170120142445588690.pdf (accessed 13 Mar. 2018), IVS 104 Bases of Value, 40.1.
68. *Ibid.*, 50.29.
69. *CMS Gas Transmission Company v. The Argentine Republic*, ICSID Case No. ARB/01/8, Award (12 May 2005), paras 430–433.

> from operations, minus interest and debt repayments), discount them at the cost of equity ('COE') and add the discounted cash flows to equity to establish the value of equity ('the direct equity value'); then, one adds the value of debt to establish the value of the firm...[70]

But when the investment was never operative or when the investment's operating history is insufficient, or profit has been wanting, tribunals have preferred not to apply the DCF method.[71]

Finally, the cost method adopts the 'economic principle that a buyer will pay no more for an asset than the cost to obtain an asset of equal utility'.[72] The cost method includes the book value,[73] a variable of this method using balance sheet data. Some scholars question the reliability of the book value method because balance sheet data usually serve financial reporting and tax purposes and because entrepreneurial precaution encourages companies to understate asset value and to overstate liabilities.[74]

Besides the objective valuation methods above, certain tribunals have also considered subjective valuation methods to calculate consequential damages such as loss of reputation, goodwill, liability of subcontractors, costs for repair and maintenance, among others.

[C] Grounds for Reducing Damages

As pointed out in §9.03 above, causality is a necessary but not a sufficient condition for reparation. This is because tribunals may reduce reparation in certain instances.

Tribunals are mindful to avoid double recovery. For instance, in *S.D. Myers v. Canada* the tribunal agreed with Canada that 'damages for breach of any one NAFTA provision can take into account any damages already awarded under a breach of another NAFTA provision; there must be no "double recovery"'.[75]

Awards have also considered contractual limitations when calculating reparation. In *Siag v. Egypt,* the tribunal relied on a sale contract concluded between

70. *Ibid.*, para. 430.
71. Henry Weisburg & Christopher Ryan, *Means to Be Made Whole*, in *Evaluation of Damages in International Arbitration* 165, 175 (Yves Derains & Richard H. Kreindler, ICC 2006). *See Metalclad Corporation v. The United Mexican States*, ICSID Case No. ARB(AF)/97/1, Award (30 Aug. 2000), paras 119-120: 'Normally, the fair market value of a going concern which has a history of profitable operation may be based on an estimate of future profits subject to a discounted cash flow analysis ... However, where the enterprise has not operated for a sufficiently long time to establish a performance record or where it has failed to make a profit, future profits cannot be used to determine going concern or fair market value'; *Southern Pacific Properties (Middle East) Limited v. Arab Republic of Egypt*, ICSID Case No. ARB/84/3, Award (20 May 1992), para. 188: 'In the Tribunal's view, the DCF method is not appropriate for determining the fair compensation in this case because the project was not in existence for a sufficient period of time to generate the data necessary for a meaningful DCF calculation.'
72. International Valuation Standards (IVS), available at http://www.cas.org.cn/docs/2017-01/20170120142445588690.pdf (accessed 13 Mar. 2018), IVS 104 Bases of Value, 60.1.
73. *See Siemens A.G. v. The Argentine Republic*, ICSID Case No. ARB/02/8, Award (17 Jan. 2007), paras 362 et seq.
74. Irmgard Marboe, *Calculation of Compensation and Damages in International Investment Law*, 5.282 (Oxford University Press 2012).
75. *S.D. Myers, Inc. v. Government of Canada*, NAFTA Partial Award (13 Nov. 2000), para. 316.

claimants' company and Egypt providing for a 50% penalty if the company disposed of the land. The tribunal therefore calculated reparation for unlawful expropriation based on the company's beneficial interest of only 50% in the land.[76]

Moreover, contributory negligence plays a role in quantifying reparation. Article 39 of the ILC Articles on State Responsibility provides that 'account shall be taken of the contribution to the injury by wilful or negligent action or omission of the injured State or any person or entity in relation to whom reparation is sought'. The *Occidental v. Ecuador* tribunal held, for instance, that 'the Claimants have contributed to the extent of 25% to the prejudice which they suffered', reducing by a 25% factor claimant's damages for expropriation.[77]

A further element affecting reparation is proportionality between reparation and the gravity of the breach.[78] Failure to mitigate damages by a party may also preclude recovery.[79] Finally, damages should not be 'too speculative, remote, or uncertain'.[80]

[D] Valuation Dates

In expropriation cases, the valuation date is the date of the taking, but indirect or creeping expropriation poses complex questions for fixing the valuation date.[81]

Indirect expropriation typically is an internationally wrongful[82] series of actions or omissions (composite acts) that 'interfere with property rights to such an extent that these rights are rendered so useless that they must be deemed to have been expropriated [even if] the legal title to the property formally remains with the original owner'.[83] Article 15 of the ILC Articles on State Responsibility on breaches consisting of composite acts provides as follows:

> 1. The breach of an international obligation by a State through a series of actions or omissions defined in aggregate as wrongful occurs when the action or omission occurs which, taken with the other actions or omissions, is sufficient to constitute the wrongful act.

76. *Waguih Elie George Siag & Clorinda Vecchi v. Arab Republic of Egypt*, ICSID Case No. ARB/05/15, Award (1 Jun. 2009), paras 577–584.
77. *Occidental Petroleum Corporation and Occidental Exploration and Production Company v. Republic of Ecuador*, ICSID Case No. ARB/06/11, Award (5 Oct. 2012), paras 687, 825. *See also MTD Equity Sdn. Bhd. and MTD Chile S.A. v. Republic of Chile*, ICSID Case No. ARB/01/7, Award (25 May 2004), paras 242–243.
78. *See* ILC, Draft Articles on Responsibility of States for Internationally Wrongful Acts With Commentaries, adopted by the International Law Commission at its fifty-third session (2001), p. 94, para. 14.
79. *Ibid.*, p. 93, para. 11. On the duty to mitigate damages from a contractual perspective, *see* Yasuhei Taniguchi, *The Obligation to Mitigate Damages*, in *Evaluation of Damages in International Arbitration*, 79 et seq. (Yves Derains & Richard H. Kreindler, ICC 2006).
80. *Murphy Exploration and Production Company International v. Republic of Ecuador [II]*, PCA Case No. 2012-16 (formerly AA 434), Partial Final Award (6 May 2016), para. 487.
81. Abby Cohen, *Principles of Compensation in Investment Arbitration*, 22 ICSID Rev. 1, 10 (2007).
82. Most indirect expropriation cases are of unlawful expropriation leading to the application of the full reparation rule of *Chorzów Factory*.
83. *Starrett Housing Corporation, et al. v. The Government of the Islamic Republic of Iran*, Iran-US Claims Tribunal, Partial Award (19 Dec. 1983), 23(5) ILM 1090, 1115.

2. In such a case, the breach extends over the entire period starting with the first of the actions or omissions of the series and lasts for as long as these actions or omissions are repeated and remain not in conformity with the international obligation.

Pursuant to Article 15(2) above, the start date of an indirect expropriation coincides with the first wrongful action or omission lasting for the duration the international breach is repeated. The valuation date coincides therefore with the date of the first wrongful action or omission, valuation at this date representing the minimum valuation for reparation purposes.

Nevertheless, the tribunal in *Starrett Housing v. Iran* disregarded actions and omissions before the temporary manager's nomination by the Revolutionary Council on 30 January 1980 – the formal expropriation date. Thus, this tribunal held that '30 January 1980 must be considered as the date of the taking [and] for ease of accounting the Tribunal decides that 31 January 1980 shall be considered as the date of taking'.[84]

A further discussion about the valuation date is whether calculation should consider forecasted data at the valuation date (*ex ante*) or data on subsequent developments not known or knowable at the valuation date (*ex post*). As a rule, reparation calculation considers the effects of the harm at the date of the harm (*ex ante*). But sometimes tribunals move the valuation date to include events by the time of the award, or adjust reparation in the light of certain events by the time of the decision (*ex post*).

This has been discussed by Professors Franklin Fisher and Craig Romaine[85] with an anecdote about a stolen and destroyed yearbook of the school where Janis Joplin studied, containing her signature. On the date of the theft, the signed yearbook cost USD 5 (it was not known or knowable that Janis Joplin would become famous). However, at the time of judgment on the theft, the signed yearbook was valued at USD 1,000. The question whether damages for the yearbook's theft should be calculated at USD 5 or USD 1,000 illustrates the *ex ante v. ex post* dilemma.

Damages for lawful expropriation have been calculated with forecasted data at the valuation date (*ex ante*). Tribunals apply the same rational to unlawful expropriation, if the investment is completely lost, or if, but for the taking, the investors would have retained their investment.[86]

The *ex ante* approach has also been applied to other unlawful acts breaching treaty standards. The *Murphy v. Ecuador* tribunal disagreed with the *ex post* approach

84. *Ibid.*, 1117.
85. Franklin M. Fisher & R. Craig Romaine, *Janis Joplin's Yearbook and the Theory of Damages*, 5(1–2) J. Acctg. Auditing & Fin. 145, 153–156 (1990).
86. *Ioannis Kardassopoulos and Ron Fuchs v. The Republic of Georgia*, ICSID Case Nos. ARB/05/18 and ARB/07/15, Award (3 Mar. 2010), para. 514: 'In certain circumstances full reparation for an unlawful expropriation will require damages to be awarded as of the date of the arbitral Award. It may be appropriate to compensate for value gained between the date of the expropriation and the date of the award in cases where it is demonstrated that the Claimants would, but for the taking, have retained their investment. For the reasons set out herein, however, this is not the case on the facts of these arbitrations.'

when quantifying reparation for Ecuador's breach of the FET obligation, applying the *ex ante* approach:[87]

> [N]otwithstanding the issue raised above concerning the inappropriateness of *ex post* data in this case, the Tribunal has considered the information that became known after the valuation date. Specifically, the Tribunal has examined whether the assumptions on the development of oil prices and oil production levels, on which the *ex-ante* appraisal of Murphy Ecuador's fair market value is based, should be adjusted in the light of actual ex-post data. This approach is consistent with the general requirement for awarding damages for violations of international obligations that any compensable damage must not be too speculative, remote, or uncertain. The Tribunal's conclusion is that it is neither necessary nor justified to adjust the *ex-ante* calculation of damages as of 12 March 2009...[88]

But this has not been consistent,[89] investors sometimes seek the *ex post* calculation to increase their recovery. This is because *ex post* calculation with real data on subsequent developments not known or knowable at the date of harm may provide a higher reparation. In *Quiborax v. Bolivia,* the claimants sought an *ex post* valuation divided in two periods:

> (i) from the date of the expropriation to the date of the award (or current date), and (ii) from the date of the award (or current date) until the end of the life of the Concessions. The value of the Concessions during the first (past) period is calculated *ex post*, using all information available as of current date. The second (future) period is valued as of [the] current date, using the DCF method. Hence, the *ex post* valuation combines two different valuation methods for two different time periods, marked by the date of the award.[90]

87. Supporting the *ex ante* approach, *see* Diora M. Ziyaeva, *Arbitral Tribunals Tend to Pay Lip Service to the Chorzów Factory Full Reparation Principle, Disregarding the Context and Full Implication of the Dictum*, in *Investment Treaty Arbitration and International Law*, 119, 131–42 (Ian A. Laird, Borzu Sabahi, Frédéric G. Sourgens &Todd J. Weiler, Juris 2016): 'The [PCIJ] was clear that the normal valuation date is the date of dispossession and that, in the normal case, if the expropriation is legal but for the payment of compensation, the traditional valuation date would hold... [S]everal modern arbitral tribunals ... have moved the date of valuation to date of award, and have chosen to interpret Chorzów Factory as if it requires them to grant the expropriated party the benefit of any favorable post-taking changes and to insulate the same party from any negative post-taking changes. To use such discretion is a fundamentally flawed approach ...' (pp. 132–133); Franklin M. Fisher & R. Craig Romaine, *Janis Joplin's Yearbook and the Theory of Damages*, 5(1–2) J. Acctg. Auditing & Fin. 145, 153–156 (1990): '[O]ur position is that hindsight should not be used. Rather, the stream of returns should be estimated using the information available at the time of violation. Indeed, as we shall see, expectations as of that time are particularly relevant... Suppose that the asset destroyed was the opportunity to enter into a long-term contract thought at the time to be valuable. Suppose, however, that, with the benefit of hindsight, we now know that the contract would have been a disaster, losing money for the plaintiff. Surely, one would not assess negative damages, having the plaintiff pay the defendant.' (pp. 153, 155).
88. *Murphy Exploration and Production Company International v. Republic of Ecuador [II]*, PCA Case No. 2012-16 (formerly AA 434), Partial Final Award (6 May 2016), para. 487.
89. For tribunals applying the DCF method with an *ex post* approach, *see Quiborax S.A., Non Metallic Minerals S.A. and Allan Fosk Kaplún v. Plurinational State of Bolivia*, ICSID Case No. ARB/06/2, Award (16 Sep. 2015), paras 377–385; *ADC Affiliate Limited and ADC & ADMC Management Limited v. The Republic of Hungary*, ICSID Case No. ARB/03/16, Award (2 Oct. 2006), paras 497–499, 502.
90. *Quiborax S.A., ibid.*, para. 368.

The *Quiborax* tribunal found that the *ex post* approach was appropriate, noting that claimants would have been in possession of their investment '[h]ad the expropriation not occurred'.[91]

§9.05 INTEREST

Interest often represents an important portion of reparation. This is because 'a significant amount of time often elapses between the date on which a claimed injury occurs and the date on which an arbitral award is issued'.[92] Article 38(1) of the ILC Articles on State Responsibility provides that interest be paid to ensure full reparation:

> Interest on any principal sum due under this chapter shall be payable when necessary in order to ensure full reparation. The interest rate and mode of calculation shall be set so as to achieve that result.

Interest therefore seeks to prevent unjust enrichment by compensating the creditor's financial disadvantage of not disposing the claimed amount while the debtor having financially benefited from withholding this amount.[93] Some tribunals have used the same pre-award and post-award interest rate,[94] while others have fixed different pre-award and post-award rates.[95]

Tribunals have fixed interest rates on a case-by-case basis, Article 38 of the ILC Articles on State Responsibility being silent on this issue. Tribunals have considered relevant legal rates (domestic, fixed statutory rate), agreed rates applying to the parties' agreements, and market borrowing rates (including prime rates, government bonds' rates and floating interbank rates like LIBOR)[96] and cost of capital rates,[97] among others).[98] Some tribunals have also discussed whether to apply risk-free interest rates or 'forced loan' interest rates, the latter being higher than the former.[99]

---

91. *Ibid.*, para. 385.
92. Henry Weisburg & Christopher Ryan, *Means to be Made Whole*, in *Evaluation of Damages in International Arbitration*, 165, 180 (Yves Derains & Richard H. Kreindler, ICC 2006).
93. Irmgard Marboe, *Calculation of Compensation and Damages in International Investment Law*, 6.05–6.06 (Oxford University Press 2012).
94. Pre-award interest (compensatory interest) is the interest rate ranging from the start accrual date until the award date. Post-award interest (moratory interest) is the interest rate ranging from the award date until the payment date. *See Tenaris S.A. and Talta – Trading e Marketing Sociedade Unipessoal Lda. v. Bolivarian Republic of Venezuela*, ICSID Case No. ARB/11/26, Award (29 Jan. 2016), para. 595 (Using the same pre- and post-award interest rate, but granting Venezuela a six month grace period for payment.).
95. *Emilio Agustín Maffezini v. The Kingdom of Spain*, ICSID Case No. ARB/97/7, Award (13 Nov. 2000), paras 96–97 (Fixing as pre-award interest the LIBOR rate compounded annually and as post-award interest a 6% rate compounded monthly.).
96. London Interbank Offered Rate (LIBOR).
97. For instance, a cost of capital rate could take into account the weighted average cost of capital (WACC). *See* James Dow, *Interest*, in *The Guide to Damages in International Arbitration*, 271, 274 (2nd ed., John A. Trenor, Global Arbitration Review 2018).
98. Irmgard Marboe, *Calculation of Compensation and Damages in International Investment Law*, 6.44–6.161 (Oxford University Press 2012).
99. James Dow, *Interest*, in *The Guide to Damages in International Arbitration*, 271, 277 et seq. (2nd ed., John A. Trenor, Global Arbitration Review 2018). *See Railroad Development Corporation v. Republic of Guatemala*, ICSID Case No. ARB/07/23, Award (29 Jun. 2013),

Accrual of interest in lawful expropriation cases starts at the expropriation date. In relation to internationally wrongful acts, Article 38(2) of the ILC Articles on State Responsibility provides that interest accrue 'from the date when the principal sum should have been paid until the date the obligation to pay is fulfilled'. Arbitral tribunals have fixed the date of the wrongful conduct,[100] the date of commencement of arbitration,[101] the date of the award, among others, as interest accrual dates.

Traditionally, awarding compound interest as opposed to simple interest was criticized; compound interest quickly leading to interest amounts exceeding the principal amount.[102] The modern trend,[103] however, is to award compound interest; interest compounded annually or semi-annually.[104]

§9.06 ARBITRATION COSTS

Arbitration costs can be divided in two types: (1) arbitration or procedural costs, including arbitrators' and arbitral institutions' fees and expenses and (2) the party's costs, including their legal costs and expenses with counsel, party-appointed experts and witnesses, among others.[105] Arbitration costs have become an increasing concern

para. 278: 'Claimant has argued for compound interest at a rate of 9.34% based on the rate that Respondent paid to private and public creditors in 2006 and on the notion of a coerced loan from Claimant to Respondent. Respondent has suggested a pre award interest rate equivalent to six-month LIBOR plus two percentage points. The Tribunal disagrees with the coerced loan rationale of Claimant to arrive at the proposed rate of interest. The rationale for pre-award interest rests on a claimant's loss for not being able to dispose of the funds awarded from the moment the breach of an international obligation has been determined in the award. Claimant would not have been able to obtain the rate of interest claimed in its normal course of business nor would have paid such rate for funds borrowed to replace those due for the breach of an obligation by Respondent.'

100. *CMS Gas Transmission Company v. The Argentine Republic,* ICSID Case No. ARB/01/8, Award (12 May 2005), para. 470 (fixing the date of breach as the date of interest accrual).
101. *CME Czech Republic B.V. v. The Czech Republic,* UNCITRA Arbitration Proceedings, Final Award (14 Mar. 2003), para. 635.
102. *See Compañia del Desarrollo de Santa Elena S.A. v. Republic of Costa Rica,* ICSID Case No. ARB/96/1, Award (17 Feb. 2000), paras 95, 106–107.
103. According to Professor Dow, in 80% of 60 ICSID decisions in which interest was awarded between 1992 and 2016 compound pre-award interest was awarded. James Dow, *Interest,* in *The Guide to Damages in International Arbitration,* 271, 279 (2nd ed., John A. Trenor, Global Arbitration Review 2018).
104. *See Siemens A.G. v. The Argentine Republic, ICSID Case No. ARB/02/8,* Award (17 Jan. 2007), para. 401 (compounding interest annually); *Crystallex International Corporation v. Bolivarian Republic of Venezuela,* ICSID Case No. ARB(AF)/11/2, Award (4 Apr. 2016), para. 937 (compounding interest annually); *Tenaris S.A. and Talta – Trading e Marketing Sociedade Unipessoal Lda. v. Bolivarian Republic of Venezuela,* ICSID Case No. ARB/11/26, Award (29 Jan. 2016), para. 594 (compounding interest semi-annually); *Suez, Sociedad General de Aguas de Barcelona S.A., and Vivendi Universal S.A. v. The Argentine Republic,* ICSID Case No. ARB/03/19, Award (9 April 2015), p. 60 (compounding interest semi-annually); I. Marboe, *Calculation of Compensation and Damages in International Investment Law,* 6.235 (Oxford University Press 2012).
105. Micha Bűhler, *Costs,* in *The Guide to Damages in International Arbitration,* 283, 284–285 (2nd ed., John A. Trenor, Global Arbitration Review 2018).

sometimes reaching millions or ten millions of dollars.[106] Allocation of arbitration costs is therefore to a great extent very important.

Arbitral tribunals have adopted three different approaches to allocating arbitration costs.[107] First, costs can be borne by the unsuccessful party pursuant to the 'costs follow the event' approach (the 'loser pays' maxim). Second, costs can also be allocated in proportion to the relative success of the parties' claims and defenses. Third, the parties can equally share costs, or they can bear their own costs.

Cost allocation will depend on the applicable arbitration rules to the investment dispute. For instance, Article 42(1) of the UNCITRAL Arbitration Rules[108] provides, in its first sentence, that the loser pays, while providing for flexibility in its second sentence, as follows:

> The costs of the arbitration shall in principle be borne by the unsuccessful party or parties. However, the arbitral tribunal may apportion each of such costs between the parties if it determines that apportionment is reasonable, taking into account the circumstances of the case.

For example, the *Methanex v. United States* UNCITRAL tribunal ordered Methanex to pay arbitration costs applying the 'loser pays' maxim.[109] The *EnCana v. Ecuador* tribunal applied the relevant treaty rules and the UNCITRAL Arbitration Rules on costs, relying on the flexibility provision under the UNCITRAL Rules to find that the 'loser pays' maxim 'is not an inflexible rule and the Tribunal has a discretion to order otherwise'.[110] The *EnCana* tribunal concluded thus that 'it would be just and equitable for Ecuador to bear the costs of the arbitration' despite the limitations preventing jurisdiction and the tribunal's rejection of *EnCana*'s expropriation claim.[111]

There are, however, arbitration rules that do not provide for substantive criteria on cost allocation. Article 61(2) of the ICSID Convention only provides that the arbitral tribunal will decide 'how and by whom' (a) expenses incurred by the parties in relation to the arbitration, (b) fees and expenses of tribunal members, and (c) ICSID charges will be paid. Neither do the ICSID Arbitration Rules[112] or the ICSID Additional Facility Arbitration Rules[113] provide for substantive criteria on cost allocation. According to Professor Schreuer, '[p]ossible principles are the costs follow the event ("loser pays")

---

106. Bernard Hanotiau, *The Parties' Costs of Arbitration*, in *Evaluation of Damages in International Arbitration*, 213 (Yves Derains & Richard H. Kreindler, ICC 2006).
107. *See* Yves Derains & Eric Schwartz, *A Guide to the ICC Rules of Arbitration*, 371 (2nd ed., Kluwer 2005).
108. UNCITRAL Arbitration Rules (with new Art. 1, Para. 4, as adopted in 2013).
109. *Methanex Corporation v. United States of America*, UNCITRAL, Final Award of the Tribunal on Jurisdiction and Merits (3 Aug. 2005), Part V, pp. 2-4.
110. *EnCana Corporation v. Republic of Ecuador*, LCIA Case No. UN3481, UNCITRAL (formerly *EnCana Corporation v. Government of the Republic of Ecuador*), Award (3 Feb. 2006), para. 201.
111. *Ibid.*, para. 202.
112. ICSID Arbitration Rule 47(1)(j) only provides that the award contain 'any decision of the Tribunal regarding the cost of the proceeding', with no substantive rules on cost allocation.
113. ICSID Additional Facility Rules, Art. 58(1): 'Unless the parties otherwise agree, the Tribunal shall decide how and by whom the fees and expenses of the members of the Tribunal, the expenses and charges of the Secretariat and the expenses incurred by the parties in connection with the proceeding shall be borne. The Tribunal may, to that end, call on the Secretariat and

maxim, the use of costs as a sanction for procedural misconduct ... or the equal sharing of costs.'[114]

In the *Crystallex v. Venezuela* arbitration, the tribunal referred to the treaty rules[115] and to Article 58(1) of ICSID Additional Facility Rules, ordering that the parties bear their own costs and equally share the arbitration costs.[116] In *Tenaris v. Venezuela* the ICSID arbitral tribunal applied the 'loser pays' maxim,[117] refusing to sanction Venezuela for procedural misconduct. According to the *Tenaris* tribunal, 'the conduct about which complaint is made would not reach the high bar set by previous ICSID tribunals and subject to which, a party might be sanctioned in costs'.[118]

Following suit, Article 38(4)–(5) of the ICC Arbitration Rules[119] does not provide for substantive criteria on cost allocation, other than the possibility to sanction for procedural misconduct,[120] in the following terms:

> 4) The final award shall fix the costs of the arbitration and decide which of the parties shall bear them or in what proportion they shall be borne by the parties.
>
> 5) In making decisions as to costs, the arbitral tribunal may take into account such circumstances as it considers relevant, including the extent to which each party has conducted the arbitration in an expeditious and cost-effective manner.

The SCC Arbitration Rules[121] cover the costs of arbitration in different provisions, including the tribunal's and the SCC's fees and expenses (Article 49), and the costs incurred by the parties in the arbitration (Article 50). Both provisions contain a rule that upon request of a party – unless otherwise agreed by the parties – the tribunal take into account 'the outcome of the case, each party's contribution to the efficiency and expeditiousness of the arbitration and any other relevant circumstances'.[122]

---

the parties to provide it with the information it needs in order to formulate the division of the cost of the proceeding between the parties.'

114. Christoph H. Schreuer, *The ICSID Convention: A Commentary*, 1228 (2nd ed., Cambridge University Press 2014).
115. Agreement between the Government of Canada and the Government of the Republic of Venezuela for the Promotion and Protection of Investments of 1 Jul. 1996, Art. XII(9): 'A tribunal may also award costs in accordance with the applicable arbitration rules.'
116. The *Crystallex* tribunal noted that even if the claimant had prevailed in jurisdiction and partially on the merits, the respondent's defenses were not frivolous, but serious. *Crystallex International Corporation v. Bolivarian Republic of Venezuela*, ICSID Case No. ARB(AF)/11/2, Award (4 Apr. 2016), paras 958, 960.
117. *Tenaris S.A. and Talta – Trading e Marketing Sociedade Unipessoal Lda. v. Bolivarian Republic of Venezuela*, ICSID Case No. ARB/11/26, Award (29 Jan. 2016), paras 622–623: 'The Tribunal recalls that whilst the Claimants have succeeded in this case in establishing an illegal expropriation, and have secured a substantial award in their favour, they have not been entirely successful. The Tribunal has found against them in respect of all pre-expropriation claims... Taking this into account, and in the circumstances of this case, the Tribunal concludes that the fairest disposition on costs is that they should lie where they fall.'
118. *Tenaris S.A. and Talta – Trading e Marketing Sociedade Unipessoal Lda. v. Bolivarian Republic of Venezuela*, ICSID Case No. ARB/11/26, Award (29 Jan. 2016), para. 618.
119. ICC Arbitration Rules (1 Mar. 2017).
120. *See* ICC Commission, *Report on Decisions on Costs in International Arbitration*, (2) ICC Dis. Res. Bull. 1, 4, 12 (2015).
121. Arbitration Rules of the Arbitration Institute of the Stockholm Chamber of Commerce (SCC) (1 Jan. 2017).
122. Article 49(6) and Art. 50 of the SCC Arbitration Rules.

§9.07 CONCLUSION

Investment tribunals often rely on international customary rules when investment treaties fail to provide for attribution and compensation criteria. They may consider the attribution rules, the causation requirement between injury and unlawful conduct, and the 'full reparation' principle enshrined in the ILC Articles on State Responsibility.

Treaties often provide for fair market value compensation in lawful expropriation cases but are silent on reparation for unlawful conduct. Tribunals have therefore relied on the customary international 'full reparation' principle for unlawful expropriation, breaches of fair and equitable, national and most-favored treatment obligations, among other treaty breaches.

In the light of the 'full reparation' principle, arbitral tribunals have calculated reparation using the market value, the income and the cost methods. There is no consensus about valuation dates for unlawful conduct reparation, which dates are fixed on a case-by-case basis, most recent awards having awarded compound interest to ensure full reparation.

In addition, arbitral tribunals have adopted different approaches when allocating arbitration costs. Tribunals have applied the 'loser pays' maxim for arbitration costs' allocation when arbitration rules thus provide. The rules being silent on substantive criteria, arbitrators have applied the 'loser pays' maxim, allocated costs in proportion to the parties' relative success or in equal shares, or ordered the parties to bear their own costs.

Questions

(1) What is the difference between primary and secondary international legal obligations in international law on State responsibility?
(2) What is the role of causation in investment arbitration reparation?
(3) Please compare the 'direct' causation and the 'proximate' causation standards, providing examples.
(4) What is the difference between lawful and unlawful expropriation for reparation purposes?
(5) What difficulties do investment arbitral tribunals face when fixing damages in indirect expropriation cases?
(6) What are the advantages and disadvantages of the *ex ante* and *ex post* calculation methods?
(7) Please distinguish between pre-award and post-award interest.
(8) Please discuss the different approaches to allocating arbitration costs.

CHAPTER 10

The Award and Enforcement Issues

Investment awards are final and binding on the parties and subject to limited challenges. Despite being final and binding, parties can apply for correction of minor deficiencies and for award interpretation.

These applications, however, are not sufficient to correct egregious errors that may threaten the legitimacy of the arbitration. In such cases, the parties may institute annulment proceedings on limited grounds. ICSID awards are subject to the self-contained annulment mechanism under the ICSID Convention. Non-ICSID awards, including ICSID Additional Facility, UNCITRAL, and SCC awards are subject to annulment or setting aside proceedings before the State courts of the arbitral seat.

Annulment differs from appeal proceedings because annulment concerns mostly the legitimacy of the decision-making and not its merits and does not lead to award modification. Although appeals are not generally accepted in international arbitration, some investment treaty practice and other initiatives have alluded to or introduced investment arbitration reforms leading, among others, to an appeals system.

When the losing party defaults, the successful party will seek investment award recognition and enforcement before State courts to obtain forced compliance with the award. Assistance of State courts is crucial because arbitral tribunals cannot enforce the award. A party may seek to recognize the award to obtain the res judicata effect if it is necessary in a particular jurisdiction or enforce it before State courts to seek seizure of assets from the defaulting party.

Most investment treaties are silent on recognition and enforcement. The ICSID Convention applies to recognition and enforcement of ICSID arbitral awards, in addition to enforcement provisions of the law of the place of enforcement. The Member States' obligation to recognize an ICSID award is unconditional under the ICSID Convention, although enforcement is subject to the law of the place of enforcement. In turn, in most jurisdictions non-ICSID awards' recognition and enforcement are subject to the New York Convention.

When enforcing an award against States or State entities, immunity from jurisdiction or immunity from enforcement or execution might be an issue. The main difference between ICSID awards and non-ICSID awards with respect to immunity is that the question of immunity from jurisdiction does not arise in the context of the ICSID Convention.

§10.01 INTRODUCTION

This chapter builds on the investment arbitration's fundamental premise that, subject to limited challenges, awards are final and binding on the parties. Article 53(1) of the ICSID Convention provides that the award shall be binding, not subject to appeal or other remedy different from those set forth in the Convention. Similarly, Article 35(6) of the ICC Rules sets forth that the award shall be binding and that the parties are 'deemed to have waived their right to any form of recourse insofar as such waiver can validly be made'.

Because of its binding effect, an award has to be well drafted, disposing of the relevant matters in a clear way allowing the reader to follow its reasoning and understand the relief granted.[1] An award may not please losing parties, who may nevertheless decide to comply freely with the award. When displeased for good reason, losing parties sometimes succeed in having possible award deficiencies adjusted or in having the award annulled. Besides formal requirements applying to ICSID and non-ICSID awards, this chapter will discuss procedures to adjust award deficiencies (§10.02) and annulment proceedings (§10.03).

When the losing party does not comply with the award voluntarily, the winning party will seek award recognition and enforcement before State courts to obtain compliance with the award. Assistance of State courts is crucial in this respect because arbitral tribunals do not have powers to enforce the award. This chapter will examine recognition and enforcement proceedings of ICSID and non-ICSID awards (§10.04), including possible impediments to award enforcement such as State immunity (§10.05).

1. John R. Crook, *Award and Discontinuance of the Proceeding*, in *Litigating Investment Disputes, A Practitioner's Guide*, 443, 444 (Chiara Giorgetti, Brill Nijhoff 2014).

§10.02 AWARD FORMALITIES, SUPPLEMENTATION OR RECTIFICATION, INTERPRETATION AND REVISION

[A] ICSID Awards

ICSID awards are subject to certain mandatory requirements under Article 48 of the ICSID Convention that cannot be subject to modification by the parties.[2] Awards have to be rendered by majority but may contain separate or dissenting opinions as attachments.[3] Awards have to be in writing and signed by the tribunal members who voted on it. Awards also have to be exhaustive, dealing with every legal question or claim submitted by the parties. The exhaustiveness requirement does not mean that the award has to discuss every argument of the parties' pleadings. For example, the tribunal does not have to discuss alternative arguments when acceptance of a party's argument leads to this party's desired relief.[4]

Moreover, awards also have to state reasons, a requirement that is consistent with contemporary international dispute resolution. An award entirely without reasons has never arisen in ICSID arbitration.[5] The *Klöckner v. Cameroon*[6] ad hoc annulment committee[7] explained that this requirement means stating reasons with substance permitting to follow the tribunal's reasoning.

Awards are deemed to be rendered 'on the date on which the certified copies were dispatched' to the parties.[8] Within forty-five days of the award's dispatch to the parties, a party may request that the same tribunal supplement omissions in the award and rectify 'clerical, arithmetical or similar error' under Article 49(2) of the ICSID Convention, subject to notifying this to the other party. The tribunal cannot supplement or rectify the award on its own without a party's request. Article 49(2), which applies to awards and to ad hoc annulment committee decisions, provides as follows:

> (2) The Tribunal upon the request of a party made within 45 days after the date on which the award was rendered may after notice to the other party decide any question which it had omitted to decide in the award, and shall rectify any clerical, arithmetical or similar error in the award. ...

The expression 'may' for supplementation requests and the expression 'shall' for rectification requests in Article 49(2) above suggest that the tribunal has an obligation

---

2. Christoph H. Schreuer et al., *The ICSID Convention: A Commentary*, 806 (2nd ed., Cambridge University Press 2014).
3. ICSID Convention, Art. 48(4).
4. Christoph H. Schreuer et al., *The ICSID Convention: A Commentary*, 817 (2nd ed., Cambridge University Press 2014).
5. *Ibid.*, 821.
6. *Klöckner Industrie-Anlagen GmbH and others v. United Republic of Cameroon and Société Camerounaise des Engrais*, ICSID Case No. ARB/81/2, Ad Hoc Committee's Decision on Annulment (3 May 1985), para. 119, in Emmanuel Gaillard, *La Jurisprudence du CIRDI* 163, 284–285 (2nd ed., Global Arbitration Review 2018).
7. When an annulment application is made before the ICSID Secretary General under Art. 52(1) of the ICSID Convention, the Chairman of the Administrative Council appoints 'from the Panel of Arbitrators an ad hoc committee of three persons' pursuant to Art. 52(3) of the ICSID Convention.
8. ICSID Convention, Art. 49(1).

to rectify clerical, arithmetical or similar errors but no obligation to supplement the award. Supplementing the award is a limited remedy intended for unintentional omissions rather than "essential" omissions justifying award annulment under Article 52.[9]

If the parties have a dispute about the meaning or the scope of an existing award, either party may at any time request the award's interpretation by application to the ICSID Secretary General under Article 50 of the ICSID Convention. If the same tribunal is no longer available, a new ICSID tribunal will be constituted to rule on the parties' interpretation dispute.[10]

Finally, a newly discovered fact decisively affecting the award can serve as a ground for an award revision application to the ICSID Secretary General under Article 51 of the ICSID Convention. Article 51(1) requires that this newly discovered fact be 'unknown to the Tribunal and to the applicant and that the applicant's ignorance of that fact was not due to negligence'. The revision application has to be made within ninety days after discovering the new fact, subject to a three-year limitation counting from the award's issuance. If the same tribunal is no longer available, a new ICSID tribunal will be constituted to rule on this application.

[B] Non-ICSID Awards

Non-ICSID awards are also subject to formal requirements. The ICC Arbitration Rules require that an award be rendered by majority,[11] that an award state reasons (Article 32(1) and (2)) and that it be signed (Article 35(1)). An award has no legal effect until approved by the ICC Court under Article 34. The ICC Court's scrutiny maximizing legal effectiveness of draft awards may include identifying defects of 'form' and drawing the tribunal's attention to points of 'substance'. This distinction between 'form' and 'substance' is crucial, because arbitrators are free to disregard the Court's observations on the award's 'substance'.[12] 'Substance' is thus the arbitrators' responsibility.

ICC draft awards should be submitted to the Court for scrutiny 'before being signed'. '[T]he scrutiny process is a cornerstone of the Rules' that the parties cannot derogate from.[13] Once scrutinized and approved, the legal effect[14] of the tribunal's signature is set forth in Article 32(3):

9. Christoph H. Schreuer et al., *The ICSID Convention: A Commentary*, 860, 864 (2nd ed., Cambridge University Press 2014).
10. Article 50 does not apply to decisions by ad hoc annulment committees.
11. Most awards are unanimous in ICC arbitration, *see* Yves Derains & Eric A. Schwartz, *A Guide to the ICC Rules of Arbitration*, 307 (2nd ed., Kluwer Law International 2005). If there is no majority, the president of the tribunal will make the award pursuant to Art. 32(1).
12. Yves Derains & Eric A. Schwartz, *A Guide to the ICC Rules of Arbitration*, 313 (2nd ed., Kluwer Law International 2005).
13. Jason Fry, Simon Greenberg & Francesca Mazza, *The Secretariat's Guide to ICC Arbitration*, 328 (ICC 2012).
14. W. Laurence Craig, William W. Park & Jan Paulsson, *International Chamber of Commerce Arbitration*, 397 (3rd ed., Oceania Publications Inc. 1998).

The award shall be deemed to be made at the place of the arbitration and on the date stated therein.

Article 32(3) requiring information on when and where the award was made seeks to dispel uncertainty because often awards are physically made in numerous places and at different times[15] and also because the mention of the place of arbitration in the award is a requisite for its validity under many national laws.

When the award is made, the ICC Secretariat will notify it to the parties that are 'bound'[16] by it under Article 35(1) and Article 35(6) of the ICC Rules. When making the award, the arbitrators are 'discharged of their office or *functus officio*'.[17] But this is subject to limited exceptions such as the tribunal's authority to make post-award corrections or to provide interpretation.

A tribunal can make corrections of 'clerical, computational or typographical error, or any errors of similar nature' on its own initiative within thirty days of the award's date under Article 36(1). A tribunal can also decide on corrections or on the interpretation of an award upon a party's application to the Secretariat, within thirty days of receiving the award under Article 36(2). If the application is granted, the tribunal's decision will take the form of an addendum to the award.

The majority rule[18] and the requirements that awards state reasons, be dated, indicate the arbitral seat, and be signed also feature in Articles 33 and 34 of the UNCITRAL Rules and in Article 42 of the SCC Arbitration Rules. Moreover, Article 34(2) of the UNCITRAL Rules and Article 46 of the SCC Rules stipulate that an award is 'final and binding' on the parties.

The UNCITRAL Rules and the SCC Rules also provide for correction and interpretation requests by a party within thirty days of receiving the award.[19] The UNCITRAL Rules and the SCC Rules set forth the possibility of corrections by the tribunal on its own motion within thirty days of the award's communication and within thirty days of the award's date, respectively.[20] Finally, Article 39 of the UNCITRAL Rules and Article 48 of the SCC Rules establish that a party may request an additional award on claims presented in the arbitration but not decided by the arbitrators within thirty days of receiving the award.[21]

15. Jason Fry, Simon Greenberg & Francesca Mazza, *The Secretariat's Guide to ICC Arbitration*, 321 (ICC 2012).
16. Article 35(6) of the ICC Rules provides that '[e]very award shall be binding on the parties.' The expression 'final was changed to 'binding' in the 1998 version of the Rules because this is sufficient for an award's enforceability under Art. III and Art. V(1)(e) of the New York Convention. *See* Yves Derains & Eric A. Schwartz, *A Guide to the ICC Rules of Arbitration*, 320 (2nd ed., Kluwer Law International 2005).
17. W. Laurence Craig, William W. Park & Jan Paulsson, *International Chamber of Commerce Arbitration*, 406 (3rd ed., Oceania Publications Inc. 1998).
18. Subject to a decision by the president failing such majority, *see* Arbitration Rules of the Arbitration Institute of the Stockholm Chamber of Commerce (SCC) (1 Jan. 2017), Art. 42(3); UNCITRAL Arbitration Rules (with new Art. 1, Para. 4, as adopted in 2013), Art. 33(2).
19. 2017 SCC Arbitration Rules, Art. 47(1); UNCITRAL Arbitration Rules, Art. 37(1) and Art. 38(1).
20. 2017 SCC Arbitration Rules, Art. 47(2); UNCITRAL Arbitration Rules, Art. 38(2).
21. The UNCITRAL Rules provide that the thirty day time limit of an additional award request counts from the date of receiving the award or the 'termination order' under Art. 39(1).

§10.03 ICSID AND NON-ICSID ANNULMENT PROCEEDINGS

Appeals are generally not accepted in international arbitration, including investment arbitration. As discussed in the section above, in ICSID and non-ICSID arbitration parties can apply for correction of minor deficiencies and award interpretation. But these applications are not sufficient to correct egregious errors threatening arbitration's legitimacy,[22] errors which due to their gravity are subject to annulment proceedings.

Annulment proceedings are part of the ICSID's self-contained nature pursuant to the exclusive-remedy rule of Article 26 of the ICSID Convention.[23] Pursuant to Article 52 of the ICSID Convention, the Centre constitutes an ad hoc committee on a case-by-case basis to rule on annulment applications.

Annulment differs from appeal because annulment concerns the legitimacy of decision-making not its merits,[24] unless the annulment is based on the incompatibility of the award with international public policy. Moreover, annulment leads to 'invalidation of the original decision' not to its modification.[25] Despite the differences between annulment and appeal, some investment treaty practice,[26] and other initiatives have alluded to [27] or introduced[28] investment arbitration reforms leading, among others, to an appeal system.

---

22. *See* Veijo Heiskanen & Laura Halonen, *Post Award Remedies*, in *Litigating Investment Disputes, A Practitioner's Guide*, 497 (Chiara Giorgetti, Brill Nijhoff 2014); Sundra Rajoo, *Annulment of Investment Arbitration Awards*, in *The Investment Treaty Arbitration Review*, 211 (2nd ed., Barton Legum, Law Business Research 2017).
23. ICSID Convention, Art. 26: 'Consent of the parties to arbitration under this Convention shall, unless otherwise stated, be deemed consent to such arbitration to the exclusion of any other remedy ...'
24. Christoph H. Schreuer et al., *The ICSID Convention: A Commentary*, 901 (2nd ed., Cambridge University Press 2014).
25. *Ibid.* Nevertheless, the *Occidental* ad hoc committee substituted the tribunal's damages calculation in the light of procedural economy, noting the need for 'a very simple arithmetic calculation and without further input from the parties'. In this case, the committee partially annulled part of the award calculating compensation for 100% of an expropriated investment, when this investment was only 60% beneficially owned by the claimants. *See Occidental Petroleum Corporation and Occidental Exploration and Production Company v. Republic of Ecuador*, ICSID Case No. ARB/06/11, Decision on Annulment of 2 Nov. 2015, paras 299–301.
26. For example, Art. 28(10) of the 2012 US Model BIT provides the following: 'In the event that an appellate mechanism for reviewing awards rendered by investor-State dispute settlement tribunals is developed in the future under other institutional arrangements, the Parties shall consider whether awards rendered under Article 34 should be subject to that appellate mechanism. The Parties shall strive to ensure that any such appellate mechanism they consider adopting provides for transparency of proceedings similar to the transparency provisions established in Article 29.' *See also* Free Trade Agreement between the United States and the Republic of Korea (30 Jun. 2007), Art. 11.20(12): 'If a separate, multilateral agreement enters into force between the Parties that establishes an appellate body for purposes of reviewing awards rendered by tribunals constituted pursuant to international trade or investment arrangements to hear investment disputes, the Parties shall strive to reach an agreement that would have such appellate body review awards rendered under Article 11.26 in arbitrations commenced after the multilateral agreement enters into force between the Parties'; Katia Yannaca-Small, *Annulment of ICSID Awards: Limited Scope But Is There Potential?*, in *Arbitration Under International Investment Agreements*, 603, 627 (Katia Yannaca-Small, Oxford University Press 2010).
27. ICSID Secretariat, Possible Improvements of the Framework for ICSID Arbitration, Discussion Paper (22 Oct. 2004), available at https://icsid.worldbank.org/en/Documents/resources/

Dissimilarly from ICSID awards (A), non-ICSID awards, including ICSID Additional Facility, UNCITRAL, and SCC awards, are subject to annulment or setting aside proceedings before the State courts of the arbitral seat (B).

[A] Annulment of ICSID Awards under Article 52 of the ICSID Convention

The 2017 ICSID Annual Report[29] states that of 555 registered arbitrations leading to 261 awards only five awards were annulled in full and another twelve were partially annulled. This shows an annulment rate of approximately 6.5% for awards and of approximately 3% for registered arbitrations. Article 52(1) of the ICSID Convention sets forth the limited annulment powers of ad hoc committees:

> (1) Either party may request annulment of the award by an application in writing addressed to the Secretary-General on one or more of the following grounds:
>
> (a) that the Tribunal was not properly constituted;
> (b) that the Tribunal has manifestly exceeded its powers;
> (c) that there was corruption on the part of a member of the Tribunal;
> (d) that there has been a serious departure from a fundamental rule of procedure; or
> (e) that the award has failed to state the reasons on which it is based

The annulment ground under Article 52(1)(a) on improper constitution of the tribunal has been interpreted to include the party's confidence in the independence and impartiality of arbitrators under Article 14(1)[30] of the ICSID Convention. The ad hoc committee in *Suez et al. v. Argentina* held that:

> [T]he Committee agrees with Respondent that the parties' confidence in the independence and impartiality of the arbitrators deciding their case is essential for ensuring the integrity of the proceedings and the dispute resolution mechanism as such; thus, in principle, a lack of the qualities in Article 14(1) may serve as ground for annulment under Article 52(1)(a). This conclusion is in line with the finding

Possible%20Improvements%20of%20the%20Framework%20of%20ICSID%20Arbitration.pdf (accessed 25 Oct. 2018), paras 20–23 and Annex 1(discussing the creation of a single Appeals Facility with a fifteen member Appeals Panel to decide on appeals for a clear error of law or any of Art. 52(1) annulment grounds); Council of the European Union, Negotiating directives for a Convention establishing a multilateral court for the settlement of investment disputes of 20 Mar. 2018, available at http://data.consilium.europa.eu/doc/document/ST-12981-2017-ADD-1-DCL-1/en/pdf (accessed 26 Apr. 2018), para. 10 (providing for a multilateral court with an appeal tribunal to decide on appeals for 'errors of law or manifest errors in the appreciation of facts, or, as appropriate, serious procedural shortcomings').

28. *See* Free Trade Agreement between the EU and Vietnam of 2016 and Canada-EU Comprehensive Economic and Trade Agreement ('CETA') of the same year, even if they do not resort to a proper arbitration system but to a permanent court.
29. ICSID 2017 Annual Report (6 Sep. 2017), pp. 38–39, available at https://icsid.worldbank.org/en/Documents/icsiddocs/ICSID%20AR%20EN.pdf (accessed 24 Apr. 2018).
30. ICSID Convention, Art. 14(1): 'Persons designated to serve on the Panels shall be persons of high moral character and recognized competence in the fields of law, commerce, industry or finance, who may be relied upon to exercise independent judgment ... .'

made by the *ad hoc* committee in *EDF v. Argentina* and also with the apparent intention of the drafters of the ICSID Convention.[31]

Article 52(1)(b) on manifest excess of powers is a recurrent ground than Article 52(1)(a) above. Parties have relied on Article 52(1)(b) to argue that the tribunal (a) lacked or exceeded jurisdiction; (b) failed to exercise jurisdiction; and/or (c) failed to apply the proper law.[32] For example, in *Occidental v. Ecuador* the ad hoc committee found that the tribunal exceeded jurisdiction compensating an investor for an expropriated investment that was 40% beneficially owned and controlled by a Chinese non-protected investor under the US-Ecuador BIT.[33]

Moreover, in *Venezuela Holdings et al. v. Venezuela* the ad hoc committee partially annulled the award for manifest excess of powers for failure to apply the proper law. In the ad hoc committee's view, the tribunal made a mistake when holding that customary international law governed compensation for investment expropriation in the Cerro Negro Project.[34] The ad hoc committee concluded that the tribunal should have applied the relevant BIT compensation standard on expropriation, not customary international law.

Parties have seldom relied on corruption of a tribunal member under Article 52(1)(c) to challenge ICSID awards. For example, in *Aguas del Aconquija and Vivendi* Argentina withdrew the Article 52(1)(c) challenge before the ad hoc committee could rule on it.[35]

On Article 52(1)(d), the ad hoc committee in *TECO v. Guatemala* noted that '[a] departure from a rule of procedure may lead to the annulment of an award only if the departure is serious and the rule of procedure that was not complied with is fundamental.'[36] Applying this standard, the committee found that the tribunal erred when denying TECO's claim for interest on historical damages on unjust enrichment grounds. In the committee's view, the tribunal surprised the parties when relying on unjust enrichment, which was never alluded by the parties or the tribunal. Consequently, the tribunal breached the parties' 'right to be heard' on unjust enrichment.[37]

31. *Suez, Sociedad General de Aguas de Barcelona S.A. and Vivendi Universal S.A v. Argentine Republic*, ICSID Case No. ARB/03/19, Decision on Annulment (5 May 2017), para. 77 (the annulment application was denied). *See also EDF International S.A., SAUR International S.A. and León Participaciones Argentinas S.A. v. Argentine Republic*, ICSID Case No. ARB/03/23, Decision on Annulment (5 Feb. 2016), paras 126–127 (The annulment application was also dismissed in this case.).
32. Christoph H. Schreuer et al., *The ICSID Convention: A Commentary*, 908 et seq. (2nd ed., Cambridge University Press 2014).
33. *Occidental Petroleum Corporation and Occidental Exploration and Production Company v. Republic of Ecuador*, ICSID Case No. ARB/06/11, Decision on Annulment (2 Nov. 2015), paras 257 et seq.
34. *Venezuela Holdings B.V. and others (formerly Mobil Corporation and others) v. Bolivarian Republic of Venezuela*, ICSID Case No. ARB/07/27, Decision on Annulment (9 Mar. 2017), para. 188(a).
35. *Compañía de Aguas del Aconquija S.A. and Vivendi Universal S.A. v. Argentine Republic*, ICSID Case No. ARB/97/3, Decision on Annulment (10 Aug. 2010), para. 201.
36. *TECO Guatemala Holdings, LLC v. Republic of Guatemala*, ICSID Case No. ARB/10/23, Decision on Annulment (5 Apr. 2016), para. 81.
37. *Ibid.*, paras 189–191.

Finally, when seeking annulment under Article 52(1)(e), parties have made arguments on (a) the absence of reasons; (b) insufficient and inadequate reasons; (c) contradictory reasons; or (d) the tribunal's failure to deal with questions.[38] Noting that ad hoc committees do not have authority to review the merits,[39] the *Tidewater et al. v. Venezuela* committee held that stating reasons is a crucial duty of tribunals:

> [T]he statement of reasons is one of the central duties of arbitral tribunals. An award is not a discretionary *fiat* but the result of the process of weighing evidence and applying and interpreting the law and subsuming the facts thus established under the law as interpreted by the Tribunal. The legitimacy of the process depends on its intelligibility and transparency. The statement of reasons allows the Parties to understand the process through which the tribunal makes its findings...[40]

Applying this standard, the *Tidewater* committee annulled part of an award quantifying reparation for expropriation on Article 52(1)(e) grounds. According to the ad hoc committee, the tribunal's contradictory reasoning when calculating reparation cancelled out the tribunal's previous reasoning about the same reparation.[41] Also, the ad hoc committee in *TECO v. Guatemala* annulled part of an award for the tribunal's failure to deal with evidence on the loss of value claim pursuant to Article 52(1)(e).[42]

When an annulment application is made before the Secretary General under Article 52(1), the Chairman of the Administrative Council will 'appoint from the Panel of Arbitrators an ad hoc Committee of three persons' pursuant to Article 52(3). None of the ad hoc committee appointed members can be a national of the State party to the dispute or by the State of the investor's nationality or be designated to the Panel of Arbitrators by these States. The ad hoc members cannot have acted as an arbitrator or a conciliator in the same dispute.

The annulment application must be made within 120 days of the award's dispatch to the parties. This is so, except when the annulment application alleges corruption of an arbitrator; then, the 120-day time limit counts from discovery of corruption under Article 52(2).

[B] Annulment of Non-ICSID Awards

Like ICSID awards, non-ICSID awards, including ad hoc UNCITRAL awards, and awards made under institutional rules such as ICSID Additional Facility, ICC and SCC Rules are not subject to appeal on the merits. But they can be set aside pursuant to the

38. Christoph H. Schreuer, *The ICSID Convention: A Commentary*, 908 et seq. (2nd ed., Cambridge University Press 2014).
39. *Tidewater Investment SRL and Tidewater Caribe, C.A. v. Bolivarian Republic of Venezuela*, ICSID Case No. ARB/10/5, Decision on Annulment (27 Dec. 2016), para. 167.
40. *Ibid.*, para. 163.
41. *Ibid.*, para. 196.
42. *TECO Guatemala Holdings, LLC v. Republic of Guatemala*, ICSID Case No. ARB/10/23, Decision on Annulment (5 Apr. 2016), paras 123 et seq.

arbitral seat's law, which may vary depending on the jurisdiction. The arbitral seat plays a major role in the annulment of non-ICSID awards.[43]

Despite some variations, most States adopt laws with annulment grounds similar to the ones provided in the UNCITRAL Model Law.[44] The UNCITRAL Model law seeks to provide a suggested pattern for lawmakers when adopting their domestic arbitration legislation. To date, eighty States have adopted legislation based on the UNCITRAL Model Law,[45] including its Article 34(2) on annulment, which reads that:

> (2) An arbitral award may be set aside by the court specified in article 6 only if:
>
> (a) the party making the application furnishes proof that:
>   (i) a party to the arbitration agreement referred to in article 7 was under some incapacity; or the said agreement is not valid under the law to which the parties have subjected it or, failing any indication thereon, under the law of this State; or
>   (ii) the party making the application was not given proper notice of the appointment of an arbitrator or of the arbitral proceedings or was otherwise unable to present his case; or
>   (iii) the award deals with a dispute not contemplated by or not falling within the terms of the submission to arbitration, or contains decisions on matters beyond the scope of the submission to arbitration, provided that, if the decisions on matters submitted to arbitration can be separated from those not so submitted, only that part of the award which contains decisions on matters not submitted to arbitration may be set aside; or
>   (iv) the composition of the arbitral tribunal or the arbitral procedure was not in accordance with the agreement of the parties, unless such agreement was in conflict with a provision of this Law from which the parties cannot derogate, or, failing such agreement, was not in accordance with this Law; or
>
> (b) the court finds that:
>   (i) the subject-matter of the dispute is not capable of settlement by arbitration under the law of this State; or
>   (ii) the award is in conflict with the public policy of this State.

Article 34(2)(a) above provides for the annulment grounds to be raised by a party. In addition, Article 34(2)(b) sets forth the grounds that State courts of the arbitral seat may raise on their own motion. Pursuant to Article 34(3) of the UNCITRAL Model Law, the annulment application shall be made within three months from the date of receiving the award or receiving the decision on the request for correction, interpretation or the additional award.

---

43. *See* Juan Fernández-Armesto, *Different Systems for the Annulment of ICSID Awards*, 26(1) ICSID Rev. 128, 133 (2011); Kaj Hobér & Nils Eliasson, *Review of Investment Treaty Awards by Municipal Courts*, in *Arbitration Under International Investment Agreements*, 635, 668 (Katia Yannaca-Small, Oxford University Press 2010).
44. UNCITRAL Model Law on International Commercial Arbitration of 1985 (with amendments adopted in 2006).
45. States enacting legislation based on a model law have, however, the flexibility to depart from its text.

In the US, eight States have adopted the UNCITRAL Model Law, including California, Connecticut, Florida and Texas;[46] others such as the District of Columbia and the State of New York have not adopted the UNCITRAL Model Law. In *Mesa Group v. Canada,* the dispute under the UNCITRAL Arbitration Rules was about Canada's incentives to renewable energy producers. After the *Mesa Group v. Canada* tribunal's dismissing all investor's claims and awarding the arbitration costs to Canada,[47] Mesa Group instituted annulment proceedings before the US District Court for the District of Columbia, the arbitral seat being Miami, Florida. Canada opposed the annulment, counter-petitioning the award's enforcement. The parties diverged about the applicable law. Canada favored the application of the law of Florida's Circuit (11th Circuit); Mesa Power sustained the application of the law of the District of Columbia's Circuit. The DC court stated in an obiter dictum that Mesa Power's claims failed under either law.[48] The questions before it having federal character, the court assumed that the law of the District of Columbia's Circuit, the Federal Arbitration Act (FAA), applied to annulment.[49]

According the DC court, under the FAA a court must confirm a foreign arbitral award except if it finds a ground for refusal under this Act or under the New York Convention.[50] Section 10 of the FAA reads that:

> § 10. Same; vacation; grounds; rehearing
>
> (a) In any of the following cases the United States court in and for the district wherein the award was made may make an order vacating the award upon the application of any party to the arbitration –
> (1) where the award was procured by corruption, fraud, or undue means;
> (2) where there was evident partiality or corruption in the arbitrators, or either of them;
> (3) where the arbitrators were guilty of misconduct in refusing to postpone the hearing, upon sufficient cause shown, or in refusing to hear evidence pertinent and material to the controversy; or of any other misbehavior by which the rights of any party have been prejudiced; or
> (4) where the arbitrators exceeded their powers, or so imperfectly executed them that a mutual, final, and definite award upon the subject matter submitted was not made ...

The DC court rejected Mesa Power's allegations that the tribunal erred when (a) interpreting the 'procurement' exception to jurisdiction under Article 1108 NAFTA, and (b) giving 'deference' to Canada under Article 1105 NAFTA on minimum standard of treatment. Consequently, the court rejected the FAA section 10(3) and (4) annulment grounds on prejudice to rights and excess of jurisdiction; the DC court also

46. UNCITRAL Model Law on International Commercial Arbitration of 1985 (with amendments adopted in 2006), Status, available at http://www.uncitral.org/uncitral/en/uncitral_texts/arbitration/1985Model_arbitration_status.html (accessed 26 Apr. 2018).
47. *Mesa Power Group, LLC v. Government of Canada,* UNCITRAL, PCA Case No. 2012-17, Award (24 Mar. 2016), para. 706.
48. *Mesa Power Group, LLC v. Government of Canada,* US District Court for the District of Columbia, Civil Action No. 16-1101 (JDB), Decision (15 Jun. 2017), p. 9.
49. *Ibid.,* pp. 7–8.
50. *Ibid.,* pp. 7–8.

rejected the additional annulment ground on manifest disregard of the law, applicable in addition to statutory FAA grounds in the District of Columbia's Circuit.[51]

Canadian provinces and territories have adopted legislation based on the UNCITRAL Model Law.[52] To illustrate, the British Columbia province has enacted the International Commercial Arbitration Act (ICAA).[53] In the *Mexico v. Metalclad* annulment proceedings, Mexico sought to annul an ICSID Additional Facility award made in Vancouver, British Columbia. In the arbitration, the tribunal found that Mexico had breached the FET obligation and had expropriated Metalclad's landfill investment in San Luis Potosí under Article 1105 and Article 1110 of NAFTA.[54] The annulment proceedings took place before British Columbia courts because the arbitral seat was Vancouver.

Rejecting other annulment grounds, the Supreme Court of British Columbia found that the NAFTA tribunal exceeded its jurisdiction under Article 34(2)(a)(iv) ICAA.[55] The court noted that the tribunal could not include transparency obligations under Chapter 18 into Article 1105 NAFTA on FET let alone decide on this basis.[56] The Supreme Court of British Columbia also found that the tribunal's 'analysis of Article 1105 infected its analysis of Article 1110'[57] on expropriation for the period before adoption of the ecological decree of September 1997. Therefore, the court annulled the award, except for part of the expropriation decision founded on this ecological decree.[58] When partially annulling the award, the court clarified that it set aside from the reparation calculation interest before September 1997 and that if the parties failed to agree on the interest recalculation 'the matter was remitted back to the Tribunal'.[59]

France has not adopted the UNCITRAL Model Law. The French Civil Procedure Code provides in Articles 1518 and 1519 that setting aside proceedings of an award made by an international arbitral tribunal seated in France be instituted within one month from the award's notification. Article 1520 sets forth five annulment grounds, as follows:

(1) the arbitral tribunal wrongly upheld or declined jurisdiction; or

51. *Ibid.*, pp. 12–20.
52. UNCITRAL Model Law on International Commercial Arbitration of 1985 (with amendments adopted in 2006), Status, available at http://www.uncitral.org/uncitral/en/uncitral_texts/arbitration/1985Model_arbitration_status.html (accessed 26 Apr. 2018).
53. British Columbia (Canada), International Commercial Arbitration Act ('ICAA'), RSBC 1996, Ch. 233. The British Columbia legislature passed the International Commercial Arbitration Amendment Act on 12 Apr. 2018 amending the ICAA, to come into effect once this bill receives royal assent. Article 34 ICAA on annulment was not amended.
54. *Metalclad Corporation v. The United Mexican States*, ICSID Case No. ARB(AF)/97/1, Award (30 Aug. 2000), paras 101, 112.
55. ICAA, Art. 34(2)(a)(iv): 'the arbitral award deals with a dispute not contemplated by or not falling within the terms of the submission to arbitration, or it contains decisions on matters beyond the scope of the submission to arbitration, provided that, if the decisions on matters submitted to arbitration can be separated from those not so submitted, only that part of the arbitral award which contains decisions on matters not submitted to arbitration may be set aside …'.
56. *The United Mexican States v. Metalclad Corporation*, 2001 BCSC 664, para. 70.
57. *Ibid.*, para. 78.
58. *Ibid.*, para. 83.
59. *Ibid.*, para. 134.

(2) the arbitral tribunal was not properly constituted; or
(3) the arbitral tribunal ruled without complying with the mandate conferred upon it; or
(4) due process [*le principe de la contradiction*] was violated; or
(5) recognition or enforcement of the award is contrary to international public policy.[60]

In *Venezuela v. Gold Reserve* the Paris Court of Appeal rejected all annulment grounds raised by Venezuela under Article 1520(1) and Article 1520(3)-(5) above. This was after the ICSID Additional Facility arbitral tribunal found that Venezuela had breached the FET provision[61] under the Canada-Venezuela BIT.[62] First, the French court found that the tribunal rightly upheld jurisdiction under Article 1520(1) because: (a) the Canadian investor and its investment qualified under the BIT jurisdictional requirements, and (b) Venezuela failed to establish abuse of process by the investor.[63] Second, the Court of Appeal found that the tribunal organizing the evidentiary hearing, its reparation calculation and its dismissal of an additional hearing request by Venezuela after the awards rendering were all consistent with due process under Article 1520(4)-(5).[64] Third, the Court of Appeal rejected Venezuela's Article 1520(3) challenge that the tribunal had decided *ex aequo et bono* or had awarded punitive damages.[65] Finally, Venezuela's challenge failed on Article 1520(1), (3) and (5) because (a) Gold Reserve's reparation of loss incurred as the owner and majority shareholder of its Venezuelan branch was consistent with the BIT, and because (b) Venezuela had renounced its argument under Article XII(9)[66] on claims for loss suffered by an affiliate company at the hearing.

Nevertheless, the Paris Court of Appeal annulled pursuant to Article 1520(5) of the French Code of Civil Procedure a UNCITRAL award made under the Latvia-Kyrgyzstan BIT[67] against Kyrgyzstan.[68] This arbitration was about a Latvian banker's

60. Code of Civil Procedure (*Code de procédure civile*), Art. 1520 (translation by Emmanuel Gaillard et al., *Code of Civil Procedure, Book IV, Arbitration*, in *ICCA International Handbook on Commercial Arbitration*, 1, 14 (Jan Paulsson & Lise Bosman, Kluwer Law International, Supplement No. 64, May 2011). For a discussion of annulment decisions of investment awards in France from 2008 to 2017, *See* Laurent Gouiffes & Lucie Chatelain, *L'annulation en France des sentences arbitrales rendues sur le fondement de traités d'investissement*, 2017(3) Revue de l'Arbitrage 840 et seq.
61. *Gold Reserve Inc. v. Bolivarian Republic of Venezuela*, ICSID Case No. ARB(AF)/09/1, Award (22 Sep. 2014), para. 863.
62. Treaty between the Government of Canada and the Government of Venezuela for the Promotion and Protection of Investments of 1 Jul. 1996.
63. *République du Kirghizistan v. Valeriy Belokon*, 15/01650, Cour d'appel de Paris, Pôle 1, Chambre 1, Judgment (21 Feb. 2017), pp. 4-5.
64. *Ibid.*, pp. 5-6.
65. *Ibid.*, p. 7.
66. Treaty between the Government of Canada and the Government of Venezuela for the Promotion and Protection of Investments of 1 July 1996, Article XII(9): '...Where an investor brings a claim under this Article regarding loss or damage suffered by an enterprise the investor directly or indirectly owns or controls any award shall be made to the affected enterprise'.
67. Agreement between the Government of the Republic of Latvia and the Government of the Kyrgyz Republic on the Promotion and Protection of Investments (22 May 2008).
68. *République Bolivarienne du Venezuela v. Gold Reserve Inc*, 14/21103, Cour d'appel de Paris, Pôle 1, Chambre 1, Judgment (7 Feb. 2017).

investment in Manas bank, placed under government control with the Kyrgyz political turmoil in 2010 and subject to administrative and criminal investigations by Kyrgyz authorities for money laundering. The arbitral tribunal rejected the allegation about Manas bank's engaging in illegal activity when failing to act and to report suspicious money laundering activities for lack of 'concrete and decisive evidence'.[69] The tribunal granted the claimant compensation for expropriation of its investment, and for unfair, inequitable, arbitrary and unreasonable treatment by the host State.[70] The Paris court decided to annul the award whose recognition and enforcement was contrary to international public policy. According to the court, the arbitral decision awarded the Latvian banker compensation for illegal activities by Manas bank, in manifest, effective and concrete breach of international public policy as understood by French law (recognizing or enforcing the award '*viole de manière manifeste, effective et concrète l'ordre public international*').[71]

§10.04 AWARD RECOGNITION AND ENFORCEMENT

Once an investment award is issued and is not voluntarily complied with, the interested party may seek to recognize it to obtain res judicata effect if it is necessary in a particular jurisdiction and enforce it before State courts to seek seizure of assets from the award's debtor. Recognition seeks to give legal effect to an award in a national legal system, including to obtain the res judicata effect in this national legal system. In turn, enforcement is the 'court's action to compel a person to comply with the terms of the [award]'.[72] Execution, often used as a synonym to enforcement in relation to awards granting pecuniary relief, is '[j]udicial enforcement of a money judgment ... by seizing and selling the judgment debtor's property.'[73]

As a rule, a party may seek award recognition and enforcement once receiving the definitive award from the investment tribunal. Nevertheless, some investment treaties may require that a time limit elapse before a party can seek award recognition and enforcement.

For example, Article 34(6)(a) of the 2012 US Model BIT sets forth a 120-day time limit between the tribunal's dispatching the award and the date when ICSID award recognition and enforcement proceedings can be pursued. Article 34(6)(b) sets forth a 90-day time limit for non-ICSID awards. The 120-day and 90-day time limits correspond to the time period for institution of annulment proceedings under the ICSID Convention and the UNCITRAL Model Law, respectively. These time limits apply when there has been no revision or annulment requests. Alternatively, pursuant to Article 34(6)(a) and Article 34(6)(b) recognition and enforcement can be sought (a) after the revision or

69. *Valeri Belokon v. Kyrgyz Republic*, UNCITRAL, Award (24 Oct. 2014), para. 163.
70. *Ibid.*, para. 335.
71. *République du Kirghizistan v. Valeriy Belokon*, 15/01650, Cour d'appel de Paris, Pôle 1, Chambre 1, Decision (21 Feb. 2017), p. 15.
72. Bryan A. Garner (ed.), *Black's Law Dictionary*, 295 (5th pocket ed., Thomson Reuters 2016): 'enforcement of judgment. (1815) A court's action to compel a person to comply with the terms of judgment ...'.
73. *Ibid.*, p. 314.

annulment decision on ICSID awards and (b) after no appeal is allowed against a revision or annulment decision on non-ICSID awards, respectively.

Nevertheless, most investment treaties are silent on recognition and enforcement. The ICSID Convention applies to recognition and enforcement of ICSID arbitral awards, in addition to enforcement provisions of the law of the place of enforcement. Non-ICSID awards are subject in most jurisdictions to the New York Convention, which is in force in 159 States.[74] For these reasons, recognition and enforcement of ICSID awards (A) and non-ICSID awards (B) differ in many respects, which will be discussed, in turn.

[A] ICSID Awards

Pursuant to Article 53(1)[75] of the ICSID Convention an award is binding on all parties to the proceeding. Article 53(2) sets forth that an 'award' 'include[s] any decision interpreting, revising or annulling such award pursuant to Articles 50, 51 or 52'. Only final awards are subject to recognition and enforcement. Decisions preliminary to awards such as decisions affirming jurisdiction and recommending provisional measures, and procedural orders are not awards.[76] But if these preliminary decisions are incorporated into the award, they are also subject to recognition and enforcement.

Upon a request for award interpretation under Article 50(2),[77] a tribunal may stay enforcement of the award. A tribunal may stay enforcement on its own motion when seized of a request for award revision under Article 51(4);[78] yet, if a party requests a stay, the tribunal shall grant it until it rules on the revision. The effect of annulment proceedings on enforcement under Article 52(5)[79] is similar to the one of revision requests. The ad hoc committee may stay enforcement on its own motion and shall stay enforcement until its decision if a party so requires.

Article 54(1) of the ICSID Convention sets forth the Member States' unconditional obligation to 'recognize' the award as a 'final judgment' of their courts, as follows:

74. Status of the New York Convention, available at http://www.uncitral.org/uncitral/en/uncitral_texts/arbitration/NYConvention_status.html (accessed 1 May 2018).
75. ICSID Convention, Art. 53(1): 'The award shall be binding on the parties and shall not be subject to any appeal or to any other remedy except those provided for in this Convention. Each party shall abide by and comply with the terms of the award except to the extent that enforcement shall have been stayed pursuant to the relevant provisions of this Convention.'
76. Christoph H. Schreuer et al., *The ICSID Convention: A Commentary*, 1114 (2nd ed., Cambridge University Press 2014).
77. ICSID Convention, Art. 50(2): '... Tribunal may, if it considers that the circumstances so require, stay enforcement of the award pending its [interpretation] decision'.
78. ICSID Convention, Art. 51(4): 'The Tribunal may, if it considers that the circumstances so require, stay enforcement of the award pending its [revision] decision. If the applicant requests a stay of enforcement of the award in his application, enforcement shall be stayed provisionally until the Tribunal rules on such request.'
79. ICSID Convention, Ar. 52(5): 'The [*ad hoc*] Committee may, if it considers that the circumstances so require, stay enforcement of the award pending its decision. If the applicant requests a stay of enforcement of the award in his application, enforcement shall be stayed provisionally until the Committee rules on such request.'

> Each Contracting State shall recognize an award rendered pursuant to this Convention as binding and enforce the pecuniary obligations imposed by that award within its territories as if it were a final judgment of a court in that State.

The recognition obligation under Article 54(1) extends to the whole award leading to res judicata effect of the entire award in the State where recognition is sought. The enforcement obligation under the same provision extends only to pecuniary obligations. It does not extend to other obligations under the award such as restitution and specific performance.[80]

Although the recognition obligation is unconditional, the enforcement obligation under Article 54 is subject to the law of the forum State under Article 54(3).[81] The UK High Court decision[82] in *Micula et al. v. Romania and European Commission* illustrates the distinction between the recognition and enforcement obligations under Article 54 of the ICSID Convention.

Relying on tax incentives, the claimants in *Micula et al. v. Romania*[83] heavily invested in a food production operation in the Ștei-Nucet-Drăgăneşti region, Romania, in the 2000s. In 2004, Romania passed legislation repealing most tax incentives because of EU State aid regulation, leading to an ICSID arbitration instituted in 2005 under the Sweden-Romania BIT.[84] In the same year, the claimants registered the ICSID award with the High Court, the UK's 'designated authority' under Article 54(2).[85] Romania, supported by the European Commission, applied for refusal of registration or of enforcement of the ICSID award. Among other things, Romania argued that the UK proceedings be stayed because whether State courts could give res judicata effect to an award circumventing EU State aid law had been raised before the CJEU in the

80. Professor Schreuer explains that the restriction to pecuniary relief sought to ensure that every legal system could enforce it (for instance, in some States 'courts may not have the power to order specific performance'). He also states that a party could rely on the New York Convention to enforce non-pecuniary obligations. *See* Christoph H. Schreuer et al., *The ICSID Convention: A Commentary,* 1137–1139 (2nd ed., Cambridge University Press 2014).
81. ICSID Convention, Art. 54(3): 'Execution of the award shall be governed by the laws concerning the execution of judgments in force in the State in whose territories such execution is sought.'
82. *Micula et al. v. Romania and European Commission,* High Court of Justice, Queen's Bench Division, Commercial Court, Case No: CL-2014-000251, Judgement (20 Jan. 2017) [2017] EWHC 31 (Comm).
83. *Ioan Micula, Viorel Micula, S.C. European Food S.A, S.C. Starmill S.R.L. and S.C. Multipack S.R.L. v. Romania,* ICSID Case No. ARB/05/20, Award (11 Dec. 2013).
84. Agreement between the Government of the Kingdom of Sweden and the Government of Romania on the Promotion and Reciprocal Protection of Investments (29 May 2002).
85. ICSID Convention Art. 54(2): 'A party seeking recognition or enforcement in the territories of a Contracting State shall furnish to a competent court or other authority which such State shall have designated for this purpose a copy of the award certified by the Secretary-General. Each Contracting State shall notify the Secretary-General of the designation of the competent court or other authority for this purpose and of any subsequent change in such designation.' *See also* Arbitration (International Investment Disputes) Act of 13 Dec. 1966 [Act implementing the ICSID Convention], section 1: '1 Registration of Convention awards.... (2) A person seeking recognition or enforcement of such an award shall be entitled to have the award registered in the High Court subject to proof of the prescribed matters and to the other provisions of this Act. ... (4) In addition to the pecuniary obligations imposed by the award, the award shall be registered for the reasonable costs of and incidental to registration ... .'

annulment proceedings.[86] The CJEU annulment proceedings sought to annul a European Commission's decision[87] finding that payment of compensation awarded to the claimants in the arbitration was State aid breaching EU law.

According to the High Court, the European Commission's decision only prohibits the award's payment by Romania; hence, simple award registration or recognition does not create a risk of conflict between decisions of domestic and EU institutions.[88] Yet, the High Court favored staying enforcement to prevent conflicting decisions inconsistent with Article 351[89] of the Treaty on the Functioning of the EU (TFEU). Therefore, the court dismissed Romania's application for setting aside the registration order and stayed the award's enforcement pending the resolution of the claimants' CJEU proceedings seeking annulment of the European Commission's decision.[90]

[B] Non-ICSID Awards: The New York Convention

Non-ICSID awards are subject, in most jurisdictions, to the New York Convention. Pursuant to its Article I(1)[91] the New York Convention applies to recognition and enforcement of awards 'made in the territory of a State other than the State where recognition and enforcement of such awards are sought'. The New York Convention also applies to 'awards not considered as domestic awards in the State where their recognition and enforcement are sought' under Article I(1).

Some Contracting States[92] of the New York Convention, including the US, have made a declaration under Article I(3) to limit its application 'only to differences arising

86. *Micula et al. v. Romania and European Commission*, High Court of Justice, Queen's Bench Division, Commercial Court, Case No: CL-2014-000251, Judgement (20 Jan. 2017) [2017] EWHC 31 (Comm), para. 111.
87. Commission Decision (EU) 2015/1470 of 30 Mar. 2015 on State aid SA.38517 (2014/C) (ex 2014/NN) implemented by Romania — *Arbitral award Micula v. Romania* of 11 December 2013, OJ L 232, 4 Sep. 2015, p. 69.
88. *Micula et al. v. Romania and European Commission*, High Court of Justice, Queen's Bench Division, Commercial Court, Case No: CL-2014-000251, Judgement (20 Jan. 2017) [2017] EWHC 31 (Comm), para. 126.
89. Treaty on the Functioning of the European Union, Art. 351: 'The rights and obligations arising from agreements concluded before 1 January 1958 or, for acceding States, before the date of their accession, between one or more Member States on the one hand, and one or more third countries on the other, shall not be affected by the provisions of the Treaties. To the extent that such agreements are not compatible with the Treaties, the Member State or States concerned shall take all appropriate steps to eliminate the incompatibilities established. Member States shall, where necessary, assist each other to this end and shall, where appropriate, adopt a common attitude.'
90. *Micula et al. v. Romania and European Commission*, High Court of Justice, Queen's Bench Division, Commercial Court, Case No: CL-2014-000251, Judgment (20 Jan. 2017) [2017] EWHC 31 (Comm), para. 203.
91. New York Convention, Art. I(1): 'This Convention shall apply to the recognition and enforcement of arbitral awards made in the territory of a State other than the State where the recognition and enforcement of such awards are sought, and arising out of differences between persons, whether physical or legal. It shall also apply to arbitral awards not considered as domestic awards in the State where their recognition and enforcement are sought.'
92. Among the parties making the Art. I(3) Declaration are Afghanistan, Algeria, Antigua and Barbuda, Argentina, Armenia, Bahrain, Barbados, Bhutan, Bosnia and Herzegovina, Botswana, Burundi, Central African Republic, China, Croatia, Cuba, Cyprus, Denmark, Djibouti, Greece,

out of legal relationships, whether contractual or not, which are considered as commercial under the national law of the State making such declaration'. This declaration is not necessarily incompatible with ICSID Additional Facility arbitrations not arising directly out of an investment under Article 2(b) of the ICSID Additional Facility Rules. Article 4(3)[93] of the ICSID Additional Facility Rules on access to these rules requires that an Article 2(b)[94] arbitration have an underlying transaction distinguishable from an ordinary commercial transaction; however, 'commercial' under Article I(3) of the New York Convention has been broadly interpreted.

Moreover, Article III[95] of the New York Convention prohibits Contracting States from imposing more onerous conditions on recognition or enforcement of foreign arbitral awards than domestic arbitral awards. This means that Contracting States cannot discriminate against foreign awards. Article IV of the New York Convention on formal conditions requires that the party applying for recognition and enforcement supply the original award or a certified copy, the original arbitration agreement or a certified copy, including sworn translations if needed.

Article V on substantive conditions provides for grounds to be raised by the party resisting enforcement in paragraph (1), and by the courts on their own motion in paragraph (2), as follows:

> 1. Recognition and enforcement of the award may be refused, at the request of the party against whom it is invoked, only if that party furnishes to the competent authority where the recognition and enforcement is sought, proof that:
>
> (a) The parties to the agreement referred to in article II were, under the law applicable to them, under some incapacity, or the said agreement is not valid

Guatemala, Holy See, Honduras, Hungary, India, Indonesia, Iran, Jamaica, Madagascar, Malaysia, Monaco, Mongolia, Montenegro, Nepal, Nigeria, Philippines, Poland, Republic of Korea, Romania, Saint Vincent and the Grenadines, the former Yugoslav Republic of Macedonia, Trinidad and Tobago, Tunisia, Turkey, United States, Venezuela, and Vietnam. *See* Status of the New York Convention on the Recognition and Enforcement of Foreign Arbitral Awards, available at http://www.uncitral.org/uncitral/en/uncitral_texts/arbitration/NYConvention_status.html (accessed 3 May 2018).

93. ICSID Additional Facility Rules, Art. 4(3): 'In the case of an application based on Article 2(b), the Secretary-General shall give his approval only if he is satisfied (a) that the requirements of that provision are fulfilled, and (b) that the underlying transaction has features which distinguish it from an ordinary commercial transaction.'

94. ICSID Additional Facility Rules, Art. 2: 'The Secretariat of the Centre is hereby authorized to administer, subject to and in accordance with these Rules, proceedings between a State (or a constituent subdivision or agency of a State) and a national of another State, falling within the following categories: (a) conciliation and arbitration proceedings for the settlement of legal disputes arising directly out of an investment which are not within the jurisdiction of the Centre because either the State party to the dispute or the State whose national is a party to the dispute is not a Contracting State; (b) conciliation and arbitration proceedings for the settlement of legal disputes which are not within the jurisdiction of the Centre because they do not arise directly out of an investment, provided that either the State party to the dispute or the State whose national is a party to the dispute is a Contracting State; and (c) fact-finding proceedings ... .'

95. New York Convention, Art. III: 'Each Contracting State shall recognize arbitral awards as binding and enforce them in accordance with the rules of procedure of the territory where the award is relied upon, under the conditions laid down in the following articles. There shall not be imposed substantially more onerous conditions or higher fees or charges on the recognition or enforcement of arbitral awards to which this Convention applies than are imposed on the recognition or enforcement of domestic arbitral awards.'

under the law to which the parties have subjected it or, failing any indication thereon, under the law of the country where the award was made; or

(b) The party against whom the award is invoked was not given proper notice of the appointment of the arbitrator or of the arbitration proceedings or was otherwise unable to present his case; or

(c) The award deals with a difference not contemplated by or not falling within the terms of the submission to arbitration, or it contains decisions on matters beyond the scope of the submission to arbitration, provided that, if the decisions on matters submitted to arbitration can be separated from those not so submitted, that part of the award which contains decisions on matters submitted to arbitration may be recognized and enforced; or

(d) The composition of the arbitral authority or the arbitral procedure was not in accordance with the agreement of the parties, or, failing such agreement, was not in accordance with the law of the country where the arbitration took place; or

(e) The award has not yet become binding on the parties, or has been set aside or suspended by a competent authority of the country in which, or under the law of which, that award was made.

2. Recognition and enforcement of an arbitral award may also be refused if the competent authority in the country where recognition and enforcement is sought finds that:

(a) The subject matter of the difference is not capable of settlement by arbitration under the law of that country; or

(b) The recognition or enforcement of the award would be contrary to the public policy of that country.

A party can rely on lack of legal capacity or 'subjective' non-arbitrability as a ground for non-recognition or enforcement, capacity meaning the ability of natural or legal persons to conclude and be party to an arbitration agreement under Article V(1)(a). As a rule, party capacity is subject to personal law. Consequently, a natural person's capacity is subject to the law of the State of his or her nationality or domicile, whereas a legal person's capacity is subject to the law of the State of its seat or its place of incorporation or formation.

In a treaty-based arbitration, an investor resisting recognition and enforcement for its own lack of capacity under Article V(1)(a) would prove contradictory because usually the investor consents to investment treaty arbitration by commencing it.

In addition, self-imposed restrictions on Sovereigns' capacity to arbitrate under constitutional and legislative provisions may be relevant under Article V(1)(a), including when the capacity to arbitrate under national law is conditional on legislative and regulatory authorizations. Yet, States' and State entities' objections to grant recognition and enforcement because of their purported incapacity to arbitrate under their own laws may not prevail in some forum States. Article 177(II)(2)[96] of the Swiss Federal

96. Swiss Federal Law on Private International Law (Loi fédérale sur le droit international privé) (18 Dec. 1987) as amended, Art. 177(2): 'If a State, a State-owned company, or a State-controlled entity is a party to an arbitration agreement, this party cannot rely on its own law to challenge the arbitrability of the dispute or its capacity to arbitrate.' (Free translation from the authors). The original reads as follows: 'Si une partie à la convention d'arbitrage est un

Law on Private International Law provides that a State or a State entity cannot rely on its personal law to challenge its legal capacity to arbitrate. Article II(1) of the European Convention on International Commercial Arbitration provides for an alternative solution, affirming legal capacity to arbitrate of 'legal persons of public law'. Pursuant to Article II(1), 'legal persons considered by the law which is applicable to them as "legal persons of public law" have the right to conclude valid arbitration agreements'.[97]

Venezuela's unsuccessful litigation before US courts in *Rusoro v. Venezuela*[98] illustrates another ground for resisting enforcement: Article V(1)(c) of the New York Convention on excess of jurisdiction. This ICSID Additional Facility arbitration was about Venezuela's measures affecting Rusoro's investment in gold mining in Venezuela. Seated in Paris, the arbitral tribunal granted Rusoro compensation for expropriation,[99] damages for Venezuela's restrictions on gold export,[100] and the arbitration costs.[101]

Seeking the award's enforcement in the US, Rusoro filed a request to confirm the award with the US District Court for the District of Columbia.[102] Applying the New York Convention, incorporated in the FAA, the DC court rejected Venezuela's argument on Article V(1)(c) of the New York Convention on excess of jurisdiction. Among other things, Venezuela argued that the tribunal exceeded its jurisdiction when using valuations predating the expropriation.[103] Refusing to review the merits of the award and giving deference to the arbitral tribunal's ruling on jurisdiction pursuant to the parties' arbitration agreement, the DC court confirmed the award.[104] The DC court equally rejected Venezuela's request to suspend the DC proceedings under Article VI[105] of the New York Convention pending annulment proceedings before Paris courts.[106]

État, une entreprise dominée ou une organisation contrôlée par lui, cette partie ne peut invoquer son propre droit pour contester l'arbitrabilité d'un litige ou sa capacité d'être partie à un arbitrage.'

97. Article II(2) provides, however, that Contracting States may provide declarations limiting the right of 'legal persons of public law' to arbitrate. *See* European Convention on International Commercial Arbitration (21 Apr. 1961), Art. II: '(1) In the cases referred to in Article 1, paragraph 1, of this Convention, legal persons considered by the law which is applicable to them as "legal persons of public law" have the right to conclude valid arbitration agreements. (2) On signing, ratifying or acceding to this Convention any State shall be entitled to declare that it limits the above faculty to such conditions as may be stated in its declaration.'
98. *Rusoro Mining Ltd. v. Bolivarian Republic of Venezuela*, ICSID Case No. ARB(AF)/12/5, Award (22 Aug. 2016).
99. *Ibid.*, paras 398–410, 904.
100. *Ibid.*, paras 588–595, 904.
101. *Ibid.*, paras 863–878, 904.
102. *Rusoro Mining Ltd. v. Bolivarian Republic of Venezuela*, US District Court for the District of Columbia, Civil Case No. 16-cv-02020 (RJL), Decision (1 Mar. 2018), paras 14–15.
103. *Ibid.*, para. 17.
104. *Ibid.*, paras 19–27.
105. New York Convention, Art. VI: 'If an application for the setting aside or suspension of the award has been made to a competent authority referred to in article V (1) (e), the authority before which the award is sought to be relied upon may, if it considers it proper, adjourn the decision on the enforcement of the award and may also, on the application of the party claiming enforcement of the award, order the other party to give suitable security.'
106. *Ibid.*, paras 28–35.

In addition to the grounds (a) to (e) listed in Article V(1) to be raised by the party resisting enforcement, 'objective' non-arbitrability[107] pursuant to the law of the place of recognition and enforcement and violation of public policy may be raised by the forum courts on their own motion under Article V(2) of the New York Convention. Successful in the ICSID Additional Facility arbitration[108] seated in Washington D.C., in *Crystallex v. Venezuela* Crystallex sought the award's confirmation in the US. The DC court applied the New York Convention because the award had been made pursuant to an international treaty, the Canada-Venezuela BIT.[109] Having alleged excess of jurisdiction under Article V(1)(c) and manifest disregard of the law, Venezuela also relied on the public policy ground under Article V(2)(b) before DC courts. The courts rejected all these grounds. On public policy, the court required that Article V(2)(b) be 'construed narrowly' applying when an award 'violate[s] the forum state's most basic notions of morality and justice'.[110]

Finally, Article VII(1)[111] of the New York Convention provides for the most-favorable rule principle. French courts mostly apply French law on recognition and enforcement because it is more favorable than the New York Convention.[112] For example, they have applied French law in *Hilmarton* and *Putrabali* as the most-favorable rule recognizing awards annulled in the arbitral seat.[113] The French courts disregarded annulment by the courts of the arbitral seat because this is not an annulment ground under French law even if this could be an annulment ground under Article V(1)(e) of the New York Convention.

107. 'Objective' as opposed to 'subjective' arbitrability means that a subject matter is not capable of being decided by arbitration. For example, Article 2059 of the French Civil Code (*Code civil*) adopts the criterion of 'free disposition of rights' for 'objective' arbitrability ('Toutes personnes peuvent compromettre sur les droits dont elles ont la libre disposition'.). In turn, Article 177(1) of the Swiss Federal Law on Private International Law adopts the criterion of 'patrimonial rights' for 'objective' arbitrability ('Toute cause de nature patrimoniale peut faire l'objet d'un arbitrage'.).
108. *Crystallex International Corporation v. Bolivarian Republic of Venezuela*, ICSID Case No. ARB(AF)/11/2, Award (4 Apr. 2016).
109. *Crystallex International Corporation v. Bolivarian Republic of Venezuela*, US District Court for the District of Columbia, Civil Action No. 16-0661 (RC), Decision (25 Mar. 2017), pp. 8–9.
110. *Ibid.*, p. 28.
111. New York Convention, Art. VII(1): 'The provisions of the present Convention shall not affect the validity of multilateral or bilateral agreements concerning the recognition and enforcement of arbitral awards entered into by the Contracting States nor deprive any interested party of any right he may have to avail himself of an arbitral award in the manner and to the extent allowed by the law or the treaties of the country where such award is sought to be relied upon.'
112. Jérome Ortscheidt & Christophe Seraglini, *Droit de l'arbitrage interne et international*, 902 (L.G.D.J. 2013). *See also* Thomas Clay, *La Convention de New York vue par la Doctrine Française*, 27(1) ASA Bulletin 50, 64. The grounds for challenging recognition and enforcement are the same as the annulment grounds set forth in Art. 1520 of the French Civil Procedure Code (*Code de procédure civile*), *see* Mathias Audit, Sylvain Bollée & Pierre Callé, *Droit du Commerce International et des Investissements Etrangers*, 742 (2nd ed., LGDJ 2016).
113. *Société Hilmarton v. Société OTV*, Cour d'appel de Paris, 1re Ch. Suppl., Judgment (19 Dec. 1991), 1993(2) Revue de l'arbitrage 300; *Société PT Putrabali Adyamulla v. Société Rena Holding et Société Rena Holding et Société Mnogutia Est Epices*, Cour de cassation, Cass. civ. 1re, First Judgment (29 Jun. 2007), with comments by Emmanuel Gaillard, 2007(3) Revue de l'arbitrage 512.

§10.05 SOVEREIGN IMMUNITY

An important question about enforcement against States is whether they are subject to immunity from jurisdiction or immunity from enforcement or execution. The main difference between ICSID awards and non-ICSID awards with respect to immunity is that the question of immunity from jurisdiction does not arise in the context of the ICSID Convention.

Immunity from jurisdiction is a non-issue in ICSID arbitration because Member States have given their consent to ICSID jurisdiction under Article 25(1),[114] and have assumed the unconditional obligation to recognize ICSID awards under Article 54(1). Nevertheless, immunity from execution is subject to the law of the forum State under Article 55, which provides that:

> Nothing in Article 54 shall be construed as derogating from the law in force in any Contracting State relating to immunity of that State or of any foreign State from execution.

Article 55 provides a clarification to Article 54(3) on execution being subject to the law of the State where execution is sought. Article 55 clarifies that this law includes the law on State immunity. Article 55 only applies to immunity from execution. It does not apply to immunity from jurisdiction, because the obligation to recognize the award as binding is unconditional. State immunity law does not therefore affect the res judicata effect of an ICSID award, once it is recognized.[115]

Irrespective of the forum State's law on immunity from execution, ICSID Member States have the obligation to comply with the award under Article 53(1) of the ICSID Convention. Alternatively, a party seeking payment can seek diplomatic protection under Article 27(1),[116] and a Member State can resort to the ICJ under Article 64[117] of the ICSID Convention if there is a dispute with another Member State about award execution.

Immunity from jurisdiction may arise in relation to non-ICSID awards, although many jurisdictions provide exceptions on arbitration-related proceedings (A). But enforcing an investment award against States may not be immune from State courts'

114. ICSID Convention, Art. 25(1): 'The jurisdiction of the Centre shall extend to any legal dispute arising directly out of an investment, between a Contracting State (or any constituent subdivision or agency of a Contracting State designated to the Centre by that State) and a national of another Contracting State, which the parties to the dispute consent in writing to submit to the Centre. When the parties have given their consent, no party may withdraw its consent unilaterally … .'
115. Christoph H. Schreuer et al., *The ICSID Convention: A Commentary*, 1153 (2nd ed., Cambridge University Press 2014).
116. ICSID Convention, Art. 27(1): 'No Contracting State shall give diplomatic protection, or bring an international claim, in respect of a dispute which one of its nationals and another Contracting State shall have consented to submit or shall have submitted to arbitration under this Convention, unless such other Contracting State shall have failed to abide by and comply with the award rendered in such dispute.'
117. ICSID Convention, Art. 64: 'Any dispute arising between Contracting States concerning the interpretation or application of this Convention which is not settled by negotiation shall be referred to the International Court of Justice by the application of any party to such dispute, unless the States concerned agree to another method of settlement.'

execution. This will require examining contractual waivers (B) and distinguishing between property intended for commercial use and property designated for sovereign or official activities (C).

[A] Immunity from Jurisdiction and Arbitration-Related Exceptions

Immunity from jurisdiction prevents a sovereign State from being sued before the courts of another sovereign State without its consent. In other words, immunity from jurisdiction is an exemption from jurisdiction of foreign national courts, which can be waived.[118] As discussed, immunity from jurisdiction is a non-issue for ICSID awards.

To illustrate, section 1604[119] of the US Foreign Sovereign Immunities Act (FSIA) sets forth that 'a foreign state shall be immune from the jurisdiction of the courts of the United States and of the States' subject to the exceptions under sections 1605–1607. Section 1605(a)(6) provides that a foreign State shall not be immune from jurisdiction in relation to certain arbitration-related proceedings. This arbitration exception includes State court proceedings to confirm an award made pursuant to an arbitration agreement concluded 'by the foreign state with or for the benefit of a private party.' This provision requires that the dispute's subject matter be arbitrable under US law and arise from a legal relationship, contractual or not, provided that:

> (A) the arbitration takes place or is intended to take place in the United States, (B) the agreement or award is or may be governed by a treaty or other international agreement in force for the United States calling for the recognition and enforcement of arbitral awards, (C) the underlying claim, save for the agreement to arbitrate, could have been brought in a United States court under this section or section 1607, or (D) paragraph (1) of this subsection is otherwise applicable.

Moreover, Article 12 of the European Convention on State Immunity[120] of 1972 provides that State immunity from jurisdiction does not apply in relation to certain arbitration-related proceedings, including setting aside proceedings, as follows:

> 1 Where a Contracting State has agreed in writing to submit to arbitration a dispute which has arisen or may arise out of a civil or commercial matter, that State may not claim immunity from the jurisdiction of a court of another Contracting State on the territory or according to the law of which the arbitration has taken or will take place in respect of any proceedings relating to:
>
> a the validity or interpretation of the arbitration agreement;
> b the arbitration procedure;

118. *See* Foreign Sovereign Immunities Act of 1976 (28 USC Ch. 97), section 1605(a)(1): '(a) A foreign state shall not be immune from the jurisdiction of courts of the United States or of the States in any case— (1) in which the foreign state has waived its immunity either explicitly or by implication, notwithstanding any withdrawal of the waiver which the foreign state may purport to effect except in accordance with the terms of the waiver; ... .'
119. *Ibid.*, section 1604: 'Subject to existing international agreements to which the United States is a party at the time of enactment of this Act a foreign state shall be immune from the jurisdiction of the courts of the United States and of the States except as provided in sections 1605 to 1607 of this chapter.'
120. European Convention on State Immunity (16 May 1972) ETS 74.

c the setting aside of the award, unless the arbitration agreement otherwise provides.

2 Paragraph 1 shall not apply to an arbitration agreement between States.

This provision does not include recognition and enforcement proceedings. It also contains an exception to arbitration agreements between States in paragraph (2).

[B] Waivers from State Immunity from Execution

Successful allegation of State immunity from execution of investment awards is high. Nevertheless, immunity from execution can be waived contractually. The ICSID Model Clause 15 illustrates a waiver clause, as follows:

> The Host State hereby waives any right of sovereign immunity as to it and its property in respect of the enforcement and execution of any award rendered by an Arbitral Tribunal constituted pursuant to this agreement.[121]

Article 23 of the European Convention on State Immunity provides for this possibility, subject to the conditions that the waiver be (a) express, (b) written and (c) specific to a particular case.

Article 18(1)(a) of the ILC Draft Articles on Jurisdictional Immunities of States and Their Property[122] also provides for the States' waiving from 'measures of constraint, such as attachment, arrest and execution' by 'express' consent to these measures. Consent can be given by (a) an international agreement, (b) an arbitration agreement or written contract or (c) a declaration before a court or a written communication after the dispute arises. Article 19(a)[123] of the UN Convention on Jurisdictional Immunities of States and Their Property, not yet in force,[124] has retained this waiver provision.[125]

In France, Article L111-1-2(1) of the Code of Civil Procedures of Execution[126] also provides for the possibility of 'express' waiver from immunity from execution.

121. ICSID Model Clauses, available at https://icsid.worldbank.org/en/Pages/resources/ICSID-Model-Clauses.aspx (accessed 4 May 2018).
122. ILC Draft Articles on Jurisdictional Immunities of States and Their Property (1991).
123. United Nations Convention on Jurisdictional Immunities of States and Their Property (2 Dec. 2004), Art. 19(a): 'No post-judgment measures of constraint, such as attachment, arrest or execution, against property of a State may be taken in connection with a proceeding before a court of another State unless and except to the extent that: (a) the State has expressly consented to the taking of such measures as indicated: (i) by international agreement; (ii) by an arbitration agreement or in a written contract; or (iii) by a declaration before the court or by a written communication after a dispute between the parties has arisen; ... .'
124. *See* Status of the United Nations Convention on Jurisdictional Immunities of States and Their Property of 2 Dec. 2004, available at https://treaties.un.org/Pages/ViewDetails.aspx?src=IND&mtdsg_no=III-13&chapter=3&lang=en (accessed 4 May 2018).
125. Christoph H. Schreuer et al., *The ICSID Convention: A Commentary*, 1176 (2nd ed., Cambridge University Press 2014).
126. Code of Civil Procedures of Execution (*Code des procédures civiles d'exécution*), Art. L111-1-2(1): 'Conservatory or forced execution measures in relation to property owned by a foreign State cannot be authorised by a judge unless one of the following conditions is satisfied: (1) the relevant State has expressly consented to the application of such measure.'

Nevertheless, waivers in relation to property used or to be used in foreign States exercising diplomatic or consular functions, their special missions and missions in international organizations, including bank accounts, shall be 'express' and 'special' under Article L111-1-2(3) of the same Code.

Similarly, section 1609[127] FSIA provides for foreign States' immunity from attachment, arrest and execution, subject to exceptions including waivers. Section 1610(a)(1) FSIA provides that a foreign State's property 'used for commercial activity in the United States' shall not be immune from 'attachment in aid of execution, or from execution' upon a US judgment if this foreign State has waived its immunity.

Under section 1610(a)(1) FSIA this waiver can be explicit or implicit 'notwithstanding any withdrawal of the waiver the foreign state may purport to effect except in accordance with the terms of the waiver'. In any event, a waiver from immunity from execution under section 1610(a)(1) is subject to the requirement that the foreign State's property be 'used for commercial activity'. The notion of property with use for commercial purposes appear in international instruments and national legislation as an exception to immunity from execution and, in the case of FSIA, features as an express requirement to a valid waiver.

[C] Property with Use for Commercial Purposes

In addition to waivers, international instruments and certain national laws provide for exceptions to immunity from execution in relation to property with use for commercial purposes. For example, Article 18(1)(c) of the ILC Draft Articles on Jurisdictional Immunities of States and Their Property provides for this exception requiring that property be (a) 'in use or intended for use' other than for government non-commercial purposes, (b)in the territory of the forum State and (c) in connection with the claim object of the proceeding or with the State entity against which the proceeding is directed.[128]

Article 19(c) of the UN Convention on Jurisdictional Immunities of States and Their Property has not retained the requirement that property be in connection with the claim object of the enforcement proceedings, as follows:

> No post-judgment measures of constraint, such as attachment, arrest or execution, against property of a State may be taken in connection with a proceeding before a court of another State unless and except to the extent that:

(Free translation of the original: 'Des mesures conservatoires ou des mesures d'exécution forcée visant un bien appartenant à un État étranger ne peuvent être autorisées par le juge que si l'une des conditions suivantes est remplie: 1° L'État concerné a expressément consenti à l'application d'une telle mesure'). This provision was created by Art. 59 of Law No. 2016-1691 (9 Dec. 2016).

127. Foreign Sovereign Immunities Act of 1976 (28 USC Ch. 97), section 1609: 'Subject to existing international agreements to which the United States is a party at the time of enactment of this Act the property in the United States of a foreign state shall be immune from attachment arrest and execution except as provided in sections 1610 and 1611 of this chapter.'

128. ILC Draft Articles on Jurisdictional Immunities of States and Their Property (1991), Art. 18(1)(c).

> ... (c) it has been established that the property is specifically in use or intended for use by the State for other than government non-commercial purposes and is in the territory of the State of the forum, provided that post-judgment measures of constraint may only be taken against property that has a connection with the entity against which the proceeding was directed.[129]

As for national laws, the US FSIA Section 1610(a)(2) also provides for the exception in relation to property that 'is or was used for the commercial activity upon which the claim is based'. In France, the Article L111-1-2(3)[130] of the Code of Civil Procedures of Execution establishes this exception, requiring that property be used or be intended for use for commercial purposes and be connected with the entity against which execution is sought. Article L111-1-2(3) sets forth a non-exhaustive list of property that is considered used or intended for use for sovereign, public service purposes such as embassy bank accounts, military property, cultural heritage, and tax or social credits of foreign States.

Section 13(4) of the UK State Immunity Act of 1978 equally provides for the exception on property that 'is for the time being in use or intended for use for commercial purposes'. However, among other exemptions from Section 13(4), Section 14(4) sets forth that '[p]roperty of a State's central bank or other monetary authority shall not be regarded for the purposes of subsection (4) of section 13 above as in use or intended for use for commercial purposes.' To illustrate, in *AIG et al. v. Kazakhstan*[131] the UK High Court distinguished between commercial and sovereign bank assets. AIG Group had entered into a joint venture to develop a residential housing complex in Almaty, Kazakhstan. Kazakhstan cancelled the project because the land concerned was required for a national arboretum, passing a resolution ordering the transfer of the project property to the City of Almaty, without compensation to the joint venture. Successful in the ICSID arbitration, the claimants sought the award recognition and enforcement in the UK.

After obtaining leave to register the award in the High Court under the Arbitration (International Investment Disputes) Act 1966, the claimants sought to enforce the award through third-party debt and charging orders against assets of the National Bank of Kazakhstan (NBK) held by private banks in London. These assets were held by the ABN AMRO Group under a Global Custody Agreement concluded with the National Fund of Kazakhstan (a natural resources fund), NBK being the assets' beneficiary.[132] According to the High Court, the NBK assets in the London banks were owned by NBK, not by Kazakhstan itself. Whether Kazakhstan ultimately had a beneficial interest in the assets was irrelevant. The UK court went on to cite to Section 14(4)[133] of the UK

129. United Nations Convention on Jurisdictional Immunities of States and Their Property (2 Dec. 2004), Art. 19(c).

130. Code of Civil Procedures of Execution (*Code des procédures civiles d'exécution*), Art. L111-1-2(3). This provision was created by Art. 59 of Law No. 2016-1691 (9 Dec. 2016).

131. *AIG Capital Partners and other v. Kazakhstan, ABN AMRO et al. (National Bank of Kazakhstan Intervening)*, High Court of Justice, Queens' Bench Division, Commercial Court, Case No: 2004/536, Judgment (20 Oct. 2005), [2005] EWHC 2239 (Comm).

132. *Ibid.*, paras 8–18.

133. UK State Immunity Act (1978), section 14(4): 'Property of a State's central bank or other monetary authority shall not be regarded for the purposes of subsection (4) of section 13 above

State Immunity Act, noting that property of a State's central bank or other monetary authority benefited from 'complete immunity from the enforcement process in the United Kingdom courts'[134] under Section 14(4) of the UK State Immunity Act. The High Court therefore refused to grant the third-party debt and charging orders.

§10.06 CONCLUSION

Despite the fact that awards are final and binding on the parties, the issuance of an investment award is only the first step to obtaining satisfaction on your claim. After its issuance, the award is subject to recognition and enforcement.

Most investment treaties are silent on recognition and enforcement, the ICSID Convention governs recognition and enforcement of ICSID arbitral awards, in addition to the laws on enforcement of the forum State. Under the ICSID Convention the recognition obligation is unconditional, although ICSID award enforcement is conditional on the law of the place of enforcement. In contrast, non-ICSID awards' recognition and enforcement are subject to the New York Convention in most jurisdictions.

Once rendered, investment awards are subject to limited challenges. When faced with serious errors that threaten the arbitration's legitimacy, the parties may commence annulment proceedings on limited grounds.

The ICSID Convention provides for a self-contained annulment mechanism. Non-ICSID awards are subject to annulment proceedings before arbitral seat's State courts.

When enforcing an award against States or State entities immunity from jurisdiction and/or immunity from execution might be an issue (though in relation to ICSID awards immunity from jurisdiction is a non-issue). The success rate for a State's alleging State immunity from execution of investment awards is high. Nevertheless, immunity from execution can be waived contractually in certain situations.

Questions

(1) Are ICSID Additional Facility awards subject to the provisions on recognition and enforcement of the ICSID Convention?
(2) Is it possible to enforce a decision upholding jurisdiction under the ICSID Convention?
(3) Are UNCITRAL investment awards subject to ICSID annulment proceedings?

---

as in use or intended for use for commercial purposes; and where any such bank or authority is a separate entity subsections (1) to (3) of that section shall apply to it as if references to a State were references to the bank or authority.

134. *AIG Capital Partners and other v. Kazakhstan, ABN AMRO et al. (National Bank of Kazakhstan Intervening)*, High Court of Justice, Queens' Bench Division, Commercial Court, Case No: 2004/536, Judgment (20 Oct. 2005), [2005] EWHC 2239 (Comm), para. 57.

(4) What are the advantages of ICSID enforcement if compared to enforcement under the New York Convention?
(5) What is the difference between recognition and enforcement of investment awards?
(6) What is a 'commercial relationship' declaration under the New York Convention?
(7) What is the difference between immunity from jurisdiction and immunity from execution?
(8) Discuss the distinction between commercial and sovereign bank accounts, taking into account, for instance, (a) their intended uses, (b) their future use, (c) their designation for special public activities or function, and (d) their possible mixed character.

ANNEX IBA

Guidelines on Conflicts of Interest in International Arbitration

Part II: Practical Application of the General Standards

1. If the Guidelines are to have an important practical influence, they should address situations that are likely to occur in today's arbitration practice and should provide specific guidance to arbitrators, parties, institutions and courts as to which situations do or do not constitute conflicts of interest, or should or should not be disclosed. For this purpose, the Guidelines categorize situations that may occur in the following Application Lists. These lists cannot cover every situation. In all cases, the General Standards should control the outcome.

2. The Red List consists of two parts: 'a Non-Waivable Red List' (*see* General Standards 2(d) and 4(b)); and 'a Waivable Red List' (*see* General Standard 4(c)). These lists are non-exhaustive and detail specific situations that, depending on the facts of a given case, give rise to justifiable doubts as to the arbitrator's impartiality and independence. That is, in these circumstances, an objective conflict of interest exists from the point of view of a reasonable third person having knowledge of the relevant facts and circumstances (*see* General Standard 2(b)). The Non-Waivable Red List includes situations deriving from the overriding principle that no person can be his or her own judge. Therefore, acceptance of such a situation cannot cure the conflict. The Waivable Red List covers situations that are serious but not as severe. Because of their seriousness, unlike circumstances described in the Orange List, these situations should be considered waivable, but only if and when the parties, being aware of the conflict of interest situation, expressly state their willingness to have such a person act as arbitrator, as set forth in General Standard 4(c).

3. The Orange List is a non-exhaustive list of specific situations that, depending on the facts of a given case, may, in the eyes of the parties, give rise to doubts as to the arbitrator's impartiality or independence. The Orange List thus reflects situations that would fall under General Standard 3(a), with the consequence that the arbitrator has a

duty to disclose such situations. In all these situations, the parties are deemed to have accepted the arbitrator if, after disclosure, no timely objection is made, as established in General Standard 4(a).

4. Disclosure does not imply the existence of a conflict of interest; nor should it by itself result either in a disqualification of the arbitrator, or in a presumption regarding disqualification. The purpose of the disclosure is to inform the parties of a situation that they may wish to explore further in order to determine whether objectively – that is, from the point of view of a reasonable third person having knowledge of the relevant facts and circumstances – there are justifiable doubts as to the arbitrator's impartiality or independence. If the conclusion is that there are no justifiable doubts, the arbitrator can act. Apart from the situations covered by the Non-Waivable Red List, he or she can also act if there is no timely objection by the parties or, in situations covered by the Waivable Red List, if there is a specific acceptance by the parties in accordance with General Standard 4(c). If a party challenges the arbitrator, he or she can nevertheless act, if the authority that rules on the challenge decides that the challenge does not meet the objective test for disqualification.

5. A later challenge based on the fact that an arbitrator did not disclose such facts or circumstances should not result automatically in non-appointment, later disqualification or a successful challenge to any award. Non-disclosure cannot by itself make an arbitrator partial or lacking independence: only the facts or circumstances that he or she failed to disclose can do so.

6. Situations not listed in the Orange List or falling outside the time limits used in some of the Orange List situations are generally not subject to disclosure. However, an arbitrator needs to assess on a case-by-case basis whether a given situation, even though not mentioned in the Orange List, is nevertheless such as to give rise to justifiable doubts as to his or her impartiality or independence. Because the Orange List is a non-exhaustive list of examples, there may be situations not mentioned, which, depending on the circumstances, may need to be disclosed by an arbitrator. Such may be the case, for example, in the event of repeat past appointments by the same party or the same counsel beyond the three-year period provided for in the Orange List, or when an arbitrator concurrently acts as counsel in an unrelated case in which similar issues of law are raised. Likewise, an appointment made by the same party or the same counsel appearing before an arbitrator, while the case is ongoing, may also have to be disclosed, depending on the circumstances. While the Guidelines do not require disclosure of the fact that an arbitrator concurrently serves, or has in the past served, on the same Arbitral Tribunal with another member of the tribunal, or with one of the counsel in the current proceedings, an arbitrator should assess on a case-by-case basis whether the fact of having frequently served as counsel with, or as an arbitrator on, Arbitral Tribunals with another member of the tribunal may create a perceived imbalance within the tribunal. If the conclusion is 'yes', the arbitrator should consider a disclosure.

7. The Green List is a non-exhaustive list of specific situations where no appearance and no actual conflict of interest exist from an objective point of view. Thus, the arbitrator has no duty to disclose situations falling within the Green List. As

stated in the Explanation to General Standard 3(a), there should be a limit to disclosure, based on reasonableness; in some situations, an objective test should prevail over the purely subjective test of 'the eyes' of the parties. The borderline between the categories that comprise the Lists can be thin. It can be debated whether a certain situation should be on one List instead of another. Also, the Lists contain, for various situations, general terms such as 'significant' and 'relevant'. The Lists reflect international principles and best practices to the extent possible. Further definition of the norms, which are to be interpreted reasonably in light of the facts and circumstances in each case, would be counterproductive.

1. **Non-Waivable Red List**

1.1 There is an identity between a party and the arbitrator, or the arbitrator is a legal representative or employee of an entity that is a party in the arbitration.
1.2 The arbitrator is a manager, director or member of the supervisory board, or has a controlling influence on one of the parties or an entity that has a direct economic interest in the award to be rendered in the arbitration.
1.3 The arbitrator has a significant financial or personal interest in one of the parties, or the outcome of the case.
1.4 The arbitrator or his or her firm regularly advises the party, or an affiliate of the party, and the arbitrator or his or her firm derives significant financial income therefrom.

2. **Waivable Red List**

2.1 Relationship of the arbitrator to the dispute

2.1.1 The arbitrator has given legal advice, or provided an expert opinion, on the dispute to a party or an affiliate of one of the parties.
2.1.2 The arbitrator had a prior involvement in the dispute.

2.2 Arbitrator's direct or indirect interest in the dispute

2.2.1 The arbitrator holds shares, either directly or indirectly, in one of the parties, or an affiliate of one of the parties, this party or an affiliate being privately held.
2.2.2 A close family member [footnote omitted] of the arbitrator has a significant financial interest in the outcome of the dispute.
2.2.3 The arbitrator, or a close family member of the arbitrator, has a close relationship with a non-party who may be liable to recourse on the part of the unsuccessful party in the dispute.

2.3 Arbitrator's relationship with the parties or counsel

2.3.1 The arbitrator currently represents or advises one of the parties, or an affiliate of one of the parties.
2.3.2 The arbitrator currently represents or advises the lawyer or law firm acting as counsel for one of the parties.
2.3.3 The arbitrator is a lawyer in the same law firm as the counsel to one of the parties.
2.3.4 The arbitrator is a manager, director or member of the supervisory board, or has a controlling influence in an affiliate [footnote omitted] of one of the parties, if the affiliate is directly involved in the matters in dispute in the arbitration.
2.3.5 The arbitrator's law firm had a previous but terminated involvement in the case without the arbitrator being involved himself or herself.
2.3.6 The arbitrator's law firm currently has a significant commercial relationship with one of the parties, or an affiliate of one of the parties.
2.3.7 The arbitrator regularly advises one of the parties, or an affiliate of one of the parties.
2.3.8 The arbitrator has a close family relationship with one of the parties, or with a manager, director or member of the supervisory board, or any person having a controlling influence in one of the parties, or an affiliate of one of the parties, or with a counsel representing a party.
2.3.9 A close family member of the arbitrator has a significant financial or personal interest in one of the parties, or an affiliate of one of the parties.

3. **Orange List**

3.1 Previous services for one of the parties or other involvement in the case

3.1.1 The arbitrator has, within the past three years, served for as counsel one of the parties, or an affiliate of one of the parties, or has previously advised or been consulted by the party, or an affiliate of the party, making the appointment in an unrelated matter, but the arbitrator and the party, or the affiliate of the party, have no ongoing relationship.
3.1.2 The arbitrator has, within the past three years, served as counsel against one of the parties, or an affiliate of one of the parties, in an unrelated matter.
3.1.3 The arbitrator has, within the past three years, been appointed as arbitrator on two or more occasions by one of the parties, or an affiliate of one of the parties.[footnote omitted]
3.1.4 The arbitrator's law firm has, within the past three years, acted for or against one of the parties, or an affiliate of one of the parties, in an unrelated matter without the involvement of the arbitrator.
3.1.5 The arbitrator currently serves, or has served within the past three years, as arbitrator in another arbitration on a related issue involving one of the parties, or an affiliate of one of the parties.

3.2 Current services for one of the parties

3.2.1 The arbitrator's law firm is currently rendering services to one of the parties, or to an affiliate of one of the parties, without creating a significant commercial relationship for the law firm and without the involvement of the arbitrator.
3.2.2 A law firm or other legal organization that shares significant fees or other revenues with the arbitrator's law firm renders services to one of the parties, or an affiliate of one of the parties, before the Arbitral Tribunal.
3.2.3 The arbitrator or his or her firm represents a party, or an affiliate of one of the parties to the arbitration, on a regular basis, but such representation does not concern the current dispute.

3.3 Relationship between an arbitrator and another arbitrator or counsel

3.3.1 The arbitrator and another arbitrator are lawyers in the same law firm.
3.3.2 The arbitrator and another arbitrator, or the counsel for one of the parties, are members of the same barristers' chambers.
3.3.3 The arbitrator was, within the past three years, a partner of, or otherwise affiliated with, another arbitrator or any of the counsel in the arbitration.
3.3.4 A lawyer in the arbitrator's law firm is an arbitrator in another dispute involving the same party or parties, or an affiliate of one of the parties.
3.3.5 A close family member of the arbitrator is a partner or employee of the law firm representing one of the parties, but is not assisting with the dispute.
3.3.6 A close personal friendship exists between an arbitrator and a counsel of a party.
3.3.7 Enmity exists between an arbitrator and counsel appearing in the arbitration.
3.3.8 The arbitrator has, within the past three years, been appointed on more than three occasions by the same counsel, or the same law firm.
3.3.9 The arbitrator and another arbitrator, or counsel for one of the parties in the arbitration, currently act or have acted together within the past three years as co-counsel.

3.4 Relationship between arbitrator and party and others involved in the arbitration

3.4.1 The arbitrator's law firm is currently acting adversely to one of the parties, or an affiliate of one of the parties.
3.4.2 The arbitrator has been associated with a party, or an affiliate of one of the parties, in a professional capacity, such as a former employee or partner.
3.4.3 A close personal friendship exists between an arbitrator and a manager or director or a member of the supervisory board of: a party; an entity that has a direct economic interest in the award to be rendered in the arbitration; or

any person having a controlling influence, such as a controlling shareholder interest, on one of the parties or an affiliate of one of the parties or a witness or expert.

3.4.4 Enmity exists between an arbitrator and a manager or director or a member of the supervisory board of: a party; an entity that has a direct economic interest in the award; or any person having a controlling influence in one of the parties or an affiliate of one of the parties or a witness or expert.

3.4.5 If the arbitrator is a former judge, he or she has, within the past three years, heard a significant case involving one of the parties, or an affiliate of one of the parties.

3.5 Other circumstances

3.5.1 The arbitrator holds shares, either directly or indirectly, that by reason of number or denomination constitute a material holding in one of the parties, or an affiliate of one of the parties, this party or affiliate being publicly listed.

3.5.2 The arbitrator has publicly advocated a position on the case, whether in a published paper, or speech, or otherwise.

3.5.3 The arbitrator holds a position with the appointing authority with respect to the dispute.

3.5.4 The arbitrator is a manager, director or member of the supervisory board, or has a controlling influence on an affiliate of one of the parties, where the affiliate is not directly involved in the matters in dispute in the arbitration.

4. **Green List**

4.1 Previously expressed legal opinions

4.1.1 The arbitrator has previously expressed a legal opinion (such as in a law review article or public lecture) concerning an issue that also arises in the arbitration (but this opinion is not focused on the case).

4.2 Current services for one of the parties

4.2.1 A firm, in association or in alliance with the arbitrator's law firm, but that does not share significant fees or other revenues with the arbitrator's law firm, renders services to one of the parties, or an affiliate of one of the parties, in an unrelated matter.

4.3 Contacts with another arbitrator, or with counsel for one of the parties

4.3.1 The arbitrator has a relationship with another arbitrator, or with the counsel for one of the parties, through membership in the same professional association, or social or charitable organization, or through a social media network.

4.3.2 The arbitrator and counsel for one of the parties have previously served together as arbitrators.

4.3.3 The arbitrator teaches in the same faculty or school as another arbitrator or counsel to one of the parties, or serves as an officer of a professional association or social or charitable organization with another arbitrator or counsel for one of the parties.

4.3.4 The arbitrator was a speaker, moderator or organizer in one or more conferences, or participated in seminars or working parties of a professional, social or charitable organization, with another arbitrator or counsel to the parties.

4.4 Contacts between the arbitrator and one of the parties

4.4.1 The arbitrator has had an initial contact with a party, or an affiliate of a party (or their counsel) prior to appointment, if this contact is limited to the arbitrator's availability and qualifications to serve, or to the names of possible candidates for a chairperson, and did not address the merits or procedural aspects of the dispute, other than to provide the arbitrator with a basic understanding of the case.

4.4.2 The arbitrator holds an insignificant amount of shares in one of the parties, or an affiliate of one of the parties, which is publicly listed.

4.4.3 The arbitrator and a manager, director or member of the supervisory board, or any person having a controlling influence on one of the parties, or an affiliate of one of the parties, have worked together as joint experts, or in another professional capacity, including as arbitrators in the same case.

4.4.4 The arbitrator has a relationship with one of the parties or its affiliates through a social media network.

Index